RECONSTRUCTION
AND EMPIRE

RECONSTRUCTING AMERICA
Andrew L. Slap, series editor

Reconstruction and Empire

The Legacies of Abolition and Union Victory for an Imperial Age

David Prior, Editor

FORDHAM UNIVERSITY PRESS
NEW YORK   2022

Copyright © 2022 Fordham University Press

All rights reserved. No part of this publication may be reproduced, stored in a retrieval system, or transmitted in any form or by any means—electronic, mechanical, photocopy, recording, or any other—except for brief quotations in printed reviews, without the prior permission of the publisher.

Fordham University Press has no responsibility for the persistence or accuracy of URLs for external or third-party Internet websites referred to in this publication and does not guarantee that any content on such websites is, or will remain, accurate or appropriate.

Fordham University Press also publishes its books in a variety of electronic formats. Some content that appears in print may not be available in electronic books.

Visit us online at www.fordhampress.com.

Library of Congress Cataloging-in-Publication Data

Names: Prior, David (College teacher), editor.
Title: Reconstruction and empire : the legacies of abolition and Union victory for an imperial age / David Prior, editor.
Description: First edition. | New York : Fordham University Press, 2022. | Series: Reconstructing America | Includes bibliographical references and index.
Identifiers: LCCN 2021054451 | ISBN 9780823298648 (hardback) | ISBN 9780823298655 (paperback) | ISBN 9780823298662 (epub)
Subjects: LCSH: Reconstruction (U.S. history, 1865–1877) | Imperialism—History—19th century. | United States—Foreign relations—1865–1921. | United States—Politics and government—1865–1933. | United States—Social conditions—1865–1918. | United States—Territorial expansion.
Classification: LCC E668 .R36 2022 | DDC 973.8—dc23/eng/20211129
LC record available at https://lccn.loc.gov/2021054451

Printed in the United States of America

24 23 22   5 4 3 2 1

First edition

for Isaac's grandparents, with love

Contents

Introduction
David Prior | 1

1 The Last Filibuster: The Ten Years' War in Cuba and the Legacy of the American Civil War
Andre M. Fleche | 27

2 "What Hinders?": African Methodist Expansion from the U.S. South to Hispaniola, 1865–1885
Christina C. Davidson | 54

3 Domestic Stability and Imperial Continuities: U.S.–Spanish Relations in the Reconstruction Era
Gregg French | 79

4 "Their very sectionalism makes them cultivate that wider and broader patriotism": Southern Free Trade Imperialism Survives the Confederacy
Adrian Brettle | 105

5 James Redpath, Rebel Sympathizer
Lawrence B. Glickman | 136

6 "Our God-Given Mission": Reconstruction and the Humanitarian Internationalism of the 1890s
Mark Elliott | 161

7 Connected Lives: Albert Beveridge, Benjamin Tillman, and the Grand Army of the Republic
David V. Holtby | 191

8   The Lynching of Frazier Baker:
    Violence from Reconstruction
    to Empire
    DJ Polite | 214

9   "The Same Patriotism . . . as Any
    Other Americans": Reconstruction,
    Imperialism, and the Evolution
    of Mormon Patriotism
    Reilly Ben Hatch | 239

10 Schooling "New-Caught, Sullen
    Peoples": Illustrating Race
    in U.S. Empire
    Brian Shott | 264

11 An Empire of Reconstructions:
    Cuba and the Transformation of
    American Military Occupation
    Justin F. Jackson | 297

    Afterword
    Rebecca Edwards | 317

List of Contributors   327
           Index   329

Reconstruction and Empire

Introduction

David Prior

Within a period of just over thirty years, the United States government went from conducting one of the most radical experiments in the history of democracy to constructing a racist empire. In 1867, Union soldiers were enforcing a congressional mandate that former Confederate states, long led by a powerful slaveholding class, rewrite their constitutions with African American men, overwhelmingly enslaved but a few years earlier, participating in the process. The result was a fragile interracial and multi-party democracy in a war-torn region with an embittered white supremacist majority. By 1898, that same military was occupying Spain's colonies in the Pacific and Caribbean. Over the next few months and years, it would crush a fledgling Filipino state, enforce restrictions on Cuban sovereignty, and commandeer Spain's other colonies as well as the Hawaiian Islands. But the relationships between these two developments, and their broader political and cultural moments, have largely eluded attention.[1] As this volume demonstrates, this neglect is unfortunate, for even if we define the ever-evolving terms "Reconstruction" and "Empire" narrowly, the history of the former has much to tell us about the course of the latter.[2]

The disconnect is perplexing given the proximity of and commonalities between these two moments. Reconstruction—understood as a series of possibilities and conflicts emerging from the twin pivots of emancipation and Union victory—did much to alter the course of events in and beyond the United States. African Americans—former slaves and the minority born free—fought to secure personal autonomy, legal equality, and political power. Northern churches and humanitarians supported an ambitious, if halting, campaign to transform Southern society, often in the face of reactionary violence. The Republican Party, committed to an antislavery reunion but internally divided over racial equality and the extent of Congress's constitutional authority, embraced both in the face of white supremacist intransigence, including that of Abraham Lincoln's successor as president, Andrew Johnson. Republicans' core legislative measures, including the Fourteenth and Fifteenth Amendments, dramatically expanded civil and political rights, but also precipitated divisions among reformers over the nexus of gender and racial oppression. A Southern wing of the party composed of African Americans, a minority of discontented whites, and Northern migrants governed briefly across much of the South. Soon, however, Southern Republicans were on their back foot before more numerous Southern white supremacists and their Northern Democratic allies. Historians do not agree on exactly why Northern Republicans became less willing or able to intervene in Southern politics, but already by 1874 Southern white paramilitaries acted with near impunity. The final Republican state governments in the South fell in 1877, although this was no unqualified victory for racists. African American political participation persisted in many locales, as did educational, religious, social, and civic institutions unthinkable under slavery. The amended Constitution, moreover, included the legal foundations for the later victories of the modern civil rights movement. Finally, the South was firmly within the Union with slavery abolished. But Southern white supremacists had gained regional control. A new Jim Crow order built around segregation, ritualistic acts of sadism, state-sanctioned convict-lease systems, debt peonage, and formal disenfranchisement spread across the South, winning federal sanction and national connivance by century's end.[3]

Things were just as complicated with the place of the United States in a world that was increasingly interconnected and suffused with imperial power and violence. Immediately following the Civil War, leading Republicans variously eyed territorial acquisitions, supported commercial expansion across the western territories and abroad, and worked to enforce the Monroe Doctrine. The United States government acquired Alaska and the Midway Atoll and pressured the French imperial government to abandon its puppet monarchy in Mexico. But it also demurred from annexing the Dominican Republic and the Danish West Indies and from supporting raids by Irish-American Fenians into Canada. Both Republican and Democratic politicians supported wars with diverse Native American groups that lived within or astride the internationally recognized boundaries of the United States, enforcing confinement on reservations and seeking to undermine Indigenous cultural resilience. Steam power, telegraphy, and cheap print rendered an interconnected world, granting easy access to information and misinformation from around the globe and fueling U.S. evangelicals' ambitions to convert the human race. By the Civil War's end, a new industrial capitalism centered on the North Atlantic was transforming the world, spawning a small globe-trotting class of super-rich U.S. citizens, fueling the growth of more modest forms of tourism, and employing millions of immigrant laborers under harsh conditions. Corporate behemoths insinuated themselves into the halls of power in Washington, D.C., and sequestered resources abroad. These forces of change culminated at the turn of the century. In 1898, a clique of Republican politicians, empire-hungry and self-consciously masculine, both blustered and stumbled into two of the Spanish government's colonial stalemates while also annexing Hawaii. The ensuing globe-straddling conflict yielded a distinctive moment in the United States' long and complicated history of violent expansion in the name of democracy and progress. The United States occupied and, excepting the quasi-independent nation-state of Cuba, formally annexed far-flung overseas Spanish colonies whose inhabitants were culturally diverse and putatively racially distinct from those deemed "white" and "Anglo-Saxon." The imposition of U.S. authority prompted democratic resistance in Cuba, a series of anticolonial wars in the Philippines, and a patchwork anti-imperialist movement of racists and Northern egalitarians at home. Federal officials and colonial denizens navigated an ambiguous and impromptu legal regime. In the following years and decades, U.S. politicians would practice rampant interventionism, especially in Latin America and the Caribbean, going so far as to dispossess Colombia of the Isthmus of Panama.[4]

Common themes—violence and military power, citizenship and sovereignty, discourses of race, gender, religion, and national identity, economic transformations, and claims to equality and progress—connected and evolved through these two historical moments. Yet although linkages abound, they defy easy summation, with the two stories having many common parts, but arranged differently. Northeastern and midwestern Republicans authored Reconstruction's key legislation and launched turn-of-the-century overseas imperialism, but generational change transformed their party over this same period.[5] Severe economic recession struck twice over this period (1873–1877 and 1893–1897), providing one of Reconstruction's endpoints but preceding the War with Spain and granting it a nervous energy.[6] The cause of reconciliation among white Northerners and Southerners found a qualified affirmation in the "War with Spain," but the conflict also pulled U.S. politics out from the shadow of the Civil War.[7] Abolition and Union victory as well as later imperial occupations intensified debates over the meaning of race, but that concept was itself unstable, with nativist responses to European "new immigrants" and theories of evolution transforming it.[8] U.S. overseas imperialism also saw domestic racism inflicted on colonial subjects but simultaneously divided African American opinion and, ironically, helped forge connections between African Americans and Afro-Cubans.[9] Gender norms that had long been integral to the abolitionist movement, including those lauding manly self-restraint and the nurturing nature of women, also suffused the imperial project and popular prejudices against the colonized other.[10] Both moments witnessed currents of humanitarian reform swirling around U.S. military conflicts but in two contexts set apart by the rise of professionalization and the authority of scientific expertise.[11] And yet with both conflicts, invasions spurred on health crises that undermined the conqueror's claims of benignity and competence.[12] The grassroots white-supremacist violence of the postbellum South and the U.S. military's use of torture and reconcentration in the Philippines were, like campaigns against Native American communities, harbingers of a coming century of world history marked by the proliferation of civilian atrocities.[13] Across this period, a faith in the distinction between civilized progress and retrograde barbarism transcended the political and intellectual landscape, but with the identity of civilization's barbarian others subject to shifting lines of contestation.[14] In both contexts, concepts of civilization and barbarism sustained elaborate metaphors and world-straddling comparisons in which Southern whites were equated with Mormons and Turks, the South with tropical colonies, Cubans with Armenians and Haitians, and the colonies with crowded ethnic quarters of cities.[15]

Given the complexity of these issues and their importance to understanding the decades following the Civil War, one wonders whether there isn't an alternative historiographical universe where a long-standing interpretive paradigm of "Reconstruction & Empire" reigns in place of our own "Gilded Age & Progressive Era." Indeed, early-twenty-first-century scholarly debates over how to define, label, and segment the history of the late-nineteenth- and early-twentieth-century United States suggest that just such a paradigm may come into vogue.[16] Of particular interest, Heather Cox Richardson, Elliott West, and Richard White have attempted to expand the definition of Reconstruction so that it encompasses the U.S. conquest and incorporation of its western territories. Especially with Richardson and White, this approach bridges the ending of the Civil War and developments at the turn of the century, with Richardson concluding her narrative of Reconstruction with the United States' wars in the Spanish colonies.[17] One of the hitches with this approach, however, is that it raises the question of whether and how Reconstruction mattered to the trajectory of U.S. power abroad if we do not first redefine it—if we contain it, as Rachel St. John has put it.[18] How did the sweeping economic, cultural, and political transformations embedded in and stemming from abolition and Union victory condition, inhibit, or facilitate the various manifestations of U.S. power at century's end? How tightly tethered were

INTRODUCTION   5

these two political and cultural moments, each centered on its own complex fusing of conquest and liberation?

To understand how historians ended up neglecting these questions, and how much room there is for sustained debate about them, we should revisit W. E. B. Du Bois's once forgotten but now canonical *Black Reconstruction in America* (1935). As Moon-Ho Jung and Eric Foner have pointed out, *Black Reconstruction* trenchantly situated the broader drama of Reconstruction, especially the white supremacist reaction to African American freedom and empowerment, as a critical moment in the United States' route to racial imperialism.[19] Du Bois—the most prominent and accomplished African American intellectual of his day and a pivotal figure in American sociology, literature, and history—only sketched his argument about Reconstruction and empire. But the result was striking and original in ways that can still help us think through the complex connections between the two.

Du Bois wrote, revised, and edited the massive, polemical volume from 1931 to 1935, amid a global Great Depression, the highwater mark of European empires, and Jim Crow as a national institution.[20] A kind of evocative moral history rare in the profession today, *Black Reconstruction* combined detailed critiques of early-twentieth-century racist scholarship, ruminations on the centrality of labor to politics in the North and South, and lyrical passages on the experiences and hopes of Southern freedpeople during and after emancipation.[21] Du Bois, who spent pivotal parts of his life and career in the South but was born and raised in the North, sometimes wrote of Southern freedpeople with a touch of distance, perhaps even talented-tenth elitism.[22] But overwhelmingly his book struggled against a tide of white supremacist scholarship to uphold Southern African Americans as the heroes of one of the most promising and tragic moments in the history of the United States, and indeed of the modern world.

Black Reconstruction addressed this last topic by arguing that twentieth-century European and Euro-American geopolitical power rested on and was committed to the thralldom of the world's nonwhite peoples. Merging concepts of capitalism and empire in a heterodox Marxism, Du Bois contended that the modern analog of the antebellum slave was "the yellow, brown and black laborer in China and India, in Africa, in the forests of the Amazon." He argued—building on his broader turn-of-the-century career advocating for civil rights, anti-imperialism, and radical reform—that these oppressed laborers toiled to generate the surplus value that sustained "world power and universal dominion and armed arrogance in London and Paris, Berlin and Rome, New York and Rio de Janeiro." Du Bois urged, as he would for the rest of his remarkable life, that "the emancipation of man is the emancipation of labor and the emancipation of labor is the freeing of that basic majority of workers who are yellow, brown and black."[23]

The historical narrative that Du Bois had in mind came across in brief passages. Ending his second chapter, "The White Worker," for example, Du Bois sketched the transition from Reconstruction—here rhetorically subsumed within a broadened Civil War—to empire, writing:

> Then came this battle called Civil War, beginning in Kansas in 1854, and ending in the presidential election of 1876—twenty awful years. The slave went free; stood a brief moment in the sun; then moved back again toward slavery. The whole weight of America was thrown to color caste. The colored world went down before England, France, Germany, Russia, Italy and America. A new slavery arose. . . . Democracy died save in the hearts of black folk.

More details then emerged in the chapter titled "The Counter-Revolution of Property." During the contested election of 1876, he claimed, Northern capitalists and poorer Southern whites joined with Southern barons in their long-running campaign to deny Southern freedpeople education, autonomy, and guidance—or has he put it, "Light and Land and Leading." The South, with Black voting suppressed but its federal representation increased by the end of the three-fifths clause, reinforced Northern pro-business conservativism and a new industrial imperialism that "degraded colored labor the world over." This Southern white supremacist triumph wrought a sweeping and "spiritual" change on the United States, transforming it into "a reactionary force."[24]

In *Black Reconstruction*, Du Bois drew attention to the broader ascent of the United States as a capitalist power under the leadership of white supremacists; he did not focus on a single imperial event or conflict.[25] Du Bois saw this ascent as earth-changing, and if anyone missed the boldness of his argument, he laid it bare in his conclusion to "The Counter-Revolution of Property." "God wept," he opened, "but that mattered little to an unbelieving age. . . . For there began to rise in America in 1876 a new capitalism and a new enslavement of labor." To this momentous change Du Bois attributed World War I, brought on, he averred, by imperial competition, and then the ensuing global Great Depression. A more robust and enduring post–Civil War expansion of African American rights, especially one that saw widespread land redistribution, could have, Du Bois argued, "made a basis of real democracy in the United States that might easily have transformed the modern world."[26] For Du Bois, the Southern freedpeople's quest for local autonomy and national citizenship, and the radical postbellum moment centered on these, pointed the way to global peace and equality.

There is much to be said about *Black Reconstruction*'s imperial thesis, so much so that scholars tend to either glance over it or tip their hats to it in passing. In fact, Du Bois's argument was provocative and insightful but also cryptic. Many of its details warrant debate and fuller explanation, including the idea that imperialism caused World War I and therefore the Great Depression. Du Bois also relied on the assumption that Southern freedpeople and their children would necessarily act as a class of workers to explain why, if not disenfranchised, they would have opposed the federal government's or U.S. corporations' exercises of power abroad.[27] Finally, Du Bois's analysis, like those of many other historians, at times became ensnared in the befuddling terms "Reconstruction," "empire," and "imperialism," which all had complex etymologies. At moments he took "Reconstruction" as a straightforward concept, whereas at others, some deep in the text, he grappled with its definition.[28] He also at points used "empire" and "imperialism" in an older sense meaning not colonial conquest but the anti-democratic consolidation of power, suggesting that the assault on Black voting constituted—not just caused—imperialism.[29]

But none of that is to deny the trenchancy of Du Bois's imperial thesis (or this volume's debt to it). As he made clear, the egalitarian and at times radical impulses of the immediate postbellum moment, as well as the contests they provoked, left profound legacies for the industrializing nation. His volume's imperial thesis could have inaugurated a wider debate about these topics and thereby shaped the evolution of historical writing on the late-nineteenth- and early-twentieth-century United States. Indeed, it nearly did. Although white supremacy, near the height of its intellectual authority in the 1930s, created serious hurdles to *Black Reconstruction*'s scholarly influence, there were several other factors working in its favor. One was that Du Bois's imperial thesis came as a rebuttal to *Reconstruction and the Constitution* (1902), by the arch-racist John W. Burgess, and therefore formed a part of an emerging debate within the field. Burgess argued that Republicans had erred in extending suffrage across the color line but had hence, through imperialism, embraced the white man's burden. Quoting and refuting Burgess's argument, Du Bois countered that the fulfillment of Reconstruction's promise would have prevented racist terrorism abroad.[30] These opening salvos linking Reconstruction and empire could have easily fed into what was then considerable interest in how the economic processes at work in the postbellum South dovetailed with the rise of industrial capitalism. Du Bois found fault with other scholars working in this vein, including Charles and Mary Beard and Howard K. Beale, and elicited critiques for his quasi-Marxian analysis from otherwise sympathetic, pro–civil rights scholars.[31] *Black Reconstruction*, moreover, came out right as an eclectic cohort of historians—such as Francis Butler Simkins, A. A. Taylor, Robert Hilliard Woody, John Hope Franklin, and William Hesseltine—joined earlier African American historians and memoirists in dissenting from racist interpretations of Reconstruction.[32] A young C. Vann Woodward, who would become the single most influential figure in the evolution of Southern historical scholarship, wrote to Du Bois in 1938 to praise *Black Reconstruction* and share his own work.[33] As David Levering Lewis and others have noted, *Black Reconstruction* met with positive reviews and garnered, if briefly, some critical acclaim.[34] The field was primed for discussion of the nexus of Reconstruction, economic change, and imperialism, which is exactly what *Black Reconstruction* offered.

So why did *Black Reconstruction* not emerge as the focal point for precisely such a field-defining scholarly debate? Along with racism in and beyond the academy, a confluence of factors came to bear. *Black Reconstruction* had the poor luck of being published during the Great Depression and just before World War II. Although universities in the United States by no means closed shop, widespread unemployment, falling tax revenues, and then national mobilization disrupted scholarly production.[35] Depression conditions limited sales, in part because the bulky volume was a touch expensive.[36] Post–World War II Consensus scholarship, although more complex than is sometimes acknowledged, showed little interest in the topic of race and was unlikely to inspire renewed interest in Du Bois's volume.[37] In a fairly remarkable series of coincidences, by the mid-1950s some of the scholars who had favorably reviewed *Black Reconstruction* retired, passed away, or took a conservative turn in their thinking, limiting the roster of scholars who might have called for renewed attention to it.[38] Finally, the intellectual climate of the early Cold War discouraged the public discussion of Left-leaning critiques of the United States, including its racism. A testament to Du Bois's refusal to buckle, in 1949 he was still condemning the United States, stating in one speech, with clear echoes of *Black Reconstruction*, that the country was "leading the world to hell in a new colonialism with the same old human slavery which once ruined us."[39] Such unapologetic criticisms, as well as growing ties to Far Left writers and thinkers, put Du Bois on the margins of the day's academic life. They also, however, meant that he anticipated the emergence of a thread of more critical and radical work in the late 1950s and 1960s. Du Bois would visit the Soviet Union and communist China before passing away in Ghana in 1963.[40]

These forces came to a head in the late 1950s and 1960s, a pivotal moment in the evolution of the historical profession as universities and colleges in the United States expanded.[41] A handful of well-placed scholars authored influential studies, offered new interpretations, and trained small armies of PhDs who went on to their own distinguished careers. In this key period, *Black Reconstruction* received only checkered attention in undergraduate and graduate classrooms.[42] The volume was reissued in 1956 and garnered at least occasional discussion on the political Left.[43] But *Black Reconstruction* did not make a deep imprint on the changing historiographies of Reconstruction and U.S. empire, which were both going through major revisions.

Those revisions were, in and of themselves, amenable to Du Bois's imperial thesis. With Reconstruction, a tremendous volume of thorough pro–civil rights scholarship reexamined abolition, enfranchisement, and white supremacist reaction in the South, often with an emphasis on local history from the bottom up.[44] In diplomatic history, meanwhile, a series of sweeping reinterpretations by William Appleman Williams and his students attributed U.S. overseas imperialism to the boom-and-bust cycle of industrial capitalism and the need, or perceived need, to acquire export markets.[45] It is surprising that scholars working in both of these veins rarely if ever discussed or even cited *Black Reconstruction* despite his emphasis on grassroots African American politics and the driving force of industrial capitalism.[46] It is far from absurd to imagine the leftist Williams reading and engaging with *Black Reconstruction*'s critical view of industrial capitalism, or the pro–civil rights syntheses of Reconstruction from the 1960s addressing its long-term impact on the globe with Du Bois in mind.[47] *Black Reconstruction*'s imperial thesis, in part because it was in need of elaboration and deliberation, was ideally suited for sustaining discussion between these two increasingly distant bodies of scholarship. Instead, Reconstruction scholars and diplomatic historians seemed to move in different worlds, with the gulf enduring until this century. It is telling that few of the many excellent historiographical essays reviewing the origins of the United States' turn-of-the-century overseas empire mention either Du Bois or Reconstruction even in passing.[48] Likewise, the period from 1940 to 1990 witnessed only a handful of diplomatic studies that framed themselves as about Reconstruction, with Reconstruction studies returning the favor.[49]

If earlier scholarship missed the opportunity to explore the connections between these two topics, historians are now primed to revisit them. Three early-twenty-first-century trends, in particular, have laid the foundation for broader debates about how Union victory and abolition contoured the rise of the United States as a regional hegemon with an overseas empire. In bringing these three trends into a common conversation, we would be well served to keep Du Bois's imperial thesis in mind. Although scholars will no doubt disagree about it, its clarity, sweep, and originality make it ideal for thinking through the big picture.

First, the diplomatic history of U.S. imperialism—both as a broader phenomenon and as it pertains to the turn-of-the-century expansionism in particular—has increasingly merged the social and the cultural with the political and administrative. No longer just "maps and chaps," diplomatic history constitutes an eclectic and expansive field of study.[50] Often concerned with the agency of the colonized and the permeability of national and cultural borders, scholarship from the late 1990s to the present shows us a global landscape replete with diverse actors capable of operating against, around, and through imperial power. Afro-Cubans and Filipino students studying in the United States, Filipino musicians touring the United States with an African American conductor, and interracial couples settling the imperial frontier in the Philippines all point to patterns of relations that existed within and alongside the formal structures of U.S. colonial administrations.[51] Together, this literature tends to add needed nuance to Du Bois's emphasis on unremitting domination by European and American industrial powers while also affirming his concerns with their common investment in racial ideologies and with the nexus of economic and military power. This scholarship has, moreover, fleshed out an ideological portrait of a U.S. empire that fused Jim Crow racism, humanitarian ambitions, and progressive reform.[52] A synthesis awaits of the Reconstruction-era experiences of the foot soldiers, administrators, boosters, and critics of the United States' overseas empire.[53]

Second, Reconstruction scholarship, which has long been thematically expansive but geographically focused, has recently taken interest in transnational connections. Post-emancipation struggles in the South remain integral to the field, but now so too is Reconstruction's embeddedness within a globalizing world. Immigrants who played active roles in Reconstruction's political battles, the global resonances of domestic struggles over slavery and democracy, and reactions to events abroad have all elicited sustained attention.[54] The cosmopolitan expansionist William H. Seward, secretary of state from 1861 to 1869, once seemed ahead of his time—a lonely harbinger of empire out of place during a period when domestic political turmoil drew national energies inward. Now, he seems much more like a representative figure of a mid-century political culture obsessed with and divided over the United States' place in the world and transitioning from proslavery antebellum land grabs to steam-driven commercial imperialism.[55] As yet, however, we lack a composite picture from this growing literature. Perhaps earlier debates among Reconstruction scholars over whether the changes shaping postbellum Southern history were radical and sweeping or limited and tenuous are already being recapitulated among scholars who take a global angle.[56] Is postbellum U.S. engagement with the world—diplomatic, cultural, and intellectual—best understood for its egalitarian, emancipatory declarations or a deeper-lying conservatism? Du Bois saw the overthrow of interracial democracy in the postbellum South as a key moment in the United States' embrace of a global imperial order centered on racism and economic exploitation. Yet some might argue that the trends heading in that direction were already sufficiently in place by the 1860s to ensure such an outcome. Still others might call attention to the persistence of reform currents and humanitarian ideals well after the white-supremacist victories of 1876–1877. Either way, these two historiographical trends make clear that there is now plenty of thematic and topical overlap between scholarship on Reconstruction and turn-of-the-century U.S. imperialism, however exactly scholars attempt to define and redefine those terms.

Third, the early twenty-first century has seen the proliferation of wide-ranging narrative histories. Their sweeping, distinctive, and sometimes contending interpretations deliberately connect oft-siloed subjects, laying the foundation for a series of broader interpretive debates about the decades following the Civil War. With an eye on the differences between works such as David Blight's *Race and Reunion*, Heather Cox Richardson's *West from Appomattox*, and Caroline Janney's *Remembering the Civil War*, we should continue to debate the extent to which Southern white supremacists were successful in shaping the culture and politics of the late-nineteenth-century United States.[57] Similarly, Steven Hahn's *A Nation without Borders*, Richard White's *The Republic for Which It Stands*, and Charles Postel's *Equality* should leave us pondering whether the day's leading social and political movements and diverse cultures of work and leisure were opposed to industrial capitalism itself, or just particular features of it.[58] These works give ample reason to consider Du Bois's argument that the United States went through a spiritual change and became a reactionary force in the world. Borrowing from him, we might ask whether, if there was a turning away from the radical possibilities of the 1860s, this change wasn't instead doctrinal in nature, with slight modifications in specific beliefs entailing dramatic real-world consequences. Nina Silber, in reviewing scholarship on postbellum sectionalism, has pointed to works showing that "even relatively subtle changes in thinking, including attitudes about race, may have opened intellectual doors to reconciliation." No doubt the same case could be made for views of industrialization, big business, and empire.[59] Either way, the remarkable lives of Albert Parsons, the ex-Confederate who married across the color line and became an anarchist martyr, and William Ellis, the former slave who passed as Mexican, married across the color line in the other direction, and became a celebrity businessman, remind us that attitudes toward opportunities and risks reflected complex life histories that often ran back to the twin pivots of abolition and Union victory.[60]

These three trends provide grounds for a closing thought experiment: imagining how scholars might have built—and might still build—a larger scholarly debate around Du Bois's imperial thesis through good-faith challenges to it. One potential counterargument would be that Reconstruction mattered to the evolution of U.S. global power because, from some perspectives, it was a success.[61] The reunion of the North and South on antislavery terms, but without full racial equality, was precisely what many moderate Northern Republicans wanted. Slavery was out of the South, the South was in the Union. The postbellum settlement, this line of thinking might go, therefore left Northern Republicans confident in their moral authority and happy to attribute postbellum shortcomings to the backwardness of Southerners, Black and white. Northern Republicans' imperialism would echo this view, promising uplift but writing off those who seemed to stand in its way.[62]

Another approach would be to turn Du Bois's references to industrial and colonial enslavement on their head. As some of his critics at the time pointed out, *Black Reconstruction* tended to elide technical distinctions among different modes of labor exploitation. Indeed, Du Bois's usage of the term "slavery" to describe industrial and colonial labor regimes can be vexing, sometimes seeming metaphorical and at other times literal. That ambiguity leaves room to present a countervailing emphasis on how the Civil War, in a process consummated by Reconstruction, destroyed chattel slavery in the United States right before industrial capitalism's decades'-long ascent. Much to the modern world's benefit, some could stress, the postbellum expansion of civil and political rights capped off the foreclosing of a bleak and once-imminent historical trajectory in which a powerful class of pro-imperial slaveholders survived into a very different gilded age.[63] For all the welcomed debate about whether Confederates won the peace, we should remember that secessionists had wanted to preserve not only white supremacy but also their absolute legal right for themselves and their descendants to own another class of human beings in perpetuity. Just as the South's former slaveholders never closed all the doors that Reconstruction opened for African Americans, they never opened all the doors it shut on them.

Finally, there is room to challenge Du Bois's imperial thesis by calling attention to the late-nineteenth-century triumph of antislavery norms. Scholars such as Eric Foner and Barbara Gannon have stressed that Northern attitudes to race and slavery were related but distinct topics. Even many Northerners who openly expressed doubts about or distaste for African Americans celebrated the Union's destruction of slavery as a triumph.[64] After the Civil War, slavery as an institution was broadly stigmatized while the mid-nineteenth-century counterweight to racism, Christian notions of human equality, waned in intellectual authority. As a result, late-nineteenth-century conservatives turned to antislavery rhetoric to advance causes such as Chinese exclusion and preventing Philippine independence.[65] Perhaps, moreover, Northerners' self-congratulatory embrace of antislavery principles at once secured the place of humanitarian ideals in the mainstream and made it difficult for them to own up to their own complicity in the oppression and exploitation of others.[66]

No doubt still other alternative narratives of the path from Reconstruction to empire exist. Constructing them should help bridge the gap between the scholarship on these two topics, and hopefully render a sharper understanding of the postbellum, post-abolition United States and the increasingly imperial world it was embedded in.

The chapters here offer fine-grained studies that explore the manifold ways that the developments stemming from Union victory and abolition anticipated, shaded into, and intersected with the geopolitical rise of the United States. They show the complex political divisions and cultural changes of the late-nineteenth-century United States as forming a part of a contentious world of empires, colonies, and nation-states. The composite portrait is one of diverse actors, shifting ideologies, and contradictory continuities operating form a domestic landscape struck through with global connections. The chapters appear in a roughly chronological order.

Andre Fleche, in his "The Last Filibuster," explores the careers of two Civil War veterans, one Union and one Confederate, in Cuba's Ten Years' War (1868–1878). Federico Fernández Cavada, a Cuban-born Union soldier and, briefly, a U.S. consular official on the island, witnessed the start of the rebellion and quickly sided with it. Although the Cuban insurgents had a complicated relationship with abolition, Cavada saw in their struggle the possibility of an antislavery republic and the potential birth of a free labor empire through the island's annexation to the United States. Former Confederate general Thomas Jordan, in contrast, arrived as a soldier of fortune with a mixed band of Union and Confederate soldiers. Yet Jordan, who was a newspaper editor and an apologist for KKK-founder Nathan Bedford Forrest, also brought ideological baggage with him. Both men's Cuban careers embodied the conflicted interplay of national identity and slavery across the New World and help illuminate them.

In Chapter 2, Christina C. Davidson looks at the tenuous and sometimes fraught relationships centered on the African Methodist Episcopal Church's history in the Caribbean. This story begins in the 1820s, when African American members of the church began moving to the island of Hispaniola, then unified under Haitian control. Yet these AME communities soon languished on the largely Catholic island. As they struggled, however, the AME Church in the United States went through a sweeping transformation as abolition and civil rights opened a vast new field of missionary activity within the United States. Soon, the denomination looked outward. Hispaniola would be the first foreign missionary field for the AME Church during this new era, predating its better-known efforts to evangelize Africa. But this was an ambivalent and hesitating start to the church's missionary project, which sat awkwardly at the nexus of expanding U.S. influence and Afro-diasporic connections.

"Domestic Stability and Imperial Continuities," by Gregg French, situates the postbellum United States' relations with Spain within a longer history that featured an oft-forgotten tradition of alliance and respect. Although certain negative views of the Spanish Empire existed, in particular those stemming from the Black Legend, so too did a sense of historical connection to a European power that was credited with discovering the Americas and that had supported the American Revolution. In the postbellum United States, this tradition merged with transatlantic racial ideas and anxieties within the United States over simmering sectional animosities. The man who most fully embodied these trends was the conservative Northern secretary of state Hamilton Fish, who worked assiduously to tamp down expansionistic and anti-Spanish policy suggestions within President Ulysses S. Grant's administrations. His tenure, which saw Grant's attempts to annex the Dominican Republic and nearly the full duration of the Ten Years' War in Cuba, anticipated the inter-imperial transfer of authority that would end the Spanish-American War.

In Chapter 4, Adrian Brettle explores how Virginia conservatives forged alliances in and reconciled themselves to the Union after the Civil War, in the process sustaining elements of their older Confederate imperialism in the re-United States. Looking at the careers of individuals such as John Letcher (governor of Confederate Virginia), Robert M. T. Hunter (Confederate secretary of state and a former U.S. senator), and J. Randolph Tucker (state attorney general during the war), Brettle offers a composite picture of a depressed but ultimately resilient elite who sought the future glory of their state and section within the nation. Moods oscillated with federal politics, but Virginia conservatives took their chances when they had them, reintegrating themselves into national politics through alliances with former Whigs and then the Democratic Party. With growing enthusiasm, many sought to renew Confederate projects, including the building of a southern Pacific railroad, regional internal improvements, and international free trade.

Lawrence Glickman, in "James Redpath, Rebel Sympathizer," fathoms one abolitionist's circuitous route to sectional reconciliation by viewing it alongside his deepening opposition to the British Empire. Redpath was, as Glickman shows, a lifelong devotee to radical causes and a tireless and often ingenious entrepreneurial reformer. It is with this in mind that two of his post-Reconstruction causes seem so odd together. On the one hand, Redpath became a relentless critic of the British Empire, especially in the name of Irish independence. On the other, Redpath refrained from extending his antebellum criticisms of slavery, and in particular his interest in hearing the voices of the enslaved, into an attack on postbellum white supremacy. In fact, he expressed doubts about African Americans' capacity for equal citizenship, suggested they abandon their confrontational stance toward Southern whites, and befriended former Confederate president Jefferson Davis. Redpath still spoke in defense of the weak, including Indians and Egyptians fighting against British rule, but showed more sympathy for Southern whites than African Americans.

The sixth chapter, by Mark Elliott, examines four patriotic reformers whose careers stretched from Reconstruction to the birth of the United States' overseas empire. O. O. Howard, Julia Ward Howe, Lyman Abbott, and Clara Barton provide prominent examples of how patriotic fervor in the North merged with zeal for fighting against suffering at home and abroad. Distinguishing this humanitarian internationalism was a faith—forged in the Civil War and Reconstruction—that the federal government could and should intervene in support of just causes. Part and parcel of this humanitarian concern was a sense of cultural, national, and racial superiority that saw white Americans, especially Northerners, overseeing the uplift of the rest of the world. The complex interplay of those ideas shaped private and public campaigns in the South, Armenia, Russia, the Caribbean, and the Philippines.

In his "Connected Lives," David Holtby explores the political legacies of the Civil War and Reconstruction during a period of economic turmoil. Spanning the final third of the nineteenth century, Holtby shows how imperialism served as a generational bridge for Union veterans in the Grand Army of the Republic (GAR) and the rising midwestern Republican Albert Beveridge. This connection, and in particular the promises of commercial prosperity and national mission that Beveridge saw in U.S. empire, spoke directly to Gilded Age anxieties that Beveridge knew through his father's postbellum struggles. Holtby also shows us the interplay of enduring sectional antagonisms with reconciliationist ideas grounded in racial identities. Even as President William McKinley and Beveridge used the War with Spain to foster North-South unity, one of imperialism's major senatorial opponents would be Benjamin Tillman, a leading Southern white supremacist. Indeed, a wedge opened between Beveridge and the GAR, which held fast to its role in suppressing the Confederate rebellion.

Chapter 8, by DJ Polite, looks at Jim Crow violence, the memory of Reconstruction, and debates over imperialism. America's War with Spain began during a wave of racist terrorism in the Carolinas, including an attack on the household of Frazier Baker, the African American federal postmaster for Lake City, South Carolina. As Polite shows, these attacks evoked a longer history of violence and poignantly contradicted the emancipatory rhetoric Americans used in their war with Spain. African American newspapers demanded action, and anti-lynching crusader Ida Wells-Barnett worked with George White, the only Black member of Congress, to pressure the McKinley administration to launch a federal investigation. Tillman again played a key role, raising the specter of a return to carpetbag rule while railing against American imperialism, although his fellow South Carolina senator, John McLaurin, ultimately outmaneuvered him.

Reilly Ben Hatch, in his "Reconstruction, Imperialism, and the Evolution of Mormon Patriotism," analyzes the place of the war with Spain and the occupation of the Philippines in the Church of Jesus Christ of Latter-day Saints. Hatch analyzes Mormon doctrine concerning patriotism, religious freedom, and violence, as well as popular anti-Mormon sentiment. As he shows, the wars came only eight years after the church hierarchy suspended the practice of polygamy and only two years after Utah's statehood, which contemporaries and now historians view as capping off a Mormon Reconstruction. Mormons were initially ambivalent about the War with Spain, unsure of how to reconcile their brand of patriotism with holy peacemaking. The Mormon leadership divided but then embraced military service, with an outpouring of volunteering from Mormon communities across Utah. The experience of war, including the occupation of the Philippines, would prove more trying and divisive, but afforded a chance for Mormons to move toward the U.S. mainstream.

In the tenth chapter, Brian Shott takes Louis Dalrymple's 1899 *Puck* cartoon, "School Begins," as a vantage point from which to consider the polyvalent place of racial ideas and identities in turn-of-the-century politics and culture. Featuring a stern Uncle Sam as a schoolteacher and four sullen, dark-skinned children representing the Philippines, Hawaii, Puerto Rico, and Cuba, the cartoon seems a racist, pro-imperial piece. Shott calls into question just how straightforward it is, illuminating that while racism is clearly central to it, what precisely the author intended and how audiences would have received it is harder to fathom. If hardly anti-imperial, the piece was layered with symbols, including an African American child with a bucket, evoking Booker T. Washington, and a well-kempt Chinese child excluded from the classroom. Especially viewed alongside other nineteenth-century cartoons featuring racial politics, "School Begins" invites a second look for its ambiguities and nuances.

Justin Jackson, in "An Empire of Reconstructions," examines together the histories of U.S. military occupations in the South after the Civil War and Cuba following the defeat of Spain. His comparisons between the two military administrations explore important continuities and changes in the culture of armed occupation, as well as their implications for the hemispheric history of racial equality. The two took place in different contexts, but also shared divisive questions over race, political power, reform, and control of economic resources. The two episodes in military government highlight important shifts in ideas about sovereignty and governance in the United States. Perhaps no single event marked more clearly the subtle but important ideological drift shaping U.S. occupations than the evolution of "reconstruction" itself. Associated with a radical commitment to social change before the Civil War, the occupation of Cuba remade reconstruction into a postwar mode of foreign rule involving commitments to capitalist development.

In her Afterword, Rebecca Edwards surveys the volume and its place in scholarship on the late-nineteenth- and early-twentieth-century United States.

Notes

1. Literary historians, legal scholars, and biographers have done important work pointing the way toward better linking these two subjects. Representative works include Amy Kaplan, *The Anarchy of Empire in the Making of U.S. Culture* (Cambridge, Mass.: Harvard University Press, 2002); Brook Thomas, *The Literature of Reconstruction: Not in Plain Black and White* (Baltimore: Johns Hopkins University Press, 2017); and Sam Erman, "The Constitutional Lion in the Path: The Reconstruction Constitution as a Restraint on Empire," *Southern California Law Review* 91, no. 6 (2018), 1197–1222. For an interesting argument linking turn-of-the century anti-imperialism with Civil War–era abolitionism, see Manisha Sinha, *The Slave's Cause: A History of Abolition* (New Haven, Conn.: Yale University Press, 2016).

2. This scholar is skeptical that singular definitions of "empire," "imperialism," and "Reconstruction" will ever prevail in academic usage. To the extent that this volume uses what might be called conventional and restricted definitions of the terms, it is to make the point that even when these are in effect, there is still good reason to study the United States' Reconstruction and its empire together. It is true by definition that expanding the meaning of these terms so that they encompass more of U.S. history, as the contributors sometimes do, magnifies the number of thematic and causal linkages between the historical processes they refer to. For a helpful cautioning against an uncritical embrace of narrow definitions of "empire," see Paul A. Kramer, "How Not to Write the History of U.S. Empire," *Diplomatic History* 42, no. 5 (2018), 911–931. On the complex history of these terms, see Mark F. Proudman, "Words for Scholars: The Semantics of 'Imperialism,'" *Journal of the Historical Society* 8, no. 3 (2008), 395–433; Andrew Heath, "'Let the Empire Come': Imperialism and Its Critics in the Reconstruction South," *Civil War History* 60, no. 2 (2014), 152–189; David Prior, "Reconstruction, from Transatlantic Polyseme to Historiographical Quandary," in *Reconstruction in a Globalizing World*, ed. David Prior (New York: Fordham University Press, 2018), 172–208; Rachel St. John, "The Case for Containing Reconstruction," in *Reconstruction and Mormon America*, ed. Brian Q. Cannon and Clyde Milner II (Norman: University of Oklahoma Press, 2019), 181–191; David Moltke-Hansen, "Confederate Reconstructions: Generations of Conflict," in *Reconstruction at 150: Reassessing America's "New Birth of Freedom"* (volume under revision); and Brook Thomas, "Reconstruction and World War I: The Birth of What Sort of Nation(s)?" *American Literary History*, 30, no. 3 (2018), 559–583.

3. For surveys of these developments, see Eric Foner, *Reconstruction: America's Unfinished Revolution, 1863–1877* (New York: Harper and Row, 1988); Mark Wahlgren Summers, *The Ordeal of the Reunion: A New History of Reconstruction* (Chapel Hill: University of North Carolina Press, 2014); and Faye Dudden, *Fighting Chance: The Struggle over Woman Suffrage and Black Suffrage in Reconstruction America* (New York: Oxford University Press, 2011).

4. For introductions to these developments, see Ian Tyrrell, *Transnational Nation: United States History in Global Perspective since 1789* (Basingstoke: Palgrave Macmillan, 2007); Kristin L. Hoganson, *Fighting for American Manhood: How Gender Provoked the Spanish-American and Philippine-American Wars* (New Haven, Conn.: Yale University Press, 1998); Elliott West, *The Last Indian War: The Nez Perce Story* (New York: Oxford University Press, 2011); Thomas Bender, *A Nation among Nations: America's Place in World History* (New York: Hill and Wang, 2006); and Matthew Frye Jacobson, *Barbarian Virtues: The United States Encounters Foreign Peoples at Home and Abroad, 1876–1917* (New York: Hill and Wang, 2000).

5. See especially Chris Fobare, "A Generational Divide: The Reconstruction of American Party Politics, 1865–1912" (PhD diss., University of Massachusetts Amherst, 2019).

6. Summers, *The Ordeal of the Reunion*, chaps. 14–15 and Robert Dallek, "National Mood and American Foreign Policy: A Suggestive Essay," *American Quarterly* 34, no. 4 (1982), 339–361.

7. See David C. Turpie, "A Voluntary War: The Spanish-American War, White Southern Manhood, and the Struggle to Recruit Volunteers in the South," *Journal of Southern*

History 80, no. 4 (2014), 859–892; David W. Blight, *Race and Reunion: The Civil War in American Memory* (Cambridge, Mass.: Harvard University Press, 2000), 346–353; Barbara A. Gannon, *The Won Cause: Black and White Comradeship in the Grand Army of the Republic* (Chapel Hill: University of North Carolina Press, 2011), 174–76; Heather Cox Richardson, *West from Appomattox: The Reconstruction of America after the Civil War* (New Haven, Conn.: Yale University Press, 2007), esp. chap. 9; Caroline Janney, *Remembering the Civil War: Reunion and the Limits of Reconciliation* (Chapel Hill: University of North Carolina Press, 2013), 222–231.

    8. See B. Ricardo Brown, *Until Darwin: Science, Human Variety and the Origins of Race* (London: Pickering & Chatto, 2010); Jacobson, *Barbarian Virtues*; and Alison Clark Efford, "Civil War–Era Immigration and the Imperial United States," *Journal of the Civil War Era* 10, no. 2 (2020), 233–253. For the role of racism in inhibiting imperialism, see Eric T. L. Love, *Race over Empire: Racism and U.S. Imperialism, 1865–1900* (Chapel Hill: University of North Carolina Press, 2004).

    9. See Willard B. Gatewood Jr., *Black Americans and the White Man's Burden, 1898–1903* (Urbana: University of Illinois Press, 1975); Michele Mitchell, *Righteous Propagation: African Americans and the Politics of Racial Destiny after Reconstruction* (Chapel Hill: University of North Carolina Press, 2004), 61–69; and Frank Andre Guridy, *Forging Diaspora: Afro-Cubans and African Americans in a World of Jim Crow and Empire* (Chapel Hill: University of North Carolina Press, 2010).

    10. See Hoganson, *Fighting for American Manhood*; Kaplan, *The Anarchy of Empire*; Allison L. Sneider, *Suffragists in an Imperial Age: U.S. Expansion and the Woman Question, 1870–1929* (New York: Oxford University Press, 2008); and Gail Bederman, *Manliness and Civilization: A Cultural History of Gender and Race in the United States, 1880–1917* (Chicago: University of Chicago Press, 1996). For a helpful overview of this literature, see Sarah Steinbock-Pratt, "New Frontiers beyond the Seas: The Culture of American Empire and Expansion at the Turn of the Twentieth Century," in *A Companion to U.S. Foreign Relations: Colonial Era to the Present*, ed. Christopher R. W. Dietrich, vol. 1 (Hoboken, N.J.: Wiley, 2020), 233–251. For a recent call for renewed attention to the feminist study of U.S. empire, broadly construed, see Laura Briggs, "Imperialism as a Way of Life: Thinking Sex and Gender in American Empire," *Radical History Review* 2015, no. 123 (2015), 9–31.

    11. On professionalization within the U.S. military, see Graham A. Cosmas, "The Spanish-American and Philippine Wars, 1898–1902," in *A Companion to American Military History*, ed. James C. Bradford (Malden, Mass.: Blackwell, 2009), 139–152, 139, 142–144; David J. Silbey, *A War of Frontier and Empire: The Philippine-American War, 1899–1902* (New York: Hill and Wang, 2007), 19–26; and David Axeen, "'Heroes of the Engine Room': American 'Civilization' and the War with Spain," *American Quarterly* 36, no. 4 (1984), 481–502.

    12. See, for example, Jim Downs, *Sick from Freedom: African-American Illness and Suffering during the Civil War and Reconstruction* (New York: Oxford University Press, 2012); John M. Gates, "War-Related Deaths in the Philippines, 1898–1902," *Pacific Historical Review* 53, no. 3 (1984), 367–378; and Daniel C. Immerwahr, *How to Hide an Empire: A History of the Greater United States* (New York: Farrar, Straus and Giroux, 2019) on the need for care in assessing the complex causes of disease outbreaks and deaths.

13. Consider Stephen V. Ash, *A Massacre in Memphis: The Race Riot That Shook the Nation One Year after the Civil War* (New York: Hill and Wang, 2013); Peter Cozzens, *The Earth Is Weeping: The Epic Story of the Indian Wars for the American West* (New York: Vintage, 2017); and the careful analysis in Iain R. Smith and Andreas Stucki, "The Colonial Development of Concentration Camps (1868–1902)," *Journal of Imperial and Commonwealth History* 39, no. 3 (2011), 417–437. The U.S. Civil War, in contrast, witnessed little deliberate, strategic violence against civilians in the campaigns of Union and Confederate forces against each other; consider Mark E. Neely Jr., "Was the Civil War a Total War?" *Civil War History*, 37, no. 1 (1991), 5–28.

14. See, for example, Frank Ninkovich, *Global Dawn: The Cultural Foundations of American Imperialism, 1865–1890* (Cambridge, Mass.: Harvard University Press, 2009); Jacobson, *Barbarian Virtues*; Bederman, *Manliness and Civilization*; Daniel E. Bender, *American Abyss: Savagery and Civilization in the Age of Industry* (Ithaca, N.Y.: Cornell University Press, 2009); Jay Sexton, "William Seward in the World," *Journal of the Civil War Era* 4, no. 3 (2014), 398–40; and David Prior, *Between Freedom and Progress: The Lost World of Reconstruction Politics* (Baton Rouge: Louisiana State University Press, 2019).

15. See especially Louis A. Pérez Jr., *Cuba in the American Imagination: Metaphor and the Imperial Ethos* (Chapel Hill: University of Chapel Hill Press, 2008); Prior, *Between Freedom and Progress*; Natalie J. Ring, *The Problem South: Region, Empire, and the New Liberal State, 1880–1930* (Athens: University of Georgia Press, 2012); and Bender, *American Abyss*.

16. See Rebecca Edwards, "Politics, Social Movements, and the Periodization of U.S. History," *Journal of the Gilded Age and the Progressive Era* 8, no. 4 (2009), 463–473; Rebecca Edwards, *New Spirits: Americans in the Gilded Age, 1865–1905* (New York: Oxford University Press, 2006); Richard Schneirov, "Thoughts on Periodizing the Gilded Age: Capital Accumulation, Society, and Politics, 1873–1898," *Journal of the Gilded Age and Progressive Era* 5, no. 3 (2006), 189–224 and the following responses by James Huston and Rebecca Edwards in the same issue; Heather Cox Richardson, "Reconstructing the Gilded Age and Progressive Era," in *A Companion to the Gilded Age and Progressive Era*, ed. Christopher McKnight Nichols and Nancy Unger (Malden, Mass.: Wiley Blackwell, 2017), 7–20; Elliott West, "Reconstructing Race," *Western Historical Quarterly* 34, no. 1 (2003), 6–26; Stacey L. Smith, "Beyond North and South: Putting the West in the Civil War and Reconstruction," *Journal of the Civil War Era* 6, no. 4 (2016), 566–591; Elliott West, "Reconstruction in the West," *Journal of the Civil War Era*, online forum, https://www.journalofthecivilwarera.org/forum-the-future-of-reconstruction-studies/reconstruction-in-the-west/; Fobare, "Generational Divide"; and Pekka Hämäläinen, "Reconstructing the Great Plains: The Long Struggle for Sovereignty and Dominance in the Heart of the Continent," *Journal of the Civil War Era* 6, no. 4 (2016), 481–509.

17. For these authors' narrative histories, see Elliott West, *The Last Indian War*; Richardson, *West from Appomattox*; and Richard White, *The Republic for which it Stands: The United States during Reconstruction and the Gilded Age, 1865–1896* (New York: Oxford University Press, 2017).

18. See St. John, "The Case for Containing Reconstruction."

19. Eric Foner, "*Black Reconstruction*: An Introduction," *South Atlantic Quarterly* 112, no. 3 (2013), 411; Moon-Ho Jung, "*Black Reconstruction* and Empire," ibid., 465–471; and Moon-Ho Jung, *Coolies and Cane: Race, Labor, and Sugar in the Age of Emancipation* (Baltimore: Johns Hopkins University Press, 2006).

20. On the writing of *Black Reconstruction*, see David Levering Lewis, *W. E. B. Du Bois: A Biography* (New York: Henry Holt, 2009), 581–583; and Claire Parfait, "Rewriting History: The Publication of W. E. B. Du Bois's *Black Reconstruction in America*," *Book History* 12 (2009), 266–294, 273–274.

21. Foner, "*Black Reconstruction*." For the concept of evocative history, see Edward Baptist, *The Half Has Never Been Told: Slavery and the Making of American Capitalism* (New York: Basic Books, 2016). For Du Bois as a moral historian, see Edward J. Blum, *W. E. B. Du Bois: American Prophet* (Philadelphia: University of Pennsylvania Press, 2007), 103, 221; and Lewis, *W. E. B. Du Bois*, 590.

22. Du Bois, for example, felt more comfortable than most scholars today likely would in describing Southern freedpeople as ignorant and in attributing a lack of ambition, self-respect, and refinement to Black life in the South in the decades following the Civil War. Du Bois's point in doing so was to illustrate the oppressive nature of white supremacist rule, but more recent scholarship tends to accentuate the sagacity and resilience of Southern freedpeople and their children. Du Bois also addressed the religious meanings of emancipation in ways at once sympathetic yet distant from his own and presumably his readers' beliefs. See, for example, W. E. B. Du Bois, *Black Reconstruction in America, 1860–1880* (1935; New York: Free Press, 1992), 124, 605–607, 611, 618, 701. For a brief comment on Du Bois's views of religion and his idea of the talented tenth in *Black Reconstruction*, see Foner, "*Black Reconstruction*," 416–417. For a statement on Du Bois's enduring faith in middle-class black leadership in the 1930s, see Manning Marable, *W. E. B. Du Bois: Black Radical Democrat* (Boston: Twayne, 1986), 143, 147–148.

23. Du Bois, *Black Reconstruction*, 9, 15–16. On Marxism and *Black Reconstruction*, see Cedric J. Robinson, "A Critique of W. E. B. Du Bois' *Black Reconstruction*," *Black Scholar* 8, no. 7 (1977), 44–50; Marable, *W. E. B. Du Bois*, 146; Foner, "*Black Reconstruction*," 413–416; Lewis, *W. E. B. Du Bois*, 582. On Du Bois's broader engagement with socialism in the period before the publication of *Black Reconstruction* and his earlier statements that anticipate his thesis in *Black Reconstruction*, see Marable, *W. E. B. Du Bois*, 103, 107, 108, 110; Lewis, *W. E. B. Du Bois*, 577; and Jung, "*Black Reconstruction* and Empire," 469–470. On the origins of Du Bois's intellectual inspiration in *Black Reconstruction* in his earlier literary and sociological career, see especially Thomas C. Holt, "'A Story of Ordinary Human Beings': The Source of Du Bois's Historical Imagination in *Black Reconstruction*," *South Atlantic Quarterly* 112, no. 3 (2013), 419–435.

24. Quotations from Du Bois, *Black Reconstruction in America*, 30, 633, 630–631; see also 704. Foner, "*Black Reconstruction*," 414–15.

25. Indeed, for that reason scholars continue to see *Black Reconstruction*, along with Du Bois's other works, as relevant to understanding events today; see Anthony Monteiro, "Race and Empire: W. E. B. Du Bois and the U.S. State," *Black Scholar: Journal of Black Studies and Research* 37, no. 2 (2007), 35–52.

26. Quotations from Du Bois, *Black Reconstruction in America*, 634–635, 602; see also 706, 708. On the origins of Du Bois's argument about imperial competition and World War I, see Marable, *W. E. B. Dubois*, 93–94.

27. For works treating the broader history of African American opinions about and engagement with late-nineteenth-century empires, see Gatewood, *Black Americans and the White Man's Burden*; Jeannette Eileen Jones, "'The Negro's Peculiar Work': Jim Crow and Black Discourses on U.S. Empire, Race, and the African Question, 1877–1900," *Journal of American Studies* 52, no. 2 (2018), 330–357; Mitchell, *Righteous Propagation*, chap. 2; and Andrew Zimmerman, *Alabama in Africa: Booker T. Washington, the German Empire, and the Globalization of the New South* (Princeton, N.J.: Princeton University Press, 2012). For an article assessing Du Bois's earlier relationship with imperial Germany, see Kenneth Barkin, 'W. E. B. Du Bois' Love Affair with Imperial Germany,' *German Studies Review* 28, no. 2 (2005), 285–302.

28. See, for example, Du Bois, *Black Reconstruction in America*, 717 versus 673–74. Also of note, Du Bois's original title for the volume, *Black Reconstruction of Democracy in America*, arguably conveyed a slightly different meaning than the "reconstruction in" of the final, published title, the subtitle of which also used the verb "reconstruct." See David Levering Lewis, introduction to *Black Reconstruction in America*, by W. E. B. Du Bois (New York: Free Press, 1992), ix, and Lewis, *W. E. B. Du Bois*, 582. Also of note, Du Bois started but did not finish a manuscript titled "The Negro and Social Reconstruction," which evoked pre–Civil War meaning of the term "reconstruction" as a radical, grassroots transformation. On the manuscript, see Marable, *W. E. B. Du Bois*, 144–145, 148–149. On scholarly disagreement over the term's meaning, see Prior, "Reconstruction."

29. For Civil War–era meanings of "imperialism" and "empire," see Heath, "'Let the Empire Come.'" For Du Bois's uses of these earlier meanings, see Du Bois, *Black Reconstruction in America*, 584, 586, 596, 605.

30. John W. Burgess, *Reconstruction and the Constitution, 1866–1876* (New York: Charles Scribner's Sons, 1902), viii–ix, 217–218; Du Bois, *Black Reconstruction in America*, 719. On Burgess, see Shepherd W. McKinley, "John W. Burgess, Godfather of the Dunning School," in John David Smith and J. Vincent Lowery, *The Dunning School: Historians, Race, and the Meaning of Reconstruction* (Lexington: University Press of Kentucky, 2013), 49–76; and Thomas, *The Literature of Reconstruction*, 6–8, 83–90.

31. See Prior, "Reconstruction," 183–185; Thomas, *The Literature of Reconstruction*, 258–259; Lewis, *W. E. B. Du Bois*, 579–580, 590–591; Lewis, introduction to *Black Reconstruction in America*, by Du Bois, ix; Parfait, "Rewriting History," 281–282; Foner, "*Black Reconstruction*," 412; Bernard A. Weisberger, "The Dark and Bloody Ground of Reconstruction Historiography," *Journal of Southern History* 25, no. 4 (1959), 427–447, esp. 444; Du Bois, *Black Reconstruction*, 714–715, 716; A. A. Taylor, Review of W. E. B. Du Bois, *Black Reconstruction in America*, published in the *New England Quarterly* 8, no. 4 (1935), 608–612, esp. 610; and Rayford W. Logan, Review of W. E. B. Du Bois, *Black Reconstruction in America*, published in the *Journal of Negro History* 21, no. 1 (1936), 61–63, esp. 62–63.

32. Peter Novick, *That Noble Dream: The "Objectivity Question" and the American Historical Profession* (New York: Cambridge University Press, 1988), 224–234; Lewis, *W. E. B. Du Bois*, 585–586.

33. C. Vann Woodward to W. E. B. Du Bois, April 3, 1938, in *The Letters of C. Vann Woodward*, ed. Michael O'Brien (New Haven: Yale University Press, 2013), 60; Lewis, *W. E. B. Du Bois*, 591–592; Lewis, introduction to *Black Reconstruction in America*, by Du Bois, xvi.

34. On the reception of *Black Reconstruction*, see especially Lewis, introduction to *Black Reconstruction in America*, by Du Bois, xi–xvi; Parfait, "Rewriting History," 277, 279–283; Prior, "Reconstruction," 204n92.

35. For general background, see Novick, *That Noble Dream*, 169–175, 204–205, 302–303.

36. Parfait, "Rewriting History," 283–287.

37. Richardson, "Reconstructing the Gilded Age and Progressive Era," 8.

38. A. A. Taylor, who reviewed the volume in the *New England Quarterly* 8, no. 4 (1935), 608–612, passed away in 1954; see John Hope Franklin, "Personal: Alrutheus Ambush Taylor," *Journal of Negro History* 39, no. 3 (1954), 240–242. Arthur C. Cole, who reviewed the volume in *The Mississippi Valley Historical Review* 23, no. 2 (1936), 327–328, retired in 1957; see "Arthur C. Cole, 89, Dead," *New York Times*, February 28, 1976, 25; Francis Butler Simkins, who reviewed the volume in the *Journal of Southern History* 1, no. 4 (1935), 530–532, became racially conservative and died in 1966; see James Scott Humphreys, *Francis Butler Simkins: A Life* (Gainesville: University Press of Florida, 2008), chap. 13.

39. Quotations from Lewis, *W. E. B. Du Bois*, 687.

40. Lewis, *W. E. B. Du Bois*, chaps. 21–22.

41. Novick, *That Noble Dream*, 362, 377.

42. Consider Foner, "*Black Reconstruction*," 417; Holt, "'A Story of Ordinary Human Beings,'" 420; Lewis, introduction to *Black Reconstruction in America*, by Du Bois, xvi; and Lewis, *W. E. B. Du Bois*, 694.

43. For some brief comments on the book's influence on the radical Left, see Robert Greene II, "The Legacy of *Black Reconstruction*," *Jacobin*, August 27, 2018, https://www.jacobinmag.com/2018/08/web-du-bois-black-reconstruction-civil-rights; Ferrucio Gambino, "Reading *Black Reconstruction* on the Eve of 1968," *South Atlantic Quarterly* 112, no. 3 (2013), 529–535; and Lewis, *W. E. B. Du Bois*, 670.

44. Many historiographical essays review this literature. See especially Stephen A. West, "'A General Remodeling of Every Thing': Economy and Race in the Post-Emancipation South," and John C. Rodrigue, "Black Agency after Slavery," both in *Reconstructions: New Perspectives on the Postbellum United States*, ed. Thomas J. Brown (New York: Oxford University Press, 2006), 10–39, 40–65; and Eric Foner, "Reconstruction Revisited," *Reviews in American History* 10, no. 4 (1982), 82–100.

45. See the historiographical essays cited in note 47 below and Don H. Doyle, "Reconstruction and Anti-Imperialism: The United States and Mexico," in *United States Reconstruction across the Americas*, ed. William Link (Gainesville: University Press of Florida, 2019), 47–80, esp. 47–48.

46. For example, the following classic studies do not include *Black Reconstruction* in their bibliographies or bibliographic essays and do not have an index entry for either Du Bois or *Black Reconstruction*: Willie Lee Rose, *Rehearsal for Reconstruction: The Port*

Royal Experiment (New York: Oxford University Press, 1964); LaWanda Cox and John H. Cox, *Politics, Principle, and Prejudice, 1865–1866: Dilemma of Reconstruction America* (1963; New York: Atheneum, 1969); Joel Williamson, *After Slavery: The Negro in South Carolina during Reconstruction, 1861–1877* (Chapel Hill: University of North Carolina Press, 1965).

47. On Du Bois and Williams, see also Jung, "Black Reconstruction and Empire," 468. For an essay that can help scholars think through how Williams might have drawn on Du Bois's work in his own analyses, see Richard A. Melanson, "The Social and Political Thought of William Appleman Williams," *Western Political Quarterly* 31, no. 3 (1978), 392–409. On the pro–civil rights syntheses: Kenneth M. Stampp referred to *Black Reconstruction* as "disappointing" in his bibliographic essay in his *The Era of Reconstruction: 1865–1877* (New York: Vintage, 1965), 218; John Hope Franklin, devoted but one sentence to *Black Reconstruction* in the suggested readings for his *Reconstruction: After the Civil War* (Chicago: University of Chicago Press, 1961), noting its "strong Marxist bias throughout," 236. See also Holt, "'A Story of Ordinary Human Beings,'" 422–423; Parfait, "Rewriting History," 285–286.

48. See, for example, Eric Rauchway, "The Global Emergence of the United States, 1867–1900," in *A Companion to Nineteenth-Century America*, ed. William L. Barney (Malden, Mass.: Blackwell, 2001), 104–117; Allan E. S. Lumba, "Empire, Expansion, and Its Consequences," in *A Companion to the Gilded Age and Progressive Era*, ed. Christopher M. Nichols and Nancy Unger (Malden, Mass.: Wiley Blackwell, 2017), 399–409; Frank Ninkovich, "The United States and Imperialism," in *A Companion to American Foreign Relations*, ed. Robert Schulzinger (Malden, Mass.: Wiley Blackwell, 2003), 79–102; and Joseph A. Fry, "In Search of an Orderly World: U.S. Imperialism, 1898–1912," in *Modern American Diplomacy* , ed. John M. Carroll and George C. Herring (1986; Wilmington, Del.: SR Books, 1996), 1–23. For essays that offer brief exceptions to this rule, see Joseph A. Fry, "Phases of Empire: Late Nineteenth-Century U.S. Foreign Relations," in *The Gilded Age: Perspectives on the Origins of Modern America*, ed. Charles W. Calhoun, 2nd ed. (Lanham, Md.: Rowman & Littlefield, 2007), 307–332, 312, and Steinbock-Pratt, "New Frontiers beyond the Seas," 234, 243.

49. See Rembert W. Patrick, "Foreign Affairs," chapter 9 in his *The Reconstruction of the Nation* (New York: Oxford University Press, 1967), 194–209; Dale Roger Steiner, "'To Save the Constitution': The Political Manipulation of Foreign Affairs during Reconstruction" (PhD diss., University of Virginia, 1973); James Burke Chapin, "Hamilton Fish and American Expansion" (PhD diss., Cornell University, 1971). For an essay urging scholars of Reconstruction to attend to diplomatic history, see Mark M. Smith, "The Past as a Foreign Country: Reconstruction, Inside and Out," in *Reconstructions*, ed. Brown, 117–140. For a recent overview of Reconstruction-era diplomacy and expansionism, see Summers, *The Ordeal of the Reunion*, chap. 9.

50. For the broader transformation of the history of U.S. foreign relations, see Susan Brewer, "'As Far as We Can': Culture and U.S. Foreign Relations," in *A Companion to American Foreign Relations*, ed. Robert Schulzinger (Malden, Mass.: Blackwell, 2003), 15–30; Michael J. Hogan, "The 'Next Big Thing': The Future of Diplomatic History in a Global Age," *Diplomatic History* 28, no. 1 (2004), 1–21; Thomas W. Zeiler, "The Diplo-

matic History Bandwagon: A State of the Field," *Journal of American History* 95, no. 4 (2009), 1053–1073, and the following responses by Fredrik Logevall et al., ibid., 1074–1091; and Kramer, "How Not to Write the History of U.S. Empire."

51. The examples here are from Guridy, *Forging Diaspora*; Sarah Steinbock-Pratt, "'It Gave Us Our Nationality': U.S. Education, the Politics of Dress, and Transnational Filipino Student Networks, 1901–1945," *Gender & History* 26, no. 3 (2014), 565–588; Cynthia Marasigan, "Race, Performance, and Colonial Governance: The Philippine Constabulary Band Plays the St. Louis World's Fair," *Journal of Asian American Studies* 22, no. 3 (2019), 349–385; and Tessa Ong Winkelmann, "Rethinking the Sexual Geography of American Empire in the Philippines: Interracial Intimacies in Mindanao and the Cordilleras, 1898–1921," in *Gendering the Trans-Pacific World*, ed. Catherine Ceniza Choy and Judy Tzu-Chun (Leiden, The Netherlands: Brill, 2017), 39–76. See also Ian Tyrrell, *Reforming the World: The Creation of America's Moral Empire* (Princeton, N.J.: Princeton University Press, 2010).

52. For an excellent review of recent literature, see Steinbock-Pratt, "New Frontiers beyond the Seas."

53. See, for example, how Rebecca J. Scott connects the lives of civil rights activists in southern Louisiana to the imperial moment in 1898, in *Degrees of Freedom: Louisiana and Cuba after Slavery* (Cambridge, Mass.: Belknap Press of Harvard University Press, 2008).

54. Smith, "The Past as a Foreign Country"; Andrew Zimmerman, "Reconstruction: Transnational History," in *Interpreting American History: Reconstruction*, ed. John David Smith (Kent, Ohio: Kent State University Press, 2016), 171–196; David Prior, ed., *Reconstruction in a Globalizing World* (New York: Fordham University Press, 2018); and Prior, *Between Freedom and Progress*.

55. See Ernest N. Paolino, *The Foundations of the American Empire: William Henry Seward and U.S. Foreign Policy* (Ithaca, N.Y.: Cornell University Press, 1973); Don H. Doyle, *The Cause of All Nations: An International History of the American Civil War* (New York: Basic Books, 2015); Doyle, "Reconstruction and Anti-Imperialism"; Sexton, "William Seward in the World"; Prior, *Between Freedom and Progress*; Jay Sexton, "Toward a Synthesis of Foreign Relations in the Civil War Era, 1848–1877," *American Nineteenth Century History* 5, no. 3 (2004), 50–73; George C. Herring, *From Colony to Superpower: U.S. Foreign Relations since 1776* (New York: Oxford University Press, 2008), chaps. 5–7; and Walter Nugent, *Habits of Empire: A History of American Expansion* (New York: Vintage, 2008), 237–244.

56. The classic treatment of this earlier literature is Foner, "Reconstruction Revisited."

57. Blight, *Race and Reunion*; Richardson, *West from Appomattox*; Janney, *Remembering the Civil War*; and Nina Silber, "Reunion and Reconciliation, Reviewed and Reconsidered," *Journal of American History* 103, no. 1 (2016), 59–83.

58. Steven H. Hahn, *A Nation without Borders: The United States and its World in an Age of Civil Wars, 1830–1910* (New York: Penguin, 2017); White, *The Republic for Which It Stands*; Charles Postel, *Equality: An American Dilemma, 1866–1896* (New York: Farrar, Straus and Giroux, 2019).

59. See Silber, "Reunion and Reconciliation, Reviewed and Reconsidered," 73.

60. See Scott Miller, *The President and the Assassin: McKinley, Terror, and Empire at the Dawn of the American Century* (New York: Random House, 2013); and Karl Jacoby, *The Strange Career of William Ellis: The Texas Slave Who Became a Mexican Millionaire* (New York: W.W. Norton, 2016).

61. For Reconstruction as a success on these terms, see Summers, *The Ordeal of the Reunion*.

62. On Northern views of the South as defined by economic, educational, and racial problems and as sharing features with the colonized global South, see Ring, *The Problem South*. On "the federal government's soaring confidence in its ability to reconstruct societies and regions" in the postbellum decade, see Hämäläinen, "Reconstructing the Great Plains," 488.

63. Eric Hobsbawm, while viewing the bourgeois West of the mid-nineteenth century as generally hostile to slavery, noted that "Northern capitalism, whatever the private views of businessmen, might well have found it as possible and convenient to come to terms with and exploit a slave South as international business has with the 'apartheid' of South Africa"; see E. J. Hobsbawm, *The Age of Capital, 1848–1875* (London: Weidenfeld and Nicolson, 1975), 141. Scholars willing to engage in the counterfactual exercise might ask whether the union-busting, vertically integrated corporate behemoths of the late nineteenth century would not have utilized human chattel as strikebreakers and in place of high-wage skilled workers if they could have, and whether Maryland or South Carolina state legislatures could not have reworked state laws to lure in corporate headquarters. For interesting takes on proslavery imperialism before the Civil War, see Matthew Karp, *This Vast Southern Empire: Slaveholders at the Helm of American Foreign Policy* (Cambridge, Mass.: Harvard University Press, 2016); and Walter Johnson, *River of Dark Dreams: Slavery and Empire in the Cotton Kingdom* (Cambridge, Mass.: Harvard University Press, 2017). For one vision of what a victorious, industrialized post–Civil War Confederacy would have looked like, see *C.S.A.: The Confederate States of America*, directed by Kevin Willmott (2004; Lawrence, Kansas; Hodcarrier Films, distributed by IFC Films, 2006), DVD.

64. See Eric Foner, *The Fiery Trial: Abraham Lincoln and American Slavery* (New York: W. W. Norton, 2010); and Gannon, *The Won Cause*.

65. Stacey Smith, *Freedom's Frontier: California and the Struggle over Unfree Labor, Emancipation, and Reconstruction* (Chapel Hill: University of North Carolina Press, 2013); and Michael Salman, *The Embarrassment of Slavery: Controversies over Bondage and Nationalism in the American Philippines, 1896–1916* (Berkeley: University of California Press, 2001).

66. On the fusing of mid-nineteenth-century emancipatory ideals with U.S. national identity and how these may have obscured from American eyes their own involvement in forms of oppression other than chattel slavery, it is worth reading David M. Potter, "The Civil War in the History of the Modern World: A Comparative View," in David M. Potter, *The South and the Sectional Conflict* (Baton Rouge: Louisiana State University Press, 1968), 287–299, alongside Walter Johnson, "The Pedestal and the Veil: Rethinking the Capitalism/Slavery Question," *Journal of the Early Republic* 24, no. 2 (2009), 299–308.

1

The Last Filibuster

The Ten Years' War in Cuba and the Legacy of the American Civil War

Andre M. Fleche

On the night of October 9, 1868, the Cuban planter Carlos Manuel de Céspedes gathered his slaves and offered freedom to any who would fight alongside him in a war for independence from Spain. The ensuing conflict came to be known as the Ten Years' War, and, though Céspedes might not have known it, the war he inaugurated initiated a debate that would engage issues of race, slavery, and citizenship in Cuba, the United States, and Spain. The Ten Years' War called into question the future of human bondage in Cuba at the very moment politicians and the general public in the United States debated the policies of postwar Reconstruction. The Civil War, the Emancipation Proclamation, and the Thirteenth Amendment to the Constitution had destroyed slavery in the United States but had not settled the future of coerced labor in the Western world. When President Ulysses S. Grant took office in 1869, many white Southerners continued to violently resist federal laws that had granted equal citizenship rights to African Americans. Profitable slave regimes continued to exist in Brazil, Puerto Rico, and Cuba. Though the Confederacy had met a decisive military defeat during the Civil War, the verdict of arms had not so clearly addressed the future of slave labor, let alone racial equality, in the Western Hemisphere.

The Ten Years' War offered observers the opportunity to reflect on the legacy of the Civil War, including both its promises and its limitations. Hundreds of U.S. citizens volunteered to fight in Cuba, and two of them—Federico Fernández Cavada, a Union veteran, and Thomas Jordan, an ex-Confederate general—would each briefly hold the rank of general-in-chief of the insurgency. The experiences and actions of the two soldiers in Cuba would shed light on the politics of Reconstruction, the future of American empire, and, ultimately, the meaning and legacy of the Civil War.

For Cavada, the Union victory in the Civil War opened the door for the U.S. to establish a political economy in the Caribbean based on republican government and free labor. The abolition of slavery in the United States, he believed, would inevitably lead to the demise of human bondage in Cuba. Even more important, he imagined liberal reform of the island's economy would weaken Spanish rule and strengthen Cuba's ties to the U.S. When rebellion eventually broke out, Cavada consistently argued that only an aggressive war against slavery would secure Cuban independence. Thomas Jordan, for his part, preferred to limit the impact of the Cuban conflict on the social and racial order as much as he could. Though the actions of the rebels and the outcome of the American Civil War had forced him to reconcile himself to emancipation and even Black military service, as general-in-chief, Jordan fought for an independent Cuba that would continue to preserve racial hierarchies.

The two men had real differences but also similarities that have much to teach about the legacy of the Civil War. Cavada and Jordan agreed that white Americans would take the lead in shaping the Western Hemisphere, but they adapted in very different and telling ways to the promise of emancipation. The disagreement between the two veterans over Cuban policy mirrored the differences of opinion held by citizens of the United States over Reconstruction, the future of the Union, and the progress of American empire. Radical Republicans worked to ensure that the Civil War would give birth to an interracial democracy in which African Americans would enjoy civic, if not necessarily social, equality. White Southerners and Northern Democrats fought to maintain racial subordination even as they came to grips with the reality of emancipation. The two competing visions even came to divide the cabinet of President Ulysses S. Grant—as Gregg French explores further in his chapter in this volume. Grant himself had backed the abolition of slavery and supported the Fourteenth Amendment's guarantee of equal citizenship for all Americans regardless of race. With the questions of slavery and political equality settled, he believed it had become desirable to acquire racially diverse territories in the Caribbean, including Cuba, Puerto Rico, and the Dominican Republic. For that reason, he and Secretary of War John A. Rawlins favored intervention on behalf of the rebels in the Ten Years' War. Secretary of State Hamilton Fish worked hard to stave off these aggressive impulses. The conservative ex-Whig, reluctant Republican, and one-time admirer of the Reconstruction policies of President Andrew Johnson, opposed action in Cuba for a number of reasons. He wished to avoid war with Spain, especially after it briefly became a republic. He also opposed the acquisition of Cuba because of its religious and linguistic differences with the U.S., and because he disapproved of adding nonwhite populations to the Union. As a result, the debate over Cuba came to reflect competing views on the politics of Reconstruction and the legacy of the Civil War.[1]

Several historians have noted parallels between the Civil War, Reconstruction, and the Ten Years' War in Cuba. Ada Ferrer and Rebecca Scott have noted that in both the United States and Cuba slaves and free people of color fought to gain emancipation and equal rights amid the crisis of war.[2] Matt Childs argues that the outcome of the American Civil War itself contributed to the gradual erosion of slavery in Cuba.[3] Jay Sexton notes that U.S. foreign policy came to embrace antislavery in the years after the Civil War. "American statesmen," Sexton concludes, "viewed the Cuban rebellion through a lens tinted by Reconstruction, the meaning of the Civil War, and an evolving and contested idea of national mission."[4] Greg Downs argues that the Civil War–era struggle over Cuba formed part of a revolutionary wave that swept Mexico, Spain, Cuba, and the United States, eventually promising to transform the Atlantic system of the mid-nineteenth century.[5]

Most of the historians who have examined U.S. involvement in the Cuban insurrection have focused mostly on its importance as an episode of formal state-to-state diplomacy.[6] Historians of the domestic politics of Reconstruction have rarely drawn connections between developments at home and abroad.[7] As the story of Cavada and Jordan shows, however, Reconstruction-era debates over race relations, slavery, and citizenship transcended U.S. borders and held important implications for the development of the Western Hemisphere.

A consideration of U.S. policy toward Cuba can demonstrate just how much the Civil War had reoriented American approaches to hemispheric affairs. Cuba had for many years played an outsized role in American imperial imaginings. Its proximity, profitability, and vulnerability to European control convinced many Americans that its future would prove vital to the security of the United States.[8] Before the Civil War, planters in the Mississippi Valley believed control of Cuba would ensure the preservation of slavery in the Americas.[9] Private armies of adventurers made several ill-fated attempts to invade the island during the 1850s. These men were known as "filibusters," and most of them assumed Cuba would become a slave state.[10] The outcome of the Civil War ensured that no new slave territory would be added to the Union, but it did little to address the future of Cuba. Would Cuba also become free soil? This was a pressing question, because Cuba remained central to American imperial ambitions. It would be up to men like Jordan and Cavada—among the last of the filibusters—to help decide the future of American empire in a multiracial world. In the process, they would also demonstrate different ways of thinking about the Civil War and its meaning.

Cavada and a Free Labor Empire

In January 1865, during the waning months of the Siege of Petersburg, Federico Fernández Cavada returned to the land of his birth. The Cuban-born Union veteran awaited an appointment by the Lincoln administration as the new U.S. consul in the city of Trinidad de Cuba. As Cavada prepared to take his post, the geopolitical future of the Western Hemisphere stood poised to undergo breathtaking change. In the United States, Confederate armies slowly disintegrated in the trenches of Virginia, ex-slaves fought for freedom from their one-time masters, and the most radical members of the Republican Party prepared a final push for the adoption of the Thirteenth Amendment to the U.S. Constitution, which would abolish slavery in all of the states of the Union. Cavada reported that public thinkers in his native land immediately grasped the implications these developments might have for the future of Cuba.[11] "The ultimate extinction of the institution of slavery over the whole Western Hemisphere," he marveled, "seems to be accepted as an inevitable sequel to its extinction in the United States."[12] The "colored population," he reported, "are not in the dark as to these great issues." According to Cavada, even some slaveholders in Cuba had come to believe that emancipation was now inevitable.[13]

For Cavada, the destruction of slavery everywhere in the Western Hemisphere would serve as a necessary first step in the "regeneration" of the region. Like many moderate free-soilers and radical abolitionists, he believed that the institution of slavery had undermined confidence in the viability of free labor. He reported that the end of slavery in the United States had caused Cubans to begin to question the opinion that "the white race cannot labor in the fields of Cuba," a misconception he believed needed to be dispelled.[14] He imagined that the victorious Yankees would reinvigorate the tropics with industry and trade, thereby threatening the backward imperialism of the Spanish Empire while also revealing the limitations of his thinking on the potential of the Cuban people themselves. Though the appointment as consul was a minor diplomatic posting, Cavada held excellent credentials to advance his understanding of the Civil War. Cavada presented himself to William Henry Seward, the U.S. secretary of state, as an expert on Cuba and as an enthusiastic supporter of Seward's goals to expand American influence in Latin America. During the early 1850s, Cavada had served on Col. John C. Trautwine's expedition to survey a route for a railroad across Panama, a key step in advancing the goals of American imperialists who sought to make the United States a true two-ocean power. Like many Unionists, both Cavada and Seward believed that U.S. interests in Latin America would be best served by establishing a network of free republics committed to free labor. With slavery destroyed, those countries might safely become new states for the American Union.[15]

Still, Cavada found neither political nor human freedom in the Caribbean. When he arrived in Cuba, the island remained the most important possession in Spain's diminished but still dynamic empire. In 1860, Cuba's plantations produced between 30 and 40 percent of the world's cane sugar, and well more than 300,000 men, women, and children, almost one-third of the total population, continued to labor as slaves. Over the course of the decade, Cubans imported more than 30,000 more enslaved human beings from Africa.[16] Planters also experimented with Chinese contract laborers, who toiled as unpaid apprentices while working off their terms of service. For a time, it appeared that the American Civil War might augur the return of Old World empire in the hemisphere, not the end of monarchy and slavery. In 1861, Spain re-annexed the Dominican Republic. The Lincoln administration remonstrated but dared not intervene due to the growing secession crisis.[17]

The year 1865, though, offered hope for dramatic change. That year, the Spanish Abolition Society held its first meeting in Madrid. In Cuba, the pace of slave importation remained significant but had begun to decline. During the war, Seward had agreed to cooperate with Great Britain in cracking down on the illicit slave trade that had sustained Cuba's plantations.[18] The Spanish Empire also faced setbacks in the Caribbean. A violent guerrilla insurgency emerged in the Dominican Republic, and in 1865, the Spanish army began a withdrawal.[19]

Despite these encouraging events, Cavada's Cuba seemed to remain firmly in the grip of Spanish colonialism. As a U.S. consul, he repeatedly came up against the barriers of Spanish imperial law. In 1866, for example, he scrambled to secure a civil marriage for a young American couple. As Americans and presumably Protestants, the pair could not find a priest willing to perform a ceremony. Cavada bemoaned the lack of separation between the Roman Catholic Church and the state, which made it "impossible" for them "to conform to the religious requirements of this country."[20] Cavada grew even more frustrated with Cuba's imperial administrators when he attempted to have his brother, Adolfo, commissioned as a consular agent. Adolfo, who had served in the Union army and earned a position on the staff of General Andrew A. Humphreys, had taken a job in a merchant house in Cienfuegos. Despite the fact that he was, as Federico explained to Seward, "an American citizen, who served with credit throughout the late war," Spain refused to accept him as a representative of the United States because he had been born a Spanish subject and considered him one in perpetuity.[21] Cavada raged against the new policy, claiming it made his work increasingly "difficult."[22]

Cavada did not have long to wait to strike a blow against the Spanish Empire. Céspedes's declaration of independence, known in Cuba as the "Grito de Yara," promised to upend what Cavada believed had been centuries of misrule. On February 5, 1869, he wrote to Seward to resign his diplomatic commission so that he might volunteer to serve the rebellion.[23] The insurgency quickly developed into a full-fledged war. In April, Horatio Fox, Cavada's successor, reported from Trinidad to Hamilton Fish, the new U.S. secretary of state, that "the insurrection in this neighborhood is still in full force, although the Gov^ment continues to make strong efforts to suppress it."[24] Spanish authorities rounded up American citizens and Cubans suspected of aiding the rebellion. Cavada did not number among the detained. He made his way to rebel lines, and rebel authorities promptly commissioned him a general in the district of Trinidad.[25] He later explained his decision to enlist, speaking often about his desire to "put an end to the atrocious Govt of Spain in Cuba."[26] The imperial government, he implied, had routinely denied basic civil liberties, which were worth risking death to fight for. "Today the Cuban in Cuba," he wrote, "suffers but speaks,—dies but kills."[27]

The Cuban insurgency also offered the hope that an independent Cuba might become a partner and perhaps even a possession of the United States. On May 4, 1869, Henry Ward Beecher, William Cullen Bryant, and Charles A. Dana hosted a mass meeting at the Cooper Institute in New York. The assembly celebrated the "Cuban revolution for freedom and independence" and urged the U.S. government to extend recognition and belligerent rights to the rebels seeking to "throw off the Spanish yoke." The speeches that followed offered the standard American critique of monarchy. The speakers praised the rebels for seeking to establish "republican institutions, and for those principles of freedom, progress, and humanity, the establishment of which will make Cuba a worthy sister Republic of the United States." Orators depicted a struggle between "foreign despotism" and American liberty. Stewart Woodford, a Union Army veteran, ex-officer in the United States Colored Troops, and current lieutenant governor of New York, called attention to the antislavery character of the rebellion. He invoked the memory of the "martyred Lincoln" who, like the rebels, "proclaimed the liberty of the black man" in order to "save the liberty of this nation."[28]

One did not have to listen hard to realize that these boosters linked the spread of liberty to the spread of American influence in Latin America. The organizers adorned the meeting hall with portraits of George Washington, who had established the New World's first republic, Ulysses S. Grant, who had saved it from destruction, and, tellingly, Zachary Taylor, who had led troops into Mexico in a war of imperial conquest. The Democrat John McKeon called attention to the strategic location of Cuba. If it lay in the hands of a power like Great Britain, he explained, it would "command the Gulf of Mexico" and threaten the outlet of the Mississippi. If, however, a liberal regime governed Cuba and relieved the territory of colonial taxes, the island, and presumably American farmers, manufacturers, and merchants, would stand to enjoy fabulous economic growth. Stewart Woodford concluded with the hope that the successful rebels would petition for admission to the Union, where their new republic would be welcomed with "liberty, prosperity, justice and equal rights."[29] Woodford's wishes soon moved toward realization. In April 1869, an assembly of revolutionary delegates at Guáimaro drafted a constitution for the republic and began consideration of a petition in favor of U.S. annexation. The new government also adopted the banner of the famous antebellum filibuster, Narciso López, as the flag of the republic.[30]

Thomas Jordan and the Politics of Race

Although it was not the intention of the Cuban rebels at Guáimaro, who also moved to abolish slavery in the republic, the choice to adopt the flag of the filibusters might have called attention to the fact that in the years before the U.S. Civil War, most of the interest in acquiring Cuba came from slaveholders intent on strengthening the institution in the Caribbean. White Southern leaders, as key members of the Democratic Party, which controlled the executive branch more often than not during the antebellum era, developed what one historian has called a "foreign policy of slavery." Slaveholding secretaries of state, navy, and war expanded U.S. armed forces and provided intellectual and military support to slaveholding regimes in Cuba, Brazil, and Texas.[31] Antebellum filibusters represented the most aggressive proslavery expansionists.[32]

Though the Civil War destroyed slavery in the U.S., it did not destroy American interest in Cuba. The Thirteenth Amendment had ended the possibility of adding the territory to the Union as a slave state, but the future of race relations in Cuba remained uncertain. In the postwar United States, many former adherents of the Confederacy continued to struggle to preserve a hierarchical racial order at home, and like-minded men would certainly not hesitate to do the same abroad. As Cuban rebels offered freedom to slaves who would fight against Spain, rifle clubs and the Ku Klux Klan in the American South took up arms against freedmen and their white supporters. Other Southern whites left for Latin America in search of hospitable social, economic, and political regimes. In the months after Appomattox, hundreds of former Confederate citizens fled to Cuba, Mexico, Venezuela, Brazil, and beyond. Some sought new economic opportunities; most, though, also realized that relocation offered the chance to preserve regimes of racial control. Maximilian, the emperor of Mexico, allowed white immigrants to bring African American "apprentices" who could be held to labor for five to ten years.[33] One Southern settler in Venezuela hoped to find a haven there for the preservation of the white race "uncontaminated by admixture with inferior blood."[34] Those who fled to Brazil needed no reminder that slavery remained legal there. "Slavery will not be abolished soon in this country," one migrant to Brazil reported. "Negroes are advancing in price, and southerners are all wanting to buy."[35]

The war in Cuba might do quite a bit to settle the future of race relations in the Americas, and proslavery U.S. Americans prepared to participate. The very same issue of the *New York Times* that covered Charles A. Dana's pro-Cuba rally also carried another announcement: General Thomas Jordan had just sailed for Cuba "with sixty-two ex-officers of the United States and Confederate armies."[36] Although the expedition attracted its share of Union veterans, its leader, Jordan, had been a devoted Confederate. A native of the Luray Valley, Virginia, he had attended West Point, been commissioned in the U.S. Army, and fought in the Mexican War. When his home state seceded in 1861, he knew exactly where his allegiance would lie. He had spent long hours while stationed in Oregon in the 1850s contemplating the role that cotton cultivation would play in peopling "the solitudes of the great West."[37] America's agricultural might, he believed, would inevitably facilitate the subjugation of the continent. He argued that the London's World's Fair of 1851 had announced America's arrival as a global power. The U.S. exhibit, which had included corn, pork, and cotton bolls, had been placed next to Russia's display, which featured "malachite furniture, mosaics," and "splendid stuffs of gold and silver."[38] Though the world had come away impressed with the Russians, Jordan held that the United States would ultimately triumph. "While those sumptuous articles of furniture and raiment," he wrote, "could only serve the uses of the Czar, the monarchs, and the great nobles of Europe, cotton, corn, and meat clothe and feed millions of an empire resting on the shores of two oceans."[39] Slavery, Jordan believed, had made it all possible. "Divine economy," he wrote, had reserved cotton for the profit of the "great Anglo-Teutonic race" whose "mighty destiny" would lead to the "progress of mankind."[40]

In 1861, Jordan published his thoughts on slavery, cotton, and empire as a defense of secession under the title *The South: Its Products, Commerce, and Resources*. He joined the Confederate army and served on the staff of General Pierre Gustave Toutant Beauregard. His faith in the power of "King Cotton" failed him, as it did so many other Confederate volunteers. The collapse of his army, however, did not shake Jordan's conviction of the justness of his cause. After the war, he took a post as editor of the *Memphis Appeal* and contributed some of the earliest writings in the literature of the Lost Cause. Although Jordan initially angered some Confederate veterans by criticizing Jefferson Davis, he went on to play a part in developing the postwar Southern white orthodoxy on Confederate soldiers.[41] Jordan believed that, though defeated, Confederates had fought bravely for the cause of independence and self-government. "The Confederate story of the war should be told without delay," Jordan explained.[42] During the mid-1860s, he took up his pen in defense of one of the most controversial of living Confederates, General Nathan Bedford Forrest. After the war, Forrest approached Jordan and an acquaintance, J. B. Pryor, with his papers and notes, hoping that the "accomplished writers" might tell his tale.[43] Forrest, a Confederate cavalry commander, had earned notoriety for his role in one of the war's most infamous crimes. When his command overran Fort Pillow along the Mississippi River, his men reportedly gunned down scores of Union soldiers—most of them African Americans—as they attempted to surrender. After the war, Forrest helped establish the original Ku Klux Klan. Jordan and Pryor's laudatory biography of Forrest included a vigorous defense of his record, including his actions at Fort Pillow, in which the authors claimed that the only casualties had been incurred before the surrender.[44] The men dedicated their work to "the memory of the [Confederate] dead" and celebrated the "valor" and "manhood" of the Confederate soldier and his "heroism in the face of prodigious odds."[45]

With the bulk of the book complete, Jordan left Tennessee behind. In 1868, he moved to New York, where he made contact with a group of exiled Cuban patriots called the Cuban Junta, which had been active in the city for decades. During the antebellum era, the group had dedicated itself to the cause of Cuban independence. From the relative safety of the United States, it raised funds and recruited soldiers of fortune for a proposed invasion of the island. The junta had supported the filibusters Narciso López and John Quitman, and had often approached slaveholding Southerners, including Robert E. Lee. The junta itself was divided on the long-term future of slavery in Cuba, as well as on possible annexation by the United States, but all the members of the group agreed to prioritize independence from Spain. By 1868, the group sought to recruit to their cause former supporters of both the Union and the Confederacy.[46]

In May 1869, newspapers in New York and Memphis received word that Jordan, the newest filibuster, had set sail for Cuba. Before Jordan departed, he announced to his readers in Tennessee that he was "about to go to Cuba to take part in the revolutionary movement," noting that "the cause"—which of course once again included national independence—"is one with which my sympathies may be fairly enlisted."[47] He predicted that "success" might also win him "distinction and perhaps fortune."[48] "Jordan's command" successfully landed that June with a force made up of "ex-Federal and Confederate" soldiers.[49] The *New York Sunday News* reported that the troops included Americans, Germans, Irishmen, and Englishmen, "some of whom have undergone 'the baptism of blood' from Chattanooga to Atlanta; others who have breasted the tempest of battle from the Wilderness to the Five Forks."[50] The *Sunday News*'s correspondent praised the performance of "our veterans of the Army of the Potomac" whose experience in "the use of the spade" allowed them to quickly excavate defensive works.[51] An Alabamian in the unit may not have thought quite as much of the "boys in blue," but held out hope that his present cause would not be lost: "The Spaniards don't fight as well as the Yankees," he asserted.[52]

Though Jordan commanded veterans from both sections and both political parties, he did what he could to personally appeal to ex-Confederates.[53] While organizing his command, he reached out to the survivors of Nathan Bedford Forrest's cavalry, imploring them to come to Cuba and offering them a place in his unit. "The country is the noblest I ever saw and worth fighting for," he insisted. "With 3000 Americans to form a nucleus for the people to rally around, there will be no trouble to drive the Spaniards out of the island."[54]

Indeed, Jordan's campaign in Cuba got off to an auspicious start. In July, the revolutionary government named him chief commander for the eastern district, and his soldiers performed well in several skirmishes with the Spanish.[55] The Havana correspondent for the *New York Herald* reported that "he has formed a large camp of instruction" and had begun "thoroughly organizing, drilling, disciplining, and arming some 6000 picked men."[56] In August, Jordan's command repulsed several attacks by the Spanish and won a major victory at Holguín.[57] That fall, the revolutionary high command recognized his exploits by making him military chief-of-staff of the republic.[58] General Jordan, the *Memphis Daily Appeal* concluded, was "applying his Confederate experience with good purpose to the cause of Cuba."[59]

The editors of the *New York Times* agreed with the *Memphis Daily Appeal* that Jordan's command was one of the best in Cuba, "due, doubtless," one writer remarked, "to the infusion of a good deal of the American spirit by the general."[60] His men, another article declared, "are well organized, well drilled, and fight like demons."[61] While the *Memphis Daily Appeal* linked the general's success to his Confederate training, the *New York Times* increasingly emphasized that Jordan led an interracial army. The paper reported that rebel forces had liberated a cargo of slaves that had landed along the Cuban coast, and that escapees from loyalist plantations constantly augmented Jordan's ranks.[62] In the victory at Holguín, a militia unit made up of free people of color, which had been impressed into service by Spanish forces, broke and defected to Jordan's command at the height of the battle. "Slaves throughout the island," the *New York Times* reported, "are joining the Cubans by hundreds and thousands." Such men, the reporter had heard, "make good and efficient soldiers."[63]

As the *New York Times* noted, growing numbers of former slaves, Chinese contract laborers, and free people of color had begun to join the Cuban war for independence. These men and women struggled to push the revolution toward a more complete embrace of emancipation and equality. Their actions increasingly undermined slavery in areas on the island where the rebels operated. In the immediate aftermath of the Grito de Yara, enslaved men and women began leaving the plantations and seeking shelter in rebel lines. Revolutionary bands sacked the estates of loyalists and freed the slaves who remained. Before the end of the year 1868, Carlos Manuel de Céspedes authorized the rebels to confiscate for the use of the republic slaves owned by active enemies of the revolution. His government also agreed to indemnify owners who freed their slaves for service in the rebel armies. In February 1869, revolutionary authorities in Camagüey announced the abolition of slavery in the province with indemnities for owners and requirements that freedpeople work for the republican cause, either in the ranks or in the fields. When delegates met in April in Guáimaro to draft a constitution for an independent Cuba, they adopted a similar plan. The new constitution abolished slavery in the republic, but required the newly freed—now classed as *"libertos"*—to work as soldiers or laborers for the duration of the conflict.[64]

Thomas Jordan and any American who joined the revolution would need to reconcile themselves to emancipation, as they had to do in the U.S. In November 1869 Jordan wrote a letter to the *New York Times* pleading for donations of arms to support the rebels. In making his appeal, he assured his New York audience that "slavery was abolished when the standard of revolt was raised, and again by the twenty-fourth article of the Constitution of this Republic." He reported that "there are 40,000 liberated slaves now following our camps." If properly armed, he implied, they might prove a powerful force in striking a blow for Cuban independence. "Thousands of them," Jordan explained "are armed with machetas [sic], a half hatchet and a half meat ax. They have shown a willingness to meet the enemy in the open field with such weapons only as these."[65] By early the next year, even the Memphis papers acknowledged that Jordan's force included "negroes and Chinese," and, what's more, the general himself declared that "none fought better" than they.⁶⁶ In an 1870 retrospective interview with the *New York Tribune*, Jordan himself admitted that when he first arrived in Cuba, he thought "the patriots should set free their slaves, but he had no faith in the policy of arming the blacks." Their performance in battle changed his mind, but not his belief in racial hierarchy. By the time Jordan's command began its campaigns against the Spanish, the promise of freedom and equality for the republic's slaves remained limited, as the Guáimaro Constitution had made clear.⁶⁷ Subsequent events would show that whatever his views on emancipation and military service, Jordan clearly preferred any policy that limited opportunities for nonwhites and kept plantations intact.

Jordan's opinions were consequential because his successes in the field led to his rapid rise through the ranks. In January 1870, Manuel de Quesada stepped down as general-in-chief, after losing a power struggle with the revolutionary legislature. Jordan took his place. Although Céspedes and the legislature hoped Jordan would help the republic move past the divide between Quesada's allies and enemies, Jordan's service in Cuba quickly became mired in controversy.⁶⁸ In the spring of 1870, the *New York Times* printed an account by an anonymous and disillusioned "volunteer in Cuba" who had recently returned from the fray. The young man had made his way to Jordan's headquarters, but found the general recovering from an illness and wishing that more Americans had joined his forces. Most of Jordan's soldiers, the observer explained, "were negroes and Chinamen of the very lowest types." The fact that many of the revolution's soldiers showed signs of demanding social and political equality troubled the young veteran even more. "The negroes," the man reported, "would serve themselves first and the officers afterwards." General Jordan, the American volunteer discovered, "was not in full favor with the Cubans."⁶⁹

Indeed, the American observer arrived in Cuba in the midst of a debate between Jordan and his associates over race, slavery, military tactics, and the future of the war. When Carlos Manuel de Céspedes issued his initial call to arms, he had indicated that he held a general commitment to eventual emancipation and equality for all Cubans. He phrased his sentiments as hopes rather than commands, however, and consistently held that the Cuban people would make all decisions regarding slavery and citizenship rights only after the triumph of the revolution. Less conservative revolutionaries did not wish to wait so long. A reform-minded faction of leaders from Camagüey Province, including "the Young Bolívar," Ignacio Agromonte, had been the driving force behind the republic's abolition of slavery in the Guáimaro Constitution. As a young student, Agromonte had been influenced by the liberal ideals of the European revolutions of 1848, and in a prewar address delivered at the University of Havana he had asserted the fundamental equality of all human beings. As a major-general in Camagüey, he envisioned fighting the war with an irregular cavalry force, which would include people of color, many of whom had begun to push for equal treatment and positions of authority.[70]

Thomas Jordan quickly became one of Agromonte's chief political rivals.[71] When the ex-Confederate arrived in Cuba, he had hoped to fight a conventional war. In announcing his promotion to chief-of-staff of the army in October 1869, he declared his determination to "introduce military organization to the Cuban troops."[72] Jordan's preferences had been conditioned by his Confederate convictions. During the Civil War, most Confederate commanders had rejected guerrilla tactics and had instead sought to fight regular battles with a traditional army. In a war for national independence, they reasoned, the maintenance of a well-disciplined army would go a long way toward convincing the powers of the world that their new nation could command the popular loyalty and order expected of legitimate governments.[73] That approach did not win the Confederacy full recognition as an independent country, but Jordan evidently remained convinced that it had been right. When he took command of the insurgency, he noted that he had had "experience in the organization of troops of a determined people in a great war and in circumstances very like those" in Cuba. He insisted that he would use only those methods that had proved acceptable to the "volunteer forces of both sides" in the United States' "recent" and "unfortunate civil war." In a direct equation of the Cuban and Confederate causes, he promised to introduce only those tactics that had been already "effectively tried on the forces" of a people "in a struggle for its liberty and independence."[74] He fully planned to employ irregular troops, including men who had fought with Nathan Bedford Forrest, but only as supplements to a traditional, concentrated campaign, which Jordan believed essential to winning recognition and independence.

Jordan's task did not go as smoothly as he had hoped. He did not believe that a rebel army of patriotic planters, former slaves, Chinese contract laborers, free people of color, and white volunteers could be easily melded into a cohesive unit. Two months after he had been appointed chief-of-staff of the army, Jordan continued to plead with his colleagues for an orderly approach: "It is of the utmost importance that the troops of the republic are organized and instructed at once," he wrote.[75] When he oversaw the creation of a cavalry force that winter, he again stressed that its success depended on "organization."[76] In January 1870, after his appointment as general-in-chief, he finally lost his patience. When President Céspedes questioned the progress of the troops, Jordan responded with a defensive outburst, blaming his lack of clear success on the fault of "organization in all the branches of the army" that had existed on the date he had taken command. In a closing salvo, he sullenly claimed that he had never sought to serve as general-in-chief in the first place.[77]

As the *New York Time*'s anonymous informant explained, Jordan believed in "concentration" of forces, not a diffuse guerrilla campaign.[78] In holding these views, he remained convinced that a unified army defending key strategic locations would eventually achieve the rebels' military and political goals. Though guerrillas might be used as auxiliaries, only a traditional army defending a capital could convince foreign powers that the Cuban insurgents had erected a legitimate government worthy of recognition. The ex-Confederate believed he drew from the lessons of the Civil War.[79] In February 1870, he advocated a vigorous defense of Camagüey, which had housed the original rebel government. Camagüey, he maintained, was "for the island of Cuba . . . what Virginia was for the Confederate States during the American Civil War." Though Union forces had made countless incursions into the Confederate countryside, Jordan believed that Richmond had always been the key to the war. "When the ultimate seat of government was expelled from Virginia and the arsenals destroyed," he explained, "the revolution did not survive anywhere for more than fifteen days."[80]

Many of Jordan's subordinates evidently disagreed. As Jordan labored to build a regular army, his regional commanders used small units to burn the fields and homes of loyalists and to liberate their slaves. Jordan deemed such tactics uncivilized and unfit for a people determined to seek independence. Throughout his tenure, Jordan strictly forbade any "unnecessary and prejudicial" fires, insisting that any acts of deliberate destruction of civilian property had been carried out "without the sanction or the participation" of the army.[81]

The racial makeup of the armies bothered Jordan most, however. Jordan accepted emancipation and the service of nonwhite troops, but he remained committed to white supremacy. In December 1869, a few short months after taking his post as chief-of-staff of the army, Jordan confessed to the secretary of state of the republic that on reviewing his men he was "surprised to find much more than half of them negroes (including many Africans) and Chinese."[82] He did not understand why, with the country "full of able bodied white men," the "ranks of the army were full of stupid looking negroes and chinos."[83] "Be assured, Mr. Secretary," he declared, "this is a great evil which should be speedily corrected . . . before it shall be too late."[84]

According to Jordan, military success depended on securing for the country what he called "the best men in it for the army."[85] He advocated several measures that might help him procure what he called "a considerable body of good men . . . in place of so much of the defective material that now swell [the] ranks."[86] First off, he advocated passing a draft law that would bring the "white sons of Camagüey to the armed services."[87] He explained that the reluctance of whites to serve "permitted the spectacle of an army formed almost exclusively of negroes and chinos, while . . . young, healthy, and robust men . . . avoided service to the country."[88] Jordan was also disturbed to find that among those who did serve, "whites or the better class of men of color" had disproportionately sought to serve in noncombat roles, especially as couriers and postmen.[89] To free these men up for the front, Jordan recommended that the army recruit boys between the ages of sixteen and eighteen to serve in their stead.[90] Jordan assured the authorities that the Confederacy had successfully employed such a practice when "the need for the best men for the army was not more exigent than here."[91] He attested to the fact that the valor of boys in their teens had been "conspicuously illustrated on the peculiarly bloody fields of the late war in the United States, by the youths of the Southern States."[92] "Surely," he admonished, "you will be able to find among the *white* youths of the country, the equal fully in that respect to the mass of those now employed."[93] "It was this policy," he concluded, "that enabled my countrymen to maintain for four years their gigantic war with the United States."[94]

As for nonwhites who wished to serve the rebel cause, Jordan preferred to keep them in a state as close to slavery as possible. In his positions as chief-of-staff and general-in-chief, he directed the *libertos* to serve as agricultural laborers, thereby keeping them from the ranks of the army. In general, as escaped slaves came into rebel lines, Jordan preferred to apportion them to labor on the plantations in the neighborhood.[95] For example, in February 1870, he directed that a group of newly arrived *libertos* be put to work in the fields "under the direction of government administrators."[96] Only the whites, he explained, had been "called in the first place to conquer the independence of their country."[97]

Despite Jordan's efforts, a predominantly white force failed to materialize. Free people of color, who in 1862 made up almost 17 percent of Cuba's population, provided the rebels with an important base of support.[98] Slaves, who made up another 27 percent of the population, increasingly became a source of soldiers and laborers.[99] Though no definitive study exists of the exact racial breakdown of the rebel army, one American observer estimated its composition at two-thirds nonwhite.[100] Historian Rebecca J. Scott concedes that the American's estimate might have undercounted men who self-identified as white, but she still warns that it would be a mistake to assume that whites formed the preponderance of the army.[101] Either way, Jordan remained unhappy with his units. The *New York Times*'s informant reported that the general's patience reached its end during an attack on a railroad between Puerto Principe and Nuevitas. The troops went in "like a mob," he explained, and when Jordan ordered them to charge a strong point, they refused. The American volunteer recounted that "after this fight Jordan got disgusted and resigned . . . and left for parts unknown."[102] Whether or not the *Times*'s correspondent had accurately described Jordan's motives, he correctly reported that the former Confederate's time in Cuba had come to an end. In early February 1870, Jordan announced his intention to resign the moment he could be relieved. Jordan himself explained his decision in terms that lent credence to the *New York Times*'s report. The general-in-chief complained that "the officials and people of this country seem to have no desire to obtain military organization or to make war as soldiers do."[103] He confessed that he "knew no other way" to fight, grumbled that he "had not come [to Cuba] to learn new methods," and, as a result, warned that he would be leaving for the United States at the first opportunity.[104]

Cavada and the War against Slavery

Jordan's departure proved consequential. As Jordan stepped down, a very different soldier with very different understandings of war prepared to take his place. Like Jordan, Federico Cavada experienced a meteoric rise after casting his lot with the rebels. He fought hard and successfully as a general in the Trinidad district, and then earned promotion to general-in-chief of all operations in Cinco Villas.[105] From his position of authority, Cavada began to impose his own vision of Cuba's future. It included a respect for civic institutions and a hatred for imperial values and the Catholic Church. During the midsummer of 1869, he charged his brother Adolfo, who had also joined the rebellion, with bringing order to his district. "I claim," Adolfo Cavada wrote, "the honor of being the first to establish the Republican government in Cinco Villas."[106] Adolfo immediately established public schools in the area and introduced civil marriages. He expressed pride at his orders stamping out old "vices" and that "our countrymen have at last awakened to the necessity of bettering their condition."[107] He felt especially gratified when individuals showed signs of willingness to suffer for the cause. "Farmers well off and living in commodious houses," he asserted, "have destroyed their homes . . . freed their slaves and fled to the hills."[108] Such patriots, he contended, consoled themselves "with the thought that the hated enemy cannot shelter his head beneath his roof."[109] Though he hoped Cubans and Spaniards might someday meet as friends, he looked forward to a day in which all patriots might "celebrate the independence of Cuba."[110]

The Cavada brothers proved much more comfortable than Jordan had been with relying on nonwhite troops. In the midst of the fighting, Federico reported to his mother in the United States about the progress of the war in Cuba. He urged her to encourage the Cuban Junta in the U.S. to send proclamations to Havana addressed to the free colored "class" of the city, whose long-standing militias, he worried, were being employed by Spain.[111] He left little doubt that he saw the world differently than his one-time superior. Jordan could be trusted to continue to advocate for the cause, he advised his brother Emilio, but his racial views, he noted, were "of course, some what prejudiced."[112]

In the meantime, Federico Cavada came to embrace a harder war against loyalists than Jordan had, especially the prosperous sugar planters who formed the backbone of Cuban support for Spain. As a revolutionary leader, Cavada issued orders to destroy the buildings and machinery of pro-Spanish planters and to set fire to the cane fields in an effort to destabilize slave-based agriculture.[113] He defended his actions with an appeal to patriotism. "Those Cubans who are really in favor of our independence will not grumble at their losses," he wrote, but those who sought only to protect their property might be "Cubans indeed, but very far from being patriots."[114]

Cavada came to the conclusion that, as in the American Civil War, it would be necessary to destroy the power of the planters in order to ensure victory for patriots. In a letter to his brother, he asserted that "many of our countrymen, among the planters, are bitter enemies of our cause."[115] In July 1869, as general-in-chief of the state of Las Villas, he had issued a stern warning to the planters of the province. "Do you think," he asked them, "of defiantly returning to mix the sweat of your slaves with the juice of the cane?"[116] Though the planters might hope to make enough money to buy "the protection of the Spanish government," Cavada predicted that the rebels would exact a more fearsome price: "You will see yourself stripped of your slaves, you will see your fields turned into ashes and you will weep when it is already too late [to prevent] the irreparable loss of your fortunes."[117]

As many Northerners in the United States had in the years before the Civil War, Cavada feared that the institution of slavery created a selfish interest among the planting class that competed with loyalty to the nation. The love of money, he implied, competed with love of country and led men to cooperate with the otherwise discredited policies of imperialism. "Remember," he admonished the island's planters, "your gold is the gold that feeds the worn-out coffers of Spain."[118]

He asked planters to decide whether they could, without shame and regret, continue to give their money and support to the "barbarous foreigner" who spilled Cuban blood.[119] "Remember," he added, "that you are sons of this land and that you are our brothers."[120] Decide, he implored them, if "you feel in your breast this mysterious chord that they call fraternity."[121]

Federico Cavada did not live to realize his vision for Cuba. The following summer, Spanish forces captured the general-in-chief. When news arrived in the United States, Oliver Wilson Davis, a prominent Philadelphia lawyer and friend of Cavada's, began a frantic campaign to save his life. He reached out to a number of his contacts close to the Grant administration, including General Dan Sickles, who then served as ambassador to Spain, General Phil Sheridan, and, ultimately, the president himself. He urged them to intervene with the Spanish to secure good treatment for the captured commander. He had acted too late. On July 1, 1871, days before Davis had even received news of his friend's capture, Spanish forces executed Cavada by firing squad.[122] On the morning of his execution, authorities allowed him to write a final letter to his family. He assured them that he felt "calm and resigned," but he confessed that his idealism had been shattered.[123] He advised his son to "leave to others the difficult project of reforming the world."[124] His love for his native land had not withered, however. His final words were, "Adios Cuba, para siempre."[125]

The Ten Years' War brought still more pain and suffering to the Cavada family. In December 1871, Adolfo died in battle on a coffee plantation outside Santiago. The rebellion lasted well into the late 1870s, but the Spanish Army ultimately defeated the rebels. The result included neither immediate abolition nor independence. Still, the insurgency had fatally weakened slavery on the island.[126] In the years after Jordan's departure, increasing numbers of nonwhite Cubans achieved positions of leadership in the revolutionary armies, including Antonio Maceo, who shared Cavada's commitment to emancipation and guerilla war. Given the destruction of slavery in the United States and the disintegration of the plantation sector in Cuban war zones, few imagined that human bondage could regain the hemispheric strength it had enjoyed during the 1850s. A former Cuban slave succinctly described the situation in an interview with the *New York Times*. "You see, master," he said, "when the North triumphed [in the U.S. Civil War], we all know that the hour of liberty would soon come." The hundreds of ex-slaves fighting in the Cuban rebel armies, he explained, fought for nothing less than "universal liberty." He expressed faith that no matter which side won, the victor would have no choice but to acknowledge slavery's end.[127]

Increasingly, many observers shared the man's faith. In December 1873, the *New York Times* reported that the Spanish government had warned Cuban slaveholders to prepare for emancipation.[128] By this time, even that news did not placate some supporters of Cuba. "Nothing save immediate and unconditional abolition," the paper declared, "will benefit the slave in the slightest degree."[129] The Cuban Junta had come to agree. Later that year, speakers at a mass meeting on Cuba pressed for the total abolition of slavery on the island. The emancipation of the slaves, the speakers argued, would destroy the loyalist planting class, thereby securing Cuban independence, just as the decimation of the American South's slave society had saved the Union. "It was the slaveholders who were the cause of all the trouble," one speaker concluded, "and when slavery was abolished it would be impossible for them to remain on the island."[130]

As for Thomas Jordan, when he returned to New York he continued to lobby on behalf of the rebels, as Cavada predicted he would. Shortly after his homecoming, the Cuban Junta feted Jordan at a banquet at Delmonico's, an event at which he lobbied for the abrogation of the Neutrality Act, urged the sale of arms to the rebels, denounced Spanish tyranny, and announced his intention to return to the isle. He insisted that he had "come back to try and procure arms for the patriots, and not because he was discouraged in the cause."[131] Indeed, rumors held that he had attempted several return expeditions, and American authorities hauled him into court at least once for violations of the Neutrality Act.[132] In the meantime, he continued his support activities. Jordan and his wife, for example, actively worked on behalf of the American Women's Aid Society for the Relief of Cuban Women and Children by leading collection drives to procure clothes, food, and supplies for displaced civilians.[133]

Increasingly, Jordan's continued support of the cause forced him to make peace with the interracial character of the Cuban republic. The end of May 1870 found Jordan in Washington lobbying Republican lawmakers and advocating the Cuban cause in a private audience with President Grant.[134] By 1873, some of the mass meetings Jordan attended were racially integrated and included former slaves from Cuba.[135] In July 1870, at a pro-Cuba rally at the Academy of Music in Brooklyn, Jordan reminded his Northern audience that the rebels "inaugurated their movement for national independence by a manumission of all their slaves, which they confirmed in their Constitution."[136] He averred, in contrast with what his own policies on the island had been, that "Negroes have not only been set free, but have been allowed equal political rights and privileges with whites wherever the patriot cause has prevailed."[137] In the end, the one-time Confederate admitted that "no class entered into the revolution with more earnestness or a higher appreciation of the interests involved than they, and they have fought manfully side by side with white men."[138]

Jordan's apparent conversion did not convince everyone in the United States. During congressional debates on the Cuba issue during the summer of 1870, memories of the Civil War remained raw. John F. Farnsworth, an ex-Union officer and Republican representative from Illinois, confessed he had lost patience with Jordan's lobbying. "This Gen. Jordan," he complained, "had been so faithless to his own oath and duty as to resign his position in the United States Army . . . and had, as Chief of Staff to Beauregard . . . done as much as perhaps any man to aid the rebellion."[139] When that cause failed, Farnsworth pointed out, Jordan "joined the still more desperate cause of the adventurous filibusters and guerrillas."[140] Farnsworth concluded by sarcastically asserting that "when the American filibusters and the men who had fought for the Southern Confederacy were withdrawn from Cuba, there would be but few left to fight against Spain."[141]

In the meantime, the Grant administration remained neutral. U.S. officials worked consistently to prevent filibusters from sailing to Cuba from ports in the United States. Secretary of State Fish successfully prevailed on the president to pursue a policy of nonintervention in the Cuban insurrection. Fish argued that the rebels had not proved worthy of recognition because they had organized neither a legitimate government nor a conventional army, a position Jordan had feared foreign powers might take. Fish also worried about war with Spain, and he opposed the addition of Spanish-speaking Catholics to the United States. Fish's racial views also proved important. Privately, he abhorred the possibility of admitting additional nonwhite populations to the Union, an opinion of his which had been long-standing. After a trip to Cuba in the 1850s, he came away with impressions that continued to guide his policy during the 1870s. "With its present population," he wrote, "the island of Cuba will be anything else than a desirable acquisition to the United States. . . . I can see no means of getting rid of a population of some 450,000 called *white* but really of every shade and mixture of color, who own *all* the land on the island."[142]

It is important to note that Ulysses S. Grant did not share Fish's concerns. In cabinet meetings, he often leaned toward intervention in the rebellion. For Grant, as for Cavada, neither the tactics of the rebels nor the multiracial character of the population dampened his enthusiasm for the possible achievement of a free Cuba. Ultimately, Grant chose to follow Fish's advice in part because he wished to avoid war with Spain and because he feared jeopardizing ongoing negotiations with Great Britain over the *Alabama* Claims, which sought to punish Britain for alleged violations of neutrality during the United States' own Civil War. Still, in talks with the Spanish government, the administration insisted on the abolition of slavery as the price of U.S. nonintervention.[143]

The actions of the Spanish government did not completely satisfy Grant. The end of slavery in Cuba was a slow, painful, and imperfect process. In 1870, as a result of the pressure supplied by the rebels and the threat of U.S. intervention, the Spanish government passed the Moret Law, which granted freedom to all slave children in Cuba and Puerto Rico born after 1868 and to all slaves over the age of sixty. Still, Cuban officials refused to publish the law in the colonies for two more years. In 1873, the Spanish government agreed to full abolition of slavery in Puerto Rico. Slavery in Cuba, though weakened, outlasted the Grant administration and the Ten Years' War. It would not be until 1886 that Spain completely abolished slavery on the island.[144]

A consideration of the role that Cavada and Jordan played during the Ten Years' War can teach many things. It demonstrates the degree to which Reconstruction-era debates over slavery, race, and labor transcended U.S. borders. Such figures as Cavada and Jordan thought hard about how abolition and the possibility of racial equality should be applied both to the United States and to Cuba. In so doing, they contributed to debates over the future trajectory of American empire. The actions of Cavada and Jordan illustrate the degree to which the Civil War reoriented American policy toward abolition in the hemisphere. Whereas Thomas Jordan's predecessors had assumed that the expansion of slavery would accompany the expansion of American influence abroad, when the last of the filibusters left Cuba, they had no choice but to fight a war against slavery as a part of an interracial army, a reality that Cavada but not Jordan readily embraced. Still, even Cavada assumed that a free Cuba would become a partner or even an appendage of the United States. That even Cavada, a naturalized American from Cuba with abolitionist politics, could not help thinking of the island's incorporation into the United States foreshadows the troubled trajectory of U.S.–Cuba policy in the late nineteenth and twentieth centuries. Then, as right after the American Civil War, Cuba's northern neighbors seemed incapable of disentangling their humanitarianism from their nationalism.

Notes

1. For the debate in Grant's cabinet, see Stephen McCullough, *The Caribbean Policy of the Ulysses S. Grant Administration: Foreshadowing an Informal Empire* (New York: Lexington Books, 2018); Allen Nevins, *Hamilton Fish: The Inner History of the Grant Administration*, 2 vols. (New York: Frederick Ungar, 1936); Jay Sexton, "The United

States, the Cuban Rebellion, and the Multilateral Initiative of 1875," *Diplomatic History* 30, no. 1 (2006), 335–365; Andrew Priest, "Thinking about Empire: The Administration of Ulysses S. Grant, Spanish Colonialism and the Ten Years' War in Cuba," *Journal of American Studies* 48, no. 2 (2014), 541–558; James B. Chapin, "Hamilton Fish and the Lessons of the Ten Year's War," in *Perspectives in American Diplomacy: Essays on Europe, Latin America, China, and the Cold War*, ed. Jules Davids (New York: Arno Press, 1976), 131–163; Chapin, "Hamilton Fish and American Expansion," in *Makers of American Diplomacy: From Benjamin Franklin to Henry Kissinger*, ed. Frank J. Merli and Theodore A. Wilson (New York: Charles Scribner's Sons, 1974), 227–249; Eric T. L. Love, *Race over Empire: Racism and U.S. Imperialism, 1865–1900* (Chapel Hill: University of North Carolina Press, 2004).

2. Ada Ferrer, *Insurgent Cuba: Race, Nation, and Revolution, 1868–1898* (Chapel Hill: University of North Carolina Press, 1999); Rebecca J. Scott, *Slave Emancipation in Cuba: The Transition to Free Labor, 1860–1899* (Princeton, N.J.: Princeton University Press, 1985).

3. Matt D. Childs, "Cuba, the Atlantic Crisis of the 1860s, and the Road to Abolition," in *American Civil Wars: The United States, Latin America, Europe, and the Crisis of the 1860s*, ed. Don H. Doyle (Chapel Hill: University of North Carolina Press, 2017), 204–221.

4. Jay Sexton, "The United States, the Cuban Rebellion, and the Multilateral Initiative of 1875," *Diplomatic History* 30, no. 1 (2006), 339–340.

5. Gregory P. Downs, *The Second American Revolution: The Civil War–Era Struggle over Cuba and the Rebirth of the American Republic* (Chapel Hill: University of North Carolina Press, 2019).

6. Nevins, *Hamilton Fish*; Jay Sexton, "The United States, the Cuban Rebellion, and the Multilateral Initiative of 1875," *Diplomatic History* 30, no. 1 (2006), 335–365; Richard H. Bradford, *The Virginius Affair* (Boulder: Colorado Associated University Press, 1980).

7. Andrew Zimmerman, "Reconstruction: Transnational History," in *Interpreting American History: Reconstruction*, ed. John David Smith (Kent, Ohio: Kent State University Press, 2016), 171–196; David Prior, ed., *Reconstruction in a Globalizing World* (New York: Fordham University Press, 2018).

8. Louis A. Pérez, Jr., *Cuba in the American Imagination: Metaphor and Imperial Ethos* (Chapel Hill: University of North Carolina Press, 2008).

9. Matthew Pratt Guterl, *American Mediterranean: Southern Slaveholders in the Age of Emancipation* (Cambridge, Mass.: Harvard University Press, 2008); Walter Johnson, *River of Dark Dreams: Slavery and Empire in the Cotton Kingdom* (Cambridge, Mass.: Harvard University Press, 2013); Robert E. May, *The Southern Dream of a Caribbean Empire, 1854–1861* (Baton Rouge: Louisiana State University Press, 1973).

10. Robert E. May, *Manifest Destiny's Underworld: Filibustering in Antebellum America* (Chapel Hill: University of North Carolina Press, 2002), 20–36; May, *John A. Quitman, Old South Crusader* (Baton Rouge: Louisiana State University Press, 1985), 275–291; Charles H. Brown, *Agents of Manifest Destiny: The Lives and Times of the Filibusters* (Chapel Hill: University of North Carolina Press, 1980), 39–144.

11. Oliver Wilson Davis, *Sketch of Frederic Fernandez Cavada, A Native of Cuba* (Philadelphia: James B. Chandler, 1871), 23–25.

12. Ibid.
13. Ibid.
14. Ibid.
15. Ibid., 20–21, 23–25; for the views of many Unionists on race and slavery, see Gary W. Gallagher, *The Union War* (Cambridge, Mass.: Harvard University Press, 2012).
16. Christopher Schmidt-Nowara, *Empire and Antislavery: Spain, Cuba, and Puerto Rico, 1833–1874* (Pittsburgh: University of Pittsburgh Press, 1999), 4, 16; Schmidt-Nowara, "From Aggression to Crisis: The Spanish Empire in the 1860s," in *American Civil Wars: The United States, Latin America, Europe, and the Crisis of the 1860s*, ed. Don H. Doyle (Chapel Hill: University of North Carolina Press, 2017), 125–146.
17. Anne Eller, "Dominican War, Slavery, and Spanish Annexation, 1844–1865," in Doyle, ed., 147–166.
18. Schmidt-Nowara, 100–125; Matt D. Childs, "Cuba, the Atlantic Crisis of the 1860s, and the Road to Abolition," in Doyle, ed., 204–221.
19. Eller, 147–166.
20. Federico Fernández Cavada to Thomas Savage, October 21, 1866, Records of Foreign Service Posts, Consular Posts, Trinidad, Cuba, National Archives, College Park, Maryland (hereafter NA).
21. Federico Fernández Cavada to William H. Seward, February 9, 1867, April 28, 1868, Despatches from U.S. Consuls, Trinidad, Cuba, 1824–1876, NA. For understandings of citizenship in this era, see Christian G. Samito, *Becoming American under Fire: Irish Americans, African Americans, and the Politics of Citizenship in the Civil War Era* (Ithaca, N.Y.: Cornell University Press, 2009).
22. Federico Fernández Cavada to William H. Seward, May 4, 1868, Despatches from U.S. Consuls, Trinidad, Cuba, 1824–1876, NA.
23. Federico Fernández Cavada to William Henry Seward, February 5, 1869, Despatches from U.S. Consuls, Trinidad, Cuba, 1824–1876, NA.
24. Horatio Fox to Hamilton Fish, April 16, 1869, Despatches from U.S. Consuls, Trinidad, Cuba, 1824–1876, NA.
25. Davis, 31.
26. Federico Cavada to "Netts," August 12, 1869, Fernando Fernández-Cavada Collection, Cuban Heritage Collection, University of Miami Libraries, Coral Gables, Florida (hereafter FFC).
27. Federico Cavada to C. Fernando Escobar, July 22, 1870, FFC.
28. "Cuban Independence," *New York Times*, May 5, 1869.
29. Ibid.
30. Ramiro Guerra, *Guerra de los Diez Años*, 2 vols. (Havana: Instituto Cubano del Libro, 1972), 1:256, 301–304. See also Antonio Pirala, *Anales de la Guerra de Cuba*, 3 vols. (Madrid: Felipe González Rojas, 1895).
31. Matthew Karp, *This Vast Southern Empire: Slaveholders at the Helm of American Foreign Policy* (Cambridge, Mass.: Harvard University Press, 2016), 7, 32–124, 199–225.
32. Robert E. May, *Manifest Destiny's Underworld: Filibustering in Antebellum America* (Chapel Hill: University of North Carolina Press, 2002), 20–36; Robert E. May, *John A. Quitman, Old South Crusader* (Baton Rouge: Louisiana State University Press, 1985),

275–291; Charles H. Brown, *Agents of Manifest Destiny: The Lives and Times of the Filibusters* (Chapel Hill: University of North Carolina Press, 1980), 39–144; Linda S. Hudson, *Mistress of Manifest Destiny: A Biography of Jane McManus Storm Cazneau* (Austin: Texas State Historical Association, 2001), 90–101, 110–111; Tom Chaffin, *Fatal Glory: Narciso López and the First Clandestine U.S. War against Cuba* (Charlottesville: University of Virginia Press, 1996).

33. See William Clark Griggs, *The Elusive Eden: Frank McMullan's Confederate Colony in Brazil* (Austin: University of Texas Press, 1987); Laura Jarnagin, *A Confluence of Transatlantic Networks: Elites, Capitalism, and Confederate Migration to Brazil* (Tuscaloosa: University of Alabama Press, 2008); Andrew F. Rolle, *The Lost Cause: The Confederate Exodus to Mexico* (Norman: University of Oklahoma Press, 1965); Todd W. Wahlstrom, *The Southern Exodus to Mexico: Migration across the Borderlands after the American Civil War* (Lincoln: University of Nebraska Press, 2015); Alfred Jackson Hanna and Kathryn Abbey Hanna, *Confederate Exiles in Venezuela* (Tuscaloosa: Confederate Publishing Company, 1960); Cyrus B. Dawsey and James M. Dawsey, eds., *The Confederados: Old South Immigrants in Brazil* (Tuscaloosa: University of Alabama Press, 1995); Daniel E. Sutherland, "Exiles, Emigrants, and Sojourners: The Post–Civil War Confederate Exodus in Perspective," *Civil War History* 31, no. 3 (1985), 237–256; Guterl; Eliza McHatton Ripley, *From Flag to Flag: A Woman's Adventures and Experiences in the South during the War, in Mexico, and in Cuba* (New York: D. Appleton, 1889), 125–132, 149–155.

34. Venezuelan settler quoted in Hanna and Hanna, *Confederate Exiles*, 27.

35. Brazilian migrant quoted in Laura Jarnagin, "Fitting In: Relocating Family and Capital within the Nineteenth-Century Atlantic World Economy: The Brazilian Connection," in Dawsey and Dawsey, 69.

36. "Rumored Sailing of an Expedition for Cuba," *New York Times*, May 5, 1869.

37. Thomas Jordan, *The South: Its Products, Commerce, and Resources* (London: William Blackwood and Sons, 1861), 3, 6.

38. Ibid., 5.

39. Ibid.

40. Ibid., 7. During the mid-twentieth century, Cuban biographers of Jordan writing in the mode of the Lost Cause denied Jordan had been a supporter of slavery, but the evidence presented here suggests otherwise. See, for example, Herminio Portell Vilá, "Thomas Jordan, general del Ejército Libertador Cubana," in Vilá, *Vidas de la Unidad Americana: Veinte y Cinco Biografías de Americanos Ilustres* (Havana: Editorial Minerva, 1944), 149–163; Victor Vega Ceballos, *Thomas S. Jordan, Jefe del Estado Mayor del Ejército Libertador de Cuba, 1869–1870* (Havana: Sociedad Colombista Panamericana, 1953), 9.

41. Thomas Jordan, "Jefferson Davis," *Harper's New Monthly Magazine*, October 1865. See also John George Ryan, *Life and Adventures of Gen. W. A. C. Ryan, the Cuban Martyr* (New York: Scully, 1876), 86.

42. Thomas Jordan and J. B. Pryor, *The Campaigns of Lieut.-Gen. N. B. Forrest and Forrest's Cavalry* (Memphis: Blelock, 1868), vii.

43. Ibid., viii.

44. Ibid., 424–453.

45. Ibid., v, vii–viii.

46. Chaffin, 44–50; May, *John A. Quitman*, 236–252, 272–282; Karp, 187.
47. "Ho! For Cuba," *Memphis Daily Appeal*, March 17, 1869.
48. Ibid.
49. *Memphis Daily Appeal*, June 4, 1869; "Telegrams," *New York Times*, June 4, 1869.
50. *New York Sunday News*, quoted in "Jordan's Cuba Expedition," *Memphis Daily Appeal*, June 6, 1869.
51. Ibid.
52. "A Letter from General Jordan's Command," *New York Times*, July 18, 1869.
53. Ryan, 95–96.
54. "Forrest's Men," *Memphis Daily Appeal*, September 13, 1869.
55. *New York Times*, July 5, 1869.
56. *Herald* correspondent, quoted in "The Cuban War," *Memphis Daily Appeal*, July 28, 1869.
57. "Cuba," *New York Times*, August 4, 1869; "Cuba," *New York Times*, August 13, 1869; "Mail Intelligence," *New York Times*, August 16, 1869; "Cuban Victories," *New York Times*, August 20, 1869; *New York Times*, August 24, 1869.
58. Guerra, 1:313; "Cuba and Spain," *New York Times*, January 4, 1870; *Memphis Daily Appeal*, November 27, 1869.
59. *Memphis Daily Appeal*, September 21, 1869.
60. "Affairs in Cuba," *New York Times*, August 6, 1869.
61. "Cuba," *New York Times*, August 4, 1869.
62. "Cuba," *New York Times*, August 13, 1869.
63. "Mail Intelligence," *New York Times*, August 16, 1869.
64. Guerra, 1:107, 109, 126–128; Ada Ferrer, *Insurgent Cuba: Race, Nation, and Revolution, 1868–1898* (Chapel Hill: University of North Carolina Press, 1999), 24–27; Rebecca J. Scott, *Slave Emancipation in Cuba: The Transition to Free Labor, 1860–1899* (Princeton, N.J.: Princeton University Press, 1985), 45–62.
65. "What General Jordan Says of the Army," *New York Times*, November 8, 1869.
66. "From Cuba," *Memphis Daily Appeal*, March 20, 1870.
67. See Ferrer, 28; Scott, 45–62.
68. Guerra, 1:318–321; "Cuba and Spain," *New York Times*, January 4, 1870; *Memphis Daily Appeal*, January 30, 1870.
69. "A Volunteer in Cuba," *New York Times*, April 30, 1870. A Republican in the unit, General William A. C. Ryan, also attested to racial egalitarianism in the unit, but chose to put a positive spin on the situation. See Ryan, 142.
70. Guerra, 1:43, 49, 90–99, 109; 2:3–10.
71. Ibid., 2:3–10.
72. Thomas Jordan to General Agromonte, October 1, 1869, Colección Fernández Duro, Real Academia de la Historia, Madrid, Spain (hereafter FD). Unless otherwise noted, the letters in this collection are written in Spanish and translated by the author.
73. For Confederate military strategy, see Gary W. Gallagher, *The Confederate War* (Cambridge, Mass.: Harvard University Press, 1997), 115–153.
74. Thomas Jordan to General Agromonte, October 1, 1869, FD.

75. Thomas Jordan to General Vicente García, December 2, 1869, FD.
76. Thomas Jordan to General Cornelio Porro, February 18, 1870, FD.
77. General del Ejército to Presidente de la Republica, January 21, 1870, FD.
78. "A Volunteer in Cuba," *New York Times*, April 30, 1870.
79. See Gallagher, *The Confederate War*, 115–153.
80. General del Ejército to Secretario del Ejército, February 11, 1870, FD.
81. General del Ejército to Secretario del Ejército, February 25, 1870, FD.
82. Thomas Jordan to Eduardo Agromonte, December 16, 1869 [original written in English], FD.
83. Ibid.
84. Ibid.
85. Ibid.
86. Ibid.
87. Thomas Jordan to the governor of Camagüey, November 26, 1869, FD.
88. Ibid.
89. Thomas Jordan to Eduardo Agromonte, December 16, 1869 [original written in English], FD.
90. Ibid.
91. Ibid.
92. Ibid.
93. Ibid.
94. Ibid.
95. See, General del Ejército to Governador Civil, February 19, 1870, FD; Thomas Jordan to Pedro Romero, December 24, 1869, FD; General del Ejército to Gobernador, February 22, 1870, FD.
96. General del Ejército to unspecified, February 19, 1870, FD.
97. Ibid.
98. For Cuba's population figures, see Schmidt-Nowara, *Empire and Antislavery*, 16. For analysis of various populations' support for the insurgency, see Scott, *Slave Emancipation in Cuba*, 56–57.
99. Ibid.
100. Scott, *Slave Emancipation in Cuba*, 57.
101. Ibid.
102. "A Volunteer in Cuba," *New York Times*, April 30, 1870.
103. Letter of the General del Ejército, February 5, 1870, FD.
104. Ibid.
105. Davis, 31–32.
106. Adolfo Cavada to "Friends," August 7, 1869, FFC.
107. Ibid.
108. Ibid.
109. Ibid.
110. Ibid.
111. Federico Cavada to "My Dear Mother," August 27, n.d., FFC.
112. Federico Cavada to "Netts," March 21, 1870, FFC.

113. Declaration to the Cuban Hacendados of Las Villas, July 28, 1869, FFC. See also Ryan, 180.
114. Federico Cavada to "Netts," September 28, 1869, FFC.
115. Ibid.
116. Declaration to the Cuban Hacendados of Las Villas, July 28, 1869, FFC.
117. Ibid.
118. Ibid.
119. Ibid.
120. Ibid.
121. Ibid.
122. Davis, 33–57.
123. Federico Cavada to "Netts," July 1, 1871, FFC.
124. Ibid.
125. Davis, 55–56.
126. Scott, 63–83, 141–171.
127. "Cuban Affairs," New York Times, June 10, 1870.
128. "The Situation in Havana," New York Times, December 24, 1873.
129. Ibid.
130. "The Cuban Junta," New York Times, December 4, 1873.
131. "Banquet to General Jordan," New York Times, May 13, 1870.
132. "General Jordan Arrested," New York Times, December 7, 1870; "Senor Ruiz to Surrender Himself," New York Times, December 9, 1870; "Preparations for a Cuban Expedition," New York Times, February 1, 1874; New York Times, March 14, 1871; New York Times, December 27, 1874.
133. "Aid for Cuban Women," New York Times, May 18, 1870; "Aid for Cuban Women and Children," New York Times, October 10, 1870.
134. "Gen. Jordan in Washington," New York Times, May 27, 1870.
135. "The Cuban Junta," New York Times, December 7, 1873.
136. "The Cuban Cause," New York Times, July 8, 1870.
137. Ibid.
138. Ibid.
139. "Forty-First Congress, Second Session," New York Times, June 15, 1870.
140. Ibid.
141. Ibid.
142. Fish quoted in Chapin, "Hamilton Fish and the Lessons of the Ten Years' War," 137. For more on his views on race and the revolution in Cuba see McCullough, 131–143; Nevins, 1:125, 128–129, 176–200, 238; Sexton, 335–365; Priest, 546–556; Chapin, "Hamilton Fish and American Expansion," 227–249.
143. For the dynamic in the Grant cabinet and the importance of antislavery, see Gregg French's chapter in this volume; McCullough, 131–143; Priest, 554–555; Nevins, 1:239–240, 243–247, 345–350, 354, 359, 2: 625–634, 885. The ongoing Alabama Claims also influenced Grant's decision not to recognize the Cuban rebels, because the case in part hinged on the U.S. objection to Great Britain's recognition of Confederate belligerency.
144. Scott, 63–83, 141–171.

2

"What Hinders?"

African Methodist Expansion from the U.S. South to Hispaniola, 1865–1885

Christina C. Davidson

As the first Black denomination (est. 1816) and the largest independent Black Methodist group in the United States in 1880, the African Methodist Episcopal (AME) Church stood as a potent symbol of Black achievement. In the fifteen years since the end of the U.S. Civil War (1861–1865), the AME Church had gained over two hundred thousand members. Black missionaries from the North had flocked south and west to evangelize the formerly enslaved population and to take advantage of new possibilities. They had experienced tangible success: the transfer of whole congregations; the acquisition of church property; and the recognition of white Methodists and other Protestants, some of whom had supported their cause. Considering the thousands of African Americans across the U.S. South and West who joined the denomination in the early years of Reconstruction, many clergy and lay members felt that the time was right to expand the church abroad. "We must engage in the work of Foreign Missions," one article in the AME Church's official newspaper, the *Christian Recorder*, exhorted in 1869.[1] Its author explained: "The Lord has given us fifty years training, and now he throws open the gate to His 'fields ripe for the harvest,' and calls upon us to enter." Manifest destiny, while birthed in the minds of white Americans, transformed geographic expansion into a measuring stick for Black American Protestants after the Civil War.

Yet not everyone agreed with AME expansion. Although many African Americans felt that the AME Church had matured as an institution through its missionary efforts in the U.S. South, others cautioned against the pursuit for greater presence abroad. "There are some things we cannot rationally be expected to do; and among them is the inauguration and support of missions in foreign lands," another editorialist reasoned. Describing the denomination as "too infantile," they concluded: "sharing our bread with Hayti [sic] is the utmost anyone can reasonably expect of us."[2] This second *Christian Recorder* author worried that the AME Church would spread its financial resources too thin if it expanded to too many regions beyond the continental United States. Instead of worldwide growth, he advocated for foreign missions on one Caribbean island: "Hayti," or Hispaniola, home of the present-day countries of Haiti and the Dominican Republic. As the site of the only successful slave rebellion in modern world history, the location of two "black republics," and the place where African Americans had forged both imaginary and physical ties throughout the nineteenth century, Hispaniola represented more than Black self-determination; it also signified U.S. Blacks' deep faith in the Protestant God who had brought them out of slavery and established Haiti—the modern country—as a Black "Promised Land."[3] Saving "Hayti"—meaning the island of Hispaniola and, more broadly, the nexus of symbolic meanings that African Americans associated with it—took priority over anywhere else.[4]

The discrepancy between these two visions of AME Church missions highlights a crucial paradox for African American religious leaders living in the Reconstruction period and during the emerging age of U.S. empire. On the one hand, African American missionaries aimed to spread the Christian Gospel and thereby "uplift" the race by promoting Western education and Protestant conversion among all African descendants. This work was dismissive of non-Western cultures and therefore inherently imperialistic and racist.[5] On the other hand, foreign missionary work evoked a long history of Afro-diasporic connections through which Black people forged racial and political solidarities against white supremacy. For centuries, African descendants had built Protestant networks to fight racial oppression. Hispaniola likewise existed as a crucial site of Black solidarity throughout the nineteenth century.[6] Indeed, African Americans emigrated en masse to the island, advocated for U.S. recognition of Haiti and the Dominican Republic, and promoted the island's welfare in the Black press. Thus, during the postbellum period, the quandary of where to direct the AME Church's limited financial resources exposed an inherent contradiction. Steeped in U.S. Black Protestant supremacy and U.S. chauvinism, AME missions existed simultaneously as an extension of U.S. racial empire and as a potential site of Black racial solidarity on Hispaniola and elsewhere.

Scholars of AME history have examined this paradox through the lens of the church's African missions.[7] They have noted, for example, how AME discourse of the 1880s–1930s reproduced U.S. imperialist and racist attitudes that cast Africans as uncivilized heathens in need of spiritual and social redemption.[8] As Lawrence Little has argued, this discourse became most apparent in AME leaders' writings and ideas about the "dual impulse of evangelism and emigration" to Africa at the turn of the twentieth century.[9] By enacting African missions and advocating emigration as a civilizing tool, AME leaders upheld white Euro-American culture as the only proper "civilizing" model. Thus they collaborated—sometimes purposefully and sometimes inadvertently—with U.S. and European imperial aims in the late nineteenth century.

In contrast to the traditional historiographical focus on Africa, this chapter shifts the locus of scholarly attention to the Caribbean island of Hispaniola where the AME Church established churches and schools in the 1870s and 1880s prior to enacting a robust missionary program on the African continent. Building on Dennis C. Dickerson's history of the AME Church and Brandon R. Byrd's study of African Americans' internationalist visions of Haiti, both published in 2020,[10] I argue that the AME Church's foray into foreign missions was a direct outgrowth of the denomination's expansion to the U.S. South during Reconstruction. "Going South and going to the Caribbean and [then to] Africa," as Dickerson asserts, "were integral to the Atlantic history of the denomination."[11] This trajectory also paralleled U.S. expansionist goals during Reconstruction as the United States considered annexing the Dominican Republic and other Caribbean territories.[12] Thus, this chapter explores the intersection of Reconstruction and U.S. empire through the AME Church's expansion from the U.S. North to the U.S. South, and then to Port-au-Prince and Santo Domingo. I demonstrate that the AME Church's relationship to Hispaniola shifted in the postbellum period as AME leaders sought to proselytize the whole island and the United States sought to annex the Dominican Republic (1868–1872).[13] Just as Reconstruction-era expansionism inspired AME Church leaders to begin missions on Hispaniola, a new form of Black nationalist evangelism would push the denomination toward the African continent by 1885. These shifts became apparent in AME Church leaders' evangelical discourse, missionary financial priorities, and inattention to African American immigrants and missionaries operating locally in Port-au-Prince and Santo Domingo in the early 1880s.

AME Church Expansion and Christian Missions

The AME Church began when free Black people in Philadelphia walked out of St. George's Methodist Episcopal Church in 1787 in protest of racial discrimination and formed their own institution under the leadership of the formerly enslaved preacher Rev. Richard Allen. Inspired by this action and the Haitian Revolution (1791–1804), other free Blacks formed independent churches across the U.S. Northeast. In 1816, Black Methodist congregations united as the African Methodist Episcopal Church, the first independent Black denomination in the United States, and they elected Richard Allen as the AME Church's first bishop. Early ties between the AME Church and Haiti began a few years later in 1824, when Haitian President Jean-Pierre Boyer sent his agent Jonathas Granville to the United States to recruit Black settlers to the island, which Haiti governed from 1822 until Dominican independence in 1844. Granville traveled first to Philadelphia where he met Allen and other AME leaders who expressed initial skepticism regarding emigration because of the American Colonization Society's concurrent efforts to rid the United States of free Black people by sending them to Liberia. Yet after discussing Haitian emigration with Granville, AME leaders decided to support the project, and the AME Church ultimately helped organize an emigration movement that sent upwards of thirteen thousand Blacks to Hispaniola in the early 1820s.[14]

At first, the AME Church tried to maintain a relationship with those who left for Haiti by commissioning preachers to care for Methodist immigrant societies on the island, but these ties could not be sustained.[15] The reasons for the lack of connection are obvious. The institution of slavery threatened the movement of free people of color, whom bounty hunters could kidnap and sell illegally into slavery. The independent Black denomination did not have access to large funding sources, and communication across great distances remained difficult for those who lacked the institutional means for large-scale organization. Thus, despite sporadic moments of contact, it was not until after the U.S. Civil War that African Americans and immigrant communities reestablished formal religious ties through the AME denomination.[16]

From the perspective of AME leaders in the United States, the Civil War and Reconstruction brought new opportunities for AME Church expansion. The 1864 Bishops' address to the General Conference reported that "the changes produced by the war in the South have again opened our churches in that region."[17] As AME clergy ministered to newly freed people, the denomination's membership increased.[18] The AME Church had but 16,190 communicants in 1846, but, by 1866, the denomination consisted of 50,000 members and 286 churches.[19] During Reconstruction, the *Christian Recorder* reported that "the AME Church is increasing so rapidly in extent and membership that it is almost impossible for us to keep up."[20] By the 1868 General Conference, AME congregations formed in all the former Confederate states and Kentucky, and four years later the church comprised seven episcopal districts representing twenty-eight states.[21] By 1876, the AME Church reported 206,730 members and 1,642 churches nationwide, with properties valuing $3,129,196.00.[22] In other words, church membership had increased over 413 percent since the end of the American Civil War.

Considering the AME Church's successful evangelistic efforts in the U.S. South, its rapid growth, and the development of its institutional organization, many AME leaders believed that the denomination should spread to foreign lands. For example, months before the 1872 General Conference, the *Christian Recorder* proclaimed, "Our Church is fast rising up to the full conception of her duty in the premises ... already has she no little zeal for the salvation of her heathen kindred."[23] The editorialist declared that the AME Church awaited "some great organizing spirit, to put in shape and order the already existing missionary force."[24] Thus, African Methodists held of utmost importance the election of the denomination's first Missionary Secretary in 1864 and the organization of the church's Finance Department in 1872.[25] With these advancements, AME leaders could activate the "latent missionary power of the Church," as the editorialist and other leaders demanded.[26]

For AME leaders, Hispaniola represented the natural progression of the denomination's missionary efforts in the U.S. South. They believed that, like the formerly enslaved population which Northern leaders evangelized, Haiti and the Dominican Republic needed education and Protestant religion in order to "uplift" the two predominantly Catholic nations from recurring wars and political instability.[27] They saw their role in filling this presumed need as both logical and urgent. AME intervention on Hispaniola seemed logical because African Americans believed both Haiti and the Dominican Republic to be "black republics."[28] This perspective on Haitians' and Dominicans' racial status reflected the opinions of mainstream U.S. society, which often conflated the Dominican Republic with Haiti even while the Dominican Republic's Europhile elites attempted to whitewash their country's African heritage and historical connection to Haiti.[29] As independent Black republics, both Haiti and the Dominican Republic represented Black self-determination and existed as important symbols of Black progress for African Americans. Yet the constant political instability on the island cast this symbol in doubt as white Americans ridiculed Black rule.[30] Consequently, AME leaders deemed racial uplift through missions as an urgent solution to the island's problems.

The timing for AME missions seemed especially serendipitous in the early 1870s for a couple of reasons. First, the United States considered annexing the Dominican Republic between 1869 and 1871 (a topic discussed further by Gregg French in this volume). The United States' potential expansion to the young nation brought the Dominican Republic to the forefront of Americans' minds. Second, in 1872, the AME Church received a noteworthy call for aid from African American immigrants in Santo Domingo. This request and the AME Church's subsequent response demonstrated the significance of AME missions to both African American immigrants and African Methodists in the United States. Like other such letters sent sporadically throughout the nineteenth century, it also betrayed the shifting visions of AME Church leaders and the distinct priorities of immigrant communities on the island.

A Missionary Call and Response

African Methodist leaders and congregants followed the national debate over the United States' proposed annexation of the Dominican Republic with interest. While many African Americans opposed the measure because they feared it would lead to a U.S. takeover of Haiti, most AME leaders supported the initiative because they believed it would spark the Protestant evangelization of Catholic Dominicans and incite racial uplift.[31] For example, in January 1869 one article in the *Christian Recorder* declared that support for Dominican annexation was "the sentiment that should predominate in the heart of every civilized and Christian Negro of the world."[32] A month later, another letter stated that annexation would bring about the end of war and "anarchy" on the island, instill economic stability and trade, and lead to the opening of schools and the free circulation of the Bible.[33] Yet another editorialist declared: "Open up [the Dominican Republic] for the Protestant Church of the land!"[34] If missionaries were to enter the country, AME leaders asserted that Dominican children would "no longer grow up to ignorant manhood," and "the religion of the Bible would have fair chance."[35] According to these letters and others, racial uplift would only come with the Protestant-based spiritual conversion of Hispaniola. "Incalculable would be the benefit, which that fruitful island and its people would realize," claimed another letter, which concluded that "the colored people of the States could not do a better thing, than roll up long petitions to our Congress, praying that these 200,000 people—'our kinsmen according to the flesh,' be taken under the starry flag."[36]

African Americans paid such close attention to eastern Hispaniola during the annexation debate because they considered Dominicans to be Black "kinsmen." They classified the Dominican Republic as a Black nation like Haiti and believed that the two nations' fates were necessarily intertwined. Indeed, some articles in the *Christian Recorder* barely distinguished between the two nations. "Almost at our doors there are two Negro Republics, Haiti and Dominica, both of these are located on the large and fertile island of San Domingo," stated one article before asking, "What shall be done for the religious welfare of these two Republics?"[37] Another article written by an AME church committee actually subsumed the Dominican Republic under Haiti. "The island of Haiti is appealing for help," it stated while referring to both countries. "The island is principally inhabited by the Negro race. It is divided into the Spanish and French portions."[38] These descriptions indicate that some African Americans thought little of the political divide between the two nations. From their perspective, both countries were independent Black republics, and the whole island of Hispaniola—whether dubbed "Hayti" or "San Domingo"—was a symbol of Black self-determination and racial equality. Consequently, both the Dominican Republic and Haiti mattered to African Americans, as they identified racially with the island and debated Hispaniola's fate as well as their own.

Given their support for annexation, AME leaders—much like Samuel and Julia Howe, as discussed by Mark Elliott in his chapter in this volume—felt bitterly disappointed when the effort failed in 1871.[39] Nevertheless, they continued to advocate for the expansion of U.S. capitalism and Protestantism on the island. For example, an 1873 article supporting the American Samaná Bay Company's lease of the Samaná Peninsula declared, "As we favored the annexation 'scheme' of the President, so we favor this commercial 'scheme' of these New York capitalists."[40] This article explained that "in fact, we would favor almost anything, that promised to bring Dominica within the influence of our goodly institutions, anything to infuse in it a new life."[41] Like white humanitarians who envisioned the United States "a benevolent, liberating force" in the world, AME leaders perceived Protestant missions on Hispaniola to be the particular responsibility of the AME denomination for the spiritual and social uplift of the island.[42] "It is the important duty of the AME Church to provide for the mission of San Domingo and Haiti," stated one church committee in 1872.[43] "[God] did not say, if ye are rich, go; nor white, go; but go ye unto all nations. Go is the command," it exhorted, warning readers against concerns over finances. As the AME Church's official organ made clear, African Methodists believed themselves to play a special role in drawing closer ties between the island and the United States for the benefit of both Dominicans and Haitians.

Operating within this worldview, AME leaders expressed particular excitement over a petition that arrived from Santo Domingo city in 1872. The supplicants, African American immigrants who left the United States for Hispaniola nearly fifty years prior, declared their allegiance to the AME Church. "We the members of the African Methodist Episcopal Church of this city, emigrated to this country from the United States in the years 1824, 1825, and 1826," they wrote. Claiming that they had always maintained an affiliation with the AME denomination, they explained that "on arriving here we immediately established our church, under the name BETHEL, and we have kept our language and religion to the present." The "Bethel" congregation was named after the first AME Church in Philadelphia, and its members proudly reminded African Americans in the United States of their joint heritage. They hoped that their ethnic and religious ties to the United States would inspire AME leaders to send a missionary to the Dominican Republic and sustain contact with Black Protestant communities on the island.[44]

Compared with other known African American communities on the island, particularly those in Samaná (the northeastern peninsula) little is known about the immigrants in the Dominican Republic's capital.[45] There is no data regarding the occupational composition of the immigrants and their descendants, although it is almost certain that most of the immigrants were impoverished. Regarding African American immigrants, sociologist Harmannus Hoetink claimed that racial discrimination blocked their advancement in Dominican society.[46] Immigrants in Santo Domingo felt such discrimination more acutely than those in Samaná since African American immigrants made up less than 8 percent of the capital's population compared to 50–60 percent in Samaná in the early 1870s.[47] Moreover, as in Haiti, the Catholic Church played a large role in Dominican public life, running schools and charities in the city's capital, with Protestants lacking access to such services. To overcome this disadvantage, Protestants in the capital founded a mutual aid society, the "Society of the Bible," which worked to educate the immigrants' children, take care of orphans and the sick, and bury the dead.[48] *Capitaleño* Protestant religious meetings also provided a sense of unity and spiritual support within the immigrant community, although the immigrants in Santo Domingo never benefited directly from missionary groups that organized in Port-au-Prince, Samaná, and along the island's northern coast. Such groups included the British Wesleyan Missionary Society, the American Baptist Church, and the Episcopal Church, and operated among African American immigrants and Anglophone Caribbean migrants living in these regions. Their statistical reports, missionary letters, and travel narratives are why scholars know more about African American immigrant communities in places outside of the Dominican capital.

Perhaps because of the lack of connection to the kind of Protestant societies that would have provided valuable material and spiritual support, the African American immigrant community in Santo Domingo experienced a rapid decrease in its church membership by the early 1870s. Only eighteen of the original immigrants remained alive. Reverend Isaac Miller, whom Bishop Morris Brown of the AME Church had ordained, had trained additional preachers before his death. Yet in 1872 only Reverend John Hamilton, a seventy-three-year-old ailing deacon, remained among the clergy. On the other end of the generational spectrum, the children and grandchildren of the immigrants were leaving Methodism for Catholicism. Their parents accused the Catholic Church of enticing the children away because Catholics supposedly were permitted to "dance, gamble and indulge in licentionment [sic]."[49] Immigrant parents also lamented their children's assimilation into Dominican society. By 1872 immigrant children spoke more Spanish than English and considered themselves to be Dominicans despite their parents' foreign birth.[50] Considering these conditions, the elder members of the American community feared that their congregation would soon cease to exist.[51]

It was at this juncture that members of the Protestant congregation in the capital wrote to the AME Church in the United States for aid. In the 1872 letter Protestants in Santo Domingo claimed allegiance to the AME Church and requested that their "brethren" send a minister to their religious society. This was an extraordinary request since there had been little recorded contact between the immigrants and leaders in the AME Church in the preceding decades. Indeed, in 1841 the Baltimore Conference declared that its branches on Hispaniola were lost.[52] Moreover, the Santo Domingo immigrant community had formerly reached out to the British Wesleyan Methodist Missionary Society already organized in Samaná.[53] This fact suggests that—while living in a Catholic country—immigrants desired to reinforce their Protestant faith even if it meant aligning with a white English institution rather than a Black American one. In either hypothetical case, immigrants would remain in the Methodist tradition and could continue religious instruction in English, enabling them and their children to maintain two traditions (religion and language) that distinguished them from the Catholic Spanish-speaking majority population. It also suggests that, contrary to what immigrants wrote, denominational identity (whether AME or Wesleyan) actually mattered little to the immigrants. In 1872 the immigrant congregation in Santo Domingo was desperate for aid. Thus, the community's elders expressed hope that their extreme poverty would persuade AME Church leaders in the United States to rejuvenate the church through missionary work.

The letter from Santo Domingo excited AME Church leaders in the United States, who interpreted the immigrants' request as further proof that the time was ripe for foreign missionary work. Yet as the AME Church prepared to send a missionary to the island of Hispaniola, its leaders did not consider the nuanced desires of the African American immigrant communities on the island. Instead, most AME leaders focused on a big-picture idea of racial affinity with the island rather than the AME Church's historical connections to Hispaniola via African American emigration. In fact, only a few *Christian Recorder* articles noted that

Black free people had immigrated from the United States to Haiti throughout the nineteenth century and continued to reside on both sides of the island. Thomas S. Malcom, for example, wrote, "There are faithful Methodists in Port au Prince, the Capital of Haiti, and there are others at Samna [sic] Bay in Dominica." He then asked, "Who will visit them and encourage their efforts for Christ?"[54] Another article noted the immigrants' presence on the island when it recounted that "early in the history of our church our fathers sent missionaries to this island; there they planted the banner of Christ, and the African M.E. Church."[55] Said "missionaries" likely referred to the AME ministers who immigrated to the island along with the first wave of immigrants in the 1820s. In an account of events since the 1820s, the author reported that "the French portion formed an independent church, while the Spanish part remained true amid the trials of years."[56] This overgeneralization reflected the fact that immigrants in Port-au-Prince had indeed formed a separate church that operated in cooperation with other Protestant groups.[57] Immigrants in Santo Domingo had also organized independently but did not have access to other Protestant groups and could thus claim that they had retained their "true" identity as African Methodists. Likely referring to the 1872 letter from the congregation, the author lamented that "we have not answered their prayer and granted their request."[58] In emphasizing the AME Church's failure to fulfill its supposed duty to immigrants, these few articles attempted to incite church leaders to action.

Yet despite these few exceptions, AME discourse regarding missionary work on the island rarely considered the African American immigrant communities that still resided in Santo Domingo, Port-au-Prince, Samaná, and elsewhere. For example, only two months after the letter from Santo Domingo appeared in the *Christian Recorder*, the corresponding secretary of the AME Church's missionary society, Reverend Theophilus Gould Steward, addressed the AME General Conference with the suggestion that the Santo Domingo congregation should be incorporated into the Philadelphia conference. After Steward, the eminent AME bishop and scholar Daniel A. Payne also spoke about the origins of the AME church in Santo Domingo and how the immigrant community had fared since 1824. Yet details of both Steward's proposal and Payne's speech about the community did not make it into the *Christian Recorder*. Instead, editor Benjamin T. Tanner encouraged church leaders to raise the denomination from its "childhood" into full "manhood," and cast "the good old banner of African Methodism . . . to the Southern breezes."[59] As Brandon Byrd has argued, AME leaders such as Tanner ironically disregarded the fact that African Americans had once considered Haiti their "mother" country.[60]

Nearly a year later, on January 30, 1873, another reference to the correspondence from Santo Domingo appeared in the *Christian Recorder*. In response to the immigrants' request for a minister, the anonymous author asked a two-word question, "What hinders?" This question echoed a biblical passage in which a newly converted Ethiopian eunuch standing beside a body of water persuaded the apostle Philip to baptize him by asking, "What hinders?" Writing from the United States, the author used the biblical reference as a parable. "The Eunuch could not understand, why he should not be baptized," the article read, "There was water.... There also was the man of God.... Lastly the Eunuch was there, with professing lips." The author claimed that all of these components were "clearly parts of one drama, having for its object the conversion of the Eunuch, and the subsequent glory of God." Considering the AME Church's recent expansion, the advent of the Samaná Bay Company, and the immigrants' request, the author believed that it was similarly clear that the AME Church should begin missionary work in the Dominican Republic. Yet this article never directly mentioned the immigrant community in Santo Domingo. "Our kinfolk implore us to come," it declared.[61] But "kinfolk" most likely referred to the racial connection between African Americans and Dominicans, not the ethnic or denominational connection between African Americans and the immigrant community in Santo Domingo.[62]

Three additional articles written by Malcom in 1873 further demonstrate this point.[63] In the articles, Malcom reported on the travel plans of Steward, who was preparing to visit the Dominican Republic and Haiti. "The onward step taken by the African Methodist Episcopal Church in sending out Rev. T. G. Steward ... should awaken special joy, among those who desire the mental and moral elevation of persons of African descent in the republics of Santo Domingo and Haiti," Malcom wrote.[64] He encouraged AME Church members to take up an offering to help fund Steward's trip. The money would also enable Steward to sponsor young men from the island who could "be educated at Wilberforce University, in Ohio; at Lincoln University, in Pennsylvania; or at Howard University, in Washington City."[65] After their studies, these young men would advance AME missions on the island, and thus the denomination would spread throughout the two Black republics.

Steward arrived in Port-au-Prince, the first leg of his Hispaniola tour, on June 13, 1873. His experiences in the Haitian capital made plain the discrepancy between American AME leaders' ideas about missions and immigrants' understandings of their own needs. Years later, Steward wrote, "A short experience was sufficient to convince me that I had embarked upon a work with insufficient preparation and equipment."⁶⁶ During his first days on the island, Steward had "found in Port-au-Prince many interesting Christians, descendants of the emigrants of 1824."⁶⁷ After spending time with these immigrants and their children, he concluded that "my former experience among the freedmen of the South was of no value to me here. These people were not freedmen, but citizens of an independent country."⁶⁸ This statement demonstrated the discrepancy between how African American leaders thought of foreign missions and their experiences on the island as an extension of their missionary efforts in the U.S. South but failed to account for significant cultural, historical, and linguistic differences between the United States and Hispaniola. Too overwhelmed by what he had encountered in Haiti, Steward never completed his intended trip to Santo Domingo city. If he had traveled east, he likely would have faced a similar situation as in Haiti. African American immigrant communities in Hispaniola may have shared a common ethnicity and faith with African Methodists in the United States, but they were also citizens of independent nations who expected AME leaders to collaborate with them regarding the course of AME missions.

Initiating AME Missions on Hispaniola in the 1880s

Although some AME leaders hoped that Steward would become the AME Church's permanent missionary in Port-au-Prince, he refused to return to the island after his 1873 trip.⁶⁹ Due to financial deficits in the missionary budget, the AME Church did not appoint missionaries to Hispaniola until 1878, when Reverend Charles W. Mossell and his wife, Mary Ella Mossell, traveled on behalf of the denomination to Port-au-Prince.⁷⁰ The Mossells remained in Haiti for seven years and became well acquainted with Haitian society and the prominent Americans and African American immigrants who lived there.⁷¹ Reverend Mossell later wrote *Toussaint L'Ouverture, the Hero of Santo Domingo* (1896), in which he recounted his and Mary Ella's accomplishments as well as the hardships they faced: poverty, disease, death, environmental catastrophe, and political turmoil.⁷² In the late nineteenth century, Protestant missionaries across Hispaniola suffered many of the same tribulations, but AME missionaries like the Mossells saw additional trouble as the AME Church in the United States abruptly shifted its missionary focus from Hispaniola to Africa. This seemingly sudden shift found root in the AME Church's expansionist outlook developed during Reconstruction, and the change further undermined the denomination's missionary efforts on Hispaniola.

When the Mossells first arrived in Haiti, the African American immigrant community in Port-au-Prince, which had organized an independent Methodist church, initially resisted the AME Church's advances.[73] Yet by 1880 the Mossells' Haitian mission had gained over eighty members. Charles and Mary Ella had organized a Sunday school with sixty students and an industrial school. Two local preachers and a handful of teachers and other local leaders aided them in their work. Mary Ella also started a Haitian chapter of the Women's Mite Missionary Society with forty-five members.[74] With this work, the Mossells made a favorable impression on the Haitian government and society. According to a Haitian budget report cited in the *Christian Recorder*, "This church, together with its two schools, and its Mite Missionary Society, gives us reason to hope much and look favorably upon the moral and religious future of our population."[75]

Despite these advances, however, the AME mission in Port-au-Prince remained entirely dependent on the AME Church in the United States. The Haitian government offered no financial help for their schools and the church.[76] Moreover, the congregation struggled to raise $1,400 to buy the lot of land where it hoped to erect a church. Writing to AME leaders in the U.S., the Mossells requested financial aid. "We are becoming so very well known in our religious work, that a Church is a necessity," wrote Mrs. Mossell.[77] Reverend Mossell also petitioned for "an annual appropriation for two native preachers and a Church edifice."[78] Yet the Mossells would soon realize that the denomination could not provide the material support that they desperately needed.

The requirements of the Haitian congregation placed a heavy burden on the AME Church, which was struggling to raise enough funds to provide steady salaries to the Mossells and also support the immigrant minister Samuel F. Flegler in Liberia whenever possible. Still, the potential for even greater growth in Haiti inspired AME leaders to action. In June 1881 the bishops and episcopal officers of the AME Church met for the annual general board meeting, where they reiterated their commitment to provide a salary for a preacher and agreed to construct a church building in Port-au-Prince. The board's decision to honor the Haitian congregations' petition initiated a campaign to raise at least $10,000 for the AME Church's Parent Home and Foreign Missionary Society, $5,500 of which they would dedicate to the Haitian building fund.[79] The campaign, which would not only provide aid for Haiti but also Liberia, became the central goal of the missionary society for the next three years, consuming the time and effort of the whole church. In the end, however, the denomination raised barely enough money to buy an iron frame from England, which arrived in Port-au-Prince in April 1884.[80]

Ostensibly due to the difficulty of fundraising, the denomination's Board of Bishops decided to discontinue its financial commitment to missionaries on Hispaniola and move on to Africa. Bishop Richard H. Cain, who had to postpone his missionary visit to West Africa due to the financial demands of the Mossells' work on Hispaniola, explained: "After surveying the financial condition of the Church Treasury, and the pressing demands of the Haytian [here and immediately below referring to the country] work, namely, the immediate erection of the iron church there . . . it is deemed wise to wait [on African missions] until that is accomplished." The bishop then reassured the church's leaders that "the missionary society will then declare the Haytian work self-supporting and will turn the future efforts to Africa."[81] This statement, released in the church's newspaper months before the 1884 General Conference, signaled the imminent expiration of the denomination's missionary focus on Hispaniola. Yet it also came at a strange moment. While the church's polity clamored for African missions, the Board of Bishops assigned a new missionary to Hispaniola at Santo Domingo city, and the AME Church gained additional Caribbean missionary stations in Bermuda, St. Thomas, and British Guiana through the AME Church's organic union with the British Methodist Episcopal Church.[82] Moreover, not everyone agreed with the change. Thus, the early 1880s marks a brief period when AME Church leaders in the United States debated the church's missionary future.[83]

Meanwhile, missionaries on Hispaniola continued to struggle financially. A closer look at the Santo Domingo mission further evidences the challenges they faced. By 1882 a decade had passed before the Santo Domingo immigrant community's petition seemed to be answered with the foreign service appointment of Henry C. C. Astwood to the U.S. consulship in Santo Domingo.[84] An AME clergyman, Astwood received instruction from the Board of Bishops to establish a missionary station in Santo Domingo while he performed his consular duties; consequently, he met with the leaders of the immigrant community soon after his arrival.[85] As expected, the community had languished in the decade since it petitioned the AME Church for aid in 1872. According to Astwood, disease had ravaged the congregation and only a few immigrants and their descendants remained in the capital in 1882.[86] The eldest leader, Elijah R. Gross, whom Astwood called "Old Father Gross," led the community in worship, but Gross had become too old to continue his work.[87] Once a dynamic leader and a former member of the AME Church in Philadelphia, Gross had never received aid from abroad.[88] Moreover, the building where the community worshiped had fallen into further disrepair, and it was impossible to hold services in it. The Protestants had tried to collect money for repairs, but they ran out of funds in 1878.[89] Political instability in the country that year also thwarted their plans and they had to abandon the work. Having promised the Bishops of the AME Church that he would "do all in my power to help the work [to go] on here," Astwood pledged to reestablish the connection with the United States.[90] Working with the congregation, he rented a building, bought an organ and chairs, hosted Sunday worship services, and reaffiliated the congregation with the AME Church in the United States.

Yet despite the promising start of the AME organization in Santo Domingo, by the end of 1882 Astwood felt disheartened. Since his arrival he had received little correspondence from AME leaders in the United States. He cited his experience requesting AME literature as an example. In 1882 he had appealed to the AME Publishing Department for the *Child's Recorder*, but the department sent only fifty copies of back orders. "Not hearing anything more from Bishop Campbell, I became very much discouraged," he wrote. Astwood felt additional pressure as his duties as a preacher and U.S. consul increased. "It is hard work, all of the duties developing upon me," he wrote in February 1883. He then requested that the AME Church "come to the rescue" and send a regular missionary to Santo Domingo, stating that it would cost "one-half of the trouble and expense attending the work in Haiti."[91] No response to his letter appeared in the *Christian Recorder*.[92]

Astwood was not the only AME minister from Hispaniola to face difficulty raising funds in the United States. In 1880 Rev. Charles Mossell had assisted two young Haitian men, Adolphus H. Mevs and Solomon G. Dorce, in matriculating at the AME Church's Wilberforce University in Ohio. Four years later, Mevs and Dorce were newly ordained ministers of the AME Church and planned to return to the island to take over the Santo Domingo and Port-au-Prince missions respectively. In order to pay for their trip, the two missionaries visited several AME congregations across the U.S. Midwest, where they met with ministers and their parishioners and collected donations. Yet the tour was not as successful as they had initially hoped. Although both men commended the ministers and churches that aided them in their journey, there were notable exceptions. Dorce refused to write about the troubles he faced, stating that some pastors, "might get offended at me for the manner in which I would paint their own actions."[93] Mevs, however, had no such qualms. "I am certainly opposed to the idea of concealing any such mean, low, contemptible principles existing in the Christian ministry or elsewhere," he opined.[94] He then recounted how one minister lied to his face and refused to receive him. Mevs and Dorce's experiences suggest that not all AME ministers believed in the missionary cause, and some even directly opposed giving money to Haiti. Bishops and other episcopal leaders criticized naysayers who challenged their leadership and whose attitudes may have paralleled white Americans' waning enthusiasm for U.S. expansion.[95] Yet many other ministers simply did not have much to give, despite supporting missions from an ideological standpoint. Consequently, neither Dorce nor Mevs could raise much money. Facing this dilemma, Mevs "proposed to give up the struggle," but remembering his faith and others' kindness, he resolved to continue.[96]

Despite their efforts, problems persisted when the two Haitian missionaries reached the island. Months after their arrival, the Mossells returned to the United States, and both Dorce and Mevs began to worry about the AME Church's waning commitment to Hispaniola.[97] Representing the Haitian mission, Dorce explained that the congregation of eighty-five members was growing. Dorce held three services every Sunday at 10:00 AM (French), 5:00 PM (English), and 7:00pm (French).[98] These services did not include the Sunday School (which met at 8:00 AM on Sunday) and the 4:00 PM prayer meeting. During the week, the church also hosted another prayer meeting on Friday evenings and a service on Wednesday. These activities underscored the success of the AME church in the Haitian capital despite a lack of financial aid. "Our church should do much more than what she has done, and become the leading church here," Dorce explained to AME leaders in the United States, "but she cannot on account of her poverty."[99] Whereas the other Protestant denominations in Port-au-Prince received limited aid from foreign white churches, the AME Church received nothing. "We all, Church and State, think that the connection [denomination] does not care for the Haitian mission," he wrote. He then posed rhetorical questions, "Why should the AME Church missionaries be so neglected. . . . You have nobly begun; do you wish to flinch now?" Dorce cautioned: "Don't think of that."[100]

Like the AME Church in Port-au-Prince, the Santo Domingo congregation also continued to lack financial support. Before leaving Haiti, Mossell explained that between Astwood's arrival in 1882 and December 1884, the Santo Domingo congregation had bought lamps for $35.00 and Sunday School books and church literature for $200. It additionally supported the elderly minister Gross, who was too frail to work, with $350 to sustain himself; sent $60 of missionary money to the United States as part of the annual dues ("dollar money"); and repaired the old church for $1,060.00.[101] With the debt on the building totaling $610.00 in 1884, Astwood had asked the AME Church to cover the remaining amount, but there is no evidence that any money was sent.[102] In all, between 1882 and December 1884, the congregation's costs rose to $2,363.00. Mossell claimed that the local congregation raised and borrowed money to cover their needs, for as he declaimed, "More than twelve thousand dollars has been expended to aid the Haytian work [referring to the country], but no aid whatever has been extended to St. Domingo."[103] Mevs echoed this complaint over finances upon taking over the Santo Domingo post in 1886. According to Mevs, "Appeals upon appeals are being made in behalf of Africa, while Haiti and San Domingo are neglected."[104]

Mevs's lament stemmed from the AME Church's shifting priorities. True to the bishops' promise, the AME Church declared its Hispaniola missions "self-supporting" at the General Conference of 1884 in order to make Africa the denomination's primary missionary field. In the following years, the AME Church not only ramped up its efforts in Liberia but also founded missionary stations in Sierra Leone in 1887. These stations grew quickly. Bishop Henry McNeal Turner organized the Liberian and Sierra Leone missions into annual conferences, with 800 and 1,000 members respectively in 1891.[105] Then in 1893, Southern Black women organized the Women's Home and Foreign Missionary Society, whose fund-raising activities and monies Bishop Henry McNeal Turner steered toward Africa. These funds became particularly useful after the AME Church merged with the South African Ethiopian Church and founded the South African AME conference in 1896. Finances were tight for all AME foreign work, but by 1892 monies expended for the three African stations had already surpassed Hispaniola, and by 1899 the recommended budget for African missions was nearly three times the combined budget for Haiti and the Dominican Republic.[106] That year the missionary secretary Henry Blanton Parks called for one-third of the 1899 Easter Day returns ($3,421.08 out of $10,263.23), a sizable portion of the 1898–1899 missionary earnings, to be dedicated to Queenstown College in South Africa.[107] This amount could not be distributed to South Africa without detriment to the other missionary areas. Nevertheless, Parks declared the evangelization of Africa the special duty of Black Americans. "No other race can do the work as you can," Parks wrote to African Americans in his book *Africa: The Problem of the New Century* (1899). "It is the civilized, educated Negro for the manly, heathen Negro."[108] African evangelization had become the AME Church's "Black man's burden."[109]

Conclusion

This chapter has analyzed the expansionist goals and actions of the AME Church after the American Civil War (1861–1865). Aiming to convert newly freed people, AME leaders sent missionaries to the U.S. South, which enabled the denomination to grow throughout the late 1860s and 1870s. This expansion turned leaders' attention toward the foreign missionary field. Although scholars have studied the AME Church's missions in Africa, this chapter has analyzed the impetuses and development of the denomination's missions on the Caribbean island of Hispaniola, arguably the AME Church's first foreign missionary field after the Civil War. AME expansionist discourse during Reconstruction aligned with U.S. imperialist action in the Caribbean and obfuscated other impetuses for AME missionary work on Hispaniola, namely earlier nineteenth-century Afro-diasporic connections forged through Haitian emigration and the long-standing cooperation between African Americans and Haitians. The history of AME missions in Port-au-Prince and Santo Domingo recounted in this essay builds on the scholarship of other historians who have demonstrated the significance of Haiti to the African American imagination, African American political activism, and the AME Church's foreign missions in the nineteenth century.

The unstable nature of missionary work took its toll on AME missionaries operating on Hispaniola. As marginal leaders within the African Methodist denomination, missionaries such as Astwood, Mevs, Dorce, and the Mossells did not often feature in church newspapers or history books. Indeed, after arriving in Santo Domingo, Mevs wrote melancholically, "I doubt whether [the AME Church has] much of any idea concerning the place and the great difficulties under which missionaries have to labor."[110] Few people in the United States understood the degree to which AME missionaries on Hispaniola operated without financial aid and oversight from the denomination. The records that remain of these leaders' lives provide only glimpses of the hardships that they faced, which caused some AME missionaries to ultimately abandon the island. In March 1888, for example, Mevs traveled to the United States in order to seek a new appointment, and in April 1889 the missionary department sent him to the Bermuda Annual Conference.[111] Yet by November 1891 Mevs returned again to the United States to work in Arkadelphia, Arkansas.[112] Finally settled in the U.S. South, it seems that Mevs and his family never returned to Haiti or the Dominican Republic.[113] Astwood also returned to the United States after leaving his diplomatic post in 1889.[114] In subsequent years, other Dominican and Haitian missionaries followed a similar path, abandoning the islands to become ministers in America; one of them, John Hurst of Haiti, even became a bishop in the AME Church.[115]

Still, documents of the era also suggest a tenacious perseverance and ingenuity among those who remained part of the AME Church's congregations in Santo Domingo and Port-au-Prince. Without direct oversight and without money to support their salaries and church growth, these congregations survived throughout the end of the nineteenth century and during the whole of the twentieth. Thus, neither the history of the AME Church's Hispaniola missions nor their legacies in Haiti and the Dominican Republic should be overlooked. After Reconstruction, the U.S. government's racist domestic policies and its persistent aggression toward Caribbean nations motivated some AME leaders to advocate for missionary expansion to the Caribbean and Africa in order to unite the Black race against white supremacy. Others within the denomination protested the scramble for territorial gain at the expense of the AME Church's historical connection to Hispaniola and the missionaries operating there. To ignore these dissenting voices and the experiences of the AME Church's Caribbean-based missionaries is to ignore the multifaceted ways that African Americans and Afro-Caribbeans made sense of the Reconstruction era and navigated America's burgeoning empire at the end of the nineteenth century.

Notes

1. "Our Mission Work," *Christian Recorder*, February 13, 1869.
2. "The Commonest Mistake of Which Most Christian Folks are Guilty," *Christian Recorder*, December 20, 1877.
3. Laurie F. Maffly-Kipp, *Setting Down the Sacred Past: African-American Race Histories* (Cambridge, Mass.: Belknap Press of Harvard University Press, 2010), 110–111.
4. In this essay and elsewhere, I argue that African Americans often thought of the two sides of the island together and did not always distinguish between Haiti and the Dominican Republic. This stance builds on what Dixa Ramírez has described for Americans in general during the period. See Dixa Ramírez, *Colonial Phantoms: Belonging and Refusal in the Dominican Americas, from the Nineteenth Century to the Present* (New York: NYU Press, 2018), 3. For African Americans, "Hayti" could have referred both to the Haitian state and the whole island of Hispaniola. Here I use the modern spelling, "Haiti," when referring to the country. In cases where nineteenth-century African Americans use the term "Hayti" to refer specifically to the modern country, I make sure to clarify that for the reader.
5. Sylvester A. Johnson, *African American Religions, 1500–2000: Colonialism, Democracy, and Freedom* (Cambridge: Cambridge University Pres, 2015), 251–253.
6. Brandon R. Byrd, *The Black Republic: African Americans and the Fate of Haiti* (Philadelphia: University of Pennsylvania Press, 2020); Peter Wirzbicki, "'The Light of Knowledge Follows the Impulse of Revolutions': Prince Saunders, Baron de Vastey and the Haitian Influence on Antebellum Black Ideas of Elevation and Education," *Slavery & Abolition* 36, no. 2 (2014), 275–297; Millery Polyné, *From Douglass to Duvalier: U.S. African Americans, Haiti, and Pan Americanism, 1870–1964* (Gainesville: University Press of Florida, 2010); Léon Dénius Pamphile, *Haitians and African Americans: A Heritage of Tragedy and Hope* (Gainesville: University Press of Florida, 2001).
7. For key works on AME African missions see Elisabeth Engel, *Encountering Empire: African American Missionaries in Colonial Africa, 1900–1939* (Stuttgart: Franz Steiner Verlag, 2015); Nevell A. Owens, *Formation of the African Methodist Episcopal Church in the Nineteenth Century* (New York: Palgrave Macmillan, 2014), 61–118; Lawrence S. Little, *Disciples of Liberty: The African Methodist Episcopal Church in the Age of Imperialism, 1884–1916* (Knoxville: University of Tennessee Press, 2000); James T. Campbell, *Songs of*

Zion: The African Methodist Episcopal Church in the United States and South Africa (New York: Oxford University Press, 1995).

8. Owens, *Formation*, 68–76, 99–104; Little, *Disciples of Liberty*, 63–66. See also Sylvester A. Johnson, *The Myth of Ham in Nineteenth-Century American Christianity: Race, Heathens, and the People of God* (New York: Palgrave Macmillan, 2004); Michele Mitchell, *Righteous Propagation: African Americans and the Politics of Racial Destiny after Reconstruction* (Chapel Hill: University of North Carolina Press, 2004), 51–75; Tunde Adeleke, *UnAfrican Americans: Nineteenth-Century Black Nationalists and the Civilizing Mission* (Lexington: University Press of Kentucky, 1998), 92–110; Albert J. Raboteau, *A Fire in the Bones: Reflections on African-American Religious History* (Boston: Beacon Press, 1995), 54–51.

9. Little, *Disciples of Liberty*, 63.

10. Dennis C. Dickerson, *The African Methodist Episcopal Church: A History* (Cambridge: Cambridge University Press, 2020); Byrd, *The Black Republic*.

11. Dickerson, *The African Methodist Episcopal Church*, 147.

12. The United States also had its eye on Cuba during the island's Ten Years' War (1868–1878). See Don H. Doyle, *American Civil Wars: The United States, Latin America, Europe, and the Crisis of the 1860s* (Chapel Hill: University of North Carolina Press, 2017), 25–26, and Andre Fleche's chapter in this volume

13. Byrd argues that U.S. Blacks saw Haiti as a symbol of Black redemption, but these feelings changed after the Civil War as whites "maligned Haitians and African Americans in the same breath," and African Americans determined to "save" Haiti. Here I expand on Byrd's thesis by including eastern Hispaniola. Byrd, *The Black Republic*, 7.

14. Various scholars have covered the 1820s Haitian emigration movement; see, for example, Dennis Hidalgo, *La primera inmigracion de negros libertos norteamericanos y su asentamiento en la Española (1824–1826)* (Santo Domingo: Academia Dominicana de la Historia, 2016); Sara Fanning, *Caribbean Crossing: African Americans and the Haitian Emigration Movement* (New York: NYU Press, 2014); Leslie M. Alexander, "A Land of Promise: Emigration and Pennsylvania's Black Elite in the Era of the Haitian Revolution," in *The Civil War in Pennsylvania: The African American Experience*, ed. Samuel W. Black (Pittsburgh: Pennsylvania Heritage Foundation, 2013), 97–132; Maffley-Kipp, *Setting Down the Sacred Past*, 109–153; James O'Dell Jackson, "The Origins of Pan-African Nationalism: Afro-American and Haytian Relations, 1800–1863" (diss. Northwestern University, 1976), 49–117.

15. For an example of problems that impeded connection, see Leslie Griffiths, *History of Methodism in Haiti* (Port-au-Prince: Imprimerie Méthodiste, 1991), 54–55.

16. Other connections with African Americans were made when Frederick Douglass toured the Dominican Republic with the U.S. Commission of Inquiry in 1871. Christopher Wilkins, "'They had heard of emancipation and the enfranchisement of their race': The African American Colonists of Samaná, Reconstruction, and the State of Santo Domingo," in *The Civil War as Global Conflict: Transnational Meanings of the American Civil War*, ed. David T. Gleeson and Simon Lewis (Columbia: University of South Carolina Press, 2014), 213. See also April Mayes, *The Mulatto Republic: Class, Race, and Dominican National Identity* (Gainesville: University Press of Florida, 2014), 15.

17. C. S. Smith, *A History of the African Methodist Episcopal Church: Being a Volume Supplemental to A History of the African Methodist Episcopal Church* (Philadelphia: AME Book Concern, 1922), 497; Dickerson, *The African Methodist Episcopal Church*, 121. AME General Conference is the official meeting of the whole denomination and takes place on a quadrennial schedule.

18. Reginald F. Hildebrand, *The Times Were Strange and Stirring: Methodist Preachers and the Crisis of Emancipation* (Durham, N.C.: Duke University Press, 1995), 31–49; William E. Montgomery, *Under Their Own Vine and Fig Tree: The African-American Church in the South, 1865–1900* (Baton Rouge: Louisiana State University Press, 1993), 98–99.

19. "Statistics of the AME Church," *Christian Recorder*, April 7, 1866. See also Daniel Alexander Payne, *History of the African Methodist Episcopal Church* (Nashville: Publishing House of the A.M.E. Sunday School Union, 1891), 465.

20. "Our Statistics," *Christian Recorder*, May 4, 1867.

21. Smith, *History of the African Methodist Episcopal Church*, 77, 103–104.

22. "AME Church Statistics, 1875," *Christian Recorder*, March 9, 1876.

23. "The Mission Work," *Christian Recorder*, March 30, 1872.

24. Ibid.

25. Llewellyn L. Berry, *Century of Missions of the African Methodist Episcopal Church*, ix, 91; Smith, *History of the African Methodist Episcopal Church*, 79; "The Growth of AME Mission Work," in Cyril E. Griffith Papers, Box 15577, Pennsylvania State University Libraries (hereafter PSUL).

26. "The Mission Work," *Christian Recorder*, March 30, 1872.

27. Brandon Byrd, "Black Republicans, Black Republic: African-Americans, Haiti, and the Promise of Reconstruction," *Slavery & Abolition* 36, no. 4 (2015), 546–547. See also Byrd, *The Black Republic*, 49–52.

28. For example, see Dr. C. S. Smith, "A Trip to the West Indies," *Christian Recorder*, March 12, 1896.

29. For mainstream society, Ramírez, *Colonial Phantoms*, 3. For Dominican elites, Roberto Cassá, "El racismo en la ideología de la clase dominante dominicana," *Ciencia* 3, no. 1 (1976), 59–86.

30. Byrd, "Black Republicans, Black Republic," 547.

31. Lauren Whitney Hammond, "Outpost of Empire, Endpost of Blackness: African Americans, the Dominican Republic, and U.S. Foreign Policy, 1869–1965" (PhD diss., University of Texas at Austin, 2014), 24–29; Polyné, *From Douglass to Duvalier*, 38–43; Merline Pitre, "Frederick Douglass and American Diplomacy in the Caribbean," *Journal of Black Studies* 13, no. 4 (1983), 463–464.

32. "Pittsburg, PA, January 15. President Colored Men's Convention," *Christian Recorder*, January 30, 1869.

33. "Hayti at Dominica," *Christian Recorder*, February 13, 1869.

34. "Annexation of Dominica," *Christian Recorder*, April 2, 1870.

35. "Hayti at Dominica," *Christian Recorder*, February 13, 1869.

36. "Dominican Annexation," *Christian Recorder*, February 20, 1869.

37. "The Republic of Haiti," *Christian Recorder*, August 10, 1872.

38. "Among the American Indians," *Christian Recorder*, December 21, 1872.

39. The United States considered annexing the Dominican Republic at various moments over the nineteenth century. The debate of 1869–1871 took place during President Grant's administration. Annexation would turn the Dominican Republic into a U.S. territory that could then apply for statehood. The prospect of Dominican statehood drew protests from progressives who wished to protect Dominican and Haitian sovereignty and conservatives who did not want a majority African-descended country to join the Union. For more on the annexation debate, racial politics, and the Samaná Bay company, see Nicholas Guyatt, "America's Conservatory: Race, Reconstruction, and the Santo Domingo Debate," *Journal of American History* 94, no. 4 (2010), 974–1000.

40. "Dominica," *Christian Recorder*, January 23, 1873.

41. Ibid.

42. On these points, see also Mark Elliott's chapter in this volume.

43. "Among the American Indians," *Christian Recorder*, December 21, 1872.

44. "Communications," *Christian Recorder*, March 30, 1872.

45. The literature on the Samaná Americans is comparatively vast. See, for example, H. Hoetink, "'Americans' in Samaná," *Caribbean Studies* 2, no. 1 (1962), 3–22; Martha Ellen Davis, "That Old-Time Religion: Tradición y cambio en el enclave 'Americano' de Samaná," in *Cultura y folklore de Samaná*, ed. Dagoberto Tejeda Ortiz (Santo Domingo: Editora Alfa & Omega, 1984), 97–146; Valerie Smith, "Early Afro-American Presence on the Island of Hispaniola: A Case Study of the Immigrants of Samaná," *Journal of Negro History* 72, no. 1/2 (1987), 33–41; Ryan Mann-Hamilton, "Forgotten Migrations from the United States to Hispaniola," *Trotter Review* 19, no. 1 (2010),1–19; Ryan Mann-Hamilton, "What Rises from the Ashes: Nation and Race in the African American Enclave of Samaná," in *Migrant Marginality: A Transnational Perspective*, ed. Philip Kretsedemas, Jorge Capetillo-Ponce, and Glenn Jacobs (New York: Routledge, 2014), 222–238; Wilkins, "'They had heard of emancipation and the enfranchisement of their race.'"

46. H. Hoetink, *The Dominican People, 1850–1900: Notes for a Historical Sociology* (Baltimore: Johns Hopkins University Press, 1982), 96–97.

47. The U.S. Commission of Inquiry estimated 6,000 people in the capital. Samuel Hazard estimated 800–1,000 people in Samaná. The population of immigrants in Santo Domingo originally was less than the 490 who went to Samaná. See Commission of Inquiry, "Report of the Commission of Inquiry to Santo Domingo," 15; Samuel Hazard, *Santo Domingo: Past and Present, with a Glance at Hayti* (New York: Harper & Brothers, 1873), 199; Fanning, *Caribbean Crossings*, 99.

48. Commission of Inquiry, "Report of the Commission of Inquiry to Santo Domingo," 255–256.

49. "Communications," *Christian Recorder*, March 30, 1872.

50. See interviews with Elijah Gross and George Fountain, Commission of Inquiry, "Report of the Commission of Inquiry to Santo Domingo," 255, 268.

51. "Communications," *Christian Recorder*, March 30, 1872.

52. James A. Handy, *Scraps of African Methodist Episcopal History* (Philadelphia: AME Book Concern, 1902), 135; Payne, *History of the African Methodist Episcopal Church*, 478. This declaration specifies Haiti but also refers to branches established on the eastern side of the island since the whole island remained unified under Haitian government in 1841.

53. G. G. Findlay and W. W. Holdsworth, *History of the Wesleyan Methodist Missionary Society*, vol. 2 (London: Epworth Press, 1921), 493.

54. Thomas S. Malcom, "The Republic of Haiti," *Christian Recorder*, August 10, 1872.

55. "Among the American Indians," *Christian Recorder*, December 21, 1872.

56. Ibid.

57. Charles W. Mossell, *Toussaint L'Ouverture, the Hero of Saint Domingo* (Lockport, N.Y.: Ward & Cobb, 1896), 405.

58. "Among the American Indians," *Christian Recorder*, December 21, 1872.

59. "Our Missionary Work," *Christian Recorder*, May 11, 1872. See also "A Revival of Hope for Foreign Missions Occurs at the 1872 General Conference," in Cyril E. Griffith Papers, Box 15581, PSUL.

60. Byrd, *The Black Republic*, 33–34. For Tanner, see pages 28–35.

61. "What Hinders," *Christian Recorder*, January 30, 1873.

62. Owens, *Formation*, 25–36. AME leaders believed that all people of African descent were part of the Negro race descended from Noah's son Ham, and "kinfolk" likely referred to this racial connection. See also Johnson, *The Myth of Ham*.

63. Thomas S. Malcom, "The San Domingo Mission," *Christian Recorder*, May 15, 1873; Thomas S. Malcom, "Mission to Santo Domingo," *Christian Recorder*, May 22, 1873; Thomas S. Malcom, "A Self Sustaining Mission," *Christian Recorder*, June 5, 1873.

64. Malcom, "Self-Sustaining Mission," *Christian Recorder*, June 5, 1873.

65. Malcom, "San Domingo Mission," *Christian Recorder*, May 15, 1873. Malcom repeated this request in his second letter of May 22, 1873.

66. T. G. Steward, *Fifty Years in the Gospel Ministry, from 1864 to 1914* (Philadelphia: AME Book Concern, 1921), 149.

67. Ibid.

68. Ibid. Cited also in Byrd, *The Black Republic*, 54.

69. "Bishop Shorter's Testimony," *Christian Recorder*, May 13, 1880.

70. Steward was referring to Mossell when he stated, "My mission did little more than call attention to the difficulties and suggest the things necessary to be placed in the hands of the missionary going there." Steward, *Fifty Years in the Gospel Ministry*, 149; For more on Mossell see Byrd, "Black Republicans, Black Republic," 545–567

71. His acquaintances included U.S. Minister to Haiti John Mercer Langston and Bishop James Theodore Holly of the Haitian Episcopal Church.

72. Mossell, *Toussaint L'Ouverture*, 401–446.

73. Ibid., 407–409.

74. "Our Mission in Haiti," *Christian Recorder*, January 26, 1882. For Mary Ella, see Brandon R. Byrd, "The Transnational Work of Moral Elevation: African American Women and the Reformation of Haiti, 1874–1950," *Palimpsest: A Journal on Women, Gender, and the Black International* 5, no. 2 (2016), 132–136.

75. "Our Mission in Haiti," *Christian Recorder*, January 26, 1882. The article translates part of a Haitian government report for 1880 that was likely printed in a Haitian newspaper. Mossell refers to the report as "the Expose or Budget for 1880."

76. Emily J. Cooper, "Communications," *Christian Recorder*, February 3, 1881.

77. "To the Mite Societies," *Christian Recorder*, December 23, 1880.

"What Hinders?" 77

78. Ibid.
79. "Office of the Corresponding Secretary," *Christian Recorder*, December 1, 1881.
80. James Tucker, "A Voice from Port-au-Prince, Haiti," *Christian Recorder*, August 7, 1884.
81. Richard H. Cain, "The African Missionary Work," *Christian Recorder*, September 27, 1883.
82. For more on the organic union, see Christina Cecelia Davidson, "An Organic Union: Theorizing Race, Nation, and Imperialism within the Black Church," *Journal of African American History* 106, no. 4 (2021); Julius H. Bailey, *Race Patriotism: Protest and Print Culture in the AME Church* (Knoxville: University of Tennessee Press, 2012), 63–82; Dickerson, *The African Methodist Episcopal Church*, 152–153.
83. For an overview of such debates, see Bailey, *Race Patriotism*; Owens, *Formation of the African Methodist Episcopal Church*.
84. Astwood became infamous in Santo Domingo and the United States for his diplomatic antics, especially his involvement in a scheme to lease Christopher Columbus's remains. His duplicitous character, however, did not come to light until later in the 1880s and did not initially affect his missionary work. For further details on Astwood, see this author's PhD dissertation and forthcoming manuscript Christina Cecelia Davidson, "Converting Spanish Hispaniola: Race, Nation, and the AME Church in Santo Domingo, 1872–1904" (PhD diss., Duke University, 2017), 70–79. See also Dickerson, *African Methodist Episcopal Church*, 212–213.
85. H. C. C. Astwood, "Letter from Santo Domingo," *Christian Recorder*, February 22, 1883.
86. García states that the population succumbed to typhoid. José Gabriel García, *Compendio de la historia de Santo Domingo*, 3rd ed., vol. 2 (Santo Domingo: Imprenta de García Hermanos, 1894), 122.
87. Astwood, "Letter from Santo Domingo," *Christian Recorder*, February 22, 1883.
88. Ibid.
89. Joseph Prior to M. C. Osborn, April 22, 1880, Methodist Missionary Society Archives, Microfiche, General Commission on Archives and History, United Methodist Church.
90. Astwood, "Letter from Santo Domingo," *Christian Recorder*, February 22, 1883.
91. Ibid.
92. Ibid.
93. Solomon G. Dorce, "My Western Tour," *Christian Recorder*, October 2, 1884.
94. A. H. Mevs, "Notes by the Way," *Christian Recorder*, September 18, 1884.
95. Mark Wahlgren Summers, *The Ordeal of the Reunion: A New History of Reconstruction* (Chapel Hill: University of North Carolina Press, 2014), 209–210.
96. Mevs, "Notes by the Way," *Christian Recorder*, September 18, 1884.
97. Smith reports that the Mossells returned to the United States after suffering trauma during an insurrection in Haiti in 1883. Yet it is more likely that they returned because Mrs. Mossell took ill. Mrs. Mossell died from illness on June 19, 1886. Jessie Carney Smith, ed., *Notable Black American Women*, vol. 2 (Detroit: Gale Research, 1996), 485.

98. Dorce reported that the AME Church's French evening service was the largest Protestant ceremony in the city. "A Word from Haiti," *Christian Recorder*, February 18, 1886.

99. Ibid.

100. Ibid.

101. "Missionary Report of Rev. C. W. Mossell, A.M., Port-au-Prince, Haiti," *Christian Recorder*, January 8, 1885. "Dollar money" was the technical term for the Dollar Money law written into the AME Discipline. It obligated every AME member to contribute one dollar annually to the denomination.

102. "New York, September 17, 1884," *AME Church Review* 1, no. 2 (1884), 175–176. See also "Hon. H. C. C. Astwood," *Christian Recorder*, March 27, 1884.

103. "Missionary Report of Rev. C. W. Mossell, A.M., Port-au-Prince, Haiti," *Christian Recorder*, January 8, 1885. See also "San Domingo Mission Work," *Christian Recorder*, September 10, 1885.

104. A. H. Mevs, "A Word from the Santo Domingo Mission," *Christian Recorder*, July 29, 1886.

105. Dickerson, *African Methodist Episcopal Church*, 201.

106. W. B. Derrick, *Quadrennial Report of the Mission Department of the A.M.E. Church, 1888–1892* (New York: AME Missionary Department, 1892). $3,172 was given to Africa compared with $3,046 to Hispaniola. For 1899 recommendations, see H. B. Parks, *Annual Report of the Missionary Department of the African Methodist Episcopal Church, 1897–1898* (New York: AME Missionary Department, 1898), 27.

107. H. B. Parks, *Africa: The Problem of the New Century* (New York: AME Church, 1899), 41.

108. Ibid., 39.

109. Mitchell, *Righteous Propagation*, 51–75.

110. A. H. Mevs, "A Word from the Santo Domingo Mission," *Christian Recorder*, July 29, 1886.

111. "Personal," *Christian Recorder*, March 8, 1888.

112. "Off to Bermuda," *Christian Recorder*, April 11, 1889; "Rev. A. H. Mevs and Family," *Christian Recorder*, November 19, 1891.

113. In 1894, Mevs was stationed in Greenville, Mississippi. "Personals," *Christian Recorder*, April 26, 1894.

114. Astwood resided in Santo Domingo after his consular tenure ended, and he was recognized as the Santo Domingo superintendent through 1893.

115. Hurst trained at Wilberforce along with two other young men from Haiti whose last names were Guiot and Day. "Missionary Report of Rev. C. W. Mossell, A.M., Port-au-Prince, Haiti," *Christian Recorder*, January 8, 1885.

3

Domestic Stability and Imperial Continuities

U.S.–Spanish Relations in the Reconstruction Era

Gregg French

On October 18, 1873, the Spanish government invited Daniel Sickles to attend a military ceremony in Madrid. At the event, the Spanish minister of war, General José Sánchez Bregua, presented the U.S. minister to Spain with an elaborately decorated Toledo sword. The gift was offered to the former Union officer as a way for the First Spanish Republic to distance itself from earlier governments, which refused to support the Union during the American Civil War. It also provided the new Spanish President, Emilio Castelar, with an opportunity to express his desire to continue the two countries' mutually beneficial relationship, which, despite some turbulent periods, had existed since the founding of the United States.[1]

Contrary to ministerial protocol, Sickles happily received the sword.[2] Despite the questionable legality of the event, it received minimal recognition in American newspapers. This relative absence is noteworthy since many well-informed Americans had welcomed the establishment of the First Spanish Republic and were captivated by similar Spanish swords that were on display in the United States later in the century.[3] Instead, other happenings in both the United States and the Caribbean Basin overshadowed the incident. These events included the financial crisis that struck the United States a month earlier, the failure of the Enforcement Acts to curb racial violence in the American South, as well as the actions of the Spanish Navy off the coast of Cuba on October 30.[4] The last of these occurrences led to the execution of fifty-three individuals who were on board the *Virginius*, which was flying the American flag. The incident became known as the *Virginius* Affair and to many observers appeared to bring Spain and the United States to the brink of war.[5]

At first glance, the ceremony that occurred on October 18 and the eventual resolution of the *Virginius* Affair may seem to be isolated incidents. However, when placed in the context of the Reconstruction Era and the long history of U.S.–Spanish relations, these events provide scholars with insights into the internationalism of post–Civil War America, as well as the two countries' interconnected pasts.[6] Analyzing the interplay between domestic debates and interactions among U.S. officials and foreign representatives can also illuminate how influential white Americans conceptualized race, honor, and stability.[7] Finally, these incidents show how conditions in Europe and the Caribbean Basin affected Americans' perceptions of their national and imperial ethos in the years following the Civil War.[8]

This work asserts that President Ulysses S. Grant's Secretary of State, Hamilton Fish, favored domestic stability and imperial continuities over the formal expansion of the U.S. Empire into the Caribbean Basin. The question that remains to be answered is: Why? Previous historians have accurately argued that Fish preferred that the United States follow a British-style system of hegemonic control in the region. He believed this model would benefit the country by reducing the threat of a commercial conflict with the European empires. Fish also felt that U.S. hegemonic control would avoid the formal integration of those whom he perceived to be less civilized individuals into the American Union, an issue at the nexus of race and expansionism that had exacerbated antebellum political and sectional divisions.[9] Fish's beliefs were most evident during the debates surrounding the annexation of the Dominican Republic and the acquisition of Spanish Cuba, in which he endeavored to temper Grant's desire to expand the American Empire into the region.[10]

This essay positions the United States in an interconnected transatlantic world marked, throughout the nineteenth century, by beliefs in racial differences and imperial superiority. The work also examines the long history of U.S.–Spanish relations to establish a more nuanced understanding of why Hamilton Fish favored domestic stability and imperial continuities, as well as how U.S.–Spanish relations influenced Fish's perceptions of the United States, the American Empire, the balance of power in the Caribbean, and the region's inhabitants.[11] The work contends that Fish drew on the beliefs of many of his antebellum predecessors when he perceived the leaders of the Dominican Republic and the Cuban insurgent forces through a racial lens.[12] Fish was of the opinion that individuals of African descent who lived in the Caribbean Basin lacked sufficient political aptitude and consequently did not warrant inclusion in the American Union. Also influencing these views were the racial, political, and sectional divisions that continued to challenge the construction of an interracial democracy in the United States during the Reconstruction Era. In turn, Fish privately discouraged the annexation of the Dominican Republic and was satisfied with the continuation of imperial rule on Cuba, assuming that the Spanish were able to uphold their imperial responsibilities by adequately controlling the island.[13]

Fish's perceptions of the inhabitants of the Dominican Republic and the Cuban insurgent forces were undeniably complex. His views present a fascinating juxtaposition with the official claims made by the Grant administration that it supported the Reconstruction Amendments and the rise in African American officeholders. These seemingly contrasting opinions force us to reconsider how historical actors understood the Reconstruction Era and to critically examine their motives.[14] Additionally, the prominence of the Black Legend narrative in the United States, which presented the Spanish Empire as being antithetical to the emerging American republic, adds a level of international complexity. This narrative has also drawn historians to the climactic events and hyperbolic language associated with the history of U.S.–Spanish relations, overshadowing the personal bonds and pragmatic relationships that existed between representatives from the two nations.[15]

Fish was well connected with the Spanish community in the United States and in turn adopted an imperial view of the world in which the United States was a prominent, interconnected player. Consequently, as Spanish troops struggled to subdue the colonial uprising that began on Cuba in 1868, he searched for a way to end the conflict that would maintain Spanish honor and enable the Grant administration to adhere to the "no transfer" resolution of 1811, which stated that the United States would not allow a nearby Spanish territory to "pass from the hands of Spain into those of any other foreign power."[16] Fish's respect for Spanish honor, the commonalities that he saw in his Spanish counterparts, and his appreciation for the country's imperial past maintained open lines of communication between the two nations throughout Grant's time in office.[17] This relationship enabled the administration to continue to focus on addressing domestic issues, such as the rising power of Southern white supremacists and the emerging rifts in the Republican Party over racial equality.

A series of domestic and international events in the last quarter of the nineteenth century led to the United States' formal expansion into the Caribbean in 1898. These events included the removal of the majority of the federal troops who were stationed in the former Confederate states, the establishment of Jim Crow Laws, the abolition of slavery in Cuba, the so-called "closing" of the frontier, the romanticization of the Civil War by many white Americans, and the outbreak of another rebellion on Cuba in 1895. Taken collectively, these events provided the McKinley administration with the impetus to declare war on the Spanish Empire in 1898.[18] However, rather than a drawn-out conflict, the Spanish-American War was more of an inter-imperial exchange of power, which adhered to the "no transfer" resolution and maintained a degree of imperial control over the island.

This chapter begins by exploring the history of U.S.–Spanish relations prior to the American Civil War. This section provides the reader with a foundational understanding of the relationships that existed between representatives of the two nations as the United States expanded its transcontinental empire and addressed sectional divisions during the Antebellum Era. These precedents shaped Fish's understanding of U.S.–Spanish relations and the potential stability offered by the continuation of imperial rule on Cuba. The chapter then shifts to the years following the Civil War, as debates surrounding Reconstruction and African American civil rights intersected with Grant's desire to increase U.S. interests abroad, specifically, in the Dominican Republic.[19] This section illustrates how several prominent Americans, most notably Fish and five of the seven voting members of the Senate Foreign Relations Committee, were hesitant to integrate non-native-born individuals of African descent into the American Union because of their perceived racial inferiority and the belief that integration would exacerbate Reconstruction-era domestic tensions. As the next section shows, many of these arguments reemerged in American perceptions, debates, and responses toward the events in Cuba during Grant's presidency. As a result of the Ten Years' War, U.S.–Spanish relations reached a boiling point on October 30, 1873, when the Spanish captured the *Virginius*. However, drawing on precedents, as well as both domestic and international influences, U.S. and Spanish representatives were able to reach a settlement. This maintained Spanish imperial rule on Cuba and allowed Grant's administration to address the growing tensions in both the nation and the Republican Party over attempts to create an interracial democracy in post–Civil War America.

U.S.–Spanish Relations from the American Revolution to the Civil War

Caleb Cushing replaced Daniel Sickles as the U.S. minister to Spain in 1874. During his presentation ceremony to the Spanish government, both he and President Francisco Serrano noted that the two countries had been "long friends" and that their relationship had been initiated by the support that Spain provided "at the very epoch of the independence of the United States."[20] The two men drew on this record as they worked to rectify the *Virginius* Affair, which, despite the dissolution of the First Spanish Republic in December of 1874, was resolved by February of 1875.[21]

The relationship that Serrano and Cushing referenced began nearly a century earlier when Spanish representatives began unofficially supporting the American colonists during their Revolutionary War.[22] The Spanish government's informal assistance facilitated relationships between representatives of the two nations. Most notably, George Washington became close with Juan de Miralles and Francisco Rendón, both of whom served as unofficial Spanish representatives to the United States.[23] These initial relationships continued to inform the views of influential Americans in the decades to come.[24]

As elite American citizens developed the United States' national and imperial identities, they began to construct a transatlantic narrative. This semi-fictitious, imperial tale connected the United States with Spain by celebrating Christopher Columbus's "discovery" of the Americas and credited the Spanish Empire with "giving birth" to the United States.[25] The creation of this interconnected narrative influenced American perceptions of both the United States and the Spanish Empire well into the twentieth century; however, negative perceptions associated with the Black Legend narrative have long obscured this relationship.[26] This essay does not challenge that many Americans often saw Spain as a national antithesis, but contends that influential representatives also perceived racial and imperial commonalities between both countries and were willing to use these attributes to benefit their own policies throughout the long nineteenth century.[27]

As Americans moved westward after the Revolutionary War, they encountered Spanish colonists, as well as Indigenous peoples, in Louisiana and the Floridas.[28] Most notably, in March of 1818, General Andrew Jackson took it upon himself to invade East Florida and attack Spanish troops at St. Mark's. Jackson's antagonistic actions incensed President James Monroe and his secretary of war, John C. Calhoun, because they deemed them adverse to John Quincy Adams's attempt to peacefully purchase the Floridas. Despite Jackson's conduct, the long-serving Spanish ambassador to the United States, Luis de Onís, was confident that the president would right this perceived wrong.[29] Monroe rewarded Onís's patience in July of 1818, admonishing Jackson and ordering him to return the captured fort to Spanish authorities.[30] Jackson's conduct demonstrates the differences between relations in the borderlands and those among foreign policymakers in Washington, D.C., and Madrid. In spite of the incident, Adams and Onís eventually signed the Transcontinental Treaty of 1819, further expanding the U.S. Empire.

Just beyond the Floridas was Cuba. Spain had controlled the island since the late fifteenth century and, following the Spanish American wars of independence, it and Puerto Rico were the vestiges of the Spanish Empire in the region.

Consequently, U.S. debates surrounding the extension of slavery across the continent dominated antebellum politics and sparked divisions among U.S. foreign policymakers regarding Cuba.[31] Some, like John Y. Mason and Pierre Soulé, supported the acquisition of the island because they believed it would further tie the island's economy to the United States, expand the American Empire, strengthen the position of the Southern states, and safeguard slavery outside of North America.[32] However, these hostile views were tempered by the likes of John Forsyth and Daniel Webster, who were unwilling to go to war with Spain over the acquisition of the island.[33]

Slaves rebelled in Cuba throughout the 1840s and 1850s.[34] On May 14, 1846, Secretary of State James Buchanan hinted that if Spanish authorities were unable to control the conditions on the island, it might "endanger the friendly relations which we are so anxious to preserve and cherish with Spain."[35] Few white American representatives, thinking of Haiti, desired another "Africanized" state in the Caribbean, nor did they want to engage in a full-fledged war with the Spanish Empire while they addressed sectional divisions at home. Therefore, American representatives in Madrid, Havana, and Washington, most notably the famed writer and Hispanist Washington Irving, set out to maintain productive relationships with their Spanish counterparts as well as the "no transfer" resolution.[36] As part of this resolution, the United States attempted to purchase Cuba in both 1848 and 1854; however, the sale never occurred.[37]

The decades preceding the American Civil War were turbulent years in U.S.–Spanish relations. However, while pro-expansionist Americans fought against Indigenous peoples, Mexicans, and Nicaraguans, the United States never waged a war against the Spanish Empire. It is undeniable that some representatives of the United States were willing to take aggressive actions toward Spain and its colonial possessions.[38] However, historians have overemphasized this sentiment, as well as the effects of the Black Legend narrative on several former presidents, such as James K. Polk and James Buchanan. Although Polk was a fervent expansionist and Buchanan begrudgingly took part in the so-called Ostend Manifest, their writings show that both men respected the Spanish military and worked to increase their understanding of Spanish honor and traditions, as they attempted to either preserve Spanish imperial rule over Cuba or acquire the island through a peaceful transfer of power.[39]

During the Reconstruction Era, Fish and other influential Americans, most notably the majority of the Senate Foreign Relations Committee, echoed antebellum views that favored the Spanish Empire over the autonomy of Afro-descended peoples. These outlooks emerged in their response to Grant's desire to annex the

Dominican Republic, as well as Fish's determination to avoid a conflict with Spain during the Ten Years' War and the *Virginius* Affair. Furthermore, many informed Americans before and after the Civil War still recognized the military prowess of the Spanish Empire. This led to the belief that the only feasible option left to the U.S. government was to defend Spanish sovereignty until the United States could purchase the island; a transaction that American foreign policy elites believed would preserve Spanish honor and maintain stability within the United States' sphere of influence.

The relationship between the United States and Spain was again tested in the years following the Civil War. Nevertheless, influential foreign policymakers in the United States continued to favor imperial continuities in Cuba, rather than a war with the Spanish Empire, which would have exacerbated domestic political tensions during the Reconstruction Era.

Domestic Restrictions on Foreign Expansion: Grant's Failed Attempt to Annex the Dominican Republic

On March 4, 1869, Ulysses S. Grant took office as the eighteenth president of the United States. Grant inherited a federal government that had rapidly increased the scope of its powers during the Civil War. On the domestic front, he used federal troops to uphold the Reconstruction Amendments and the Enforcement Acts.[40] These actions supported African American participation in regional and national politics in the years following the Civil War. But they also created debates with Democrats, as well as among radical and moderate Republicans, regarding the role of nonwhites in the postbellum Union.[41] These disputes influenced nearly every decision made by the Grant administration.[42] Furthermore, the president also assumed three major foreign policy issues from previous administrations. The first involved poor relations between the United States and Britain in the wake of independent British shipbuilders supplying the Confederate Navy with vessels during the Civil War; the second was the ongoing political instability the existed in Spain's former colonial possession of the Dominican Republic, which threatened American commercial interests in the region; and the third issue emerged when a rebellion began in Cuba on October 10, 1868, increasing uncertainties in America's perceived sphere of influence.

Grant's overarching foreign policy was designed to reestablish the Monroe Doctrine.[43] Similar to the the Johnson administration, Grant planned to challenge Britain's hegemony over the Caribbean Basin and to promote American commercial interests abroad.[44] To carry out this agenda, Grant appointed

Hamilton Fish as his secretary of state.[45] Fish brought a unique internationalism to the position, which the State Department lacked. He was born into an elite New York family, and throughout his political career he opposed slavery. However, Fish was still influenced by beliefs surrounding racial superiority, and as debates about the integration of African Americans into the body politic continued, he opposed the annexation of predominantly nonwhite populations in the Caribbean Basin because he believed that these actions could further complicate domestic issues.[46]

At the time of his appointment in March of 1869, Fish spoke four languages and was well connected with foreign officials. He had spent most of his life in New York, and he often found himself surrounded by both Spaniards and pro-Spanish sympathizers. Most notably, his son-in-law, Sidney Webster, served as the Spanish government's legal counsel in the United States from 1869 to 1877.[47] Collectively, these individuals perceived both the Cuban rebels and their supporters as a group of disorganized guerrillas who had no legitimate claim to the island; despite the fact that the insurgents were inspired by American attempts to create an interracial democracy during the Reconstruction Era.[48] (See also Andre Fleche's discussions of Thomas Jordan's and Hamilton Fish's views on this topic in his chapter in this volume.) Fish's skills and experiences, as well as the persons he associated with, shaped his conceptualizations of race and empire as he guided the foreign policy of the United States during Grant's time in office.[49]

While Fish focused on U.S.–British relations and the ongoing conflict in Cuba, Grant fixated on the Dominican Republic.[50] The president's main goal was to acquire the nation and to eventually integrate it into the Union.[51] More specifically, in the wake of the Spanish reoccupation of the Dominican Republic (1861–1865) and the Second French Intervention in Mexico (1861–1867), he hoped that establishing a naval base at Samaná Bay would deter future European involvement in the area; he expected that a U.S. presence on the island would bring political stability and, in turn, encourage additional American investment; and he assumed that expanding U.S.–Dominican trade would reduce Cuban, Puerto Rican, and Brazilian exports to the United States, facilitating the eventual end of slavery in the Western Hemisphere.[52]

Grant also gave credence to the argument that taking possession of the Dominican Republic would provide newly freed African Americans with the opportunity to migrate to the island. He felt that this would reduce racial tensions in the United States and establish stability in the American South.[53] During the Antebellum Era, the belief that African Americans should be sent abroad had found support from the American Colonization Society, as well as Harriet

Beecher Stowe and Abraham Lincoln.[54] However, this belief created tensions between members in the reform community after the war, just as they had before it. Ultimately, Grant's various objectives intertwined Reconstruction, empire building, and race, making them inseparable from the debate over American expansion into the Caribbean Basin.[55]

Grant based his views toward the Dominican Republic on reports provided by his private secretary, Orville E. Babcock. On several occasions, Babcock met with the president of the Dominican Republic, Buenaventura Báez, and eventually, the two men established a treaty that outlined Báez's willingness to allow annexation.[56] Privately, Fish disapproved of Grant's desire to acquire the Dominican Republic. However, he publicly supported the president's ongoing endeavor by preparing the treaty for the Senate, which was submitted on January 10, 1870.[57]

During Grant's first term in office, the Republicans controlled both the House and the Senate, but the party was split between radicals and moderates. Fish feared that the annexation of the Dominican Republic would deepen this divide, which might then strengthen the hand of the Democrats. As the chair of the Senate Foreign Relations Committee, Charles Sumner led the hearings on the proposed treaty. Sumner, a Radical Republican and avid abolitionist, believed that the Reconstruction Amendments had not gone far enough to secure equality for his "colored-fellow-citizens."[58]

In the debates that followed, both pro- and anti-expansionists addressed the issues of domestic stability, race, and empire. Sumner broke with several Radical Republicans when he opposed the annexation treaty. He pointed to the financial cost he believed the Dominican Republic would place on the federal government, his lack of trust in the Grant administration, the precedent that the annexation would set in the Caribbean, as well as his lack of confidence that the people of the Dominican Republic had the ability to "make themselves useful to their country."[59] Sumner also employed the language of environmental determinism when arguing that "to the African belongs the equatorial belt, and he should enjoy it undisturbed."[60] By connecting race, climate, and empire, Sumner seemed to be attempting to differentiate between African Americans living in the United States and those individuals of African ancestry residing in the Caribbean, all the while supporting his claim that Anglo-Saxon Americans should avoid formal annexation policies in the region.[61]

Those in the Senate who supported the treaty, such as Sumner's fellow Radical Republican and Senate Foreign Relations Committee member Oliver P. Morton, criticized Sumner for having an outdated view on race.[62] Morton had previously suppressed Southern sympathizers in his home state of Indiana during the Civil

War and later went on to support both the Enforcement Act of 1871 and the Civil Rights Act of 1875.⁶³ However, he also drew on the racial beliefs of the period and his hopes for the future of the U.S. Empire. He did this by arguing that the Dominicans were a "harmless set" of people and that the United States had successfully annexed the "New Mexican population" living in the American Southwest and, in turn, could repeat this process in the Caribbean. (For additional references to the multiracial Southwest in later imperial debates, see also DJ Polite's chapter in this volume.) Here, Morton was connecting America's westward expansion across the continent to the potential creation of the country's overseas empire in the Caribbean Basin while associating the former Spanish colonial subjects in both regions with racial docility.⁶⁴

On March 15, the Senate Foreign Relations Committee met in a closed session and voted 5 to 2 against the treaty.⁶⁵ Approximately three months later, the treaty failed to receive the two-thirds majority required to pass in the Senate.⁶⁶ The president's failure to expand the U.S. Empire into the Caribbean Basin demonstrates that during the Reconstruction Era a prevailing group of politically diverse Americans preferred attempting to restore domestic stability above overseas expansion. This motley crew included House and Senate members from both parties, such as Fernando Wood (D-NY); the aforementioned Charles Sumner and fellow Republican Carl Schurz; abolitionists William Lloyd Garrison and Wendell Phillips; and Secretary of State Hamilton Fish.⁶⁷

The Dominican Republic debate illustrates the complex place of race in shaping American politics at this time—a topic also addressed by Brian Shott in this volume. Specifically, the debate presents how influential Americans perceived similarities between the nonwhite inhabitants of the American West and those living in the Caribbean Basin. At the same time, these Americans distinguished between African Americans in the United States and individuals of African ancestry living in the Dominican Republic.⁶⁸ Furthermore, as Fish accurately predicted, the debate created a schism between members of the Republican Party. This schism was exacerbated by Grant's continued push for annexation and the authorization that he received from Congress to send a formal commission to the Dominican Republic to further investigate the possibility of acquiring it. Throughout 1870, tensions also increased between Grant and Sumner, and by March of 1871 Grant had Sumner removed as chair of the Senate Foreign Relations Committee. This standoff often captures the most attention from historians, but it is the initial rejection of the treaty that is most telling. Despite the commission's report that the Dominican people favored annexation, the fraught politics concerning race and domestic stability precluded widespread support for Grant's scheme, and, ultimately, annexation never occurred.[69]

The debate also placed a geographic limitation on the ideologies associated with Reconstruction, making it clearly a domestic policy, which would not be exported abroad. Many of the racial views toward the people of the Dominican Republic, as well as the debates surrounding the American Empire's role in the Caribbean Basin, emerged in the deliberations about the Cuban rebels during the Ten Years' War. However, these debates were further complicated by the fact that the inhabitants of the island were rebelling against a European imperial power, one that had supported American independence and was essential to the development the country's historical narrative.

Maintaining U.S.–Spanish Relations during the Ten Years' War

A colonial revolution began in October 1868 between members of the creole (meaning Cuban-born) elite and the Spanish colonial forces on the island. The creoles claimed that the conflict was a result of increased taxes on sugar exports, the favored position of Spanish-born inhabitants, and the continued existence of slavery on the island.[70] By 1869, several creole leaders and American-based pro-Cuban juntas—the most active being in New York—were petitioning for recognition of belligerent status and either annexation by the United States or outright independence.[71] These juntas supported filibustering campaigns to the island, which tested U.S.–Spanish relations.[72] Additional pressure also came from the House of Representatives, which endorsed recognizing the Cuban insurgents on April 10, 1869.[73]

On August 31, President Grant and his Cabinet met to discuss the United States' potential role in the conflict. In the months leading up to the meeting, Fish had been in constant contact with the Spanish government in Madrid. In these correspondences, Fish continued to profess the willingness of the United States to act as an arbiter in a peace agreement between Spain and the Cuban insurgents, which would maintain both Spain's honor and the country's preexisting relationship with the United States.[74] At the Cabinet meeting, Secretary of War John Rawlins fervently argued in favor of Cuban independence.[75] Rawlins believed that the removal of European powers from the Western Hemisphere was essential to the future success of the United States.[76] Ultimately, Grant sided with his secretary of state and agreed that the United States would continue to offer to mediate the conflict, assuming an immediate armistice was established.[77]

Following the meeting, both Fish and Grant quickly realized that the Spanish government in Madrid would never order their colonial administrators to agree to a ceasefire unless the insurgents laid down their weapons, nor allow the United States to intervene in what they perceived as an internal issue.[78] However, late in 1869, Grant was more concerned with his attempt to annex the Dominican Republic, and despite his desire to remove European empires from the Caribbean Basin, he echoed the views of his secretary of state in his Annual Message to Congress on December 6, 1869.

In the message, Grant stated that the United States could not recognize the Cubans as belligerents because they lacked a legitimate government. This decision was rooted in both international law, which traditionally regarded "belligerents" as sovereign states, and skepticism over whether the Cuban insurgents, many with African ancestry, could establish a stable republic. Additionally, both Grant and Fish favored Spanish imperial continuities over a formal military engagement in the Caribbean Basin and, in doing so, sustained the relations that existed between Spain and the United States since the late eighteenth century.[79]

Prominent American newspapers and congressional proceedings suggested that desires to recognize the Cuban insurgents as belligerents waned in favor of addressing domestic stability and debating the annexation of the Dominican Republic in the years immediately following Grant's first Annual Message to Congress. However, in June of 1870 the House Foreign Affairs Committee, which was led by the expansionist-minded Nathaniel P. Banks, made it known that they supported recognition of the Cuban insurgents.[80] As he had a year earlier, Grant responded by stating that the Cubans lacked the structures of a legitimate government and thus could not be recognized as belligerents. Following Grant's statement, neither the House nor the Senate came out in favor of the committee's report.[81]

As the war raged on, U.S.-based filibustering campaigns continued to invade the island of Cuba, straining relations between U.S. and Spanish representatives.[82] Tensions rose on October 30, 1873, when the Spanish Navy captured the *Virginius* and its crew of American, British, and Cuban filibusters en route to support the rebellion.[83] On November 1, the *Virginius* and her imprisoned crew arrived in Santiago de Cuba. Courts martial began the following day, and on November 4 four members of the expedition were executed. Following these actions, the U.S. and British consuls in Cuba, as well as the Spanish president, demanded that the executions cease. However, it seems that the Spanish president's request never reached the island, and so the executions continued on November 7 and November 8.[84]

Reports began to arrive in the United States on November 7 that the Spanish Navy had stopped a ship that was flying the American flag and that four crew members had been sentenced to death. Some members of the American press and the general public responded by once more insisting that the United States recognize the Cuban insurgents and, if need be, declare war on Spain.[85] Similar to the debates surrounding the annexation of the Dominican Republic, diverse groups divided over further U.S. actions in the region. Demands for recognition of the Cuban insurgents came most prominently from members of Cuban juntas, African American congressmen who hoped that African Americans could participate in the conflict, as well as some white Southerners who believed the conflict would reunite the country and bring Reconstruction to an end.[86] However, these calls were less forceful than those of 1869. As the challenges of attempting to establish an interracial democracy in a deeply racist country continued to mount and the ramification of the failed annexation of the Dominican Republic reverberated throughout the nation, a growing number of writers, journalists, and congressmen were now against a conflict with Spain and the integration of Cuba into the American Union.[87] Despite these views on both sides of the issue, Fish remained unfazed by public opinion and sent a telegram to the U.S. minister in Madrid, Daniel Sickles, in which he merely requested more information from the Spanish government.[88]

After receiving this message from Fish, Sickles met with Spanish Minister of State José de Carvajal. Carvajal apologized for the executions and informed the U.S. minister that he believed that President Castelar had attempted to circumvent the death sentences. Sickles used the executions as an opportunity to insist that Spanish authorities regain control of the situation on Cuba and, ultimately, end the conflict. Hearing of this news, Fish feared that Sickles's bellicose actions might result in an armed conflict with Spain and so he asserted a more active role in the discussions.[89]

Fish began by meeting with Spanish Minister to the United States Admiral José Polo de Barnabé. Fish and other intellectual Americans demonstrated a great deal of kindness toward Polo because he represented the First Spanish Republic, which was established in February of 1873.[90] On November 12, Fish finally received news of the executions that had occurred days earlier. Fish met with Polo on the following day and fervently denounced the ongoing events in Cuba. Specifically, the secretary of state was furious with the conduct of Spanish colonial officials, which drew into question Madrid's capacity to control the situation. Fish's predecessors were able to justify and maintain a productive relationship between the United States and Spain partially because they believed that Spanish imperial stability would preclude the rise of another "Africanized" state in the Caribbean. The *Virginius* Affair brought this line of thinking into question, and Polo knew that if the Spanish government in Madrid did not address the issue it would endanger cordial relations with the United States.[91]

Polo and Fish eventually reached a temporary agreement on November 29. Spain was forced to return the *Virginius* and the ship's remaining crew to the United States, while both governments investigated the incident.[92] Although Fish received acclaim from a variety of American politicians and journalists for avoiding a conflict, the proceedings were far from over.[93] However, the task of resolving the affair was left in the hands of Hamilton Fish, Caleb Cushing, José Polo de Barnabé, and Francisco Serrano, all of whom preferred imperial continuities in the Caribbean Basin and understood the mutually beneficial relationship that existed between their countries.

By the conclusion of 1873, Sickles had resigned as the U.S. minister to Spain, and the U.S. attorney general determined that the *Virginius* had no right to be flying the American flag.[94] Seeing Sickles's resignation as a chance to appoint an individual who was more familiar with the country, Fish convinced Grant to name Caleb Cushing. Cushing had traveled throughout the country in the 1820s and possessed a great deal of affection for the Spanish people.[95] As minister, he integrated himself into Spanish society and was well liked by many members of the Spanish government.[96] A month after his arrival, Cushing wrote that "I entertain confident belief that, with steady but patient persistence of acclamation, we shall in good time reach a satisfactory solution of most, if not all, of the unsettled questions growing out of the capture of the *Virginius*."[97] The resolution came in February of 1875, and, in the end, the Spanish government agreed to pay an indemnity of $80,000, with reparations going to the families of the executed Americans. Despite the initial public outcry two years earlier, Fish was able to successfully navigate the *Virginius* Affair and uphold imperial continuities in the Caribbean Basin rather than start a war with a European power that he believed would exacerbate political and racial tensions on the home front.[98]

Conclusion

In the midst of the discussions surrounding Spain's reparation payments, the organizers of the 1876 Centennial International Exhibition invited the Spanish government to participate in the event.[99] The celebration aimed to promote domestic unity in the midst of continued white supremacist violence, political quarreling, labor unrest, and economic instabilities that continued to grip the United States throughout the 1870s.[100] The Spanish government accepted the invitation and approximately two years later played an active role in the event.[101] Judges at the exhibition were particularly impressed with the display of the Spanish War Office, which included a Toledo sword that was similar to the one that Sickles received in 1873.[102]

Spain's participation in the Centennial International Exhibition of 1876 illustrates the cordial relationship that continued in the years following the *Virginius* Affair. In 1891, Spain and the United States signed a reciprocal commercial agreement, which increased trade between Cuba and the United States.[103] Spain also continued to play an active role in future exhibitions that were held in the United States, most notably, the World's Columbian Exposition of 1893, which once again celebrated the belief that Christopher Columbus and the Spanish Empire had given birth to the United States.[104]

In February of 1895, another colonial rebellion began on the island of Cuba. Amid an economic depression, as well as ongoing class and racial tensions in the United States, President Grover Cleveland and Secretary of State Richard Onley followed the precedents set by previous administrations and responded to the rebellion by supporting Spain's attempts to suppress it.[105] By April of 1898, the conflict had dragged on for over three years and after several attempts by President William McKinley and the U.S. minister to Spain, Stewart Woodford, to avoid American involvement in the conflict, the United States declared war on the Spanish Empire.[106] U.S. action on the island of Cuba was short-lived, and following the capitulation of Santiago, Spanish and American troops reestablished their decades'-old inter-imperial relationship. While this was occurring, General Calixto García and his Cuban insurgents watched from outside the city as the United States replaced Spain as the de facto imperial ruler on the island.[107]

Both domestic and foreign events influenced why the war between the United States and Spain occurred in 1898, and not as a result of the *Virginius* Affair. By 1898, domestically, the active role of federal troops in the former Confederate states had been significantly reduced and Jim Crow laws had severely limited African American involvement in the body politic.[108] From a foreign perspective, the U.S. Navy had progressively increased the size and quality of its fleet during the last quarter of the nineteenth century. Furthermore, this time debates over annexation and racial integration would not slow the rush to war, with the Teller Amendment eventually stating that the United States would not annex the island; however, it left other Spanish colonies for the taking and did not specify how long the U.S. military could occupy Cuba.[109] Ultimately, domestic and foreign conditions differed greatly in 1898, compared with those of 1873, and enabled the

McKinley administration to finally create the United States' overseas empire at the end of the century.

Hamilton Fish's refusal to go to war with Spain over the *Virginius* Affair should not be perceived as a unique event in U.S.–Spanish relations. On the contrary, Fish followed the precedents established by earlier American representatives and shared many commonalities with the actions of McKinley's secretary of state, William R. Day, who supported the continuation of Spanish imperial control over the island of Cuba.[110] During both the Dominican Republic debate and the *Virginius* Affair, Fish found himself limited by the threat of racial, political, and sectional instability in the United States, which influenced his beliefs that the American Union was not prepared to begin an empire in the Caribbean Basin. In turn, he encouraged President Grant to maintain the status quo abroad in favor of domestic stability at home.

Notes

1. I offer my thanks to Alexander J. Cramer, who served as my Outstanding Scholars Program research assistant at the University of Windsor in 2018. "Spain: Cabinet Reclamation to France—Compliment to the American Minister," *New York Herald*, October 19, 1873, 9; Richard H. Bradford, *The Virginius Affair* (Boulder: Colorado Associated University Press, 1980), 75; James W. Cortada, "Spain and the American Civil War: Relations at Mid-Century, 1855–1868," *Transactions of the American Philosophical Society* 70, no. 4 (1980), 52–63.

2. "Will He Keep It?" *Philadelphia Inquirer*, October 21, 1873, 4.

3. Frank Ninkovich, *Global Dawn: The Cultural Foundation of American Internationalism, 1865–1890* (Cambridge, Mass.: Harvard University Press, 2009), 80–81; Daniel Sickles, "The Recognition of the Spanish Republic by the United States, February 15, 1873," in *Papers Relating to the Foreign Relations of the United States* (Washington, D.C.: Government Printing Office, 1873), 929; Francis A. Walker, ed., *United States Centennial Commission. International Exhibition: Reports and Awards, Group XVI. Military and Sporting Arms, Weapons, Explosives, Etc.* (Philadelphia, Pa.: J. B. Lippincott, 1877), 2–3; "Just Among Ourselves," *Bay View Magazine* 6, no. 5 (1899), 206.

4. John Hope Franklin, *Reconstruction after the Civil War* (Chicago: University of Chicago Press, 1961).

5. Jeanie Mort Walker, *Life of Capt. Joseph Fry: The Cuban Martyr* (Hartford, Conn.: J. B. Burr, 1875); "The Virginius Affair," *Los Angeles Herald*, November 23, 1873, 2.

6. Eliga H. Gould, "Entangled Histories, Entangled Worlds: The English-Speaking Atlantic as a Spanish Periphery," *American Historical Review* 112, no. 3 (2007), 764–786; "Interchange: Nationalism and Internationalism in the Era of the Civil War," *Journal of American History* 98, no. 2 (2011), 455–489; Gregory Downs, *The Second American Revolution: The Civil War-Era Struggle over Cuba and the Rebirth of the American Republic* (Chapel Hill: University of North Carolina Press, 2019), 1–3.

7. David Prior, ed., *Reconstruction in a Globalized World* (New York: Fordham University Press, 2018); Lacy Ford, ed., *A Companion to the Civil War and Reconstruction* (Malden, Mass.: Blackwell, 2005); Mark M. Smith, "The Past as a Foreign Country: Reconstruction, Inside and Out," in *Reconstruction: New Perspectives on the Postbellum United States*, ed. Thomas J. Brown (New York: Oxford University Press, 2006), 117–140; Andrew Zimmerman, "Reconstruction: Transnational History," in *Interpreting American History: Reconstruction*, ed. John David Smith (Kent, Ohio: Kent State University Press, 2016), 171–196; Eric T. L. Love, *Race over Empire: Racism and U.S. Imperialism, 1865–1900* (Chapel Hill: University of North Carolina Press, 2004); Jay Sexton, "The Civil War and U.S. World Power," in *American Civil Wars: The United States, Latin America, Europe, and the Crisis of the 1860s*, ed. Don H. Doyle (Chapel Hill: University of North Carolina Press, 2017), 17; Edward J. Blum, *Reforging the White Republic: Race, Religion, and American Nationalism, 1865–1898* (Baton Rouge: Louisiana State University Press, 2005).

8. Louis A. Pérez Jr., *Cuba in the American Imagination: Metaphor and the Imperial Ethos* (Chapel Hill: University of North Carolina Press, 2008), 2–7.

9. Jay Sexton, "Toward a Synthesis of Foreign Relations in the Civil War Era, 1848–77," *American Nineteenth Century History* 5, no. 3 (2004), 50–58; James B. Chapin, "Hamilton Fish and American Expansion," in *Makers of American Diplomacy: From Benjamin Franklin to Henry Kissinger*, ed. Frank J. Merli and Theodore A. Wilson (New York: Charles Scribner's Sons, 1974), 245; Stephen McCullough, *The Caribbean Policy of the Ulysses S. Grant Administration: Foreshadowing an Informal Empire* (Lanham, Md.: Lexington Books, 2018), ix–x; Jay Sexton, "The United States, the Cuban Rebellion, and the Multilateral Initiative of 1875," *Diplomatic History* 30, no. 3 (2006), 346; John C. Calhoun, "Conquest of Mexico: Speech of Mr. Calhoun, January 4, 1848," in *Appendix to the Congressional Globe*, 30th Congress, 1st Session, 49–53.

10. At the time, the Dominican Republic was often referred to as Santo Domingo or San Domingo; see Nicholas Guyatt, "America's Conservatory: Race, Reconstruction, and the Santo Domingo Debate," *Journal of American History* 98, no. 4 (2011), 974–1000; Allan Nevins, *Hamilton Fish: The Inner History of the Grant Administration* (New York: Frederick Ungar, 1936), 262.

11. Andrew Priest, "Thinking about Empire: The Administration of Ulysses S. Grant, Spanish Colonialism and the Ten Years' War in Cuba," *Journal of American Studies* 48, no. 2 (2014), 541–558.

12. Hamilton Fish to George Bancroft, February 9, 1870, Library of Congress, The Papers of Hamilton Fish, Box 67—Correspondence (January 6 to February 22, 1870); Matthew Karp, *This Vast Southern Empire: Slaveholders at the Helm of American Foreign Policy* (Cambridge, Mass.: Harvard University Press, 2016), 60–66, 187–188; Matthew Pratt Guterl, *American Mediterranean: Southern Slaveholders in the Age of Emancipation* (Cambridge, Mass.: Harvard University Press, 2008), 1–2, 85; Joseph Fry, *Dixie Looks Abroad: The South and U.S. Foreign Relations, 1789–1973* (Baton Rouge: Louisiana State University, 2002).

13. Nevins, *Hamilton Fish*, 180–181; "The San Domingo Treaty in the United States Senate," *New York Times*, March 25, 1870, 1; Jackson Lears, *Rebirth of a Nation: The Making of Modern America, 1877–1920* (New York: HarperCollins, 2009), 2; Matthew Frye

Jacobson, *Barbarian Virtues: The United States Encounters Foreign Peoples at Home and Abroad, 1876–1917* (New York: Hill and Wang, 2000), 7; Hamilton Fish, December 13, 1869, Library of Congress, The Papers of Hamilton Fish, Container No. 311, Reel No. 1, Diary (Volume 1, March 18, 1869 to September 13, 1870).

14. David Prior, *Between Freedom and Progress: The Lost World of Reconstruction Politics* (Baton Rouge: Louisiana State University Press, 2019), 3–5.

15. María DeGuzmán, *Spain's Long Shadow: The Black Legend, Off-Whiteness, and Anglo-American Empire* (Minneapolis: University of Minnesota Press, 2005); Richard L. Kagan, *The Spanish Craze: America's Fascination with the Hispanic World, 1776–1939* (Lincoln: University of Nebraska Press, 2019); M. Elizabeth Boone, *"The Spanish Element in Our Nationality": Spain and America at the World's Fairs and Centennial Celebrations, 1875–1915* (University Park: Pennsylvania State University Press, 2019); Paul A. Kramer, "Historias Transimperiales: Raíces Españolas del Estado Colonial Estadounidense en Filipinas," in *Filipinas, Un País Entre Dos Imperios*, ed. María Dolores Elizalde and Josep M. Delgado (Barcelona, Spain: Edicions Bellaterra, 2011), 125–144.

16. Congress of the United States, "The No Transfer Doctrine," in *Latin America and the United States: A Documentary History—Second Edition*, ed. Robert H. Holden and Eric Zolov (New York: Oxford University Press, 2011), 6–8; "No. 319—Mr. Fish to General Sickles—June 24, 1870," in *Papers Relating to the Foreign Relations of the United States—Correspondence Between the Department of State and the Legation of the United States at Madrid* (Washington, D.C.: Government Printing Office, 1871), 697–698.

17. "No. 423—Mr. Fish to Mr. Sickles—October 29, 1872," in *Papers Relating to the Foreign Relations of the United States Transmitted to Congress with the Annual Message of the President* (Washington, D.C.: Government Printing Office, 1873), 1315–1322.

18. Edward L. Ayers, *The Promise of the New South: Life after Reconstruction* (New York: Oxford University Press, 1993); David W. Blight, *Race and Reunion: The Civil War in American Memory* (Cambridge, Mass.: Harvard University Press, 2001); Gary Gerstle, *American Crucible: Race and Nation in the Twentieth Century* (Princeton, N.J.: Princeton University Press, 2001); C. Vann Woodward, *The Strange Career of Jim Crow* (New York: Oxford University Press, 1955); Lears, *Rebirth of a Nation*; Grace Elizabeth Hale, *Making Whiteness: The Culture of Segregation in the South, 1890–1940* (New York: Pantheon Books, 1998); Walter L. Hixson, *American Settler Colonialism: A History* (New York: Palgrave Macmillan, 2013); Louis A. Pérez Jr., *Cuba between Empires, 1878–1902* (Pittsburgh, Pa.: University of Pittsburgh Press, 1983).

19. William Javier Nelson, *Almost a Territory: America's Attempt to Annex the Dominican Republic* (Newark: University of Delaware Press, 1990); Charles Callan Tansill, *The United States and Santo Domingo, 1798–1873: A Chapter in Caribbean Diplomacy* (Baltimore: Johns Hopkins University Press, 1938).

20. Caleb Cushing to Hamilton Fish (with the Spanish President's response)—June 1, 1874, Library of Congress, Caleb Cushing Papers, Box 114—General Correspondence (1874, April–June 24), Folder: 5 (June 1–14–1874).

21. John M. Belohlavek, *Broken Glass: Caleb Cushing & the Shattering of the Union* (Kent, Ohio: Kent State University Press, 2005), 356–365.

22. Buchanan Parker Thomson, *Spain: Forgotten Ally of the American Revolution* (North Quincy, Mass.: Christopher Publishing House, 1976), 17, 51–52.

23. Gregg French, "Spain and the Birth of the American Republic: Establishing Lasting Bonds of Kinship in the Revolutionary Era," in *Spain and the American Revolution: New Approaches and Perspectives*, ed. Gabriel Paquette and Gonzalo M. Quintero Saravia (New York: Routledge, 2020), 184–196.

24. Robert Treat Paine, "Spain: An Account of the Public Festival Given by the Citizens of Boston—January 24, 1809" (Boston, Mass.: Printed by Russell and Cutler, 1809).

25. Washington Irving, *A History of the Life and Voyages of Christopher Columbus* (London, Eng.: John Murray, Albemarle-Street, 1828); William Hickling Prescott, *History of the Reign of Ferdinand and Isabella* (New York: A. L. Burt, 1838).

26. Gould, "Entangled Histories, Entangled Worlds," 766–771.

27. Claudia L. Bushman, *America Discovers Columbus: How an Italian Explorer Became an American Hero* (Hanover, N.H.: University Press of New England, 1992); Elise Bartosik-Vélez, *The Legacy of Christopher Columbus in the Americas: New Nations and a Transatlantic Discourse of Empire* (Nashville, Tenn.: Vanderbilt University Press, 2014).

28. Gene Allen Smith and Sylvia L. Hilton, eds., *Nexus of Empire: Negotiating Loyalty and Identity in the Revolutionary Borderlands, 1760s–1820s* (Gainesville: University Press of Florida, 2010); French, "Spain and the Birth of the American Republic," 192.

29. For more information: William Earl Weeks, *John Quincy Adams and American Global Empire* (Lexington: University Press of Kentucky, 1992), 165; John Quincy Adams, "Memoirs of John Quincy Adams, February 20, 1819," in *John Quincy Adams and American Continental Empire: Letters, Papers and Speeches*, ed. Walter LaFeber (Chicago: Quadrangle Books, 1965), 85–86.

30. James Monroe, "James Monroe to Andrew Jackson, July 19, 1818," in *The Papers of John C. Calhoun—Volume II, 1817–1818*, ed. W. Edwin Hemphill (Columbia: University of South Carolina Press, 1963), 402; Weeks, *John Quincy Adams and American Global Empire*, 113; Robert E. May, *Manifest Destiny's Underworld: Filibustering in Antebellum America* (Chapel Hill: University of North Carolina Press, 2002).

31. James E. Lewis Jr., *The American Union and the Problem of Neighborhood: The United States and the Collapse of the Spanish Empire, 1783–1829* (Chapel Hill: University of North Carolina Press, 1998); Louis A. Pérez Jr., *The War of 1898: The United States and Cuba in History and Historiography* (Chapel Hill: University of North Carolina Press, 1998), 2–5.

32. Robert E. May, *The Southern Dream of a Caribbean Empire* (Baton Rouge: Louisiana State University Press, 1973); Louis A. Pérez Jr., *Cuba and the United States: Ties of Singular Intimacy* (Athens: University of Georgia Press, 2003), 39; Guterl, *American Mediterranean*, 85; Karp, *This Vast Southern Empire*, 2–8; Walter Johnson, *River of Dark Dreams: Slavery and Empire in the Cotton Kingdom* (Cambridge, Mass.: Belknap Press of Harvard University Press, 2013).

33. John Forsyth, "John Forsyth to the Secretary of State, February 10, 1823," in House Document 121, 32nd Congress, 1st Session; James Buchanan, "James Buchanan to Mr. Campbell, May 14, 1846," in *The Works of James Buchanan: Comprising Speeches, State Papers, and Private Correspondence—Volume VI, 1844–1846*, ed. John Bassett

Moore (New York: Antiquarian Press Limited, 1960), 488; Daniel Webster, "Daniel Webster to the Spanish Minister, November 12, 1851," in Senate Documents, 32nd Congress, 1st Session.

34. James W. Cortada, *Two Nations over Time: Spain and the United States, 1776–1977* (Westport, Conn.: Greenwood Press, 1978), 62.

35. "James Buchanan to Mr. Campbell—May 14, 1846," in *The Works of James Buchanan: Comprising Speeches, State Papers, and Private Correspondence—Volume VI, 1844–1846*, ed. John Bassett Moore (New York: Antiquarian Press Limited, 1960), 488.

36. Karp, *This Vast Southern Empire*, 65, 187.

37. "Saturday, 17th June, 1848," in *The Diary of James K. Polk During His Presidency, 1845–1849—Volume III*, ed. Milo Milton Quaife (New York: Kraus Reprint Company, 1970), 492–493; "James Buchanan to Mr. Saunders—June 17, 1848," in *The Works of James Buchanan: Comprising His Speeches, State Papers, and Private Correspondence—Volume VIII, 1848–1853*, ed. John Bassett Moore (New York: Antiquarian Press Limited, 1960), 90–102; "The Ostend Report—October 18, 1854," in *The Works of James Buchanan: Comprising His Speeches, State Papers, and Private Correspondence—Volume IX, 1853–1855*, ed. John Bassett Moore (New York: Antiquarian Press Limited, 1960), 260–266; "London, Wednesday, Oct. 18," *Daily News*, October 18, 1854, issue 2625; "The Minstrel Returned from the War," *Boston Daily Atlas*, April 25, 1856, 2.

38. May, *Manifest Destiny's Underworld*.

39. Robert W. Merry, *A Country of Vast Designs: James K. Polk, the Mexican War, and the Conquest of the American Continent* (New York: Simon & Schuster, 2009); James K. Polk, "Friday, 9th June, 1848," in *The Diary of James K. Polk During His Presidency, 1845–1849—Volume III*, ed. Milo Milton Quaife (New York: Kraus Reprint Company, 1970), 485–487; James Buchanan, "Fourth Annual Message, December 3, 1860," in *The Works of James Buchanan: Comprising His Speeches, State Papers, and Private Correspondence—Volume XI, 1860–1868*, ed. John Bassett Moore (New York: Antiquarian Press Limited, 1960), 29. In a letter to Secretary of State William R. Macy regarding his involvement in the Ostend Manifesto, Buchanan stated that "never did I obey an instruction so reluctantly." For more information: James Buchanan, "James Buchanan to Mr. Marcy, December 22, 1852," in *The Works of James Buchanan: Comprising His Speeches, State Papers, and Private Correspondence—Volume IX, 1853–1855*, ed. John Bassett Moore (New York: Antiquarian Press Limited, 1960), 289.

40. Eric Foner, *Forever Free: The Story of Emancipation and Reconstruction* (New York: Random House, 2005); Michael Perman, *The Road to Redemption: Southern Politics, 1869–1879* (Chapel Hill: University of North Carolina Press, 1984); Kenneth M. Stampp, *The Era of Reconstruction, 1865–1877* (New York: Vintage Books, 1965); W. E. B. Du Bois, *Black Reconstruction in America: An Essay Toward a History of the Part Which Black Folk Played in the Attempt to Reconstruct Democracy in America, 1860–1880* (New York: Russell and Russell, 1935); Rembert W. Patrick, *The Reconstruction of the Nation* (New York: Oxford University Press, 1967).

41. Eric Foner, *Reconstruction: America's Unfinished Revolution, 1863–1877* (New York: Harper & Row, 1988), 35–50, 281–291, 470–472.

42. Thomas R. Pegram, "Reconstruction during the Grant Years: The Conundrum of Policy," in *A Companion to the Reconstruction Presidents, 1865–1881*, ed. Edward O. Frantz (West Sussex, UK: Wiley Blackwell, 2014), 275–294; Stephen McCullough, "Avoiding War: The Foreign Policy of Ulysses S. Grant and Hamilton Fish," in *A Companion to the Reconstruction Presidents, 1865–1881*, ed. Edward O. Frantz (West Sussex, UK: Wiley Blackwell, 2014), 311–327.

43. Jay Sexton, *The Monroe Doctrine: Empire and Nation in Nineteenth-Century America* (New York: Hill and Wang, 2011); Rubin Francis Weston, *Racism in U.S. Imperialism: The Influence of Racial Assumptions on American Foreign Policy, 1893–1946* (Columbia: University of South Carolina Press, 1972), 208–212; Pedro L. San Miguel, *The Imagined Island: History, Identity, & Utopia in Hispaniola* (Chapel Hill: University of North Carolina Press, 2005), 89.

44. Richard Zuczek, "Foreign Affairs and Andrew Johnson," in *A Companion to the Reconstruction Presidents, 1865–1881*, ed. Edward O. Frantz (West Sussex, UK: Wiley Blackwell, 2014), 85–120; Charles S. Campbell, *The Transformation of American Foreign Relations, 1865–1900* (New York: Harper & Row, 1976), 2–3; McCullough, *The Caribbean Policy of the Ulysses S. Grant Administration*, ix–x.

45. "U.S. Grant to Hamilton Fish—March 11th, 1869," in *The Papers of Ulysses S. Grant—Volume 19: July 1, 1868—October 31, 1869*, ed. John Y. Simon (Carbondale: Southern Illinois University Press, 1995), 151–152.

46. Walter LaFeber, *The New Empire: An Interpretation of American Expansion, 1860–1898* (Ithaca, N.Y.: Cornell University Press, 1963), 39; McCullough, *The Caribbean Policy of the Ulysses S. Grant Administration*, xvi–xviii.

47. Fish's network also included José Polo de Barnabé, Caleb Cushing, António Mantilla, and Benjamin Butler. Fish was criticized by pro-Cuban newspapers for his relationship with many of these individuals. For more information: "Congress and the Cuba Question," *New York Herald*, October 27, 1869, 3.

48. James B Chapin, "Hamilton Fish and the Lessons of the Ten Year's War," in *Perspectives in American Diplomacy: Essays on Europe, Latin America, China, and the Cold War*, ed. Jules David (New York: Arno Press, 1976), 144–145; Downs, *The Second American Revolution*, 7–8.

49. Jean Edward Smith, *Grant* (New York: Simon & Schuster, 2001), 491; Chapin, "Hamilton Fish and American Expansion," 223–229. These pro-Spanish sympathizers associated with both the Republican and Democrat parties. For more information: James Burke Chapin, "Hamilton Fish and American Expansion," (PhD diss., Cornell University, Ithaca, New York, 1971), 276–294.

50. Julian Go, *Patterns of Empire: The British and American Empires, 1688 to the Present* (New York: Cambridge University Press, 2011); Jay Sexton, "Steam Transport, Sovereignty, and Empire in North America, circa 1850–1885," *Journal of the Civil War Era* 7, no. 4 (2017), 620–47; Richard Huzzey, "Manifest Dominion: The British Empire and the Crises of the Americas in the 1860s," in *American Civil Wars: The United States, Latin America, Europe, and the Crisis of the 1860s*, ed. Don H. Doyle (Chapel Hill: University of North Carolina Press, 2017), 82–106.

51. G. Pope Atkins and Larman C. Wilson, *The Dominican Republic and the United States: From Imperialism to Transnationalism* (Athens: University of Georgia Press, 1998), 20–22.

52. Anne Eller, "Dominican Civil War, Slavery, and Spanish Annexation, 1844–1864," in *American Civil Wars: The United States, Latin America, Europe, and the Crisis of the 1860s*, ed. Don H. Doyle (Chapel Hill: University of North Carolina Press, 2017), 147–66; Michele Cunningham, *Mexico and the Foreign Policy of Napoleon III* (New York: Palgrave, 2001); Campbell, *The Transformation of American Foreign Relations, 1865–1900*, 51; Ulysses S. Grant, "Reasons Why Santo Domingo Should Be Annexed to the United States," in *The Papers of Ulysses S. Grant—Volume 20: November 1, 1869–October 31, 1870*, ed. John Y. Simon (Carbondale: Southern Illinois University Press, 1994), 74–76; Ron Chernow, *Grant* (New York: Penguin, 2017), 695.

53. Millery Polyné, *From Douglass to Duvalier: U.S. African Americans, Haiti, and Pan Americanism, 1870–1964* (Gainesville: University Press of Florida, 2000), 40–42; Alexander DeConde, *Ethnicity, Race, and American Foreign Policy* (Boston, Mass.: Northeastern University Press, 1992), 46; Guyatt, "America's Conservatory," 976; Millery Polyné, "Expansion Now!: Haiti, 'Santo Domingo,' and Frederick Douglass at the Intersection of U.S. and Caribbean Pan-Americanism," *Caribbean Studies* 34, no. 2 (2006), 3–45; Ulysses S. Grant, "Draft Annual Message to the Senate and House of Representatives—December 5, 1870," in *The Papers of Ulysses S. Grant—Volume 21: November 1, 1870–May 31, 1871*, ed. John Y. Simon (Carbondale: Southern Illinois University Press, 1998), 37–67.

54. Ousmane K. Power-Greene, *Against Wind and Tide: The African American Struggle against Colonization* (New York: New York University Press, 2014).

55. Merline Pitre, "Frederick Douglass and American Diplomacy in the Caribbean," *Journal of Black Studies* 13, no. 4 (1983), 459; Nelson, *Almost a Territory*; Love, *Race over Empire*, 35–37; Foner, *Reconstruction*, 494–497.

56. "Ulysses S. Grant to Buenaventura Báez—July 13, 1869," in *The Papers of Ulysses S. Grant—Volume 19: July 1, 1868–October 31, 1869*, ed. John Y. Simon (Carbondale: Southern Illinois University Press, 1995), 209.

57. William S. McFeely, *Grant: A Biography* (New York: W. W. Norton, 1981), 338–339; Love, *Race over Empire*, 39–41; Ronald C. White, *American Ulysses: A Life of Ulysses S. Grant* (New York: Random House, 2016), 508–509.

58. "Charles Sumner to Charles N. Hunter—December 29th, 1871," in *The Selected Letters of Charles Sumner—Volume Two*, ed. Beverly Wilson Palmer (Boston, Mass.: Northeastern University Press, 1990), 578.

59. "The St. Domingo Treaty under Consideration," *New York Herald*, March 25, 1870, 10; "Charles Sumner to Hamilton Fish—March 20, 1870," in *The Selected Letters of Charles Sumner—Volume Two*, ed. Beverly Wilson Palmer (Boston, Mass.: Northeastern University Press, 1990), 504; "Charles Sumner to Henry W. Longfellow," in *The Selected Letters of Charles Sumner—Volume Two*, ed. Beverly Wilson Palmer (Boston, Mass.: Northeastern University Press, 1990), 504–505; "Charles Sumner to William Lloyd Garrison—April 26, 1871," in *The Selected Letters of Charles Sumner—Volume Two*, ed. Beverly Wilson Palmer (Boston, Mass.: Northeastern University Press, 1990), 551–552.

60. "The San Domingo Treaty in the United States Senate," 1; Guyatt, "America's Conservatory," 979–982.
61. David Donald, *Charles Sumner and the Rights of Man* (New York: Alfred A. Knopf, 1970), 442–443.
62. "San Domingo the Absorbing Theme in the Senate," *New York Times*, December 22, 1870, 1.
63. For more information: William Dudley Foulke, *Life of Oliver P. Morton, Including His Important Speeches—Volume I and II* (Indianapolis: Bowen-Merrill, 1899).
64. "Senator Morton's Speech on the St. Domingo Treaty—Presidential Coup d'Etat for the Annexation of St. Domingo," *New York Herald*, March 26, 1870, 8; *The Congressional Globe*, 41st Congress, 3rd Session, December 21, 1870, 238.
65. The Senate Foreign relations committee was made up of Charles Sumner (Republican), Carl Schurz (Republican), Simon Cameron (Republican), James Harlan (Republican), Oliver P. Morton (Republican), James W. Patterson (Republican), and Eugene Casserly (Democrat). For more information: *Committee on Foreign Relations: United States Senate—Millennium Edition, 1816–2000* (Washington, D.C.: Government Printing House, 2000), 86.
66. Atkins and Wilson, *The Dominican Republic and the United States*, 26–27; White, *American Ulysses: A Life of Ulysses S. Grant*, 512.
67. McCullough, *The Caribbean Policy of the Ulysses S. Grant Administration*, 66; *Appendix to the Congressional Globe*, 41st Congress, 3rd Session, January 11, 1871, 25–34; Guyatt, "America's Conservatory," 980.
68. J. Wesley Horne, "Santo Domingo," *Christian Advocate* 46, no. 19 (1871): 145; "The San Domingo Issue," *Every Saturday: A Journal of Choice Reading* 2, no. 66 (1871): 290.
69. *Report of the Commission of Inquiry to Santo Domingo* (Washington, D.C.: Government Printing Office, 1871); Merline Pitre, "Frederick Douglass and the Annexation of Santo Domingo," *Journal of Negro History* 62, no. 4 (1977): 390–400; McFeely, *Grant*, 350–352.
70. Pérez Jr., *Cuba and the United States*, 50–56; McCullough, *The Caribbean Policy of the Ulysses S. Grant Administration*, xi–xii; Ada Ferrer, *Insurgent Cuba: Race, Nation, and Revolution, 1868–98* (Chapel Hill: University of North Carolina Press, 1999), 15–69; Luis Martínez-Fernández, *Torn between Empires: Economy, Society, and Patterns of Political Thoughts in the Hispanic Caribbean, 1840–1878* (Athens: University of Georgia Press, 1994); Jose M. Hernández, *Cuba and the United States: Intervention and Militarism, 1868–1933* (Austin: University of Texas Press, 2010).
71. Pérez Jr., *Cuba and the United States*, 50–52.
72. Henry A. Kmen, "Remember the Virginius: New Orleans and Cuba in 1873," *Louisiana History: The Journal of the Louisiana Historical Association* 11, no. 4 (1970): 313–331; Campbell, *The Transformation of American Foreign Relations, 1865–1900*, 53.
73. "Congress, the Administration and the Cuban Question—Action, Action," *New York Herald*, April 11, 1869, 8; Bradford, *The Virginius Affair*, 12.
74. Jules R. Benjamin, *The United States and the Origins of the Cuban Revolution: An Empire of Liberty in an Age of National Liberation* (Princeton, N.J.: Princeton University Press, 1990), 17–18; "No. 1—Mr. Fish to General Sickles—June 29, 1869,"

in *Correspondence between the Department of State and the United States Minister at Madrid, and the Consular Representatives of the United States in the Island of Cuba, and Other Papers Relating to Cuban Affairs* (Washington, D.C.: Government Printing House, 1870), 13–16; "No. 8—General Sickles to Mr. Fish—August 12, 1869," in *Correspondence between the Department of State and the United States Minister at Madrid, and the Consular Representatives of the United States in the Island of Cuba, and Other Papers Relating to Cuban Affairs* (Washington, D.C.: Government Printing House, 1870), 19–20.

75. White, *American Ulysses*, 506–507.

76. Charles W. Calhoun, *The Presidency of Ulysses S. Grant* (Lawrence: University Press of Kansas, 2017), 181; Don H. Doyle, "Reconstruction and Anti-Imperialism: The United States and Mexico," in *United States and Reconstruction across the Americas*, ed. William H. Link (Gainesville: University Press of Florida, 2019), 47–80.

77. Ulysses S. Grant, "Memorandum—August 31, 1869," in *The Papers of Ulysses S. Grant—Volume 19: July 1, 1868—October 31, 1869*, ed. John Y. Simon (Carbondale: Southern Illinois University Press, 1995), 238.

78. "No. 25—General Sickles to Mr. Fish—September 14, 1869," in *Correspondence between the Department of State and the United States Minister at Madrid, and the Consular Representatives of the United States in the Island of Cuba, and Other Papers Relating to Cuban Affairs* (Washington, D.C.: Government Printing House, 1870), 39; Nevins, *Hamilton Fish*, 241.

79. Ulysses S. Grant, "Annual Message—December 6, 1869," in *The Papers of Ulysses S. Grant—Volume 20: November 1, 1869—October 31, 1870* (Carbondale: Southern Illinois University Press, 1995), 25.

80. The House Foreign Affairs Committee was made up of Nathaniel Prentice Banks (Republican), Norman Buel Judd (Republican), Morton Smith Wilkinson (Republican), Porter Sheldon (Republican), Charles Wesley Willard (Republican), Jacob A. Ambler (Republican), Austin Blair (Republican), Fernando Wood (Democrat), and Thomas Swann (Democrat). For more information on Nathaniel Prentice Banks: Fred Harvey Harrington, *Fighting Politician: Major General N. P. Banks* (Westport, Conn.: Greenwood Press, 1948).

81. Campbell, *Transformation of American Foreign Relations*, 56; Nevins, *Hamilton Fish*, 353–363; James D. Richardson, ed., *A Compilation of the Messages and Papers of the President, 1789–1897—Volume VII* (Washington, D.C.: Government Printing House, 1899), 67.

82. Gerald Poyo, *With All, and for the Good of All: The Emergence of Popular Nationalism in the Cuban Communities of the United States, 1848–1898* (Durham, N.C.: Duke University Press, 1989); "The Resort to Filibustering," *Hartford Daily Courant*, June 10, 1872, 3.

83. Bradford, *The Virginius Affair*, 33–43; French Ensor Chadwick, *The Relations of the United States and Spain: Diplomacy* (New York: Russell & Russell, 1968), 316–317.

84. Walker, *Life of Capt. Joseph Fry*; McCullough, *The Caribbean Policy of the Ulysses S. Grant Administration*, 148; Nevins, *Hamilton Fish*, 667; "No. 586—General Sickles to Mr. Fish—November 7, 1873," in *Papers Relating to the Foreign Relations of the United States* (Washington, D.C.: Government Printing Office, 1874), 923.

85. Campbell, *The Transformation of American Foreign Relations*, 57.

86. Gerald Horne, *Race to Revolution: The United States and Cuba during Slavery and Jim Crow* (New York: Monthly Review Press, 2014), 16–17; McCullough, *The Caribbean Policy of the Ulysses S. Grant Administration*, 152–153; "The Yankee-Spanish War," *Atlanta Weekly Constitution*, November 25, 1873, 1.

87. "The Virginius Affair," *Wichita City Eagle*, November 20, 1873, 2; "Our Relations with Spain," *New York Tribune*, November 28, 1873, 1; George H. Gibson, "Attitudes in North Carolina Regarding the Independence of Cuba, 1868–1898, *North Carolina Historical Review* 43, no. 1 (January 1966), 50.

88. Priest, "Thinking about Empire: The Administration of Ulysses S. Grant, Spanish Colonialism and the Ten Years' War in Cuba," 549.

89. "No. 588—General Sickles to Mr. Fish—November 8, 1873," in *Papers Relating to the Foreign Relations of the United States* (Washington, D.C.: Government Printing Office, 1874), 924.

90. Nevins, *Hamilton Fish*, 620; Ninkovich, *Global Dawn*, 124–127; McCullough, *The Caribbean Policy of the Ulysses S. Grant Administration*, 175.

91. "No. 593—Mr. Fish to General Sickles—November 12, 1873," in *Papers Relating to the Foreign Relations of the United States* (Washington, D.C.: Government Printing Office, 1874), 927; McCullough, *The Caribbean Policy of the Ulysses S. Grant Administration*, 154–155.

92. "No. 663—Mr. Fish to General Sickles—November 29, 1873," in *Papers Relating to the Foreign Relations of the United States* (Washington, D.C.: Government Printing Office, 1874), 969; "No. 667—Mr. Fish to General Sickles—December 1, 1873," in *Papers Relating to the Foreign Relations of the United States* (Washington, D.C.: Government Printing Office, 1874), 970.

93. Ulysses S. Grant, "Note—November 7, 1873," in *The Papers of Ulysses S. Grant—Volume 24: 1873*, ed. John Y. Simon (Carbondale: Southern Illinois University Press, 2000), 252; Nevins, *Hamilton Fish*, 691.

94. "No. 684—Mr. Fish to General Sickles—December 20, 1873," in *Papers Relating to the Foreign Relations of the United States* (Washington, D.C.: Government Printing Office, 1874), 975.

95. Caleb Cushing, *Reminiscences of Spain: The Country, Its People, History, and Monuments—Two Volumes* (Boston: Carter, Hendee, 1833); Richard L. Kagan, "From Noah to Moses: The Genesis of Historical Scholarship on Spain in the United States," in *Spain in America: The Origins of Hispanism in the United States*, ed. Richard L. Kagan (Urbana: University of Illinois Press, 2002), 32–35.

96. Claude Moore Fuess, *The Life of Caleb Cushing—Volume II* (New York: Harcourt, Brace, 1923), 381–383.

97. Caleb Cushing to Hamilton Fish—July 3, 1874, Library of Congress, Caleb Cushing Papers, Box 115—General Correspondence (1874, June 25–July), Folder 1: June 25–30, 1874.

98. "No. 585—Mr. Cushing to Mr. Fish—February 16, 1875," in *Papers Relating to the Foreign Relations of the United States—Volume II* (Washington, D.C.: Government Printing Office, 1875), 1247.

99. Minister of State to Caleb Cushing—October 6, 1874, Library of Congress, Caleb Cushing Papers, Box 118—General Correspondence (1874, October), Folder 2: October 7—1874.

100. Robert W. Rydell, John E. Findling, and Kimberly D. Pelle, *Fair America: World's Fairs in the United States* (Washington, D.C.: Smithsonian Institution Press, 2000).

101. *Report of the United States Centennial Commission: Message from the President of the United States* (Washington, D.C.: House of Representatives, January 1875).

102. Walker, ed., *United States Centennial Commission. International Exhibition: Reports and Awards, Group XVI. Military and Sporting Arms, Weapons, Explosives, Etc.*, 2–3.

103. *Report on the Census of Cuba, 1899* (Washington, D.C.: Government Printing Office, 1900), 29.

104. H. G. Cutler, *The World's Fair: Its Meaning and Scope.* (San Francisco, Calif.: King, 1892), 10.

105. Pérez Jr., *Cuba and the United States*, 85. For more information: Richard Hofstadter, *The Age of Reform, From Bryan to F.D.R.* (New York: Vintage Books, 1955); Robert Dallek, *The American Style of Foreign Policy: Cultural Politics and Foreign Affairs* (New York: New American Library, 1983), 19–41.

106. Pérez Jr., *Cuba between Empires, 1878–1902*, 176; William McKinley, "The Decision to Act Against Spain," in *Latin America and the United States: A Documentary History—Second Edition*, ed. Robert H. Holden and Eric Zolov (New York: Oxford University Press, 2011), 71–73.

107. Joseph Smith, "'At the Wrong Place, at the Wrong Time and with the Wrong Enemy': US Military Strategy towards Cuba in 1898," in *The Crisis of 1898: Colonial Redistribution and Nationalist Mobilization*, ed. Angel Smith and Emma Dávila-Cox (New York: St. Martin's Press, 1999), 214.

108. Gregory Downs, *After Appomattox: Military Occupation and the Ends of War* (Cambridge, Mass.: Harvard University Press, 2015), 241–244.

109. The Congress of the United States, "The Teller Amendment," in *Latin America and the United States: A Documentary History—Second Edition*, ed. Robert H. Holden and Eric Zolov (New York: Oxford University Press, 2011), 73–74.

110. Fitzhugh Lee to William R. Day—January 25, 1898, Library of Congress, William R. Day Papers, Box 35, Folder: Spain-War, 1897–98 and undated.

4

"Their very sectionalism makes them cultivate that wider and broader patriotism"

Southern Free Trade Imperialism Survives the Confederacy

Adrian Brettle

Confederates' wartime visions of a future empire persisted among Virginians during Reconstruction. In the Civil War, Confederate policymakers and articulators had engaged in expansionist planning about the Confederacy's course should it survive hostilities with the Union. Would-be Confederate negotiators had sought to preserve elements of these plans in any negotiated reconstruction of the Union. These ambitions to establish a new nation-state, one with aspirations to join the select club of global powers, were very different from those expressed by elite white Southerners before the war.[1] Those antebellum sectional dreams involved annexing lands and islands to the South in order to create new slave states, forging alliances with "kindred" slave powers, and ensuring that the United States was both a racial-hierarchical, tropical civilization and a free labor Northern industrial powerhouse.[2] For Virginians who had been prominent in the Confederacy, the visions from the 1850s were anachronisms, the more recent Confederate plans seemed more relevant to their postwar purpose.

At the very beginning of Reconstruction, there was a curious lingering of abstract Confederate ideas until it sunk in that there would be no sectional negotiation about reunion as equals, no compensation for the loss of property in enslaved people, no reward for accepting emancipation. After a period of political and economic introspection punctuated by appeals for clemency and debt forgiveness, former Confederates rejoined the Democratic Party and resurrected their recent imperial ambitions. They eventually considered that it was the Radical Republicans who were the sectional party with their discriminatory tariffs, centralized government, railroad routes that circumvented the South, and taxation policies that sucked the remaining capital from the former Confederate states. Although deprived of their "cornerstone" of slavery, Confederates believed free trade, commercial expansion, and devolved government would also serve as the requisite policies for the reunited nation.

An argument for continuity has to contend with the fact that these individuals were no longer in control of events; many historians see 1865 as a rupture in Southern history. "There was no going back," Stephanie McCurry declares. "The slaveholders' stunning experiment in proslavery and antidemocratic nation building was over. Their vision of the future had been tried, and it had failed."[3] All that remained for former Confederates was delusion and irrelevance. Historians tend to agree that white Southerners surrendered—albeit after a struggle—any chance to implement their worldview in exchange for local control.

According to scholars, defeat set former Confederates apart from mainstream Americans in U.S. history, as they experienced a decisive check on optimism and progress. C. Vann Woodward argues that historians should look abroad to try to understand peoples and nations who have suffered catastrophic defeat.[4] David Brion Davis and other scholars take a comparative approach and suggest that the Southern experience from 1865 resembled "France in 1870 and Germany in 1918," and that "the defeated South temporarily became a 'dreamland' of denial."[5] White Southerners could not mistake the pervasive evidence of defeat, from emancipation to ruined infrastructure to chronic indebtedness and cash shortages. As novelist Margaret Mitchell once wrote of white Southerners, "Something had gone out of them, out of their world."[6]

Yet these individuals remained ambitious as well as downcast at the time. Rather than empathizing with the defeated French, they looked to the victorious German Empire of 1870 as an example to follow, not for its militarism but rather for its record of economic, cultural, and educational success.[7] There was a more complex adjustment. Another female novelist writing much closer in time to these events than Mitchell, Augusta Jane Evans, in *St. Elmo* (1866), told of the blank despair of the former planter St. Elmo Murray, to whom "the world is an abomination, and those who toil about it are dogs." However, the heroine, Edna Earl, persuaded him to devote himself to the improvement of the locality, "accomplishing good among the poor" and exercising a "beneficial influence especially over the young men of the community."[8] These fictional characters resemble postwar North Carolinians, as described by historian Greg Downs, who worked for a "world they could see, an imprecise but common range that urbanites and rural people both called a neighborhood."[9] Looking across the section as a whole, scholars identify Southern whites as defeated but ambitious. Dan

Carter sees a studied avoidance of the difficulties of adjusting to a biracial society as the rationale behind white Southerners' pursuit of bold commercial and infrastructure goals. It also enabled them to retain a sectional identity while becoming Americans once more.[10] As Mark Summers observes about the process of Reconstruction, it "allowed potential disunionists to channel their Confederate nationalism into a less dangerous form."[11]

White Southerners wished to influence postwar U.S. foreign policy and expansionism. Joseph Fry, Tenant McWilliams, and other scholars, argue that the long-term sectional competition at home informed the United States' global imprint.[12] On the one hand, for much of the nineteenth century, some leading Southerners were ambivalent about empire, as the inclusion of more nonwhites as U.S. citizens threatened to upset racial balance. Meanwhile, the cost of imperialism would empower central government and justify hated tariff hikes. On the other hand, Southern whites did want access to global markets, whether via an isthmian canal or transcontinental railroads, and territory on and across the Pacific.[13] Even as abolition removed the impetus for new slave states, the translation of planters from (in the words of Gavin Wright) labor lords to landlords replaced their self-regarding sense of responsibility for enslaved people with an increased focus on customer acquisition.[14] Furthermore, acts of national loyalty, whether supporting a forward policy against Spain in 1898 and volunteering to serve, might enable white Southerners to remove the taint of treason.[15] Most important to Southerners, however, was that China—that crucial market—appeared to be on the verge of partition between European powers by the end of the century. Possession of the Philippines by the United States—or at least of a naval base there—would keep the door open.[16]

The state of Virginia's experience presented a particular challenge to expansionist ex-Confederates. During the Civil War, Virginia had resumed the leadership role it had once possessed during the Early Republic, and therefore had been hit especially hard by defeat. Virginia's citizens had to reconcile to the permanent loss of the counties that became West Virginia. Long the main theater of the war, there was devastation especially in the Shenandoah Valley and across northern and central Virginia.[17] The capital was torched, and human as well as the material losses and emancipation upended the structure of society. The state swiftly became the birthplace of the backward-looking Lost Cause memory of the war.[18] In that context, it was surprising to witness leading ex-Confederates exhibit eerily identical policies to their confident wartime plans. Such repetition was in part sterile, with free trade expansionism, shorn of the Confederates' other ideological, nation-building, progressive impulses, remaining as just a knee-jerk protest against the protectionist Republican Party.[19] Possibly it was a way for ex-Rebels of the Old Dominion to prove their fealty to the Democratic Party after splitting the party. Nevertheless, the persistence of these imperial relics from the Confederacy, sustained by individuals from its self-conscious mother state, says something of the power of empire during Reconstruction.

Historians argue for the importance of former Whigs—unionist or at least reluctant secessionists—arising as the natural leaders of Virginia amid the ruins of 1865.[20] Those Virginians who were Democrats and had been enthusiastic, leading Confederates are comparatively neglected, but their experience sheds light on the process of Reconstruction. They had driven the ambitious Confederate wartime agenda for a future post–Civil War world. Although confronted in defeat with an apathetic and discontented population that demanded leadership, many former Confederates at first considered themselves disqualified on the grounds of exile, imprisonment, or alienation. They then swiftly sought indirect leadership, through these ex-Whig intermediaries, who in turn engaged with the federal authorities. Over time, this self-restraint ebbed. The shifting context, especially the end of Military Reconstruction in Virginia in 1869 and the amnesty that followed, the onset of economic depression from 1873, and the Democratic Party's retaking of the U.S. House in 1874, contributed to this self-assertion.

As early as 1865, former Confederates began promoting a vision that drew on an overlooked strain of Confederate thought, which had understood an independent Confederacy as beneficial for the United States and improving the world. These former Confederates not only resumed—in common with their ex-Whig colleagues—their championship of national infrastructure projects, but they also presented a vision of territorial and commercial expansion culminating in recommending a series of commercial treaties with neighboring nations and territories. These proposals resembled those of the earlier Confederate government, and although such consistency amounted at times to an expression of impotent defiance, it also anticipated the ambitions behind the Spanish–American War of 1898.

Confederates reacted to the surrender of Robert E. Lee and the Army of Northern Virginia, along with their government's flight, with a sense that something would still turn up out of defeat. After all, emancipation had removed the main constraint on the Confederates' standing in global public opinion. George W. Randolph, former Confederate secretary for war, general, and industrial spy, believed that the end of slavery offered white Southerners the chance of redemption. "It would be entirely impossible for you to conceive the abhorrence with which [slavery] is regarded in Europe," Randolph told his niece, Mary, in June 1865. "It poisoned all sympathy for our cause and made even our friends find consolation in our downfall." With emancipation, this anti-Southern sentiment—at least in Europe—had vanished. "So having been washed clean from your sins," he concluded, "you may prepare yourself for your European tour with less trepidation than you would otherwise have felt."[21] The end of slavery would enable international rehabilitation, which in turn was essential for flows of capital investment and (white) migrants into the state.[22]

A world of opportunities seemed to be opening up for Confederates prepared to go into exile. Service in the Confederacy had given its officials familiarity with overseas empires and colonization schemes. The renowned oceanographer Matthew Fontaine Maury had spent much of the war in Britain propagandizing on behalf of the Confederacy.[23] With peace came a new direction in his career; in the summer of 1865, Emperor Maximilian of Mexico appointed him imperial commissioner of colonization. Although some ex-Confederates who fled to Mexico doubtlessly dreamed of revenge against the United States, prominent Virginians also went there to serve a new empire. Confederate general John B. Magruder accepted a commission as a major general in Maximilian's army. Maury regarded his role as defender of the imperial cause against the liberal opposition of Benito Juárez. According to the emperor, Maury's priority for the empire was to "augment its population, without which the various sources of wealth contained in its fruitful soil cannot be made productive."[24]

Emancipation created a sense of imperial excitement across the Atlantic. Arriving in Norfolk, Virginia, from Liverpool in June 1866 was a young Englishman destined to have a profound influence on imperialism on both sides of the Atlantic. Charles Dilke headed to Richmond where he found the bars and streets full of demobilized Confederate troops, defiantly toasting the "caged eagle," as they referred to the imprisoned Jefferson Davis. Lost Cause memory had not yet taken root as these veterans blamed the loss of the war not on overwhelming Union numbers, but on the weak performance of the Deep South regiments in the Army of Northern Virginia. Dilke shared Randolph's optimism about the benefits of emancipation for Southern whites; with the end of slavery came an end to their aversion for manual labor. The Englishman then expanded on the point: "The true moral of America is the vigour of the English race—the defeat of the cheaper by the dearer race, the victory of the man whose food cost four shillings a day over the man whose food cost four pence." The end of slavery and the triumph of the Union with free labor augmented Anglo-Saxonism and gave it a global mission: "America offers the English race the moral directorship of the world, by ruling mankind through Anglo Saxon institutions and the English tongue. Through America, England is speaking to the world."[25]

Dilke's subsequent trip across the United States and around the world reinforced his racial pride. In the summer of 1867, when he had returned to London after a year's travel, he immediately sat down to write what would be a transatlantic best seller, *Greater Britain* (1868). This popularity came at a moment when imperialism was scorned in both Britain and the United States, associated with czarist and Austrian tyranny and, especially, Napoleon III's tottering despotism (his Mexican offshoot having recently collapsed).[26] *Greater Britain* began a new imperial movement in England, with Dilke influencing Joseph Chamberlain, the towering figure of the British Empire by century's end. For these two, Britain's expansion abroad was tied to a humanitarian and progressive alliance with the United States—underpinned by a shared sense of race, language, and culture—and dedicated to both stamping out of what remained of slavery abroad and the pursuit of reform at home, including adopting federal institutions and democratization.[27]

As late as 1865, Confederates had been intrigued by the British Empire and expected it to remain its key trading partner even as they found its abolitionism abhorrent. Studies of the effect of emancipation on the British and French colonies in the Caribbean had been the frequent topic of articles published before and during the war in the influential periodical *De Bow's Review*. This interest continued in a transformed context, for in the summer of 1865, Caribbean precedent informed the Virginia Assembly's Black Codes.[28]

Throughout the war, Confederates had argued that the United States was more important to their future than even Britain. The Confederacy would have a close, mutually beneficial, commercial relationship with the Union, one that would have enabled the Republican Party to more effectually realize its economic, ideological and political goals—even if the federals had been persistently blind to this appeal and needed to be taught this lesson. After defeat, former Confederates still believed they had the Union's best interests at heart. Veteran soldier and University of Virginia student Joseph Bryan received this message from the speakers who came to address his 1866 graduating class.[29] On June 6, 1866, John W. Daniel told the students that "we should not relax our efforts to build up a mighty and free republic, [just] because the republic we founded has failed to subserve its high purpose." After all, he added, "Let us not be deluded to believe that great interests involving the future of centuries, are not at stake because great armies are no longer in motion."[30]

Confederates had long persuaded themselves that economic self-interest ensured they would have a lenient return to the Union. At the very least they expected similar treatment to that given to British planters in the Caribbean: compensation to be paid to former owners for freed enslaved people and gradual emancipation. However, by the time Daniel spoke at UVA, many former Confederates saw Reconstruction policies as failing Virginia. Prominent refugees, moreover, had already begun to return, obeying the command of Robert E. Lee, backed up by economic arguments in *De Bow's Review*. Virginians recognized that their duty lay in returning to rebuild at home.[31] Meanwhile, after Maximilian reluctantly fired Maury in April 1866, the former oceanographer returned to Virginia and, until his death in 1873, focused on reestablishing Norfolk as a seaport with steamship connections to Europe.[32]

Instead of compensation and a reunion of equal partners, former Confederates were shocked that the Federals apparently relished the South's economic collapse.[33] Lawyer and former clerk in the Confederate War Department Robert Garlick Hill Kean explained the depression in postwar Lynchburg. "The most perfect stagnation prevails from several causes: one, the absolute want of money . . . two, general loss of capital and impoverishment of the whole community," especially arising from the "insolvency of the banks." More generally, Kean believed the malaise arose from "the general feeling of insecurity," which had resulted from President Andrew Johnson's Amnesty Proclamation of May 29, 1865, which excluded all individuals worth more than $20,000.[34] Former Confederate elites considered themselves the indispensable leaders of any local economic revival. The postwar recovery was now jeopardized by immediate emancipation and the uncertainty created by the risk of their remaining property being expropriated, as well as the depressive effects of taxation and legal injunctions preventing them from trading, at least across state lines.[35] Finally, the Union's blockade of Confederate ports remained in operation. In the early summer of 1865, a party of "Richmond gentlemen" waited on Johnson at the White House in order to "beseech him" to rescind this $20,000 clause. The visitors pleaded that the prevailing insecurity prevented the speedy rebuilding of Richmond. They tried a class-based argument on the tailor-turned-president, telling him that it was "the artisans and poorer classes [who] suffered in an even greater degree by the total stagnation of labor than the men of wealth whom the prescription clause was intended to punish."[36]

A sense of despair intensified when Johnson, vindictively it appeared, refused the appeal. His well-known antipathy toward slaveholders was an early indication that Federals were not interested in Southern economic prosperity. Uncertainty as to the course of Presidential Reconstruction, together with relatively high taxes, and capital scarcity discouraged immediate efforts to rebuild the Virginian economy.[37] Released from federal prison, former governor John Letcher appealed to Johnson for his parole conditions to be waived, primarily on the basis that restrictions on his movement prevented him from undertaking his law partnership's business activities. However, the U.S. authorities relaxed those impediments only slowly and haphazardly. Letcher and his correspondents recognized that Virginia's future prosperity hinged on elusive outside investment and money.[38] The Confederate adventurer Duff Green, when he met President Abraham Lincoln in Richmond in April 1865, predicted that capital shortages would afflict the postwar South, causing a prolonged economic slump.[39] Newspaper editor, statistician, and wartime cotton agent James D. B. De Bow agreed, recommending that Southerners remove themselves from political debates and concentrate on commercial development. He therefore applauded another meeting in mid-August 1865 of leading businessmen, who, instead of begging for help in Washington, stayed in Richmond and pledged their loyalty to the Union. The following month, De Bow visited Virginia's capital and was on the whole pleased with what he saw with the exception of the atrocious railroads; he still blamed their lamentable condition on neglect by Northern capitalists and the federal government.

Any apparent embrace of free labor doctrines by former Confederates was tempered by their belief that the fruits of their labor would be syphoned off to meet the demands of taxation to fund Reconstruction. "We are hopeful in regard to the future and all are striving manfully," Letcher wrote to his former cellmate and fellow ex-governor Zebulon B. Vance of North Carolina, on May 4, 1866, with the harvest crucial to success. "If we can get along safely until next spring," he added in reference to 1867, "we shall have passed the worst." Letcher's letters to his friend reveal a pastoral barter economy around Lexington (where Union troops had burned his home in 1864), even as he endeavored to practice law again. "Our fees are paid in family supplies such as Flour, Bacon, Beef, potatoes, corn, &c.," yet this agricultural plenty was not sufficient, for he added "with a bare sufficiency in money to pay Federal and State taxes."[40]

This economic contraction was inseparable from a sense of exclusion arising from the restrictions many former Confederates experienced on their political rights. Many former Virginian Confederates chose a life of isolation on their farms and wished to have nothing to do with the federal authorities and public life. Some remained under this condition voluntarily, blaming Northerners for their inertia. "I am under all the political disabilities," former clerk to the House of Delegates George W. Munford boasted to former governor John Letcher in 1871, "and shall not apply for their removal." He was skeptical about the future. "I hope to see old Virginia renovated and to take once more the lead in the nation to which she is so justly [entitled]," Munford concluded, "but the Yankees will keep her down if possible."[41]

Faced with such loss of liberty and consequent economic impoverishment, former Confederates wondered if their apathy retarded any Southern recovery. Only the rising generation, Randolph believed, unencumbered by the past, would be able to drive Virginia's resurgence, for "the very necessity for increased exertion will nerve the rising generation and give them far more energy and enterprise than we possessed." His generation's responsibility, he told his niece Sarah Nicholas, was not to "still your hopes by mourning for the past."[42] Others were less sweeping but still saw the wisdom of a less prominent role for themselves. In 1866 Letcher told Vance that, owing to their respective states' "massive contribution" to the Confederate effort, the "Northern people are prejudiced against [us]." Letcher concluded, "I could render no efficient service to my people in a political position." It was those who "had no show prior to the recent troubles" that now had to lead Virginia and the South. "I will not be in the way of any of them," he explained to Vance, and proposed they should both retire into private life.[43]

In 1867, the pursuit of political rights had become vital for former Confederates in order to address their dire economic situation. De Bow's sudden death that February meant the loss of an effective advocate for the South escaping from a looming colonial-style economic dependence on the North. De Bow's goal of obtaining sufficient Northern investment to foster Southern industrial development and economic diversification appeared impossible without a political voice in Washington.[44] Randolph's succumbing to tuberculosis in April meant he never had time to reconsider his contention that his generation should be permanently barred from public life. By the summer, however, Letcher concluded that it was time to get back politically "in the way." A pardon, Radical Reconstruction, and his own return to prosperity in Lexington propelled him to thinking once more about the future. Letcher's first priority was to end Radical Reconstruction and return Virginia to the Union. He believed it was precisely his experience in Confederate politics that qualified him to mediate with the North. He visited House Speaker Schuyler Colfax (IN-R) at the National Hotel in Washington. Letcher justified his mission by saying that "harmony and good understanding" were "indispensable" between the sections, "in order that peace and prosperity might once again pervade ... our whole country."[45] According to Speaker Colfax's recollection, shameless references by the Virginian to his service for the Confederacy spoiled the meeting. He even believed that Letcher "would gladly renew the war," if the former governor "had the power" to do so.[46] Letcher protested that Colfax mistook his pride in his past actions for a desire for revenge in the future, stating "I had nothing to repent of—that I had done what I believed to be my right at the time, and that under the same circumstances I would do the same thing." No offense at this pride-in-Confederacy should be taken by Northerners, Letcher concluded. He and his fellow former Confederates had "fully redeemed our obligations imposed upon us by the results of the struggle."[47]

The following year, with the 1868 presidential election approaching, a group of Virginian ex-Confederates representing both prewar political parties, including several former subscribers to *De Bow's Review*, pronounced their eagerness to join the Democratic Party and so reengage with national politics.[48] On August 26, at a gathering in White Sulphur Springs, a mountain resort in West Virginia, an ex-Whig from the Shenandoah Valley, Alexander H. H. Stuart, wrote a public letter sent under General Robert E. Lee's name. In addition to Letcher, other prominent Virginia Democrats Joseph R. Anderson, Thomas Branch, John Echols, and James Lyons were co-signatories. The letter was addressed to Union General and Democrat-supporter William S. Rosecrans, and through him to Horatio Seymour, the Democratic Party presidential candidate. As well as pledging the South's devotion to reunion, peace, and the Thirteenth Amendment, the public letter was a bid to boost the chances of the Democratic Party for the approaching elections. So far from seeking to reenslave freedpeople, the signatories pledged to "treat the negro with kindness and humanity." At the same time, however, they reminded Northerners of their "deep seated conviction that at present the negroes have neither the intelligence nor other qualifications which are necessary to make them safe depositories of political power."[49]

Despite the obvious partisanship of the Virginians, even Republican Party politicians appeared more prepared to accommodate the sensibilities of ex-Confederates. The death of the powerful Radical Thaddeus Stevens in the summer of 1868, as well as the election of Ulysses S. Grant, had strengthened the Republican Party's conservative and moderate wings. In November 1868 the veteran Republican politician Elihu Washburn averred to Letcher that notwithstanding the former governor's publicized altercation with Colfax, he was one of those Virginians who, "influenced by the spirit of moderation, statesmanship, and patriotism, must come to the forefront and help rebuild the structure that Civil War has shattered." Once Grant was installed as president, Washburn hoped there would be "a new departure" for Virginia, toward "that destiny of prosperity, power, and greatness that belongs to it."[50]

Notwithstanding the warm words of Washburn, the Republicans' electoral success meant that the party's commitment to African American civil and political rights remained a potential obstacle to reunion. Here, the Virginians' eagerness to achieve the goal of political rights and prosperity for Virginia meant that they had to accept that a measure of these benefits would be passed on to African Americans. In the concert hall of the Exchange Hotel in Richmond on New Year's Eve, 1868, leading Virginians gathered to continue this initiative under the banner of "universal suffrage as an equivalent for universal amnesty." In effect, they accepted the Radical Reconstruction state constitution, including African American male suffrage, in exchange for their opponents waiving the demand for former Confederates to, if they wished to resume office, take the test oath pledging that they had always been loyal unionists. The Virginia Democrats regarded taking such a test oath as an impossible condition for them to fulfill without making a mockery of the whole process. Those attending included Democrats Thomas Branch, C. C. McRae, and Daniel C. De Jarnette, together with the antebellum governor Wyndham Robertson. Under the leadership of the ex-Whigs, Stuart and Baldwin, these Virginian Democrats joined a committee of nine who then proceeded north in order to arrive at the National Hotel in Washington on January 8, 1869. Along with rival delegations from the radical and conservative Republican factions in Richmond, the committee of nine made representations to the Reconstruction Committee of the House and the Senate Judiciary Committee. Stuart and Baldwin triumphed when the moderate Republican delegation endorsed their compromise; Virginia would return to the Union and there would be an amnesty for remaining disqualified former Confederates.[51]

Parallel with this political rehabilitation, Virginian Democrats began once more to attempt to end the state's colonial economic relations, and this led the revival of the Southern commercial convention movement. A gathering of merchants in Norfolk in October 1868, possibly stirred by Maury's vision for steamship lines, petitioned for a resumption of the meetings. A swift response by the Memphis (Tenn.) Chamber of Commerce led to five conventions being held between 1869 and 1871. The conventions' resolutions affirmed the South's role in the national and global economy and expressed ambitious commercial goals. Prominent Richmond lawyer Thomas Branch, former Confederate house speaker Thomas Bocock, and the director of the Tredegar Ironworks in

Richmond, Joseph Anderson, led the delegation from Virginia. All three had been subscribers to *De Bow's Review*.[52]

The resolutions of the commercial conventions reiterated earlier Confederate objectives: a southern Pacific railroad, a regional railroad network, direct trade with Europe, promotion of mining and manufactures, and river and harbor improvements. The mission of the conventions, which included delegates from the North, but no African Americans, was "to lead the South back into the national economy." However, the conventions also hinted at subversive efforts by Confederates to establish a "Northwestern Confederacy" during the war, focused as they were on getting support from the Midwest (it met once in Cincinnati, and delegates included the notorious ex-Copperhead gubernatorial candidate Clement Vallandigham of Ohio).[53] Adhering to the policies they once espoused as Confederates, delegates were uninterested in a Southern industrial revolution. The postwar convention movement remained wedded to Confederate political economic principles of comparative advantage, free trade, and agricultural production as the basis of national wealth.[54] The movement collapsed when it failed in its principal practical purpose, which was to get Northern investment into the South.[55]

Rather than blaming their plight on low prices and a reluctance to change old habits, Virginian farmers blamed emancipation and insisted that Northern investors owed them a living. Hugh W. Sheffley of Staunton, a friend of Letcher's, told the former governor that he was on his way to Washington on December 28, 1870, to get loans as "entering wedges to further success." Sheffley emulated Green's earlier plan for a Southern revival; banks in the capital would surely lend "on the most valuable security in the shape of real estate in the Valley."[56] Problems remained. Munford in the following year complained to Letcher about continuing capital shortages that prevented investment in agricultural improvements.[57] In 1875 Letcher had presented these arguments to a meeting of the Ruffin Agricultural Club in Cumberland County, Virginia—named after a leading proponent of the antebellum Commercial Convention Movement and agricultural improvement. "Thousands of acres of land are lying idle for want of capital to improve and labor to cultivate it," the members of the club complained in the context of an economic depression, and as a result, "the future prosperity of Virginia is too far off."[58] Others worried that the consequence of this impotence, exactly that of Evans's St. Elmo Murray, would be disastrous for the future of not only the South, but also the United States. In 1876, Lucius Q. C. Lamar, in the U.S. House of Representatives, warned his fellow congressmen of a risk of recurrence of "sullen and inactive incivicism" in the South.⁵⁹ Checking this apathy would require ambitious leadership.

Although Radical Reconstruction had ended by 1873, voters appeared passive, and an epidemic of idleness, both economical and political, worried leading former Confederate Virginians. To combat this malaise, prominent ex-Confederates returned to politics and articulated expansive visions. In 1873, Wyndham Robertson speculated to Letcher about whether the most senior Virginian Confederate, Robert M. T. Hunter, once a Confederate secretary of state and before that a U.S. senator for Virginia, might be induced to take the lead in the approaching state elections in order dispel apathy and "to get the people to think themselves, and for themselves."⁶⁰ In the absence then and thereafter of any organized agrarian movement in Virginia, this indifference to politics appeared to be the biggest issue in getting poor whites to vote.⁶¹ However, Robertson also fretted that the Republican opposition in Virginia would be able to portray as reactionary the inclusion of such prominent former Confederates as Hunter. "The obstacles in his way would be insurmountable," in that eventuality, and "I prefer to turn my eyes from the past."⁶²

Hunter had already set aside his own earlier scruples and had come out of retirement and campaigned for the Democrats in the North during the 1872 presidential election. Addressing an election meeting in New York's Tammany Hall on September 13, 1872, he explained his motives. Only the return of natural leaders like him, Hunter argued, would lead to the restoration of the Democratic Party to what he saw as its proper place in Washington. As a result, the "Southern people, whom [the Republican Party] so much vilified and reproached, is bound to play an important part in the government of this Union."⁶³

Hunter assured New Yorkers that he was not proposing a return of the "Slave Power" to dominate Washington. "The South has neither sought nor taken any lead," he claimed, and he proposed to defer any leadership to Horace Greeley and the Liberal Republicans, with Southerners only in a supporting role. Although, he added, "we abandon no opinions merely because we fail to make issues upon them now when it would be vain to do so." With Greeley's defeat in the 1872 presidential election, Hunter focused on his state of Virginia. On August 22, 1873, looking forward to that year's state election and campaigning for Confederate general James L. Kemper for governor, the former senator charged that the Republican Party planned to keep "control of the State, and perhaps of persecuting us for the past." To be elected, candidates had to be "guided by Virginia principles and interests and influenced by Virginia feelings and sensibilities."⁶⁴ Kemper won the election.

Confidence among former Confederate Virginians about a national role for themselves revived after the Democratic Party won control of the U.S. House in the 1874 midterm election. Hunter wished for a Southern reassertion in the context of its Confederate past. He desired Lucius Q. C. Lamar of Mississippi, something of an intellectual and a younger man—but also a prominent Confederate, protégé of Jefferson Davis, and a fellow veteran of the Confederate state department—to act as the section's de facto leader.⁶⁵ Lamar was not selected on the basis of any willingness to compromise on Southern rights.⁶⁶ On August 2, 1876, when Lamar spoke to the House about the "present condition and future destiny" of the South, he paid tribute to its "people who even in their desolation are no unimportant element in the national life." White Southerners, he continued, "have accepted with manly sincerity" the outcome of the war, indeed with humility, as they "know that they have the confidence of the country to regain." Lamar reiterated Hunter's argument when he assured Northern representatives that "the idea that the South will . . . ever again regain the control of this giant republic and wield its destinies against the will of its mighty people" was "baseless" and a "hallucination." The majority would continue to rule. White Southerners were "impotent to protect a single interest of their own," and besides, "even if such a dream were in their mind, the occasion for it has gone."⁶⁷

The very fact of the South's feebleness meant white Southerners would now be the most loyal Americans; after all, empire has an enduring appeal to the powerless as well as for the powerful. "Their very sectionalism," Lamar explained, "makes them cultivate that wider and broader patriotism which is coextensive with the Union. They have no aspirations not bounded up by the horizon of the Union, no purpose adverse to national interests." These arguments also resembled the Confederate appeals, during the last year of the war, for negotiations with the United States on the basis of mutual expansion.⁶⁸ U.S. territorial growth and empire abroad would enable the survival of Southern sectionalism at home. The Democratic Party would take the place of commissioners and mediate between section and nation with its "national and not sectional platform."⁶⁹

Ex-Confederates based their claim for participation and leadership of the United States on more than an assurance of patriotism; they also presented policies and plans based on their Confederate experience to benefit the United States and project its power abroad. These qualities expressed themselves in a commercial worldview that combined maximum production of goods, an emphasis on federalism, and enthusiasm for interstate internal improvements at home, together with free trade imperialism abroad. In all of these policy planks, this worldview resembled contemporary agitation in Britain and Canada for empire, which grew into the Imperial Federation League of the 1880s and culminated in Chamberlain's vision of an imperial union by the 1890s. This program included an open door in China, federal structures for the self-governing colonies, and—crucially for Southerners—decentralization of the United Kingdom government.[70] In their turn, contemporary British observers also noticed how some of these expansionist ambitions in the United States had been suppressed by the Republican majority into the 1890s.[71] However, these Southern ambitions of expansion through markets also offer a tantalizing glimpse of what would become future U.S. foreign policy, foreshadowing both Secretary of State John Hay's Open Door of 1899 and, finally, the Wilsonian program of 1913.[72] For these former Confederates, what mattered was that this national vision both vindicated the Confederate experiment and provided a vision of the future.

The onset of hard times after the Panic of 1873 provoked a further reiteration of Confederate policies. Unlike the cotton mill campaign in the Deep South, which emphasized economic diversification and independence from the North, Virginians stressed the importance of maximum production enabling them to become the North's greatest customer and supplier.[73] On January 15, 1877, H. C. Marchant, the president of Charlottesville Woolen Mills, considered that the downturn confirmed the South's centrality to the U.S. economy. "No part of the country is its equal in its productive power," he argued, and its recovery would benefit Northerners, as otherwise, any "taxes, which the South, if prosperous, could help to pay have to be borne . . . by the rest of the United States." Capital shortages in the South led to unemployment in Northern cities because, Marchant wrote to Letcher, this "prosperous trade . . . will never attain its former proportions until the Southern States are given a chance to put themselves again in good condition, and are thus enabled to restore their credit."[74]

Economic recession meanwhile was evidence of the importance of the South to commercial recovery in the North. In 1874 Lamar included in his case what he alleged to be the Union's squandered opportunity in refusing the offer of a commercial pact with the independent Confederacy.[75] "The prosperity of the South may be utterly destroyed and with it no small part of that of the North." Lamar considered the depression-era debates about the money supply and joining the Gold Standard were distractions from the real, sectional, question. The "present distresses" of the United States were "not so much due to the contraction and expansion of the currency," he argued; rather hard times had arisen on account of "the rapid closing up of the North's best market, and the impoverishment of her best customers" in the South. Once there was a "true Southern renaissance, a real grand reconstruction of the South," Lamar assured his fellow representatives, "you will see at last what will be the dawn of prosperity for all the industries and enterprises of the North."[76]

Enhanced federalism would push expansion and empire from the bottom up.[77] Prosperity would return only if power was restored to the states. Hunter had made the same arguments when a states' rights–supporting senator before the war and as a would-be Confederate negotiator with Lincoln and Seward in early 1865. "Let us preserve to the people of each state," he declared in 1873, "through its special government the control of its domestic and peculiar affairs." Local autonomy would enable national unity because "harmony" would be "impossible otherwise to achieve" and, as a result, Hunter's Union would resemble a train as "State after State would wheel upon the track in one grand united progress." The threat to this future came from the Republican policy of centralization, which threatened a "change from a popular to an imperial form of government" in Washington.[78] Hunter, with Madison probably in his mind, considered the issue about whether a republic could also be an empire.[79] As historian Andrew Heath observes, individuals during Reconstruction still had in mind a usurpation of power rather than conquest of space when they referred to "imperial forms of government."[80] Empire and democracy had a fraught relationship from Ancient Athens onward. "It has always been doubted," Hunter pointed out, "whether a great country as large and with diversified interests could be ruled by a popular government with success." The naysayers were confounded by the success of the "American confederacy," Hunter believed, when, with power devolved to the states, "it became practicable for a people to govern a much greater extent of country well and efficiently," and the central government had not "been forced to regulate all the concerns of society."[81]

Given that Hunter regarded the empire of liberty in not only federal but also ideological and racial terms, it followed that he regarded its rebirth to be of global significance. Across his career, Hunter had argued that the South should pursue common objectives with the North, including the spread of U.S. democracy and commerce across the Western Hemisphere. Momentum on these missions had stalled since 1861 but could resume with a Democrat electoral victory. "It is this great American idea under whose influence our progress and prosperity from the foundation of the government up to 1860 were unparalleled in the history of the world." The "energy and dispatch were due to the form of government and its democratic spirit." As a result, Hunter continued, "Our people were planting here upon a mission of liberty and popular government not only to make a great march of human progress themselves, but to take the world along with them." Such an accomplishment would "elevate the race." In order "to write great schemes of human liberty and progress on the *tabula rasa* of a new continent," Americans had to come up with "a grander philosophy of human rights and popular government than the world had ever seen." He regretted that such claims, in the context of 1872, now appeared "extravagant"; for Hunter argued they "seemed realistic twenty years ago" and not "illusions and day-dreams at best."[82]

The biggest impetus for empire, and it had also been the case during the Confederacy, comprised the possibilities to the imagination offered by transcontinental railroads and canals.[83] These nationwide projects also stood a greater chance of funding because, along with improvements to navigating the Mississippi River, they benefited the whole country and not just the South.[84] As he deemed these interstate projects to be constitutional, Hunter was happy to compromise on states' rights to that higher priority. "The right of congress to construct not only the Pacific Railroad, but [also] the important work now completed by which the great Northwest is proposed to be united with the Atlantic through the waters of Virginia," he told a gathering of Richmond conservatives, "may easily be justified as a fair derivation from the war powers expressly granted to the general government."[85]

Once again, as they had before and during the Civil War, Hunter and Letcher campaigned for the completion of the James River and Kanawha Canal—which would connect the Ohio River to the Atlantic Ocean across Virginia.[86] Letcher recalled old Confederate expansionist ambitions for an allied northwestern confederacy, recently revived by the Southern commercial movement. On July 21, 1873, looking for funds to transport a statue of Stonewall Jackson from Nuremberg, Bavaria, to the restored Virginia Military Institute in his hometown, he appealed to the munificence of descendants of Valley families who had migrated west. They were "now embracing five great states, with more than nine millions of people and a controlling power over the continent equal to that of Virginia over her sister states in the palmiest days of her existence."[87] In 1873, the platform of the victorious conservative party in Virginia again demanded the canal's "speedy enlargement and completion" in order to "connect the waters of the Ohio with those of the Chesapeake, affording to the teeming population of the West cheap transportation of the products to the points of shipment and markets of trade in the East." The operation of the canal would provide an "additional bond of Union" between the "communities whose products and commodities would pass over the line of this great national work."[88]

Railroads had become even more important—and controversial—than canals, and the completion of the Central Pacific Railroad in 1869 running between Nebraska and Utah boosted expansionist thinking. At the same time, the route chosen increased Southern fears that their section would simply become the "eddy" around which the east-west flows of goods, people, and money would flow.[89] Letcher therefore promoted other transcontinental railroad routes that would embrace the South. Newly elected to the General Assembly to represent Rockbridge County, Letcher served as chairman of the Committee on Roads, and he was a logical choice for Governor Kemper to nominate as a delegate to a national convention at St. Louis, Missouri, on November 23, 1875, "to consider the subject of the construction of the Pacific Railroad through the states and territories of the South West and to take such action in its favor as may seem fit."[90] The various schemes of railroad routes swiftly became a matter of sectional concern. Barry Wilkes of Bedford County had a few months earlier warned Letcher about a plan of Colonel Tom Scott and the Southern Railroad Corporation. "A road which touches its territory only on its most northern boundary," Wilkes observed, "can be of no advantage to the ten cotton states it passes at such a distance." Despite the fact that Confederate General P. G. T. Beauregard had been engaged as an agent for this enterprise, Wilkes concluded that the road was "really calculated to draw trade from that section rather than develope [sic] it."[91]

Not every ex-Confederate Democrat in Virginia welcomed the prospect of a Southern Pacific Railroad. Railroad mania had also been tainted for many by its association with what individuals construed to be Radical Reconstruction governmental excess and corruption. Veteran Virginia politician and former Confederate general Henry A. Wise regarded massive railroad projects as "worse than worthless." They would saddle the indebted state of Virginia with financial white elephants because of its "want of means to utilize them" and insufficient funds "to complete them on the scale proportional to their magnitude."[92] Hence the profits from the railroads would, he feared, be syphoned off in the 1870s into the hands of outside tycoons such as Collis Potter Huntington. Yet, as governor nearly twenty years before, Wise had planned to subsidize Virginian entrepreneurs to "acupuncture" the Alleghenies.[93] Old ambitions mingled with the need to set out a postwar vision for Virginians. Even for those former Confederates who remained unreconstructed and unreconciled, the prospect of railroads to the West offered the chance "to see the dawn of a brighter future."[94] Despite his reservations, Wise told the benevolent order of the Knights of Pythias that the construction of interstate canals and railroads now in 1875 made "the Union irresistible." The railroads transcended local grievances. "They are of such vast importance," Wise continued, "as national works, affecting the interests of the interior of the continent as to commerce, agriculture, time and cheapness of transportation, mining and manufacturing."[95] State concerns as to affordability and control had to be overridden in the national interest, for it would boost growing, allied, interests elsewhere in the U.S.

A southern transcontinental railroad might finally enable the Confederate goals of maximum production and commerce by lowering costs to market, together with a new goal: boosting (white) immigration to the South.[96] On January 26, 1876, Hunter implored Lamar to champion the planned Southern Pacific Railroad from Texas to San Diego. Such a railroad would serve to "restore that section to its just share of power in the government and its fair share of influence on the public opinion of the country." He saw recovery as arising from two factors delivered by the railroad: "the additions to the wealth and influence of the South" and "the settlement of the vast territories through which it would pass by a kindred and sympathizing people." After all, Hunter explained, "if Texas, New Mexico, and Arizona and the whole of the rich country along the line were settled and teeming with resources, agricultural and mineral," then the South as a whole would "increase in political power, not only in influence but in voting power."[97] He predicted the growth in production of cotton, wool, cattle, precious metals, and even—"by means of irrigation"—wheat, from the opening of the arid Southwest. Hunter looked forward to the railroad being able to "raise up new centers of supply and establish new routes of commerce" that would transform markets in Asia and Europe, as well as the Americas.[98]

Hunter's vision resembled the wartime Confederate plans to "regenerate" Mexico, especially its northwest, by the planting of colonies of slaveholders and enslaved people, together with the construction of a transcontinental railroad.[99] The original plans for a Confederate Pacific railroad ran from San Antonio, Texas, to the Mexican Pacific Ocean port of Guaymas in Sonora. Even with the amendment of the western terminus to San Diego, Hunter believed that the operation of the railroad "will establish intimate relations of trade and commerce between eight or ten of the northern provinces of Mexico, and the people of the American territory through which it will pass."[100]

When Hunter and other former Confederates predicted that "a vast southern empire may thus arise," they meant it in terms of a sphere of influence for the South to help it serve as a counterweight to the power of the North within the Union. This plan was both a resumption of prewar sectional competition and drew on Confederate offers made to the U.S. from later in the conflict.[101] Specifically, this "cooperative-counterweight" notion had some resemblance to the dual-presidency theories of Hunter's mentor John C. Calhoun and was almost identical to the 1865 proposals made by Jefferson Davis to Francis P. Blair Sr. in Richmond and by Alexander H. Stephens (with Hunter) to Lincoln and Seward at Hampton Roads.[102] An enlarged South would benefit the United States by "helping to maintain justice and create common interests amongst the members of the present Union." Hunter drew on other Confederate diplomatic initiatives when he added that in an alternative scenario, additional southern states might assist in "establishing a new point of departure and a new balance of interests on the North American continent."[103] As Confederate secretary of state, Hunter, along with Henry Hotze, the propagandist and agent he appointed to serve the Confederacy in London, had often spoken of the need for a new balance of power in North America after the war had ended, with Canada, Maximilian's Mexican Empire, and an independent Confederacy offsetting U.S. power.[104] Now in the 1870s, Hunter was not advocating a breakup of the Union, but rather its more rapid expansion and decentralization, with an internal balance of power between multiple sections.

By the late 1870s, Virginians projected a vision of free trade imperialism abroad arising from these domestic promotions of interstate canals and railroads, maximum production of staple crops for export, and states' rights.[105] This aspiration was primarily material, but free trade imperialism did have an ideological component. It proposed a way of life with strictly limited government at home.[106] Unlike imperialism in Britain and later in the United States, there was no accompanying program of domestic reform, other than granting state and local jurisdictions greater autonomy.[107] At the same time, free trade imperialism was emphatically a present-day critique of evolving Republican Party policy geared toward protection of an industrializing national economy.[108] The economic depression of the 1870s boosted the appeal of these arguments. Hard times gave credibility in some circles to the argument that Virginian politicians should constructively champion both the conditions of the 1850s and the objectives of Confederate planners, when people looked forward to a time of freer trade and a growing importance of exports to the economy.[109] "When the national government was most under [Virginia's] influence," Hunter reminisced, "its people were most thriving and prosperous. It was under that influence that the growth of our country was most rapid and satisfactory."[110]

One lesson from the Confederate failure was the need for the United States to have a strong navy. During the 1870s, Virginians began to lobby for a navy, foreshadowing bipartisan support in the 1880s.[111] Looking to Britain with its huge trading power, as well as free institutions, also brought back memories of a time when Confederate planners looked forward to an imposing merchant marine.[112] In making his own case for free trade, Hunter recalled not only the arguments he made against the Morrill Tariff when he was still a U.S. senator in 1861, but also his memories of the wartime blockade of the Confederacy.[113] Even during the boom times of 1872, he knew some Northerners also loathed the tariff. Hunter knew his audience would respond positively when he remarked that it was "hard to address the people of New York without saying a word on free trade." He told the audience of his "experience of commerce carried by blockade running and how it compares to commerce carried on through its usual means and regular channels." Hunter had learned from these earlier restrictions and regulations that "this commerce will not long satisfy the people."[114] The economic downturn from 1873 intensified these arguments, as "the great shipping interest of the Union is most thoroughly depressed." Hunter asked in 1875: "Was such a state of things ever even possible when the country was governed according to Virginian views and principles?"[115] Confederates had campaigned for the creation of a large merchant marine with a navy to protect it, including the creation of a Virginian Volunteer Navy, championed by Robert Archer, senior colleague of Anderson and himself director of the Tredegar Ironworks, in which his son, Edward, had planned to serve as a naval officer.[116]

Even though they demanded a navy, Virginians made it clear that this ambition was compatible with their demand for reduced government, states' rights, and federalism. With an eye on Republican Party policy, Representative John Randolph Tucker, Virginia's attorney general during the Confederacy, claimed in the House on May 8, 1878, that free trade would "prevent the evils of centralism," which accompanied a high tariff policy and a well-funded federal government. Above all, tariffs divided the people against each other by rewarding one interest—or section—over the other. The choice was to either "revive the enmities and jealousies of the past" and with it "impair faith and hope in our great future" or "make our constitutional Union of States the glory of the world."[117] Moreover, tariffs were one of many "perils of a consolidated government [which] . . . make an effective discharge of our duties under the Constitution well-nigh impracticable." According to Tucker, commercial and territorial expansion would reinforce minimal government because "in the enlarged area of the country and with its increasing interests, we will have our hands full to do well what is expressly devolved upon us without attempting to exercise doubtful powers."[118] In other words, federal authorities would be distracted from enforcing a broad construction of the provisions of the Fourteenth and Fifteenth Amendments across the South—while what Tucker took to be American democratic values would spread across the globe.

Virginians would be free to maximize production and a world policy would be necessary to ensure that these crops would find sufficient markets. Tucker demonstrated that what Hunter had deemed to be Virginian "principles" might still have both national and international relevance.[119] "The aspiration of American production, of American manufactures, and of American industry should be to fill the world with the fruits of our labor, energy, and enterprise." [120] As with later historians of globalization, Tucker believed trade and technology drew nations closer together, opened new markets, and led to greater interdependence between national economies.[121] The result would be, in the context of Pax Britannica, a reduction in the size of the U.S. army and the power of the federal government.[122]

Its planners had once intended the Confederacy to be the world's supplier of raw materials to nations entering the Industrial Revolution, including the United States. It followed that Tucker specifically denounced economic isolationism, whether of the United States from the world or of the South from the United States. "We cannot if we could, and should not if we would, remain isolated and alone." Protectionist policies had divided the Union, antagonized other nations, and exacerbated Great Power rivalries, he argued, and despite the setback of Confederate defeat were, still in 1878, contrary to what Tucker believed to be long-term global development and trends. "In this era of expanding energies, of all-embracing sympathies, of far-reaching aspirations for a better and higher destiny for our race," he challenged, "are we to be told that our true policy is to . . . live within ourselves, and hugging our petty interests within the narrow circle of our contracted selfishness, close the gates of our new world to intercourse with mankind?" Tucker made a passionate plea for the economic principle of comparative advantage and derided what he called the "old idea," an "exploded doctrine," that "in all exchanges one man must be the loser and the other must be the gainer." Whereas with commerce, in "the interchange of products made more cheaply by the one than by the other," both gain, because "each makes its own profit and neither suffers cost." As with individuals, "no nation loses, both gain by the mutual exchanges." Interdependence between economies would permanently solve the problem of overproduction, which seemed so acute in the slump. "There can never come a time when home production will fill the measurement of human desire and when commerce will not invite an enlargement of our supply by exchanging our product for what others can and we cannot produce."[123]

This ambition of the Confederacy to become the world's greatest trading nation might still be realized by the United States. Tucker closed his 1878 speech with a call to "enlarge" the U.S. commercial system. If it was to end by "embracing all countries," then "our export and import trade would soon rival that of Britain." Nevertheless, despite this note of international competition, Tucker insisted that free trade, by fostering interdependency, would ensure a permanent peace. As Lamar and Hunter had earlier done, he also cited the lower tariff eras as those times when the economy grew fastest. As well as reducing the tariffs once more, Tucker called for more commercial treaties to be signed with nations. The Confederate State Department had once sought to negotiate commercial pacts with other countries, and now was the time for the U.S. to do so. "Whenever by commercial treaties, as with Canada or the Hawaiian Islands," Tucker declared, "we have established free trade with foreign countries, the immediate results have been mutually advantageous." [124] He especially noted that exports and imports in the case of the Hawaiian Islands doubled in one year. By quoting these examples, this former Confederate from Virginia also hoped to persuade fellow representatives that these benefits of open-door expansionism might be replicated domestically by a sectional pact negotiated between North and South.

By the late 1870s, former Confederates in Virginia believed that they were on the threshold of national power. These individuals based their vision on free trade imperialism and the spread of Anglo-American political values. Domestically, they reached out to potential allies and championed minimal central government, the construction of interstate infrastructure projects dedicated to boost exports, the open door abroad, and a navy sufficient to protect these interests. In the final analysis, this future was more that of Woodrow Wilson in 1913 than the Republicans of 1898. However, with the goal of worldwide commerce in view—especially the importance of the isthmian canal—as well as the promise of continued distraction of the federal government from domestic concerns, they also cheered the triumph of 1898 as a step toward grabbing a share of the China trade by keeping the open door. Whereas the origins of Southern support for these future ventures was clearly visible by the late 1870s, they were also the same as those individuals had once propounded and expected to enact as Confederate planners during the Civil War.

Notes

The quotation in the chapter title is from Lucius Q. C. Lamar, *Policy of the Republican Party and the Political Condition of the South, August 2, 1876* (Washington: John H. Cunningham, 1876), 8.

Many thanks to David Prior, DJ Polite, and Mark Power Smith for their comments on earlier drafts of this essay. I needed the guidance of Gary W. Gallagher, Elizabeth R. Varon, and the Civil War Group at the University of Virginia during the inception of this project. William B. Kurtz, Managing Director and Digital Historian at the John L. Nau III Center for Civil War History at UVA, kindly shared with me his research in the General William Starke Rosecrans papers at University of California, Los Angeles (repository hereafter cited as UCLA). Mr. and Mrs. William G. K. Merrill of Afton, Va., generously loaned me their copy of the memoir of their ancestor Joseph Bryan. Finally, I would like to express my gratitude to the staff both at the Albert and Shirley Small Special Collections library at UVA (repository hereafter cited as UVA)and the library of the Virginia Historical Society, Virginia Museum of History and Culture, in Richmond (repository hereafter cited as VHS).

1. See Adrian Brettle, *Colossal Ambitions: Confederate Planning for a Post–Civil War World* (Charlottesville: University of Virginia Press, 2020).

2. Matthew Karp, *This Vast Southern Empire: Slaveholders at the Helm of American Foreign Policy* (Cambridge, Mass.: Harvard University Press, 2016), 186. For the annexationist approach, see Robert E. May, *Slavery, Race, and Conquest in the Tropics: Lincoln, Douglas, and the Future of Latin America* (New York: Cambridge University Press, 2013); *Manifest Destiny's Underworld: Filibustering in Antebellum America* (Chapel Hill: University of North Carolina Press, 2002); and *The Southern Dream of a Caribbean Empire* (Baton Rouge: Louisiana State University Press, 1973). For the tropical civilization see Matthew Pratt Guterl, *American Mediterranean: Southern Slaveholders in the Age of Emancipation* (Cambridge, Mass.: Harvard University Press, 2008).

3. Stephanie McCurry, *Confederate Reckoning: Power and Politics in the Civil War South* (Cambridge, Mass.: Harvard University Press, 2010), 361.

4. C. Vann Woodward, *Thinking Back: The Perils of Writing History* (Baton Rouge: Louisiana State University Press, 1986), 121–133.

5. David Brion Davis, *Inhuman Bondage: The Rise and Fall of Slavery in the New World* (New York: Oxford University Press, 2006), 303.

6. Margaret Mitchell, quoted in *The Oxford Book of the American South: Testimony, Memory and Fiction*, ed. Edward L. Ayers and Bradley C. Mittendorf (New York: Oxford University Press, 1997), 257.

7. Robert Garlick Hill Kean, "On the Economy of Higher Education: Address to the Educational Association of Virginia, November 1875," *Educational Journal of Virginia* (Richmond: Educational Journal of Virginia, 1875), 11.

8. Augusta Jane Evans, *St. Elmo* (1866; reprint, Tuscaloosa: University of Alabama Press, 1992), 319, 360.

9. Gregory P. Downs, *Declarations of Dependence: The Long Reconstruction of Popular Politics in the South, 1861–1908* (Chapel Hill: University of North Carolina Press, 2011), 102.

10. Dan T. Carter, *When the War Was Over: The Failure of Self-Reconstruction in the South, 1865–1867* (Baton Rouge: Louisiana State University Press, 1985).

11. Mark Wahlgren Summers, *The Ordeal of the Reunion: A New History of Reconstruction* (Chapel Hill: University of North Carolina Press, 2014), 396. See also Anne Sarah Rubin, *A Shattered Nation: The Rise and Fall of the Confederacy, 1861–1868* (Chapel Hill: University of North Carolina Press, 2005).

12. Joseph A. Fry, *Dixie Looks Abroad: The South and US Foreign Relations, 1789–1973* (Baton Rouge: Louisiana State University Press, 2002); and "Place Matters: Domestic Regionalism and the Formation of American Foreign Policy," *Diplomatic History* 36, no. 3 (2012), 452–472; Tenant S. McWilliams, *The New South Faces the World: Foreign Affairs and the Southern Sense of Self, 1877–1950* (Baton Rouge: Louisiana State University Press, 1988).

13. For two contrasting accounts of antebellum Southern expansionism, see Karp, *This Vast Southern Empire*; and Amy S. Greenberg, *A Wicked War: Polk, Clay, Lincoln and the 1846 U.S. Invasion of Mexico* (New York: Alfred A Knopf, 2012).

14. See Gavin Wright, *Old South, New South: Revolutions in the Southern Economy since the Civil War* (Baton Rouge: Louisiana State University Press, 1997), 17–50.

15. See Gaines M. Foster, *Ghosts of the Confederacy: Defeat, the Lost Cause and the Emergence of the New South, 1865–1913* (New York: Oxford University Press, 1987).

16. Patrick Hearden, *Independence and Empire: The New South's Cotton Mill Campaign, 1865–1901* (DeKalb: Northern Illinois University Press, 1982), 125–144.

17. For an appraisal of the effect of the war in the Shenandoah Valley, see Mark E. Neely Jr., *The Civil War and the Limits of Destruction* (Cambridge, Mass.: Harvard University Press, 2007), 109–139. See also Arthur J. L. Fremantle, *Three Months in the Southern States: April–June 1863*, ed. Gary W. Gallagher (Lincoln: University of Nebraska Press, 1991), 223.

18. Gary W. Gallagher, "Shaping Public Memory of the Civil War: Robert E. Lee, Jubal A. Early, and Douglas Southall Freeman," in *The Memory of the Civil War in American Culture*, ed. Alice Fahs and Joan Waugh (Chapel Hill: University of North Carolina Press, 2004), 39–63.

19. On the Republican economic agenda, see Marc Egnal, *Clash of Extremes: The Economic Origins of the Civil War* (New York: Hill and Wang, 2009), 326–347.

20. William Blair, *Virginia's Private War: Feeding Body and Soul in the Confederacy, 1861–1865* (New York: Oxford University Press, 1998), 132–133; Edward L. Ayers, *The Thin Light of Freedom: The Civil War and Emancipation in the Heart of America* (New York: W. W. Norton, 2017), 344–460; Jane A. Townes, "The Effect of Emancipation on Large Landholdings, Nelson and Goochland Counties, Virginia," *Journal of Southern History* 45, no. 3 (1979), 403–412; Catherine S. Silverman, "Of Wealth, Virtue, and Intelligence: The Redeemers and Their Triumph in Virginia and North Carolina, 1865–1877," (PhD diss., City University of New York, 1972); Susanna Michele Lee, "Reconciliation in Reconstruction Virginia," in *Crucible of the Civil War: Virginia from Secession to Commemoration*, ed. Gary W. Gallagher and Edward L. Ayres (Charlottesville: University of Virginia Press, 2006), 188–208; Daniel W. Crofts, *Reluctant Confederates: Upper South Unionists in the Secession Crisis* (Chapel Hill: University of North Carolina Press, 1989).

21. George W. Randolph to Mary Randolph, June 27, 1865, folder 5:101, box 5 MSS 5533, The Papers of the Randolph Family of Edgehill and Wilson Cary Nicholas, UVA.

22. On tourism from the United States to Europe, see David McCullough, *The Greater Journey: Americans in Paris* (New York: Simon and Schuster, 2011).

23. See Henry Hotze, "What the North Is Fighting For," *The Index* 3, no. 58 (1863), 81.

24. Jeremy Black, *Fighting for America: The Struggle for Mastery in North America, 1519–1871* (Bloomington: Indiana University Press, 2011), 352; Emperor Maximilian to Matthew F. Maury, April 16, 1866, Box 49, Minor and Wilson Family Papers, No. 3750, UVA; Todd W. Wahlstrom, *The Southern Exodus to Mexico: Migration across the Borderlands after the American Civil War* (Lincoln: University of Nebraska Press, 2015), xiii–xxii, 13–24, 117–127.

25. Roy Jenkins, *Sir Charles Dilke: A Victorian Tragedy* (London, U.K.: Collins, 1958), 32–35, 41; Ernest R. May, *American Imperialism, A Speculative Essay* (New York: Athenaeum, 1968), 116–121.

26. May, *American Imperialism*, 95–98.

27. J. L. Garvin, *The Life of Joseph Chamberlain*, 3 vols. (London, UK.: Macmillan, 1932–34), 1:305–308. For the connection between British Anglo-Saxonism and its U.S. variant, see Paul A. Kramer, "Empires, Exceptions, and Anglo-Saxons: Race and Rule between the British and United States Empires, 1880–1910," *Journal of American History* 88, no. 4 (2002), 1315–1353.

28. Amy Kaplan, *The Anarchy of Empire in the Making of US Culture* (Cambridge, Mass.: Harvard University Press, 2002), 78. For an example of De Bow's wartime attitude to Caribbean emancipation, see "A Yankee's Travels in the British West Indies," *De Bow's Review and Industrial Resources, Statistics, etc. Devoted to Commerce, Agriculture, Manufactures (1853–1864)* 5, nos. 5–6 (1861), 570.

29. John Stewart Bryan, *Joseph Bryan: His Times, His Family, His Friends. A Memoir* (Richmond, Va.: Whittet and Shepperson, 1935), 147.

30. John W. Daniel, *The People: An Address Delivered before the Jefferson Literary Society of the UVA in the Public Hall on June 28, 1866* (Lynchburg, Va.: Johnson and Schaffter, 1866), 4–5, 23.

31. John F. Kvach, *De Bow's Review: The Antebellum Vision of a New South* (Lexington: University Press of Kentucky, 2013), 161; Wahlstrom, *Southern Exodus*, 13–24, 117–127.

32. Kvach, *De Bow's Review*, 161; Wahlstrom, *Southern Exodus*, 117–127.

33. For the postwar economic condition of the South, see Foner, *Reconstruction*, 124–128.

34. Diary entry dated June 27, 1865 from *Inside the Confederate Government: The Diary of Robert Garlick Hill Kean, Head of the Bureau of War*, ed. Edward Younger (New York: Oxford University Press, 1957), 211.

35. On the radical Republican agitation for the confiscation of Southern property in 1865 and 1866, see Hans L. Trefousse, *Thaddeus Stephens: Nineteenth-Century Egalitarian* (Chapel Hill: University of North Carolina Press, 1997), 195.

36. Henry Hotze, "President Johnson's Rule," *Index* 5, no. 170 (1865), 472.

37. On uncertainty, capital shortages, and federal taxes, see Carter, *When the War Was Over*, 96–104.

38. John Letcher, undated note, folder 432, "Imprisonment and Parole, 1865 May–July," and folder 433, "Pardon File," John Letcher Papers, Mss1 L5684 a FA2, VHS.

39. On Duff Green, see Elizabeth Brown Pryor, *Six Encounters with Lincoln: A President Confronts Democracy and Its Demons* (New York: Viking, 2017), 269–273, 313.

40. John Letcher to Zebulon Vance, May 4, 1866, folder 434, "Letters to Governor Zebulon B. Vance," John Letcher Papers, Mss1 L5684 a FA2, VHS.

41. George W. Munford to John Letcher, January 5, 1871, folder 440, John Letcher Papers, Mss1 L5684 a FA2, VHS.

42. George W. Randolph to Sarah Nicholas Randolph, July 23, 1865, group 8, box 2, No. 8935, Papers of Jefferson, Randolph, Taylor, Smith, and Nicholas Families, UVA.

43. John Letcher to Zebulon Vance, October 16, 1865, folder 434, John Letcher Papers, Mss1 L5684 a FA2, VHS.

44. Kvach, *De Bow's Review*, 170–117.

45. *Louisville Democrat*, December 26, 1868, folder 438, John Letcher Papers, Mss1 L5684 a FA2, VHS.

46. Schuyler Colfax to John Letcher, January 20, 1869, folder 438, John Letcher Papers, Mss1 L5684 a FA2, VHS.

47. John Letcher to Schuyler Colfax, January 25, 1869, folder 438, John Letcher Papers, Mss1 L5684 a FA2, VHS.

48. For Northern fears of a restored Confederacy, see Mark Wahlgren Summers, *A Dangerous Stir: Fear, Paranoia, and the Making of Reconstruction* (Chapel Hill: University of North Carolina Press, 2009).

49. Robert E. Lee to Rosecrans, August 26, September 18, 1868, box 12: Personal and Business Papers, July–December 1868, William Starke Rosecrans Papers, UCLA; *Staunton Spectator*, September 8, 1868.

50. Elihu B. Washburn to John Letcher, November 24, 1868, folder 435, John Letcher Papers, Mss1 L5684 a FA2, VHS.

51. Alexander H. H. Stuart to William Wirt Henry, March 29, 1888, Mss1 St9101 a 3–16, Manuscripts, VHS; Alexander H. H. Stuart, *A Narrative of leading incidents of the organization of the first popular movement in Virginia in 1865 to reestablish peaceful relations between the Northern and Southern States* (Richmond, Va.: William Ellis Jones, 1888), 36–41, Mss1 St9101 a 1–2 Manuscripts, VHS.

52. Kvach, *De Bow's Review*, 204. See also Vicki Vaughan Johnson, *The Men and the Vision of the Southern Commercial Conventions, 1845–1871* (Columbia: University of Missouri Press, 1992), 172–192.

53. Johnson, *The Men and the Vision*, 220–230.

54. On the theory of comparative advantage, see David S. Landes, *The Wealth and Poverty of Nations: Why Some Are so Rich and Some So Poor* (New York: W. W. Norton, 1999), 232. Also see Henry William Spiegel, *The Growth of Economic Thought* (Durham, N.C.: Duke University Press, 1983), 330–331.

55. Johnson, *The Men and the Vision of the Southern Commercial Conventions*, 239–40; see also Egnal, *Clash of Extremes*, 342–347.

56. Hugh W. Sheffley to John Letcher, December 12, 1870, folder 440, John Letcher Papers, Mss1 L5684 a FA2, VHS.

57. George W. Munford to John Letcher, January 5, 1871, folder 440, John Letcher Papers, Mss1 L5684 a FA2, VHS.
58. "A Petition from the Ruffin Agricultural Club in Cumberland Co.," folder 446, John Letcher Papers, Mss1 L5684 a FA2, VHS.
59. Lamar, *Policy of the Republican Party and the Political Condition of the South*, 24.
60. Wyndham Robertson to John Letcher, February 24, 1873, folder 440, John Letcher Papers, Mss1 L5684 a FA2, VHS.
61. On apathy, see Carter, *When the War Was Over*, 65, 247, 271. On the weakness and caution of the Cooperative Movement, Farmers Alliance, and populism in general in Virginia, see Lawrence Goodwyn, *The Populist Movement: A Short History of the Agrarian Revolt in America* (New York: Oxford University Press, 1978), 198; and *Democratic Promise: The Populist Movement in America* (New York: Oxford University Press, 1976), 123, 144, 215, 314, 366, 663n45.
62. Wyndham Robertson to John Letcher, February 24, 1873, folder 440, John Letcher Papers, Mss1 L5684 a FA2, VHS.
63. *Speech of R. M. T. Hunter of Virginia at Tammany Hall, New York, Friday Evening September 13, 1872* (Franklin, Pa.: Venango Spectator, 1872).
64. R. M. T. Hunter, *Speech of Hon. R. M. T. Hunter, Delivered at Richmond, Aug. 22, 1873: Biographical Sketches of Gen. James L. Kemper, Col. Robert E. Withers and Hon. Raleigh T. Daniel, Conservative Nominees: Platform and resolutions, Plan of Organization, State and Executive Committees* (Richmond, Va.: n.p., 1873), 4–12.
65. R. M. T. Hunter, *Letter to Rep. Lamar on the Texas and Pacific Railroad* (Richmond, Va.: n.p., 1876).
66. On Lamar's religion and philosophy, see Elizabeth Fox-Genovese and Eugene D. Genovese, *The Mind of the Master Class: History and Faith in the Southern Slaveholders' Worldview* (New York: Cambridge University Press, 2005), 532.
67. Lamar, *Policy of the Republican Party*, 8–9.
68. See Adrian Brettle, "Confederate Imagined Relations with the Federals in the Postwar Order," *Civil War History* 65, no. 1 (2019), 43–72.
69. Lamar, *Policy of the Republican Party*, 8–9.
70. Garvin, *Chamberlain*, 3:177–78, 283.
71. Viscount James Bryce, *The American Commonwealth*, 2 vols. (London, U.K.: Macmillan, 1894), 2:521–535. On Republican fears of Southern expansionism, see Robert Kagan, *Dangerous Nation: America and the World* (New York: Knopf, 2006), 278.
72. Walter LaFeber, *The New Empire: An Interpretation of American Expansion, 1860–1898* (Ithaca, N.Y.: Cornell University Press, 1998).
73. For "The New South's Struggle for Economic Independence," see Hearden, *Independence and Empire*, 37–52.
74. H. C. Marchant to John Letcher, January 15, 1877, folder 446, John Letcher Papers, Mss1 L5684 a FA2, VHS.
75. Lucius Lamar, *Misrule in the Southern States Speech of Hon L Q C Lamar on the Louisiana Contested Election in the U.S. House of Representatives June 8, 1874* (Washington: John H. Cunningham, 1874), 5.
76. Lamar, *Misrule in the Southern States*, 14.

77. Lamar, *Misrule in the Southern States*, 6. For empire from the bottom up, see William A. Williams, *The Tragedy of American Diplomacy* (New York: Norton, 1959), 23. This view contrasts with the top-down approach argued by Hearden; Hearden, *Independence and Empire*, xiii–xv, 145–60.

78. Hunter, *Speech of Hon. R. M. T. Hunter, delivered at Richmond, Aug. 22, 1873*, 9–10.

79. Publius (James Madison), *Number XIV, An Objection Drawn from the Extent of the Country Answered from the New York Packet, Friday, November 30, 1787*. From the Lillian Goldman Law Library, Yale Law School, 127 Wall Street, New Haven, CT 06511. Document was accessed through the Internet via the library's web page.

80. Andrew Heath, "'Let the Empire Come,' Imperialism and Its Critics in the Reconstruction South," *Civil War History* 60, no. 2 (2014), 152–89.

81. Hunter, *Speech of Hon. R. M. T. Hunter, delivered at Richmond, Aug. 22, 1873*, 9–10.

82. Hunter, "Speech of R. M. T. Hunter of Virginia at Tammany Hall," *Vernago Spectator*, September 26, 1872.

83. Consider the comments on the Suez Canal in Garvin, *Chamberlain*, 1:446.

84. Egnal, *Clash of Extremes*, 345–346.

85. Hunter, *Speech of Hon. R. M. T. Hunter, delivered at Richmond, Aug. 22, 1873*, 8. At this time, references to the (old) "Northwest" usually meant the states of Ohio, Illinois, and Indiana.

86. See Carol Sheriff, *The Artificial River: The Erie Canal and the Paradox of Progress, 1817–1862* (New York: Hill and Wang, 1996); Egnal, *Clash of Extremes: The Economic Origins of the Civil War* (New York: Hill and Wang, 2009); and Brettle, *Colossal Ambitions*.

87. John Letcher, July 21, 1873, "Appeal to the Descendants, in the Great North-West, of the Scotch-Irish Settlers of the Valley of Virginia," folder 440, John Letcher Papers, Mss1 L5684 a FA2, VHS.

88. Conservative party platform, August 7, 1873, 21–22, in Hunter, *Speech of Hon. R. M. T. Hunter, delivered at Richmond* (n.p., 1873).

89. Eric Rauchway, *Blessed Among Nations: How the World Made America* (New York: Hill and Wang, 2006), 76–77.

90. "Texas-Pacific Railroad," November 19, 1875 (Memphis, Tenn., 1875), folder 444, John Letcher Papers, Mss1 L5684 a FA2, VHS.

91. Barry Wilkes to John Letcher, folder 445, John Letcher Papers, Mss1 L5684 a FA2, VHS.

92. Henry A. Wise, *Address of Henry A. Wise at West Point, Virginia, December 29, 1874, to the Knights of Pythias, on their Invitation* (Richmond, Va.: n.p., 1875), 8–9.

93. Scott Reynolds Nelson, *Steel Drivin' Man: John Henry, the Untold Story of an American Legend* (New York: Oxford University Press, 2006), 11.

94. On railroad mania and its discontents, see Mark Wahlgren Summers, *Railroads, Reconstruction, and the Gospel of Prosperity: Aid under the Radical Republicans, 1865–1877* (Princeton, N.J.: Princeton University Press, 1984); Wise, *Address of Henry A. Wise at West Point*, 14.

95. Wise, *Address of Henry A. Wise at West Point*, 9.

96. On these points, consider Hearden, *Independence and Power*, 55; and Kvach, *De Bow's Review*, 161–166.

97. Hunter, *Letter to Rep. Lamar on the Texas and Pacific Railroad, January 26, 1876* (Richmond, Va.: n.p., 1876).

98. Ibid.

99. For Confederate ambitions into northwestern Mexico, see Donald S. Frazier, *Blood and Treasure: Confederate Empire in the South West* (College Station: Texas A & M University Press, 1995); Rachel St. John, "The Unpredictable America of William Gwin," *Journal of the Civil War Era* 6, no. 1 (2016), 56–84; and Brettle, *Colossal Ambitions*.

100. Hunter, *Letter to Rep. Lamar*.

101. See also Hearden, *Independence and Empire*, xiv.

102. See Brettle, "Confederate Imagined Relations with the Federals in the Postwar Order."

103. Hunter, *Letter to Rep. Lamar on the Texas and Pacific Railroad, January 26, 1876* (Richmond, Va.: n.p., 1876).

104. See Brettle, *Colossal Ambitions*.

105. On free trade imperialism, see John Gallagher and Ronald Robinson, "The Imperialism of Free Trade," *Economic History Review* 6, no. 1 (1953), 1–15.

106. For the tariff as a way of life, see Richard Franklin Bensel, *The Political Economy of American Industrialization* (New York: Cambridge University Press, 2000); for understanding the market-expansion thesis in the context of an absence of a clear U.S. foreign policy, see Robert L. Beisner, *From the Old Diplomacy to the New, 1865–1900* (Arlington Heights, Ill.: Harlan Davidson,1986), 21–31.

107. On these points, consider Robin W. Winks, "Imperialism," in *The Comparative Approach to American History*, ed. C. Vann Woodward (New York: Basic Books, 1968), 253–270; and Hearden, *Independence and Empire*, 53

108. Consider Egnal, *Clash of Extremes*, 326–347, and Hearden, *Independence and Empire*, 55.

109. On the downward pressure on tariffs during the late antebellum era, see Marc-William Palen, *The Conspiracy of Free Trade: The Anglo-American Struggle over Empire and Economic Globalisation, 1846–1896* (New York: Cambridge University Press, 2016), 3. On Confederate planning, which evolved from free trade to commercial treaties, see Brettle, *Colossal Ambitions*.

110. R. M. T. Hunter, *Address to the Alumni of the UVA at Charlottesville by Hon. R. M. T. Hunter on Wednesday, June 30, 1875* (Richmond, Va.: James E. Goode, 1875), 15.

111. On these points, consider Beisner, *Old Diplomacy to the New*, 77–83; and Kagan, *Dangerous Nation*, 341–346.

112. Consider Karp, *This Vast Southern Empire*.

113. For Hunter's earlier comments, see *The Congressional Globe*, 36th Congress, 2nd Session, December 3, 1860, to March 3, 1861, in The Official Proceedings of Congress (Washington, D.C.: John C. Rives, New Series), no. 1, 229.

114. R. M. T. Hunter, "Speech of R. M. T. Hunter of Virginia at Tammany Hall, New York, Friday Evening, September 13, 1872," *Venango (Franklin, Pa.) Spectator* September 26, 1872.

115. Hunter, June 30, 1875, *Address to the Alumni*, 15.

116. Diary entry of Edward Archer, April 27, 1865, VHS.

117. John Randolph Tucker, *John Randolph Tucker of Virginia in the House of Representatives, May, 8, 1878, on the Revision of the Tariff* (Washington, n.p., 1878), 37, 39, 40. For the parallel argument that the tariff created the Republican Party coalition, see Bensel, *The Political Economy of American Industrialization*, 1–18.

118. Tucker, May 8, 1878, *On the Revision of the Tariff*, 39.

119. Hunter, June 30, 1875, *Address to the Alumni*, 15.

120. Ibid., 23.

121. See Palen, *The Conspiracy of Free Trade*, 56–113.

122. Consider William Alan Blair, "The Use of Military Force to Protect the Gains of Reconstruction," *Civil War History* 51, no. 4 (2005), 388–402.

123. Tucker, *On the Revision of the Tariff*, 23.

124. Ibid., 36–37.

5

James Redpath, Rebel Sympathizer

Lawrence B. Glickman

Over the course of what one obituary writer called his "strange and eventful career," James Redpath (1833–1891) was the Zelig of the nineteenth century. Like the character in the Woody Allen film of the same title, Redpath found himself in historically significant situations again and again, engaging with almost every prominent social movement in the nineteenth-century Atlantic world and rubbing shoulders with the era's notables.[1] A pioneering journalist who invented the newspaper interview, he was also, by turns, an abolitionist, a Reconstruction official, the founder of a speakers' bureau, a labor advocate, and an enemy of the British Empire. He helped coin the word "boycott" in 1880 in Ireland and disseminated it in the United States.[2] He was a friend or acquaintance of Frederick Douglass, John Brown, Thomas Edison, Walt Whitman, Mark Twain, and Henry George. As "a champion of unpopular causes," he embraced almost every radical movement of his era, from abolition to Radical Reconstruction to women's rights to tenants' rights to opposition to the death penalty.[3] As his friend Whitman said, "Redpath was one of your radical crowd—he was way out and beyond in all his ideas." Redpath himself described his life's trajectory not as a matter of radicalism but as a consequence of his love of freedom; as he said in 1881: "I had always loved liberty anywhere and everywhere."[4] The title of the abolitionist newspaper he founded in Kansas in the 1850s, *The Crusader of Freedom*, would seem to encapsulate his life's work, both before and after the Civil War.[5]

At sharp odds with his embrace of radical causes and of his relationships with social and cultural radicals, toward the end of his life, Redpath formed a close bond—a "great friendship"—with Jefferson Davis. Indeed, he helped Davis, the former president of the Confederate States of America, craft and popularize essays and books that defended that short-lived slaveholding republic. More than a defense of the Confederacy, Davis's oeuvre, with its critique of Reconstruction and support for "Redemption," amounted to an endorsement of a continuing regime of white supremacy.[6] As his biographer William Cooper notes, Davis became "the living embodiment of the Lost Cause," and his unrepentant views about slavery and secession became the dominant view in the post-Reconstruction nation.[7] Such views helped justify the emerging system of Jim Crow.

Redpath's transformation and his embrace of Davis was already puzzling observers before his death in 1891, as it has historians ever since. African American commentators, including contributors to the prominent Black newspaper, the *Christian Recorder*, joined former abolitionists, Southern conservatives, and others in trying to make sense of his stances. As the obituary writer who called Redpath's career "strange" observed: "It was one of the peculiar echoes of our times that this original abolitionist and prime factor in the dreadful results of that agitation learned to look on Mr. Davis in a new light . . . and to openly admit the honesty and justice of many of the ex-Confederate's principles."[8] A writer in 1890, after reading a sympathetic assessment of Davis by Redpath, wondered how an "abolitionist and union man" became "a convert to Davis."[9]

Whether or not "convert" is the right term, Redpath did develop a sympathetic relationship with Davis and his family. Redpath first encountered Davis through his work as an impresario and editor. As with many of his business associates, Redpath developed a friendship with Davis. Redpath became acquainted with Davis in 1875 when he attempted to recruit him as a lecturer for his lyceum bureau. They reconnected later in Redpath's role as an editor when Redpath invited Davis to respond to a critical article in the *North American Review*.[10] They began a correspondence and finally met in the summer of 1888, when Redpath traveled to Davis's estate, Beauvoir, in Biloxi, Mississippi. There, Redpath helped Davis with a number of literary projects, encouraged Davis to write a history of the Confederacy, and became close with Davis's wife, Varina. The following summer, Redpath returned for three months to ghostwrite this manuscript, published after Davis had died in 1890, as *A Short History of the Confederate States of America*.[11] As one journalist commented in 1889, "The acquaintances of Mr. James Redpath, who know that he was one of John Brown's men in Kansas, are surprised at the fact" that Davis and he had been on "intimate terms for a number of years."[12]

It is notable that Redpath's ghostwritten and his signed defenses of Davis came out in 1890, the year that Mississippi became the first state to disenfranchise its Black citizens by a constitutional convention.[13] Redpath, who died the following year, could not have known, as the historian C. Vann Woodward famously put it, that the "Mississippi Plan" would become the "American Way," meaning that over the next two decades every Southern state would follow with a similar scheme to make it nearly impossible for African Americans to vote.[14] But one suspects that in other circumstances his radical self would have been on the frontlines warning of such a possibility. Rather than challenging this movement, Redpath echoed some of the arguments that the Redeemers had employed since the end of the Civil War.

This essay explains how an abolitionist and transatlantic radical wound up hobnobbing with Davis and his family and espousing what historian David Blight has called the "reconciliationist vision" that prioritized sectional peace at the expense of racial justice after the Civil War.[15] For his part, Redpath did once deny that he had shifted ideological grounds, saying of his friendship with Davis, "neither of us had changed our essential creed" but "each respected the other's convictions," adding that he hoped their relationship could become "a model for the whole country."[16] But such a statement did not capture the complexity of Redpath's evolving perspective and, what is more, concluded with an innocent-sounding wish that showed just how much his own views had changed. A helpful contrast is the admonition of Frederick Douglass in 1871 that the nation should not "in the name of patriotism . . . remember with equal admiration those who . . . fought for slavery and those who fought for liberty and justice."[17] Indeed, the reconciliationist drift of Redpath's thinking becomes even more evident when we look as well at his changing views of African Americans. The question at the heart of this essay, then, is how do we square Redpath's putative defense of the white South and seeming abandonment of the Black freedom struggle with his lifelong passion for radical causes, including his deepening commitment to anti-imperialism after the Civil War?

There is no smoking-gun evidence to answer this question definitively, and Redpath's relatively brief comments about their relationship can be read in several ways. But an examination of Redpath's post-Reconstruction career suggests that the answer lies with an ideological transformation that he began before he befriended Davis. Davis did not have to change Redpath's views; they had already been changing on their own. This transformation was complicated since he never explicitly announced a change of heart, but there is much evidence that he had one.

It is hard to reconcile Redpath's lifelong radicalism with his seeming embrace not just of Davis the person but of arguments about the legitimacy of the Confederate cause, of those who fought on its behalf, and of the need to celebrate their cause long after the war's conclusion. Within a decade of Redpath's death, several of the increasing number of Americans who sentimentalized the Civil War and celebrated reconciliation (and in so doing, accepted the racial caste system known as Jim Crow) mentioned this unlikely friendship as the embodiment of sectional reunion. A review of Thomas Nelson Page's 1899 novel, *Red Rock*, argued that Redpath was a model, noting that he "once trained with Higginson's gang, but late in life became a friend and admirer of Jefferson Davis." It was not only the friendship that was celebrated but also that Redpath accepted the view that white Southern actions before and after the war were "purely defensive."[18] In the 1960s, the Southern writer, Robert Penn Warren took this surprising turn in Redpath's life to be a sign of his maturation. He celebrated the former "ardent abolitionist" for recognizing that Davis "could not repent or recant what he believed to be true."[19] It was not just the improbable friendship that white Southern defenders of the old regime celebrated but the fact that Davis had supposedly won Redpath over to his way of thinking.

Historians have not known how to square the friendship and defense of Davis with his lifelong radicalism in general and his defense of the Southern freedpeople in particular. Redpath's leading biographer, John R. McKivigan, writes, "The unexpected friendship that developed between the former militant abolitionist and the former Confederate president between the late 1880s and early 1890s is possibly the single most uncharacteristic act of Redpath's life," and elsewhere McKivigan calls this friendship an "anomaly." Another historian called Redpath's friendship with Davis, "ironic,"[20] for Davis was not just the president of the short-lived Confederate republic but also one of the leading shapers of the postwar "Lost Cause" mythology. As David Blight writes, Davis's "fierce defense of states' rights doctrine and secession, his incessant pleas for 'Southern honor,' and his mystical conception of the Confederacy gave ideological fuel to diehards."[21]

Redpath's improbable and surprising friendship with Davis, although uncharacteristic, was rooted in the radical journalist's postwar ideas about race, imperialism, and the meaning of the Civil War. To be clear, Redpath hated slavery throughout this life and never backtracked on that core belief. He also remained an economic and cultural radical, and continued to support a variety of progressive causes, including women's rights and, most notably, the 1886 New York City Mayoral campaign of the land reformer Henry George, which mobilized the working class as few elections had before or since.[22] But toward the end of his life, the person who wrote *The Roving Editor: or Talks with Slaves in the Southern States* before the war downplayed the struggle for African American equality in the United States.[23] Redpath, moreover, developed an anti-imperialism that was not only unaccompanied by his long-standing antiracism and concern for African American freedom, but at odds with these. His acceptance of the legitimacy of, if not complete agreement with, Davis's views rested on his ideological twists and turns through the postbellum nation and world.

This becomes clear when we examine his complex postbellum understanding of the limits of Reconstruction, his ethnographic imagination, his constricted view of landlordism, his view of Irish peasants as more victimized than enslaved African Americans, and his sometimes condescending perspective on the postbellum Black freedom struggle. None of this is to suggest that Walt Whitman was wrong about Redpath's radicalism. But Redpath was also a figure of his time and place, especially in his interpretation of the meaning of the Civil War in the decades after its end. The man who, because of his fierce rhetoric, had to deny publicly that he was encouraging the murder of British landlords in 1882, never came close to hinting at a need to punish economically, let alone physically, the landowners who initiated the Jim Crow system of debt peonage and land expropriation.[24] Regularly in his postbellum periodical, moreover, Redpath expressed interest in contemporary racial theories. He spoke about "the Irish and Hebrew races," often in celebratory terms. But when he invoked racial theory about African Americans, it was almost always in the negative.[25]

These changes coincided, then, not only with Redpath's friendship with Davis but with his increasing identification with Irish and Irish American political struggles. Since the 1990s, scholars have examined "how the Irish became white" and how, as "in-between peoples," some Irish Americans, as did other not-yet-white immigrants, disparaged African Americans.[26] There is no evidence that Redpath saw his solidarity with Irish peasants and Irish American workers as coming at the expense of his sympathy for oppressed others. Indeed, anti-imperialism led him to extend his concerns. Yet he did not propose an alliance between Irish Americans and African Americans and while he compared their oppression on occasion, he usually did so to highlight the exploitation of the Irish. Redpath was far from alone in internationalizing his reform impulses during the post–Civil War years, but whereas for many others foreign entanglements represented an extension of their prewar radicalism, for Redpath the connections were more complicated.[27]

James Redpath was a transatlantic radical, a "natural agitator" "with radical views on social and economic questions," whose career linked antebellum and post–Civil War reforms.[28] Born in Berwick-on-Tweed, near the border of England and Scotland, he immigrated to Michigan as a teenager, where he found work as a printer and journalist. Just as the sectional crisis was heating up, he wound up at Horace Greeley's *New-York Tribune*. He also became "an Abolitionist of the most radical school from his earliest manhood," and much of his journalism revolved around the question of slavery.[29] He interviewed enslaved people and met John

Brown, the radical abolitionist. After Brown's death, Redpath did much to shape his legacy, with his laudatory biography, *The Public life of Capt. John Brown*.[30] During the Civil War, he covered the war with the Union Army in South Carolina, Georgia, and Tennessee. In this same period, he became a lobbyist for the Haitian government, which was seeking diplomatic recognition, and he worked on a plan to encourage African Americans to emigrate there. During the last years of the war, he published cheap paperback books, primarily for Union soldiers. Immediately after the war, he served as school superintendent, presiding over an interracial public-school system, in Charleston, South Carolina, where he supervised dozens of instructors who taught 3,500 African American and white students. Later he started a professional lecture booking agency, later known as the Redpath Lyceum Bureau, whose clients included the abolitionists Douglass, Charles Sumner, Wendell Phillips, and Anna Dickinson, as well as humorists such as Mark Twain, Josh Billings, and David R. Locke (known as Petroleum V. Nasby).

Yet in the late 1870s—the conventional end period for Reconstruction—Redpath, the former school superintendent in Charleston, blamed some of Reconstruction's failures on African Americans and apologized for former Confederates. Redpath's status as a former radical was trumpeted by Southern journalists, who often prefaced his remarks with "Even James Redpath" to suggest that if the formerly radical abolitionist had come to his senses on reconciliation between Northern and Southern whites, so should everybody else. To take one example, the *Shreveport Times* in 1876 called Redpath "one of the reddest of the original abolitionists" who was now speaking the "healthy truth" about African Americans. In this Southern view, Redpath offered a critical realism that served as a healthy response to his previous racial utopianism. That same year, a time when the retreat from Reconstruction was almost complete, Redpath said, "There is no desire among any class to secede again, or make war against the union. Therefore, there are no rebels. Let us drop the word."[31] Redpath's comments along these lines suggested the limitations of his analysis. His argument was narrowly true but raised broader structural questions: Why would white Southerners try to secede or make war when they had not only defeated Reconstruction but gotten most white Northerners to agree with their perspective, in the era that they called Redemption? Defenders of the racial caste system in the South may have lost the war, but they largely won the peace, a factor that Redpath did not take seriously in his analysis.

Redpath came to support an evolutionary view that the achievement of African American freedom was a long-term process that was in sharp contrast to the abolitionist immediatism he embraced before the war. Toward the end of Reconstruction through the era of Redemption, Redpath embraced a conservative "realism" in his approach to the possibilities of African American freedom. "We must look at the negro as he is, before we shall ever be able to aid him," he declared in 1876. "Sentimental Abolitionism was well enough in its day," he wrote, diminishing the relevance of the movement that defined him through the end of the Civil War. "Mississippi owes its present sad condition as much to sentimental Abolitionists as it does to fiendish negro haters," he wrote, suggesting that humanitarian sentimentalism was as dangerous to African Americans as the blatant and structural racism they increasingly faced as Reconstruction collapsed. (It is interesting to read Redpath's comments here alongside Mark Elliott's chapter in this volume, which points to the continued power of humanitarianism among some postbellum Northern reformers.) Redpath's conclusion did not mince words: "The blacks were ruined as good citizens by the chronic prattle about their rights and they were never roused to a noble manhood by instruction of their duties." Exactly why discussion of civil rights was "prattle" and what "duties" they were failing to perform, Redpath did not say.[32]

As the counterrevolution against Radical Reconstruction gained momentum, Redpath seemed increasingly to side with those who claimed that African Americans were not ready for freedom. In 1876 he pronounced what he took to be the "facts about the Negro in the South." He declared that the freedom movement in Mississippi was "timid, unarmed, intimidated," but rather than inquiring as to how armed white opponents using terrorist tactics contributed to that mood, he looked for cultural answers. Even where Blacks were in power—"the bottom rail on top," as the expression had it—Redpath claimed that it was a "rotten rail at that." Rather than treating violence and exploitation as tactics that needed to be opposed with government support, he declared the problems faced by Southern Blacks to be "insoluble for the present generation." He portrayed the problem as a conundrum: "Let the Negroes exercise their rights as citizens, and their government is almost sure to be corrupt; but the alternative is Hamburg massacres and virtual disfranchisement and slavery." He thus depicted the poles as either Black corruption or white violence and deemed them both repugnant. The article noted that "Mr. Redpath does not see any hope" in the short term. Any true hope was "afar off" and "consists in education and Christianization" for African Americans, which he described as "a very slow process." The author concluded by noting that "Mr. Redpath notices the ignorance of the Negro. He doesn't mention their immorality and superstition."[33] Long before Redpath met Jefferson Davis, then, he had embraced some of the central arguments of the critics of Reconstruction. By depicting African American political power as "corruption," deferring the quest for justice indefinitely, refusing to consider means to stop violence against Black people, and labeling African Americans uniquely "ignorant," Redpath's rhetoric was little different from that of a standard-issue Southern "Redeemer."

His evolutionary view that Black progress should proceed slowly was reflected in Redpath's embrace of what Booker T. Washington later came to call "industrial education" for African Americans. As editor of the *North American Review* in the 1880s he commissioned articles titled "The Folly of Trying to Make Classical Scholars of the Negroes" and "How Shall the Negro be Educated?"—both of which suggested that developing skills for the agricultural workforce was the most productive way to promote citizenship.[34] (For a similar debate centered on education in the U.S.-occupied Philippines, see Brian Shott's chapter in this volume.) In 1879, a "colored professor writing under the name Un Sang-Mele ("a mixed-race"), criticized Redpath's constricted view of Black leadership. Noting that Redpath "has long been identified with every movement to liberate, enfranchise and elevate our race," Sang-Mele expressed disappointment about Redpath's unfair criticisms of "professional colored men."[35]

Redpath made his racialist views more explicit in a piece from 1877, when he offered his perspective on the keys to Black advancement, a message much like the one that Washington was soon to popularize. His advice to Southern Blacks was "to pay less attention to politics and seek power through business." Drawing a sharp distinction between electoral battles and economic advancement, he argued that the former was not helpful. Perhaps Redpath based this calculus on a hard-headed recognition that Black political opportunities were extremely limited as Reconstruction unraveled. But he framed the advice more generally. His comparative group that had supposedly succeeded in business while eschewing politics was instructive: "Become the Jews of America." Offering his theory that every "race" faced a choice between "force and conciliation," he proposed that Blacks follow the Jews in selecting the latter option. "The black race cannot fight," he claimed, unlike the "Anglo-Saxon race." Once again, it was unclear whether this advice was tailored to the moment or was meant to be a broader generalization about the nature of the "race": "It would be exterminated if it followed that option. It must win power by the arts of peace." Redpath offered that it was best understood as advice from "Iago," but we might think him more Panglossian: "Work! Buy land! Own your homestead and patch or garden! Go to school! Get rich!" Disconnecting economic mobility from political power, Redpath also argued that African Americans should be willing to leave their beloved homestead if it proved politically difficult to hold onto it. "If a state refuses your protection, leave it and seek a home elsewhere." His final advice to African Americans was to "cease to array yourself against whites in politics."[36] This was remarkable advice as it depicted African Americans as unsuited to politics and as political competitors with whites in general—not just white supremacists. In a period of Social Darwinism, when many intellectuals employed evolutionary thinking, it is important to distinguish Redpath's views from more egregious racist perspectives. Redpath never came close to suggesting, as S. W. Moulton, the Illinois congressman, did in 1882, that "the Anglo-Saxon race is pre-eminently and infinitely the superior of the colored race."[37] Yet he did accept racial essentialism and, in some cases, a racial hierarchy, even as he claimed that these could be erased in some indistinct future.

Redpath also grew increasingly critical of the Republican Party and, for a time, in 1877 encouraged "colored people to join the Democratic Party." While Redpath may have been alienated by the Republicans' decreasing commitment to civil rights and not just his increasingly pessimistic views about the fight for racial equality, evidence suggests the latter was key. The *Mississippi Clarion-Ledger* reported with glee that this former "Kansas Shrieker" was renouncing his radical politics.[38] Redpath used his belief that Republicans did not represent African Americans well to make a broader critique of claims about disfranchisement. In 1888, he said, "There is a good deal of cant about the suppression of the Negro vote," an ambiguous statement that could be read to say that he was not particularly bothered by voter suppression or that it was not so widespread as to need to be addressed. He also wrote out of history the immense political gains made by African Americans during Reconstruction. As he put it, "The negroes never had anything to say—any influence whatever—during the Reconstruction period—about the practical management of their party or the selection of candidates."[39] He furthermore criticized carpetbaggers, despite having been one, as "honest" and "sincere humanitarians" but misdirected. Using an argument that he had made previously, he said that they "turned the negroes' head by constantly championing their rights and never or rarely explaining their duties. They consolidated the black vote as a distinct and hostile force against the white one."[40]

In the 1880s, the peripatetic Redpath, tiring of his business, returned to his roots as an activist-journalist, this time with a focus on Ireland. He traveled there several times, and he lectured widely on Irish nationalism while in the states. He also served as vice-president of the Anti-Poverty Society, an organization led by Father Edward McGlynn that focused on improving urban, ethnic (particularly

Irish) neighborhoods in New York. He launched *Redpath's Illustrated Weekly* (later *Redpath's Weekly*), which became, during its run of little more than a year, perhaps the leading anti-imperialist journal in the United States. Focusing on the evils of colonialism, it spoke particularly to an Irish American audience. Yet this transnational turn in Redpath's thinking elaborated a racial paradigm and exacerbated his negative views of African Americans. In its pages, as well as during this period of his career more broadly, we see a growing gulf in his views of African Americans and other oppressed groups, often discussed as "races," especially the Irish and Irish Americans. Yet Redpath's views were racial in inconsistent ways. Egyptians suffering under British rule and Chinese immigrants confronting prejudice from Americans, for example, still garnered Redpath's concern. His sympathy extended, in particular, to colonized peoples of the British Empire. But here too, this was often in contradistinction to his opinions of African Americans, who, as Reconstruction faded away, faced the second-class citizenship of the emerging Jim Crow system. This radical anti-imperialist newspaper rarely if ever advocated for African American civil rights.

Redpath aimed for his periodical to speak for the Irish to Irish Americans and their allies. As he wrote in the first issue, "I shall write chiefly for the native Americans, not of Irish origins, and ignorant of Irish wrongs; and for that young American generation of Irish parentage who are not so familiar with that grander Thermophalaen fight which their ancestors have maintained against vaster than Persian disparity of numbers for seven long centuries." What was notable was that the newspaper, founded for an Irish American audience, aimed its reformist animus at subjugated peoples in the entire British Empire, not just Ireland.

Redpath's anti-imperialism had many dimensions. His journalism was consistently anti-English in ways grand and petty. For example, in an article about Queen Victoria, he called her the richest and "most miserly women in the world."[41] He called the United States minister to England, James Russell Lowell, "namby-pamby" and noted that "he mingles only with the cream of the English and foreign aristocracy, and although a simple American citizen, bears the title of Excellency."[42] (One 1881 profile of the "Savage Redpath" noted not only his political radicalism but also complained that "he spoke in most derogatory terms of Queen Victoria and the Duke of Edinburgh.")[43] His critique of English civilization—Redpath generally wrote specifically about the "English" rather than British—went well beyond his dislike of the snobbery he associated with the royal family and their acolytes. He saw it as engaged in murderous exploitation. An article titled "The English Civilization Fraud" (1883), for example, focused on a famine in India in which "seven million of Hindoos perished."[44]

Redpath's Weekly regularly linked victims of British imperialism from India and Egypt to Ireland and the United States. As Redpath wrote in an early issue, "From an English point of view, you know, there are three very unreasonable nations in the world—the Irish, who refuse to starve any longer for the benefit of English absentee landlords; the Egyptians, who are unwilling to be taxed to the point of famine for the benefit of English absentee capitalists; and the Yankees, who stubbornly decline to have their native industries ruined for the benefit of English absentee manufacturers." He noted on July 22, 1882, that "the wicked human race is getting more and more disinclined to permit England to continue to be a chartered plunderer of mankind."[45] The following week Redpath pronounced, "Egypt is entitled to our sympathy." Using the racial language that he employed regularly on behalf of Egyptian independence, he claimed, "She is fighting for the right of her people to rule the land in which their race has lived long before the dawn of modern civilization." He continued, "Irish readers, who know how persistently and how wickedly England has lied about Ireland not only for the last seven centuries," should sympathize with Egyptians. He sought to encourage his readers to see themselves as linked equally with Egyptians as with the Irish as victims of imperialism. "Every person who may be killed in Egypt during this war will be murdered by England, which has no more right to rule Egypt, or to bombard Alexandria, than she has the right to rule America, or to bombard New York."[46] Redpath's anti-imperialism made him particularly sensitive to "races" ruled by foreigners, but perhaps desensitized him to the racial caste system of the United States, where African Americans were citizens, albeit second-class ones.

Redpath was particularly sensitive to negative, dehumanizing images of the Irish in popular culture. A critic of cultural stereotyping, he was also a proponent of evolutionary racial thinking. He despised the way "Irish life and affairs are represented by the English press." He explained in a typical passage that "Ireland, in the English press, is painted several degrees lower in the scale of degradation and brutality than Dahomey or Ashantee, it being an old English habit to defame and slander every people they are engaged in robbing the better to divert attention from their own crime." This is an ambiguous sentence. On the one hand, Redpath paints the Irish and two African ethnic/political groups to be equally victims of British imperialism. On the other hand, he claims that the British press depicted the Irish as more degraded than these groups, suggesting that there might have been a particular humiliation in being ranked below sub-Saharan Africans. In either reading he is defending the Irish against English critics. Later in the same article Redpath wrote, "What is true of Ireland is also true of Egypt,"

Figure 5-1. "Resources of Civilization: John Bull Defending 'British Interests' against Irish and Egyptian 'Rebels,'" *Redpath's Illustrated Weekly*, July 29, 1882, 16. Digital Library@ Villanova University, https://digital.library.villanova.edu/Item/vudl:222235#?c=&m=&s=&cv=15&xywh=-13495%2C-1%2C32031%2C6939.

mockingly noting the limits of the "account of the 'massacres' perpetuated by those terrible Egyptians on the inoffensive Europeans."[47] In an editorial cartoon (see Figure 5-1), he depicted John Bull as uncivilized in comparison with Irish and Egyptian "rebels."[48] Redpath thus linked the fates of the Irish and the Egyptians, as co-equal victims of English racial prejudice.

Moreover, Redpath repeatedly implied that the Irish, Egyptians, and Indians suffering under British rule were more oppressed than the enslaved people before the Civil War and African Americans after it, even during the height of the backlash against Reconstruction. He emphasized the need for Irish Home Rule and "self-ownership of her soil" and demands for "still further justice."[49] But he did not explicitly connect these demands for Irish emancipation to African American freedom struggles and often implicitly ranked the former above the latter. "If a community of suffering were of the nature to bring its subjects together, surely the Irish and the Africo-Americans would be the best of friends," noted an 1880 article about Redpath in the African American newspaper, the *Christian Recorder* (a publication that also features prominently in Christina Davidson's chapter in this volume). Yet after Reconstruction ended, Redpath himself rarely, if ever, made this connection among oppressed peoples. Although he argued vigorously against the view that Irish "tenants are too ignorant, lazy and improvident," he did not make the same claims on behalf of African Americans in the postbellum years.[50]

Whereas Redpath frequently referred to the Irish "race" (as well as the "Hebrew race") in positive terms and denounced the racialized stereotypes of the Irish—by, for example, condemning the ways in which the English depicted "the Irishman on the stage as only a little higher than the baboon"—he did not combat racist depictions of African Americans.[51] The *Weekly* rarely mentioned African Americans, but one article titled "A Negro Baptism in Georgia," by Redpath's close associate Christine Faber, indulged in repeated racial stereotypes, especially having to do with African Americans dressing above their station—a form of slander addressed in detail by historian Thavolia Glymph.[52] The Savannah-born Faber described the participants as representing "every shade of colored people, from the face as black as Cerberus, to the features so light that the finger nails alone betrayed their negro origin." After describing the "startling fashions," Faber noted, "One ludicrous feature seemed to be that the larger and blacker was a negress, the gaudier and most fantastic was her costume." Faber suggested that the guests may have been dressed "to copy the fashions of their 'dandified' white brethren." Faber also commented on a "gayly-bedecked negress in our vicinity impressed with her importance," who "gave herself befitting airs" and commented on her dialect.[53] Finally, despite his consistent condemnation of British racism toward its subject peoples, Redpath published some cartoons that depicted African Americans in stereotypically racist ways. In one cartoon (Figure 5-2) called, "Getting Ready for Mrs. Langtry," for example, a small Black servant, perhaps a child, helps groom a tall, foppish, white man for an audience with the famous English actress, Lily Langtry.[54] Another cartoon (Figure 5-3) contrasted "English Theory" and "Irish Reality" to show the desperate lives of Irish peasants. But there was no equivalent cartoon depicting the reality of life for African Americans in the Jim Crow era versus the way they were depicted by white Southern landowners.[55]

Moreover, Redpath's post-Reconstruction anti-imperialism sometimes led him to inadvertently compare the conditions of African American slaves with those of Irish peasants and to pronounce slavery less onerous. Looking back at his career as an abolitionist in 1882, Redpath said, with some justification, that "no one used stronger words that I used to denounce slavery in America." "No white man, I can say without boasting, knew more about slavery than I knew.

Figure 5-2. "Getting Ready for Mrs. Langtry," *Redpath's Illustrated Weekly*, November 16, 1882, 16. Digital Library@Villanova University, https://digital.library.villanova.edu/Item/vudl:222469#?c=&m=&s=&cv=15&xywh=-12966%2C0%2C30743%2C6660.

Figure 5-3. "The Lie and the Truth: English Theory and Irish Reality," *Redpath's Illustrated Weekly*, February 24, 1883, 1. Digital Library@Villanova University, https://digital.library.villanova.edu/Item/vudl:222703#?c=&m=&s=&cv=&xywh=-13015%2C0%2C30669%2C6644.

For during my journeys I did not ask only the whites about slavery—as English travelers in Ireland ask the landlords about the land agitation—but I used my own eyes and spoke with tens of thousands of slaves. Hence, I hated slavery." Redpath may have exaggerated the degree to which he was the leading white expert on slavery, but his bona fides were unquestionable. Yet in the last decade of his life, he used this knowledge not to promote civil rights for African Americans but to argue that, from a comparative perspective, Southern Blacks were less oppressed than other groups.

In 1881, in between trips to Ireland, Redpath attended a dinner in his honor in New York City. His speech that evening was telling. "I never uttered a kind word—I never expected to be able to utter a kind word—about American slavery or American slaveholders," he began, reflecting on his history and continuing identity as an abolitionist. But, he noted, after visiting western Ireland, he had changed his mind. "Compared with Irish landlords, our southern slaveholders were noble philanthropists," he declared. "I never saw a southern slave so meanly lodged, or so poorly clad, or so badly fed as three millions of industrious and virtuous Irish peasantry are lodged and clad and fed at this very hour," Redpath concluded.[56] Redpath stated as well that "as far as their animal comforts were concerned, the slaves of our Southern States were better fed and better clad, and better housed, than nearly two millions of the peasantry and farm laborers in Ireland at this hour."[57] It is unlikely that Redpath meant to genuinely praise slave owners, but this comparison served to make chattel slavery in the prewar United States seem to be a more humane system than landless peasantry in Ireland. Considering that African Americans were no longer enslaved, Redpath's suggestion was that a comparison of African Americans in the postwar South to Irish peasants was doubly unfavorable to Black people. Redpath's generalizations were based on brief visits with representatives of both groups, albeit separated by decades, and may well have reflected his observations. But even if so, the accumulated impact of such claims, which he made repeatedly, was to undermine the battle for African American equality, which he mentioned only infrequently after the end of Reconstruction.

Two final pieces of evidence capture the complex ways in which racial thinking increasingly shaped Redpath's views of African Americans during this period without quite leading him to a doctrinaire and uniform version of white supremacy. It is instructive to compare Redpath's weakening support for African American civil rights with his attitude toward the anti-Chinese movement in the United States. Anti-Chinese sentiment was strong, especially in the labor circles in which Redpath traveled. Yet in 1880 Redpath denounced Denis Kearney, the leader of the movement in California and himself an immigrant from Ireland, as a "cruel and illiterate demagogue." He said that the issue was "not a simple problem" and "not a mere question of equal rights and human brotherhood," and he noted that the movement often pitted immigrants against each other. "It is Paddy against John; still more it is Bridget against Ah Sin," he wrote, highlighting the gendered nature of the labor conflict. Nonetheless, he noted that white workers "have legitimate fears." The *Christian Recorder* praised his efforts, less because of his ambiguous defense of Chinese laborers on the West Coast and more because he accused immigrant "white" workers in California of hypocrisy for condemning another immigrant group. These people pledged "to cease to be a foreigner, and to become an American," and yet "Irishman and German rule the city of San Francisco" because politicians pander to "this alien and morally unnaturalized vote."[58] Yet Redpath did not extend this sort of sympathetic judgment to African Americans or criticize their oppressors.

A final way in which *Redpath's Weekly* hinted at his negative views of African Americans and his coming alliance with Davis came in his treatment of American culture. The theme of regional reconciliation ran through the periodical, even though it was not its primary mission. In an 1882 article Redpath noted that "Irish-Americans (like native Americans) were found bravely fighting under the Federal and Confederate flags." (In referring to "native Americans," Redpath meant native-born, not Indigenous.) He concluded that "the South has a record of Irish-American valor as well as the North." By highlighting military "valor" rather than the justice of the cause for which soldiers fought, Redpath contributed to the increasingly common reconciliationist view that all soldiers should be celebrated for their bravery. Underplaying the degree to which the Irish fought for and supported the Union side during the Civil War, Redpath contributed to the idea that fighters on both sides were noble and not fundamentally different. And in doing so, he ignored the prominent role that Irish Americans played in the New York City "draft riots" of 1863, which included significant anti-Black sentiment.[59] In the epigraph for this article, Redpath wrote, "Now that the 'cruel war is over,' America claims as her possession the renown of Grant and Lee alike."[60] Redpath also promoted the notion that the United States was made up of regions, each with its own folk customs. He compiled jokes and customs from the West, "Yankee Notions," "From Dixie's Land," "Hawk-eye-lets," "Pen-and-ink-sylvanias," and "Michigander Sauce."[61] In this geography, "Dixie" was just another region with its own quirks, on equal footing with the others. He did not mention African Americans as shapers of Dixie culture or of racial oppression as an element of this culture. Redpath's capacious and generous ethnographic imagination did not incorporate the descendants of the enslaved people whom he portrayed sympathetically in the journalism that brought him to national prominence in the 1850s.

In the postwar years, Redpath's anti-imperialism did not show much evidence of his prewar concerns for African Americans, and his pleas for religious toleration of Catholics did not include a broader call for racial justice. Nor did he match his critique of British colonialism with an understanding of internal colonialism in his adopted country of the United States. Redpath treated the problem of prejudice against the Irish as structural as well as cultural. He criticized the British on a systematic material basis. As he said in 1880, "Irish landlordism is a feudal system shorn of its feudalistic basis, which exacts all rights and duties of ownership in the soil, but recognizes no duties to the men who cultivate it."[62] He repeatedly condemned the British exercise of power, as he had not in his analysis of the American South in the late 1870s. He did not make similar critiques of anti-Black sentiment, Jim Crow laws, or Southern white supremacist terrorism.

Redpath's criticisms of African Americans, magnified by his racialist anti-imperialism, laid the foundation for his friendship with Jefferson Davis and his embrace of sectional reconciliation. If Redpath's view of slavery remained negative, his celebration of Southern soldiers' heroism showed that, notwithstanding his former abolitionism, he embraced the underpinnings of the Redemptionist worldview. In 1860, Redpath condemned those who would "cover the crimes of slavery with the mantle of legitimacy."[63] And although he never renounced his hatred of slavery, he did excuse the Confederates who fought to preserve and expand that institution and the Redeemers who wished to promote a racial caste system. And whereas before the Civil War, he made it a point of pride to "see with my own eyes the condition of the negro slaves and to hear their stories from their own mouths," this is something he appeared to stop doing after the end of the Reconstruction period, when his main informants about the realities of Southern life were reactionary white elites, such as Davis, his wife, and youngest daughter, also named Varina.[64]

After the failure of *Redpath's Weekly*, for financial support Redpath returned to editing, working with the *North American Review* and *Belford's Magazine* in the late 1880s. It was in this last phase of his life that Redpath befriended and collaborated with Jefferson Davis. Redpath usually expressed his admiration for Jefferson Davis in terms of character rather than politics, but the two became closely connected in reconciliationist mythology, which held that the proslavery cause, like the pro-union position, was led by noble people. Politics, moreover, worked its way into the profile of Davis that Redpath published in the Denver monthly, the *Commonwealth*, in 1890. Davis's face bore "emphatic evidence of gentle, refined and benignant character," according to Redpath, who noted both his "goodness" and his "intellectual integrity." Perhaps because he was speaking to an audience that might not have been predisposed to admire Davis, Redpath did not stint in his praise, "He seemed to me to be the ideal embodiment of sweetness and light." His conversation, Redpath said, unironically quoting Davis's archenemy, Abraham Lincoln, showed that he had "charity to all and malice toward none." He was a "valiant Knight" and the epitome of the "Southern character." Redpath noted that Davis never repented and that he "regarded himself as neither a traitor or a rebel."[65] Rather than challenging Davis's self-conception, Redpath accepted it, alongside the Confederate conception of history that such a view underwrote.

Although clearly Davis altered Redpath's views about the meaning and justification of the war, there is no evidence that the reverse was true. Notably, for a person who had emphasized the need to hear from the testimony of enslaved people before the war, Redpath described the South as if it were exclusively white. When he wrote in the *Commonwealth*, "We could not afford to let the brave Southern people drift into a foreign country," he did not seem to be accounting for African Americans as part of this "people." He claimed, "They are too noble a people for any Nation—or Federation—except the United States to claim." Throughout his essay, "Southerners" and the "Southern people" were assumed to be white. Moreover, following from Davis's ideas, he claimed that "it is time to drop, and drop forever, the war-cant about Rebellion and Treason," and he noted, improbably, that the South did not fight for slavery.[66]

Redpath claimed to be won over by some of Davis's arguments about the right of secession and the causes of the Civil War. But he remained steadfast in suggesting that Davis had not budged him from his antislavery, pro-freedom views. In the context of the death of Reconstruction, it is hard to read Redpath's concessions about the legal rights of Confederates as not also granting legitimacy to the views of Redeemers, who wished to make white supremacy the law of the land. This was especially so because of Redpath's view of the "South" as a white monolith—as "Dixie"—contrasted sharply with how he depicted that region prior to the War. No doubt, if Redpath felt that his interactions with Davis left his own views of race unchanged, it was in large part because he had already moved so far from his prewar stances.

Redpath's biographer, John McKivigan, has defended him against the charge that he "softened his abolitionist principles" as a result of his friendship with Davis and sympathetic treatment of the Confederacy. "Although Redpath came to respect the old Confederate's uncompromising position on the doctrine of state's rights, he never made any concession to Davis's views on race," McKivigan writes. He notes, "In private correspondence during the period, Redpath often complained about the stifling intellectual conservatism of the Davis household." Indeed, Redpath pledged, "When I get through his work I shall popularize the most radical book on Socialism that I can find." But the judgment here is harsher. There is a difference between private grousing and public statements, which have broader political significance. Moreover, it is notable that Redpath thought the proper response to the Davis family's proslavery apologetics was "socialism" and not a defense of the specific cause of Black freedom.[67] Faced with the racial conservatism of the Davis household, Redpath may have been irked by their stodginess, but he could not bring himself to speak on behalf of the Southern freedpeople whom he had long since turned his back on. Redpath may not have been fully a "convert" to Davis's philosophy, but he publicly defended it as a legitimate perspective on the United States and its recent history and made himself into a spokesperson for sectional reconciliation.

Redpath's post-Reconstruction career—with its emphasis on social reform, his continuing interactions with celebrities, and his activist journalism—seems of a piece with his roots in abolitionism. His commitment to the Irish people was so strong in the last decade of his life that many people incorrectly assumed that he was a native of Ireland.[68] One could view his sympathy with the plight of the colonized Irish and largely working-class Irish Americans, which became the leading passion of his life, as an extension of his prewar and Reconstruction work for justice for enslaved Americans and freedpeople. Yet as we have seen, he had toward the end of Reconstruction begun to revise his views about Black freedom. His work in Ireland and his anti-imperialism did not reinforce, but undermined, his commitment to Black freedom. He did remain a radical, but one whose racialism drove a wedge in his own mind between African Americans—to whom he had devoted so much of his career—and the other "races" of the world.

It is ironic that, as Caroline E. Janney has shown, some white union veterans, many of whom began their enlistments as anything but abolitionists, grew increasingly radical in their remembrance of the war as a "redemptive" victory of "free labor" whereas Redpath, the radical abolitionist, drifted from this message in later years.[69] In this context, his sympathetic appreciation of and collaboration with Jefferson Davis seem less anomalous and more consistent with his late-career commitments. It would seem hard to see how a person with his history and allegiances would come to sympathize and bond with the unrepentant leader of the Confederacy. But by the time they met Redpath had already revised his views about the fight for racial equality in light of his critique of Reconstruction and his emerging anti-imperialism.

In 1883 Redpath looked back on his thirty-five-year career of agitating "in behalf of the less favored classes of society" and saw a pattern of continuous support for the liberation of oppressed peoples. "Hardly a day, and I think never a week has passed since then, in which I have not spoken or written, or spoken and written, or done or tried to do, something to lift up an oppressed class or help an unpopular cause or to advance a boycotted truth."[70] Although Redpath continued to describe the arc of his career in these terms, in the last decade of his life he largely replaced his focus on African Americans, first with his interest in the victims of English colonialism, particularly the Irish, and second, with his sympathetic consideration of Southern whites, like Davis. Even though he frequently spoke of the need for "equal and exact justice," Redpath applied different standards in his treatment of Irish peasants and African Americans.[71] Whereas his discussion of Irish peasants was primarily structural, focusing on property ownership, poverty, and political power, his observations on Southern African Americans in the postwar years tended toward the cultural, with a focus (often condescending) on folkways and political liabilities. Whereas he found the root of Irish oppression in British landowners, he emphasized other elements than the counterrevolutionary actions of white elites and politicians in his efforts to explain African American oppression in the post-Reconstruction South.

Given the seemingly obvious parallels between the plights of two politically disfranchised agricultural people largely prevented from land ownership through a caste system, it is surprising that Redpath limited his critique of landlordism and racial stereotyping to Ireland. It is notable that whereas he remained critical of those who represented power in the British Empire, such as the queen, the final group in the United States to attract his sympathy consisted of formerly treasonous, exploitative white landowners such as Davis. His relationship with and defense of Davis do not fit easily within the rest of his career. Ex-Confederates portrayed themselves as an oppressed class, but large landowners such as Davis would hardly have qualified from Redpath's anti-landlord point of view. The resolution to the quandary lies with how Redpath, who published a book of interviews with enslaved people before the war and who worked to create interracial public education just after it, seemed to stop listening to African Americans as time passed. He denounced landlords in Ireland and New York but not in the states of the former Confederacy, where he counseled patience and industrial education, and sometimes even engaged in behavior that today we would call "blaming the victim." His most extended stays in the South after the end of Reconstruction were his visits in successive summers to Davis's plantation, where he left behind no record that I have found of his interactions with the local African American population. Well before Redpath formed a friendship with Jefferson Davis, then, he seemed to be abandoning his earlier views about the centrality of African American freedom struggles to his overall conception of social justice. This timeline suggests that his friendship and defense of Davis should not be viewed as the cause of his political transformation but as following changes that had begun in the late 1870s.

James Redpath had a remarkable career that should not be reduced to one relationship in the final, often unhappy, years of his life. It would be wrong to view him, even in the 1880s, as abandoning his previous commitments. At the same time, this essay has argued that his sympathetic portrayal of Davis is not inexplicable—that signs could be found in his reassessment of Reconstruction, his embrace of racial theories, his belief that the Irish peasantry suffered a fate worse than slavery, and his embrace of reconciliationism. Redpath spent his career sympathizing with society's underdogs. While he continued to reject the cause for which the Confederacy fought, Redpath, like many others, came to see Davis as yet another rebel who was entitled to sympathy.[72] Race clearly played a crucial role in facilitating that shift of sympathies, even if it did not produce a uniform white supremacist vision that would have excluded sympathy for the Chinese and Egyptians.

Notes

1. "The Death of James Redpath, the Noted Journalist: His Strange and Eventful Career," *Baltimore Sun*, February 11, 1891, 1. *Zelig* (1983), directed by Woody Allen).

2. On Redpath's significant role in the history of consumer activism, see Lawrence B. Glickman, *Buying Power: A History of Consumer Activism in America* (Chicago: University of Chicago Press, 2009), 111–126.

3. The quotation is from William Boyd, "James Redpath and Negro Colonization in Haiti, 1860–1862," *Americas* 12, no. 2 (1955), 176.

4. John R. McKivigan, *Forgotten Firebrand: James Redpath and the Making of Nineteenth-Century America* (Ithaca, N.Y.: Cornell University Press, 2008), 181, 161.

5. Mentioned in Charles F. Horner, *The Life of James Redpath and the Development of the Modern Lyceum* (New York: Barse & Hopkins, 1926), 88. An 1860 newspaper described Redpath as "a rather radical abolitionist." "Pen and Press," *Berkshire County Eagle*, May 10, 1860, 2.

6. "A Convert to Davis," *Manning Times*, February 26, 1890, 1.

7. Quoted in Charles McCollum, "William J. Cooper Jr. Probes Jefferson Davis's Character," *Civil War Book Review* (2001) https://digitalcommons.lsu.edu/cgi/viewcontent.cgi?article=1561&context=cwbr. See also William J. Cooper Jr., *Jefferson Davis, American* (New York: Vintage, 2001), 691–692.

8. "Death of James Redpath."

9. "Convert to Davis"; "Neither Rebel nor Traitor," *Commonwealth* (January–February 1890).

10. McKivigan, *Forgotten Firebrand*, 182–183. See also *Vermont Watchman and State Journal*, September 8, 1875, 2, which notes that "Jefferson Davis couldn't accept Mr. James

Redpath's invitation to lecture . . . but it is quite possible he will speak there at some other time."

11. "A Convert to Davis." Jefferson Davis, *A Short History of the Confederate States of America* (New York: Belford, 1890). Chapter 10 of McKivigan's biography is called "Jefferson Davis's Ghostwriter."

12. "About People and Things," *Indianapolis Journal*, July 20, 1889, 4.

13. Caroline E. Janney, *Remembering the Civil War: Reunion and the Limits of Reconciliation* (Chapel Hill: University of North Carolina Press, 2013), 199.

14. C. Vann Woodward, *Origins of the New South, 1877–1913* (Baton Rouge: LSU Press, 1951). Chapter 12 was called "The Mississippi Plan as the American Way."

15. David Blight, *Race and Reunion: The Civil War in American Memory* (Cambridge, Mass.: Harvard University Press, 2001), 2. See also Janney, *Remembering the Civil War*, 197–231.

16. James McPherson, *The Abolitionist Legacy: From Reconstruction to the NAACP* (Princeton, N.J.: Princeton University Press, 1975), 112.

17. Quoted in Blight, *Race and Reunion*, 106.

18. Wallace Reed, "Higginson and Page: Why They Disagree," *Atlanta Constitution*, March 7, 1899, 4.

19. Robert Penn Warren, *Jefferson Davis Gets His Citizenship Back* (1965; Lexington: University of Kentucky Press, 1995), 85–86.

20. McKivigan, *Forgotten Firebrand*, 181. McKivigan used the word "anomaly" in his *American National Biography* entry on Redpath. Tom Kiffmeyer, "Words Not Bullets: The Literary Career of James Redpath," *Reviews in American History* 37, no. 1 (2009), 35.

21. Blight, *Race and Reunion*, 259.

22. James Redpath, "Failure of Male Government," *Redpath's Illustrated Weekly*, September 2, 1882, 2.

23. James Redpath, *The Roving Editor, or Talks with Slaves in the Southern States*, ed. John R. McKivigan (1859; State College: Penn State University Press, 1996).

24. "Personal," *Austin Weekly Statement*, August 17, 1882, 1.

25. *Redpath's Illustrated Weekly*, July 29, 1882, 2.

26. Noel Ignatiev, *How the Irish Became White* (New York: Routledge, 1995); David Roediger, *The Wages of Whiteness: Race and the Making of the American Working Class* (New York: Verso, 1991) Matthew Frye Jacobson, *Whiteness of a Different Color* (Cambridge, Mass.: Harvard University Press, 1998); James R. Barrett and David R. Roediger, "In-Between Peoples: Race, Nationality and the 'New Immigrant' Working Class," *Journal of American Ethnic History* 16, no. 3 (1997), 3–44; Nell Irvin Painter, *The History of White People* (New York: Norton, 2010).

27. See David M. Prior, *Between Freedom and Progress: The Lost World of Reconstruction Politics* (Baton Rouge: LSU Press, 2019); Leslie Butler, *Critical Americans: Victorian Americans and Transatlantic Liberal Reform* (Chapel Hill: University of North Carolina Press, 2007).

28. The quotation is from the *Chicago Inter-Ocean*, October 25, 1880, 4.

29. "A Convert to Davis," *Manning Times*, February 26, 1890, 1.

30. James Redpath, *The Public Life of Capt. John Brown* (Boston: Thayer and Eldridge, 1860).
31. "Mississippi," *Quad-City Times*, August 16, 1876, 2.
32. "Political Notes," *Shreveport Times*, September 8, 1876, 1.
33. "The Facts about the Negro," *Independent*, August 3, 1876, 16.
34. McKivigan, *Forgotten Firebrand*, 179.
35. Un Sang-Mele, "Colored Men by Profession: A Reply to James Redpath by a Colored Professor," *New-York Tribune*, May 24, 1879, 3. This was written in response to Redpath's article "Professional Colored Men," in the May 10 issue.
36. James Redpath, "A Policy for the Blacks," *Anderson Intelligencer*, April 26, 1877, 1.
37. "The White Race Will Rule," *Austin Weekly Statesman*, August 17, 1882, 1.
38. "James Redpath's Advice to the Colored People," *Jackson Clarion-Ledger*, May 2, 1877, 2.
39. This view is belied by Eric Foner, *Freedom's Lawmakers: A Directory of Black Lawmakers During Reconstruction*, 2nd ed. (Baton Rouge: LSU Press, 1996).
40. "James Redpath," *Pensacola Commercial*, September 19, 1888, 2.
41. "The Stingiest of Women," *Redpath's Illustrated Weekly*, August 19, 1882, 11.
42. *Redpath's Illustrated Weekly*, July 29, 1882, 15.
43. "Savage Redpath," *San Francisco Bulletin*, January 12, 1881, 2.
44. "The English Civilization Fraud," *Redpath's Illustrated Weekly*, May 25, 1883, 7.
45. "Topics of the Time," *Redpath's Illustrated Weekly*, July 22, 1882, 146.
46. *Redpath's Illustrated Weekly*, July 29, 1882, 2.
47. "Notes on the Pictures," *Redpath's Illustrated Weekly*, July 29, 1882, 15.
48. "Resources of Civilization: John Bull Defending 'British Interests' against Irish and Egyptian 'Rebels,'" *Redpath's Illustrated Weekly*, July 29, 1882, 16.
49. "Topics of the Week," *Redpath's Weekly*, December 1, 1883, 3.
50. *Christian Recorder*, September 2, 1880, 2. Christian G. Samito in *Becoming American under Fire: Irish Americans, African Americans, and the Politics of Citizenship During the Civil War Era* (Ithaca, N.Y.: Cornell University Press, 2009), discusses the period before Redpath got involved in the Irish cause. See also David T. Greeson, "Securing the 'Interests' of the South: John Mitchel, A. G. Magrath, and the Reopening of the Transatlantic Slave Trade," *American Nineteenth Century History* 11, no. 3 (2010), 279–297.
51. *Redpath's Weekly*, December 22, 1883, 2.
52. For an excellent analysis of the the politics of dress in the postbellum South see Thavolia Glymph, *Out of the House of Bondage: The Transformation of the Plantation Household* (New York: Cambridge University Press, 2008).
53. Christine Faber, "Negro Baptism in Georgia," *Redpath's Weekly*, March 29, 1883, 11. See also Lynda L. Hinkle, *Reaping the Whirlwind: Regaining the Irish Catholic Literary Voice of Nineteenth-Century America through the Work of Christine Faber* (Saarbrücken, Germany: LAP Lambert, 2013).
54. "Getting Ready for Mrs. Langtry," *Redpath's Illustrated Weekly*, November 16, 1882, 16.
55. Cartoon, "The Life and the Truth," *Redpath's Illustrated Weekly*, February 24, 1883, 1.

56. McKivigan, *Forgotten Firebrand*, 161.

57. James Redpath, "In a Plague Stricken City," *Redpath's Illustrated Weekly*, September 30, 1882, 3. For very similar comments see *Proceedings of the Farewell Dinner Given by the Land League of New York for James Redpath* (New York: Bradstreet Press, 1881), 12; "Suffering Ireland," *Vermont Watchman*, May 12, 1880, 2.

58. Quotations from *Christian Recorder*, March 25, 1880, 2. See also James Redpath, "Jack Cade on the Coast," *Independent*, January 22, 1880, 4, James Redpath, "In Jack Cade's Camp," *Independent*, March 11, 1880, 2.

59. Iver Bernstein, *The New York City Draft Riots: Their Significance for American Society and Politics in the Age of the Civil War* (New York: Oxford University Press, 1990).

60. "Irishmen under Two Flags," *Redpath's Illustrated Weekly*, November 16, 1882, 8.

61. "The Merry Americans: Fun From All the Great Sections," *Redpath's Illustrated Weekly*, September 30, 1882, 11.

62. "Born to Be Fooled," *Philadelphia Times*, May 4, 1880, 2.

63. James Redpath, "John Brown's Intentions," *Liberator*, January 20, 1860, 3.

64. Redpath, "In a Plague Stricken City," 3.

65. James Redpath, "Neither Traitor Nor Rebel," *Commonwealth* (January 1890), 386.

66. Redpath, "Neither Traitor Nor Rebel," 392.

67. It is true that some critics of Reconstruction associated it with socialism, as in an article in the *Richmond Enquirer* that contrasted the "natural conservatism" of the white South with the "destructive radicalism of the socialists." Quoted in *Staunton Spectator*, January 1, 1867, 1.

68. "General News," *Kansas Catholic*, February 19, 1891, 3.

69. Janney, *Remembering the Civil War*, 202.

70. James Redpath, "Topics of the Week," *Redpath's Weekly*, December 1, 1883, 3.

71. James Redpath, "Egypt and Exodus," *Independent*, May 1, 1879, 2.

72. This was in keeping with broader cultural patterns in which Confederate soldiers and officials were seen by Northerners in sentimental terms. See Nina Silber, *The Romance of Reunion: Northerners and the South* (Chapel Hill: University of North Carolina Press, 1993), 48, 54.

6

"Our God-Given Mission"

Reconstruction and the Humanitarian Internationalism of the 1890s

Mark Elliott

In the expansionist 1890s, a growing number of Americans urged their government to use its diplomatic and even military clout to advance humanitarian causes in foreign lands. Victims of famine in Russia and India, of religious persecution in Armenia, and of imperial violence in Cuba all found sympathizers in the United States who organized relief efforts, mobilized public opinion, and lobbied the federal government for help. The expectation of support from the federal government was something new in the aftermath of the Civil War. The belief that the federal government had a responsibility to intervene in a crisis to mitigate human suffering gained tenuous ascendance. Grounded in a celebratory nationalism that understood the Union victory as a moral triumph over the illiberal forces of slavery and tyranny, *humanitarian nationalism* reinvigorated American exceptionalism.[1] Refugees, Black and white, faced homelessness and starvation in the South in the final stages of the war. Those newly emancipated left plantations en masse despite facing white violence and an uncertain future with their legal status and rights unsettled. Responding to the need for immediate action led the national government to undertake an extended occupation of the South. A similar dynamic played out in the 1890s when humanitarian nationalism had matured and Americans began to imagine obligations to act in the international realm.

This chapter explores four key figures whose lives connect the international humanitarian causes of the 1890s with the humanitarian nationalism of Reconstruction: Oliver O. Howard, Julia Ward Howe, Lyman Abbott, and Clara Barton. Each played an active role in both periods, and, through them, we can perceive the manifold ways in which Reconstruction served as a precedent, for good and ill, for overseas humanitarian aid.[2] In his 1907 autobiography General Oliver O. Howard mused about the unprecedented decision by Congress to create the Freedmen's Bureau, an unprecedented government agency, to deal with the Civil War's humanitarian crisis. Overwhelmed and lacking sufficient resources, Freedmen's Aid Societies and dozens of other private associations pressured the government to act to alleviate the deprivation, economic chaos, and violence against freedpeople. Still, the Freedmen's Bureau Bill cautiously established only a temporary federal agency. Even that was controversial among Republicans, as Howard explained: "This sort of legislation, in 1865, was quite new to our Government. It was the exercise of benevolent functions hitherto always contended against by our leading statesmen."[3] Though limited in scope, the agency would gradually expand responsibilities, taking up relief work previously left to charitable organizations and churches and establishing permanent educational institutions.

Howard felt that the Freedmen's Bureau signaled the start of a new nationalism marked by greater government responsibility for the welfare and protection of its citizens.[4] Before Reconstruction, he imagined it had been "hard to love a Government which, theoretically, was a mere machine and which could extend no sympathy to people in disaster, nor kindness to the impoverished." Perceiving the federal government as a source of emergency aid led Americans to a higher level of patriotism: "The Nation, as something to love and cherish and to give forth sympathy and aid to the destitute, began then to be more pronounced than ever before." Strengthened patriotism, he believed, brought greater national unity:

> I think we are growing to cherish more and more the idea of a single name for the Republic, and we are fast assuming that "America" should be that name. Every day we hear from the North, South, East, and West, the expression: "I am proud that I am an American."[5]

Humanitarian nationalism, to Howard, linked patriotism to deepened bonds of "sympathy" and a sense of moral responsibility between citizens. The Freedmen's Bureau disbanded after just seven years, but its mission to aid the deprived and suffering in times of disaster, and protect their most basic human rights, was becoming an expected exercise of federal power by the time of Howard's autobiography.[6] (On the linking of humanitarianism and nationalism, see also Andre Fleche's discussion of Federico Fernández Cavada in his chapter in this volume.)

Looking beyond the nation's borders, Howard regarded American overseas military interventions of the late 1890s as humanitarian acts. The occupations of Cuba, Puerto Rico, and the Philippines resembled to him the relief and educational work of the Freedmen's Bureau. Howard observed:

Our intervention in Cuba and our subsequent neighborly action toward the people of that island; our national efforts to lift up the people of Puerto Rico, and our sending instructors in large numbers to set in motion the work of education in the Philippine Islands: these and other benevolences suggested by this reference make the people of to-day feel that at last we have a Nation which cares for its children.[7]

His last point echoed the language of racial uplift, exemplified in the idea of the "white man's burden," characteristic of many white educators and missionaries, including Howard himself during Reconstruction. As we shall see, Howard actively participated in the Spanish-American War, which he celebrated as liberation from imperial tyranny. Moreover, he believed, the destinies of Cuba and Puerto Rico were to be absorbed into the United States and Cubans and Puerto Ricans to become full American citizens. He hoped the same might be true for Hawaiians and Filipinos.[8]

Many of Howard's generation of Unionists viewed the 1898 war with Spain as humanitarian in spirit. Out of the destruction of the 1860s emerged in the North new cultures of patriotism and formulations of national identity containing powerful strains of moral self-congratulation.[9] The newly integral role of women in public life, especially in patriotic remembrance of the Civil War, contributed to this phenomenon. Abundant scholarship has shown how women shaped Northern nationalism during the war and in their active role in patriotic societies afterward.[10] Women's relief work in the United States Sanitary Commission and other private and church organizations during the Civil War and Reconstruction added a gendered aspect to the Union victory as a triumph over indifference to cruelty and suffering. These organizations helped prepare the way for what Julia Irwin dubs the "new Manifest Destiny" of "benevolence and compassion" in which the United States presented itself to the world as a force for "international humanitarianism."[11] Irwin argues that this nationalist construct did not fully emerge until World War I, but the evidence in this chapter suggests it was already influential in the 1890s, and its foundations were laid in the 1860s.

Few historians have felt a need to explain why "humanitarianism" served as the central justification to invade Cuba. President McKinley's war message to Congress echoed years of editorial appeals in newspapers that called on his administration to do something to stop the carnage of the harsh Spanish suppression of the Cuban struggle for independence.[12] McKinley, a Civil War veteran, framed the war in humanitarian terms when he described intervention in Cuba as a noble and necessary act taken "in the cause of humanity and to put an end to the barbarities, bloodshed, starvation, and horrible miseries" suffered by the Cuban people.[13] Swept up in the humanitarian cause, Howard himself hoped to assume a position of command among the American invasion forces.[14] Well past his prime, the retired general settled for a position with the Christian Commission and joined American troops in the invasion of Cuba. His published memoir of his experiences during the Spanish-American War would be titled *Fighting for Humanity*.[15]

In the bitter debate over imperialism, more Americans supported American policies in Cuba and the Philippines than opposed them. More important, moralistic and humanitarian justifications could be found on both sides of the debate over empire, suggesting it was a powerful and widely shared element of nationalism. Humanitarian justifications resonated especially with Northerners who had lived through and supported Reconstruction. This rationale ought to be taken seriously and examined more deeply than it has been in the historiography.[16] The main figures in this essay all came from New England backgrounds, deplored slavery, championed emancipation, and took part in Reconstruction. They not only subscribed to what I am calling "humanitarian nationalism"; they also each contributed to its creation. Julia Ward Howe and Clara Barton especially illustrate the significance of women in this variant of nationalism. The lives of all four linked the 1860s and the 1890s and, in each decade, they urged national action on behalf of the oppressed and suffering, promoting democracy and individual rights but also, along with them, American hegemony.

As the author of "Battle Hymn of the Republic," Julia Ward Howe was an icon of the Union's victory. Though she became an active leader of the women's suffrage movement and pioneering organizer of the international peace movement, Howe remained best known for her patriotic anthem that depicted the Union Army as God's divine instrument redeeming the nation from the evils of slavery and treason. An accomplished public speaker, she never tired of reciting or performing "Battle Hymn" when called upon by admiring audiences.[17] Her famous war anthem was an imperfect reflection of her worldview as a feminist and pacifist. Like many abolitionists, however, she made an exception for the Civil War and regarded emancipation as a milestone in an unfolding global struggle against cruelty and barbarity.[18]

Julia Ward Howe's humanitarian nationalism was shaped by her marriage to Dr. Samuel Gridley Howe, who was a key architect of Reconstruction. At their marriage in 1843, Samuel was already famous as a celebrated champion of the Greek Revolution against Turkish rule, and Julia was enthralled by his reputation as a heroic and worldly crusader. Dedicating a book to him in 1868, she praised Samuel as a "strenuous champion of Greek liberty and human rights."[19] She became active in his political work, helping him edit an antislavery newspaper that urged the Lincoln administration to abolish slavery from the moment war was declared in 1861.[20] Samuel founded the Boston Emancipation League that sought to "sanctify" the Union cause and to "write Emancipation on our Banners."[21] To this purpose, Julia's "Battle Hymn of the Republic" was a powerful envisioning of the Union army as a force of liberation marching south to accomplish the divine cause of slavery's destruction.

Near the end the war, Samuel G. Howe coauthored a report on the condition of the freedpeople that has been called "the blueprint for radical Reconstruction."[22] After serving on the board of the United States Sanitary Commission during the war, which was itself a humanitarian endeavor to promote health and contain the spread of sickness and disease among soldiers, Howe was chosen by the War Department as one of three members of the Freedmen's Inquiry Commission to recommend policies for the war's aftermath providing for their "protection and improvement."[23] Because of his inclination to view things in terms of universal laws, Howe drew on academic resources, including racial science and economic theory. Howe traveled through the Union-occupied areas of the South to study the needs of the emancipated, but also to Canada West (modern Ontario) where a community of freedpeople thrived, many of whom had escaped American slavery before the war. Although his analysis was infused with dubious racial and climate theories, the conclusions were emphatic that Blacks would succeed as equal citizens if given a fair opportunity, including access to jobs and racially integrated schools. The final report suggested: "For a time we need a freedman's bureau, but not because these people are negroes, only because they are men who have been, for generations, despoiled of their rights."[24] Samuel and his colleagues warned against any well-meaning policies that would promote dependency by curtailing freedoms or equal rights, and made clear that the main threat to Black success was hostility from prejudiced whites. As the report concluded:

> Until they become a little accustomed to their new sphere of life; secure to them, by law, their just rights of person and property; relieve them, by a fair and equal administration of justice, from the depressing influence of disgraceful prejudice; above all, guard them against the virtual restoration of slavery in any form.[25]

How long this protection would be needed remained an open question. Samuel privately believed the military occupation of the South should last for many years.[26]

The guarantee of equal rights to freedpeople, as Samuel Howe hoped, became the centerpiece of Congressional Reconstruction. This principle was fully embraced by his wife, Julia, who, looking back, recalled that "I had by this time [Reconstruction] cast my lot with those to whom the right of the Negro to every human function and privilege appeared a point to be maintained at all hazards."[27] Her writings and personal journals from the Reconstruction period shows her reflecting deeply on political and moral philosophy, particularly the writings of Immanuel Kant, and developing her thoughts on the philosophical basis of universal suffrage, democratic government, and human rights. Her support of Black suffrage led directly to her embrace of women's suffrage, which Samuel also supported (although he did not support his wife's assuming a leadership role in the suffrage movement).[28] Both Julia and Samuel Gridley Howe, despite their egalitarian commitments, continued to believe in the superiority of Christian ethics. In their view, Christianity taught humane ideals and benevolent social behaviors that had paved the way for progress and the spread of democracy. Both could be harsh in their description of people they regarded as barbarous or immoral; they sometimes perpetuated racial or ethnic stereotypes and were influenced by racial/climate theories of intellectuals such as Samuel's friend Harvard professor Louis Agassiz. Nevertheless, they understood the struggle for freedom from slavery and tyranny to be universal, and they advocated for human rights everywhere.[29]

During the Reconstruction years, the Howes focused on the war for Cretan independence from Turkey (1866–1869) and afterward on the prospects of American annexation of the Dominican Republic. As David Prior has argued, they viewed these struggles through a "liberal nationalist" ideology that presumed an affinity among all peoples who sought to attain freedom from repression.[30] "Giving up the Cretans, therefore, to the Turks," Samuel told a Boston audience during Reconstruction, was "as unrighteous and cruel as seems now the proposal to give up the negroes, who fought with us and for us, to the dominion of their old masters, without even a ballot-box for defence."[31] The Howes sought independence for Crete, but supported Grant's plan to annex the Dominican Republic because they believed rights and freedoms would be best attained under American sovereignty. Julia would support American annexations in the 1890s for similar reasons. After the death of her husband in 1876, Julia carried on his internationalism but focused initially on her own concerns about international women's rights and world peace. Yet when another round of civil unrest in the Ottoman Empire turned into a major international crisis in 1894 Julia renewed her interest in the region.[32]

Sultan Hamid II presided over the brutal suppression of Turkey's Christian Armenian population, who were feared to harbor national aspirations, like the Greeks before them. As many as 300,000 Armenians in Turkey died in the Hamidian massacres from 1894 to 1896 at the hands of soldiers or villagers who seized Armenians' homes and property and left survivors to starve.[33] Thousands of Armenians fled to Boston and New York, where they found sympathizers among old abolitionists and Protestant reformers while the crisis in Turkey continued to escalate. Because of her fame and long association with the cause of Christian minorities in the Ottoman Empire, Howe found herself at the forefront of the movement for American intervention. Elected president of the Friends of Armenia association in February of 1894, she soon was calling for American warships to be sent to Turkey to "bring them to their senses."[34]

In speeches and newspaper editorials, Julia Ward Howe's case for American intervention in Turkey struck familiar notes. First, there was a humanitarian crisis that could be halted only by the action of a government with a military powerful enough to intervene to restore order. Second, there was an opportunity to "liberate" an oppressed population that she believed thirsted for liberal-democratic reforms. She emphasized that the Armenians were victims of religious persecution that deprived them of fundamental rights: "The Armenians demand only the most elementary of human rights, the right to security of life, honor and property."[35] Finally, she extolled Americanization as a solution. Speaking to an audience of Armenian émigrés, Julia welcomed their migration to America: "It is right that America should become an asylum for the oppressed of all nations. . . . I am glad there are so many Armenians in this country. You are our brothers now." She added, "I earnestly hope that we may be able to help you, and not you only, but the oppressed of all nations."[36]

In the Armenians, she saw a defenseless and pious population subjected to the "most hideous and systematic oppression," including having their "wives and sisters outraged before their eyes." Like the freedpeople in the South, they faced brutal assault against their basic human rights. In a speech at Boston's Faneuil Hall that the Massachusetts governor praised as a "prose Battle Hymn," Howe lamented the inaction of the civilized world. Reminded of how abolitionists had taken "the field for the emancipation of a despised race that had no friends," she urged Americans to "stand by our principles of civil and religious liberty" in throwing down the glove to the Turkish government. Where European powers have failed, she concluded: "I think that we, the United States, are called upon to play the part of Florence Nightingale; to take our stand and insist upon it that the slaughter may cease."[37]

Lyman Abbott, pastor of the Plymouth Church in Brooklyn, also took up the Armenian cause. Using his pulpit and also his general editorship of a popular Christian journal, *The Outlook*, Abbott was in a position to report extensively on the Armenian situation, raise substantial relief funds, and pressure the American government.[38] Abbott was a social gospel reformer whose nationalist ideals bore a strong resemblance to those of Reverend Josiah Strong, whose patriotic treatise *Our Country: Its Possible Future and Present Crisis* portrayed Americans as chosen by God to spread Christianity and democracy around the globe. Strong insisted that churches, not government, must take the lead in global proselytizing because their work would not be tainted by imperial ambitions or political interests.[39] Both held that, in Abbott's words, "the principles of religion underlie republicanism" because religion teaches love of one's fellow men and equality of all before God. Influenced by popular theories linking evolution to social progress, they believed all societies were destined to become more like America. Unlike Strong, Abbott inclined toward an activist state; he believed that government would have to be integral to this international program.[40]

Abbott's humanitarian nationalism hearkened back to Reconstruction. A newly ordained Congregationalist pastor when the Civil War broke out in 1861, Abbott took a keen interest in emancipation but cautioned that securing freedom and democracy would require a massive postwar effort. In a prescient 1864 newspaper editorial titled "Southern Evangelization" Abbott laid out a philosophy for Reconstruction that received considerable praise. The war itself, he claimed, had been only "the *preparation* for the Nation's Work."[41] In order to truly liberate the South, the government had to establish permanent institutions of freedom— "common schools and Christian churches" for Black and white alike. He announced: "We have to occupy the South not only by bayonets, but also by ideas." In 1865, General Howard entrusted Abbott with the task of coordinating the work of all the private Freedmen's Aid Societies and missionary groups so they could more effectively cooperate with the military-run Freedmen's Bureau. Abbott became secretary of the American Freedmen's Union Commission (AFUC), coordinating an array of denominations and benevolent societies while serving as editor of its publication, *American Freedmen*.[42] In 1867, assisted by General Howard, Abbott authored a detailed AFUC report on the conditions in the South based on the Freedmen's Bureau's papers. Published as *The Results of Emancipa-*

tion in the United States, it was a staunch defense of freedpeople and Howard's work. Reflecting later in his memoirs, Abbott continued to believe that, despite its faults, Reconstruction had been an unprecedented exercise in government benevolence, which ought to be considered one of the "great world movements of history."[43]

When he took up the cause of the Armenians in 1894, Abbott viewed the question of American intervention much in the same way that he had regarded the postwar South. In a sermon to the Plymouth Church on November 15, 1896, Abbott compared the violence of the Turks to "the massacres of the Ku Klux Klan in the South" against which the Grant administration had intervened with congressional backing.[44] Although Turkey was a sovereign, foreign nation, he insisted that the American missionaries and their property interests in Turkey had to be defended. He lamented: "We let our property be burned, our schools and colleges be closed, our men and women live in terror for their lives, and have as yet done nothing more than a gentle protest."[45] Although he did not directly call for military invasion, Abbott lauded instances of American military action such as when Madison sent a fleet against Algerian pirates or when "the guns of Sumter united the North." "We, as an American nation," he declared, "ought with the whole power of our government to protect American citizens on Turkish soil." He speculated that if the United States sent warships, both American citizens and Christian Armenians could be protected merely by hoisting an American flag outside their homes.[46]

Secular nationalism that asserted a special moral role for the United States in the world intertwined with Christian internationalism.[47] Ann Marie Wilson has noted in the Armenian relief campaigns the confusing and often contradictory blend of Christian universalism, religious bigotry against Islam, racism against Turks, and odes to humanity, democracy, and universal human rights.[48] Nationalism was often the ideological glue that held these disparate elements together. The secularization of Protestant reform and missionary impulses had been ongoing for decades, with Reconstruction serving as a major example of secular organizations working alongside religious ones to undertake relief work, establish schools, and cultivate democracy. Even E. L. Godkin, normally an implacable critic of both government activism and humanitarian reform, called the Armenian massacres "a crime against the human race" that every nation had a right to oppose. He added that it was the United States' particular role to do so: "There is no nation which could speak with greater force for the common rights of humanity than we could."[49] But through what agency could the nation act other than the military? One organization that embodied the humanitarian nationalism of the

Civil War which had advanced the secularization of humanitarian work was the American Red Cross.

Clara Barton, like her friend Julia Ward Howe, was a living symbol of American nationalism. Celebrated as America's "Florence Nightingale," Barton and the American Red Cross (ARC) embodied humanitarian nationalism and the expanding government responsibility for human welfare. A private organization with a government charter, the ARC aimed to provide relief to the suffering in wartime and to the victims of natural disaster. Funded by private donations, the ARC worked closely with the military and became a tool of diplomacy in the 1890s. Because it often operated alongside Christian charitable organizations, it might easily be confused for one (the ARC's cross symbol derived from the Swiss flag and was meant to indicate neutrality). Or its close association with the military might lead one to think it was a government agency, but the ARC's efforts were limited to the immediate relief of food, shelter, or medical aid rather than spreading Christian or democratic values.

Clara Barton made her name as a volunteer nurse during the Civil War, during which she was hallowed for attending to the wounded at the warfront. Though Barton had no official role in Reconstruction, she remained in the South for a year distributing supplies to refugees and then initiated a campaign to determine the fate of every Union soldier still missing in action. She testified before the Joint Congressional Committee on Reconstruction in 1866 then investigating the results of Andrew Johnson's policies. In what may have been the first female testimony ever heard by the U.S. Congress, Barton attested to the desperate condition of Blacks and to the violence of Southern whites under the new state governments.[50] Echoing the conclusions of Howe's *Report to the Freedman's Inquiry Commission*, she stated her opinion that Blacks were no different than whites would be under "similar circumstances," and that they would become capable citizens if provided with education and economic opportunity.[51] Like Howe, Barton believed that emancipation was the great moral, redeeming consequence of the Civil War.

Barton's humanitarian nationalism can be detected in her efforts to establish a chapter of the Red Cross in the United States. Barton joined the International Red Cross when she visited France during the Franco-Prussian War. She then returned home to launch a decade-long campaign to bring the Red Cross to America. She had to overcome the traditional American aversion of European entanglements to convince the government to sign the Geneva Accords of 1864. Secretary of State William Seward had refused to join the accords when urged to do so in 1866 by Henry Bellows of the U.S. Sanitary Commission. Despite the celebrated work of the USSC, Seward rejected the need for such an organization in peacetime. Barton campaigned for over a decade to reverse this decision, calling the government's failure to sign the Geneva treaty "shameful" and insisting that Americans, in her words, "would be the last to withhold recognition of a humane movement" if they understood it properly. Appealing to "patriotism and national honor," she sharply criticized Republican administrations in Washington for standing with the "barbarous nations" rather than the civilized world.[52]

Barton finally succeeded in getting the ARC a national charter in 1882 and served as its president until 1904. Her addition of an "American Amendment" to the Geneva treaty created a permanent peacetime mission for the organization by authorizing the ARC to operate not only to relieve the sufferings caused by war but also those caused by pestilence, famine, flood, earthquake, hurricane, and other natural disasters. The ARC established a mostly meritorious reputation administering domestic relief, especially following the 1889 Johnstown flood and an 1893 hurricane in South Carolina.[53] In 1892 the ARC extended relief into foreign territory for the first time, responding to widely published accounts of the suffering of millions of Russian peasants due to crop failures. The State Department authorized Barton to take the lead in coordinating American relief efforts, which saw extensive donations of corn by Iowa farmers that required shipping and delivery. Although the Senate approved allocation of funds and naval resources, the House failed to do so, and the ARC chartered a steamship on its own. Barton later included effusive letters of thanks and praise from Russian officials to the American government and its "kind-hearted" people, boosting the self-congratulatory idea of America's selflessness and generosity.[54]

The National Armenian Relief Committee and other groups aggressively recruited Barton to undertake a mission to Turkey. In January 1896, after spending a "delightful" evening hosted by Julia Ward Howe, Barton left from New York on a steamship packed with supplies and medical staff to front-page headlines and "crowded piers, wild with hurrahs."[55] Congress issued an unprecedented joint resolution in January of 1896 declaring it the "imperative duty" of the president to take the "most vigorous" and "decisive action" to stop the slaughter and protect the rights of Americans in Turkey. Pressured by the American press, foreign minister A. W. Terrell was able to get Barton a hearing in Constantinople with the Turkish minister of foreign affairs, Tewfik Pasha. Barton then used her reputation and diplomatic savvy to convince the minister to allow five separate ARC missions into the country under the protection and supervision of Turkish troops. To the dismay of some of her American backers, Barton promised to be "no respecter of persons" in distributing relief to the needy, whether Armenian or Turk, and she did not allow newspaper correspondents among her staff. "[We] shall not go home and write a book on Turkey," she told the Minister Pasha; "we are not here for that."[56] Her uniquely apolitical and secular organization helped earn her entry.

The ARC mission lasted for six months and achieved mixed success. She maintained the favor of the Turkish government by not challenging their claims of violence on both sides of a "civil war" between Christians and Muslims. Abbott's *The Outlook* reprinted each of Barton's dispatches under the title "Aid to Armenia" for months, even as she kept these nondescript but encouraging.[57] She did not witness any massacres, which had died down by the time of the ARC mission, but she did encounter immense suffering and deprivation in the survivors in Armenian villages ravaged by the attacks. The ARC worked with the American missionary organizations already in place to sustain life, rebuild communities, combat the spread of disease among survivors, and plant fields for the following year. Declaring "success more or less" in Barton's words, they departed having expended $116,000, while leaving the remaining $1,500 with American missionaries as an emergency fund.[58]

Historians have deemed the Hamidian Massacres as a transformative moment for U.S. humanitarian intervention. They raised the blunt question of whether the United States had the duty to intervene in a foreign country on behalf of the "rights of humanity," and the American press responded with a cautious "yes."[59] This question soon arose again. Even before Barton returned to the United States, a new humanitarian crisis was overtaking the press that would lead to an American armed invasion: the reconcentrados of Cuba. Long coveted by American slaveholding expansionists, the island had been the subject of various annexation schemes before the Civil War. But in 1868 a Cuban uprising against the Spanish rule attracted the sympathy of former abolitionists and antislavery leaders. Samuel Gridley Howe, Frederick Douglass, and other radical Republicans petitioned the Grant administration to extend recognition and support to the rebels, whose struggle they viewed as a logical consequence of American emancipation.[60] Spain's colonial regime survived the Ten Years' War that followed, though slavery was mortally wounded and abolished soon thereafter. When José Martí sparked the third uprising against Spanish colonial rule in 1895, the cause, "Cuba Libre," remained associated with emancipation. Cuban exiles in the United States, like the Armenian refugees, made powerful allies and found a platform for their cause in New York's popular newspapers.[61]

The outcry to intervene in Cuba intensified into a national issue in 1896 when the Spanish governor, General Valeriano Weyler, instituted his reconcentration policy to root out insurgents in the countryside. Reports peppered American newspapers of mass starvation, sickness, and the sadistic treatment of hundreds of thousands of Cuban peasants crowded into fenced encampments. In January 1897 the *New-York Tribune* was among the first to suggest that it would be an "advantage to the cause of humanity to dispatch without delay an American Red Cross mission of relief" to Cuba. "The Armenian venture," it declared, "has established the precedent" for intervention in war-torn regions even where the United States had no interests.[62] Barton gained permission to enter Cuba from the Spanish crown who accepted her "benevolent offer" based on her organization's political neutrality and admirable work in Armenia. But the mission was held up for months by President McKinley, who feared that an American presence would draw the nation into a military conflict. The fury of the press coverage of Cuba, its wild speculations about Barton's delay, and impatient calls for armed invasion led Barton to wonder, "Had the nation gone mad?"[63] When McKinley finally assented, in December of 1897, two other relief organizations had been formed that the State Department absorbed into the government-run Central Cuban Relief Committee, headquartered in New York and chaired by Stephen Barton, Clara's nephew and vice-president of the ARC. Her "benevolent" enterprise had become officially a government enterprise and a way for a Washington administration to satisfy the public demands for action.[64]

Julia Ward Howe's efforts on behalf of Armenia are well known, but she also contributed to the pressure for intervention in Cuba. One incident that particularly raised her ire was the plight of Evangelina Cisneros, the seventeen-year-old daughter of a Cuban revolutionary leader held in a Havana prison—a personification of Cuba as a damsel in distress. The reportedly beautiful "Flower of Cuba" imprisoned among "felons and outcasts" stirred action from American women. Forgetting her usual abstention from political issues, Clara Barton joined Howe in signing a petition for her release to the queen of Spain, and Howe published an impassioned appeal to Pope Leo XIII warning that the "eyes of the civilized world" were watching. Her clout was such that Pope Leo XIII graciously responded to Howe in a public letter that called upon the Spanish to employ "mercy." Cisneros later escaped to New York, with help from Hearst's newspapermen, where she used her celebrity to rally support for the Cuban revolution.[65]

Ever the internationalist, Howe sought to collaborate with Barton on another matter. Amid the Cuban controversy, another round of revolution in Crete was being put down by the Turkish government, and Howe wondered if Barton might be willing to "equip and charter a ship loaded with provisions" that could be delivered to the "starving people" of her beloved Greek isle. She hoped Barton could use her influence with the Turkish government to allow a relief mission to Crete despite there being a "blockade in full force."[66] But this plan apparently came to naught as Barton's attention remained focused on Cuba.

Barton's mission to Cuba kept the Red Cross in the spotlight throughout the final lead-up to the Spanish-American War. When the U.S.S. *Maine* exploded and sank in Havana Harbor on February 15, 1898, Barton was on the scene. Having dined on the ship just thirty hours before, she heard the explosion and raced to the scene where she administered to the survivors, cabling the president to say: "I am with the wounded."[67] Contrary to legend, the *Maine* disaster did not precipitate war. It was, as Abbott noted, humanitarian anger over the suffering on the island, conveyed by the previously anti-interventionist Senator Redfield Proctor (R-VT), that pushed America into war.[68] The testimony of Clara Barton and her ARC co-workers were prominent in Proctor's report and a fellow senator's who cited the Red Cross estimate of 420,000 Cuban deaths in the reconcentrados.[69] (Scholars estimate the lower but still substantial number of deaths from the policy at 150,000.)[70] "It must be seen with one's own eyes to be realized," Senator Proctor told the Senate, when describing emaciated women and children, huddled and naked on stone floors, overcrowded in small huts "torn from their homes, with foul earth, foul air, foul water, foul food or none, what wonder that one-half have died, and that one-quarter of the living are so diseased that they cannot be saved."[71]

Abbott, previously cautious about the furor over Cuba, found himself converted by McKinley's war message. In published sermons, especially "The Meaning of the War" in May and "The Duty and Destiny of America" in June, Abbott proclaimed the nation's emergence as "a light to the nations of the world and a salvation for all humanity."[72] After Dewey's naval victory in the Philippines, Abbott was already looking ahead to a postwar reconstruction of the Spanish colonies. Whether the United States declared a protectorate or annexed the territories or came to another arrangement was little matter in the end, he said, because the American responsibility would be to share the blessings of its civilization. The American flag, wherever planted, must "stand for the principles that are wrought into the very structure of our nation—self-government, peace, fair chance for every man, justice, mercy." Abbott understood expansion as providential—a responsibility that divine destiny thrust upon the American people: "We did not mean to free the Philippine islands but we have done it, and the responsibility of the Philippine islands is upon us whether we like it or no. The responsibility of Cuba and Puerto Rico will soon be upon us whether we like it or no. We must accept the responsibility with all that which it involves."[73] The righteous course of action was to send "an army of teachers to follow the army of occupation" and pledge them "our word to give them self-government as fast as they are prepared for it."[74] In his view, education, which had been the centerpiece of Reconstruction of the South, must be central to any society to be based on democracy and self-government.[75]

Julia Ward Howe expressed kindred sentiments in her essay "The Uses of Victory," published after the Spanish surrender in September 1898. Like Abbott, she saw a divine hand in America's military triumph. The American victory she saw as apiece with the "abolition of slavery" and "progress of the women's cause" in the unfolding of "freedom, justice, and good will among nations, classes and individuals." "Humanity at last takes the field for freedom!" she exulted about the military response to Cuba's distress call. Looking ahead to the occupation that would follow, she expressed confidence that American righteousness would prevail. "Let our efforts and our sympathies enlarge with the enlargement of our domain," she wrote, imagining a "reign of beneficence, intelligence, and justice" over the nation's new lands. This would be accomplished by an army of missionaries and educators, who, in her words, "bear no weapons" but "the spelling book, the grammar, the Psalms of David, the Promises of Christ." Whereas the soldier came to destroy, the teacher's mission "is to create citizens, which is far better." Democratic citizenship, moreover, meant a deeper cultural transformation, which Howe acknowledged when she added that their intention should be "to sweep away the accumulated moral filth of ages, to make whole races free with the freedom of the nineteenth century."[76]

The debate over imperialism began before the war itself. Some anti-imperialists such as Carl Schurz and E. L. Godkin expressed doubt about the nobility of American intentions. Others, such as Mark Twain, supported the pro-independence invasion of Cuba but reviled McKinley's annexation of the Philippines and Puerto Rico as a betrayal of national principles and prewar commitments.[77] At a mass meeting of anti-imperialists at Faneuil Hall in June 1898, a resolution urged: "A war begun as an unselfish endeavor to fulfill a duty to humanity . . . must not be perverted into a war of conquest."[78] These critics, interestingly, were most likely to draw parallels between McKinley's policies and Reconstruction. Reconstruction had not fared well in historical memory, and by the time of McKinley's presidency, it served as a powerful negative example of governmental intrusion.[79]

On the eve of war, Godkin warned that an American intervention would only result in "the opening of fresh fields to carpetbaggers, speculators, and corruptionists," and might even lead to "the admission of alien, inferior, and mongrel races to our nationality."[80] Even some staunch racial egalitarians, such as Moorfield Storey, the future president of the NAACP (National Association for the Advancement of Colored People), used Reconstruction as a cautionary tale. While assuming leadership of an anti-imperialist club, Storey sarcastically reminded his audience of the shortcomings of Reconstruction: "Shall we establish in Cuba a carpet-bag government, like those upon which we look back with such pride?" While still venerating the ideals of equality represented by emancipation and civil rights legislation, he lamented:

> Remember that when our government was at its best, fresh from the influence of Lincoln and with Sumner and his associates in the Senate, we could not give our Southern fellow-citizens, speaking our language and close at our doors, a reasonably honest government. Can we hope to succeed better with Cuba now?[81]

Quite a few prominent members of the anti-imperialist movement had been critics of Reconstruction, including Godkin, Storey, Carl Schurz, and Mark Twain, who had charged Grant and the Southern Republican governments with corruption and incompetence in the 1870s. In the 1890s, they remained deeply skeptical about the professedly selfless, benevolent purposes guiding American military occupation in Cuba, the Philippines, and elsewhere.[82]

"Benevolent assimilation" was the striking phrase McKinley famously used to describe his postwar program for the Philippines, which described plans for the other occupied territories as well. The purpose of the American occupation, he claimed, would be to prepare the former colonies for independence and self-government through a program of educational, economic, and religious "uplift." Their program recalled Reconstruction, if in complex ways. The need to provide immediate aid to the destitute, protect the rights (of some), crush a remaining insurgency, and construct the foundation for stable democratic governments—all of these had been goals of Reconstruction. Striking tones that sounded eerily familiar to the rhetoric of sectional reconciliation, McKinley insisted, "We come not as invaders or conquerors, but as friends," assuring the Philippine people that their "full measure of individual rights and liberties" would be respected.[83]

Many anti-imperialists expressed doubt about the self-governing capabilities of Cubans, Filipinos, and Puerto Ricans. Former Senator Carl Schurz expressed a dim view of tropical people and predicted civil war. "Inasmuch as in Cuba a large part of the revolutionary forces consists of negroes and mulattos," he observed, "high places of command being held by men of color, who, having done their share of fighting, will claim their share in 'running' the government, whose wars of factions are likely to become embittered by race antagonisms of peculiar acrimony." Nothing could be worse, he felt, than the United States becoming embroiled in an effort to ameliorate more "interminable race antagonisms," which were "an evil of which we already have more than enough."[84] He also responded to those sympathizers who had praised the Cuban insurgents and compared them to the American founders. The logic that "the insurgents in Cuba have exhibited splendid fighting qualities, and that they may therefore be trusted with equal capacities for self-government," he doubted.[85] The same argument for citizenship had been made on behalf of African Americans in the 1860s based on their Civil War service. In Schurz's view, this argument had been disproven. Possibly thinking back to Grant's proposal for the Dominican Republic, he warned readers that annexation would require that Cuba become a state of the union with full representation in Congress. This idea, he was sure, would be "appalling" to any who considered it.[86]

Initially, the humanitarian defenders of territorial expansion and annexation waved away concerns about the fitness of the local populations for self-government. Offering rosier estimations of local capabilities, they presumed that American occupation would be compatible with full enjoyment of individual rights. One defender of the Cuban insurgents was retired General Oliver O. Howard. In an 1897 newspaper interview Howard expressed his desire to see Cuba and Hawaii eventually annexed to the United States, though he believed it would require "the majority of the people of the islands" to favor it. He deemed Cuba more promising in that regard, and imagined that with its independence an infusion of Americans would quickly resettle there and "help create a stable government on the island and in time it will be taken into the United States."[87] Once the war broke out, General Howard preached brotherhood with Cubans and admonished American soldiers for their unwarranted "strong prejudice" against them.[88] Howard published an essay in the *Outlook* defending Cuban insurgents after the American command refused them entry to the defeated city of Santiago alongside the triumphant American forces. He was offended at the shabby treatment and American unwillingness to regard them as equals. "I cannot help feeling a strong sympathy for the sad disappointments of the Cuban patriots when we throw them off and treat them with a show of disrespect," Howard rebuked. "To despise the Philippine insurgents and the Cuban patriots and ignore all their patriotic aspirations would be a cruel abrogation of every principle for which the advocates of this war primarily contended."[89]

Howard's charges of hypocrisy mirrored those of the anti-imperialists, yet he never joined them, steadfastly championing annexation and American rule during the postwar occupations. Howard embodied many of the same contradictions as Howe and Barton. Like them, he was associated with a patriotic blend of human rights, peace work, mercy, Christian charity, and American militarism. Known as the "Christian General" for his religiosity, Howard scrupulously adhered to the Golden Rule's imperative to "love thy neighbor" and consistently preached human brotherhood.[90] But his piety never got in the way of doing his duty as a military commander during the Civil War and afterward. His experience in the West is especially instructive. After Reconstruction, Howard tried to uphold Grant's "Peace Policy" as the leader of American forces against "hostile" Indian nations who refused to remain on reservations. While he tried to coerce them peacefully—through a mixture of negotiation and intimidation—Howard did not refrain from making war on those who resisted. Reform-minded men like Howard believed that "civilizing" Indians by settling them on reservations was a humanitarian act necessary to protect them from total extermination by bellicose white settlers. Believing he understood their interests better than they did, Howard celebrated the tribes he defeated, even writing two admiring books about Chief Joseph and the Nez Perce.[91] His attitude toward the Cubans, Hawaiians, and Filipinos reflected a similar mix of sympathy and paternalistic concern for their future well-being.

Howard's expectations for postwar policies in Cuba echoed those he pursued during Reconstruction. Unfair descriptions of Cubans, he said, focused only on "the degraded masses, who in their distress, their poverty, and long oppression by cruel governors present but a sad view of humanity." Howard pointed to the many educated and propertied men among the insurgents, insisting that even the "degraded" ones would show themselves worthy under a just government.[92] "Some cry out that the Cubans are uneducated," Howard told a gathering of Congregationalists soon after McKinley's declaration of war, but he reminded them of the Americanization of Cuban refugees living in American cities: "We have been educating them for years and years. . . . I have no fear of the Cuban people not being able to govern themselves."[93] Howard's concluding statement in the *Outlook* encapsulated his humanitarian nationalist viewpoint perfectly. Describing America's postwar obligation, he wrote:

> We must lift them up by a generous, a noble, a Christian series of efforts.
>   It is our God-given mission, and the whole Christian world is watching to see if the great American Republic is equal to the strain. My own opinion

is unchanged, namely, that we should bind our allies to us by justice kindly administered, and finally, after the expulsion of the Spaniards, foster a genuine republic under a United States protectorate till a *bona fide* stability and prosperity shall be secured for the entire Cuban people.[94]

Howard felt that American kindness and benevolence would prevail despite the prejudice he had just acknowledged and condemned. But Howard's faith in American goodness would soon be tested.

Humanitarian expansionists, in presenting annexation as something other than imperialism, had to address two key points: whether the newly "liberated" people would have equal rights and whether their populations truly consented to American rule. After McKinley made the decision to annex the Philippines and Puerto Rico, his administration had to confront questions about rights and civic status. Were they Americans? Full citizens? Wards of the state? Or something in between? To the people of the Philippines, the president explained the decision to establish American governmental authority over the island in terms General Howard would applaud: "The mission of the United States is one of benevolent assimilation, substituting the mild sway of justice and right for arbitrary rule." But in order to achieve a stable and lasting government "for the greatest good of the governed" McKinley claimed that force would be necessary: "There must be sedulously maintained the strong arm of authority, to repress disturbance and to overcome all obstacles to the bestowal of the blessings of good and stable government upon the people of the Philippine Islands under the flag of the United States."[95] When insurgent leader Emilio Aguinaldo took up arms against American occupation in early 1899, the hollowness of McKinley's benevolence was revealed. Filipino democracy would have to wait until the resistance was crushed and American authorities believed the Philippine people were ready for it. The Supreme Court in the *Insular Cases* (1901) seemed to settle the question of rights by allowing Americans to administer its territories without extending full American citizenship.[96] Schurz had been wrong that the U.S. Constitution necessarily guaranteed citizenship rights to all inhabitants of American territories. Just as new legal doctrines were emerging to deny rights to American citizens at home in the Jim Crow South, the Supreme Court's invention of "non-incorporated" territory did the same for the inhabitants of the former Spanish colonies.

In the 1890s, Southern white supremacists were rolling back Reconstruction's reforms including voting rights, while many Northern Republicans looked the other way. But simultaneously, educational and missionary work endured. A consensus was emerging among white progressives that gradualist policies—

education and "uplift"—would solve the problems of racial animosity and inequality in the South. Howard's friend General Samuel Armstrong and his protégé Booker T. Washington were the most famous proponents of this viewpoint, and both Howard and Abbott were enthusiastic patrons of their schools. Benefiting from the uplifting influences of American nationalism, expansionists concluded, was an even greater blessing than immediately enjoying its citizens' vaunted rights and liberties.[97]

None of the four individuals in this essay lost faith in American benevolence after 1898, even after the annexations, the *Insular Cases*, anti-imperialist critiques, and bloody resistance by Filipino insurgents. Clara Barton had been the most circumspect about the use of military force in Cuba, which had disrupted her humanitarian mission and prevented aid from reaching thousands of needy Cubans, worsening the refugee crisis. Nevertheless, her reticence in debates over annexation and imperialism allowed the ARC to remain a symbol of American benevolence. "The army and navy embodied the power of the government in the Spanish War," Barton observed afterward, "but the Red Cross to large degree embodied the affectionate regard of the American people . . . and their great desire to mitigate in every possible way the sufferings resulting from exposure, disease and conflict."[98]

Barton never forgot the satisfaction she felt when McKinley broke precedent and chartered a U.S. Naval vessel to carry ARC relief supplies to Cuba. After the war, the United States government granted the ARC a long-sought exclusive charter enabling it to become the nation's official volunteer aid department. Senator Proctor himself introduced the bill in the Senate, and in June of 1900 McKinley happily signed it. Both wished to keep the Spanish-American War linked to Barton and her humanitarian purposes as the Philippine resistance raged on.[99] Barton was soon pressured into retirement as Washington bureaucrats seized hold of her organization, with 22 million Americans becoming members by the end of the First World War. Operating as a governmental agency, the ARC led in relief operations at home, as with the San Francisco Earthquake of 1906, and participated in relief efforts abroad in Portugal, Costa Rica, Mexico, Japan, and Russia. In 1917 the Red Cross moved into a grand, white marble headquarters close to the White House.[100]

The Spanish-American War reinvigorated Julia Ward Howe's stature. "Battle Hymn of the Republic" enjoyed renewed popularity, serving as an unofficial anthem of the war. Her powerful lines depicting American soldiers marching for God to "make men free" resonated with the popular celebration of the "selfless" cause. General Howard recounted singing Howe's "sacred" song with American soldiers about to deploy.[101] Rough Rider Theodore Roosevelt became so enamored of it that later, as president, he considered having Congress adopt "Battle Hymn" as the national anthem (until Southerners objected).[102] Conversely, Mark Twain wrote a biting anti-imperialist satire of the lyrics, opening with "mine eyes have seen the orgy of the launching of the Sword; He is searching out the hoardings where the stranger's wealth is stored."[103] Twain never published the lines, perhaps for fear of insulting the venerable American icon.[104] The *Outlook* carried a tribute to Howe on her eighty-fifth birthday in 1904, with her daughter describing her as a devoted supporter of President Roosevelt and "an imperialist, an expansionist, and a Republican dyed in the wool."[105]

Lyman Abbott continued to write nationalistic books—over twenty published after 1898—and edit the *Outlook* for another two decades until his death in 1922. In *The Rights of Man* (1902), he updated the philosophy of natural rights to fit turn-of-the-century evolutionary and scientific thought. He concluded that Reconstruction erred in giving Blacks the right to vote, commenting that "it is a mistake to suppose that every man has a right to vote in any community." Suffrage was not a natural right, but a means to protect natural rights that should be entrusted to those worthy of the responsibility. "This was our mistake," he conceded, attributing—much like James Redpath did, as Larry Glickman shows in this volume—the failure of Reconstruction to Black suffrage.[106] Yet he disdained the Jim Crow measures that allowed a "drunken white man" to vote while "the educated and cultivated Booker T. Washington" could not. Abbott believed that "the line shall not be a color line or a race line, but a line of character."[107] Abbott did not explain how character would be measured in order to exercise suffrage, but he seemed certain that, in time, American institutions would raise up all of the worthy regardless of race.

Abbott's conviction only grew over the years that there was never "a nobler war" in the "history of the world" than the Spanish-American War.[108] Colonial administration only affirmed the point. "Our government is admirably adapted for the work God has given us to do," Abbott wrote. "For our work is not to subjugate a people; it is not to govern a people; it is to develop in a people, through law, through commerce, through education, through religion, the power of self-government." He was convinced that democracy was the highest form of government because it demanded the most from its citizens. But democracy could not flourish until a nation had developed an advanced civilization. Having evolved furthest on the way to achieving this high stage of political development, the United States could now lead other societies down the same path. "No nation is better fitted, by the structure of its government," Abbott rhapsodized, "to take the lead in this great work of the world's civilization, and make of a barbaric community first a law-abiding people, then an industrious people, then an educated people, finally a self-governing people, than this our republic."[109] Unsurprisingly, he continued to support overseas interventions and in 1914 joined Theodore Roosevelt in forcefully advocating for American intervention in the First World War. When the nation finally joined the war in 1917, and President Wilson declared his intention "to make the world safe for Democracy," his appeal resonated with Abbott and echoed the interventionist justifications he had been making since 1898, and whose roots were in his plans for Reconstruction in the South.[110]

The aftermath of the Spanish-American War was not as kind to General Howard. During the occupation of the Philippines, he sacrificed something dearer than the arm he lost in 1862. Lieutenant Guy Howard, his oldest son, had served on General Howard's staff during the Indian Wars of the 1870s and as a quartermaster in the invasion of Cuba. His effectiveness in this position got him transferred to the Philippines in 1899, where he was given a difficult mission to supply General Lawton's division in a remote area of the interior of Luzon near San Isidro. Where the river got narrow, "a body of armed Filipinos, hiding in the tall grass" attacked the supply barges and fatally wounded Lt. Howard, who reportedly urged his troops to complete the mission before expiring. The news, which the general deemed "the heaviest blow our family has had," devastated the Howards.[111] His son had died fighting a people whom the general had praised as patriotic insurgents but one year earlier. Howard nonetheless steadfastly believed in the righteousness of the mission. Defending McKinley's Philippine policies, Howard stumped for the Republican's 1900 presidential campaign and openly disdained anti-imperialist criticism.[112]

Sacrifice in war often generates determination to continue fighting so that the sacrifice is not for nothing. The death of Guy Howard, in fact, would become a rallying cry to silence anti-imperialists. Frederick Chamberlin dedicated a patriotic polemic to his friend General Howard titled *The Blow from Behind, or Some Features of the Anti-Imperialist Movement* (1903). Lambasting critics of the war for cowardice, treachery, and dishonesty, Chamberlin deemed criticism of American soldiers unpatriotic, driving home his theme with a concluding account of Guy Howard's death that portrayed him as a martyr to America's world mission. After being shot, Chamberlin wrote, "Howard struggled to his feet and then," holding his hand to his chest to keep the blood from spurting out, he shouted "'whatever happens to me, keep the launch going! Keep the launch going!'—and fell over dead—his last thought of his unfinished duty."[113] "Our history records no

"Our God-Given Mission"

grander death," Chamberlin intoned. He closed by urging Americans to support the Philippine occupation:

> As she sails out on her search for American freedom, American prosperity, American ways, a Christian religion, the little red schoolhouse, and the American home; I believe the orders of the American people to her representatives who direct that voyage will be Guy Howard's immortal words "Keep that launch going! Keep that launch going!"[114]

Humanitarian nationalism led Americans to insist that their government had a moral obligation to intervene to alleviate mass suffering and slaughter. Once the door was opened, the impulse to educate, democratize, and Christianize was irresistible and seemed to many aligned with the rescue mission. The success of the "splendid little war" in 1898 only boosted the conviction that the nation was chosen to "liberate" and protect the powerless while expanding the blessings of democratic government and modernity. But the colonized had something to say about this too, turning the language of humanitarianism and democracy back on the American occupiers. After most of the insurgents laid down their arms, the Philippine Republic's democratically elected legislature began passing resolutions for independence as early as 1907, starting a process through which the United States would begin to cede autonomy beginning with the Jones Act in 1916. Cubans, against the desire of American military leaders, adopted universal suffrage and quickly voted to end the American occupation in 1902, although the United States repeatedly reoccupied the Cuban Republic.[115]

Historians have rarely taken the humanitarian rationales of the early twentieth century seriously, and typically consider them disingenuous covers for colonial ambitions and the militaristic pursuit of national self-interest. Appealing to humanitarian nationalism was nevertheless effective politics; this essay asks why it resonated with so many Americans to the extent that it could be exploited as a political tool. By tracing its roots back to the 1860s through the four subjects of this essay, the evolution of this nationalist construct becomes clearer and shows that the interventionism of the 1890s was not entirely new. It sprouted from the same ideological ground as Congressional Reconstruction, though that association was obscured because of the tarnished reputation of those policies.

Notes

1. This brand of nationalism that I trace back to Reconstruction aligns with the nationalistic ideas Susan D. Curtis has detected in Protestant Evangelical periodicals,

especially the *Christian Herald*, in the 1890s in *Holy Humanitarians: American Evangelicals and Global Aid* (Cambridge, Mass.: Harvard University Press, 2018).

2. Consider Edward L. Ayers, "Exporting Reconstruction," in *What Caused the Civil War? Reflections on the South and Southern History* (New York: W. W. Norton, 2005), 145–166.

3. O. O. Howard, *Autobiography of Oliver Otis Howard, Major General, United States Army* (New York: Baker & Taylor, 1907), 203.

4. For the Freedmen's Bureau as a pivotal antecedent of the welfare state, see Michele Landis Dauber, *The Sympathetic State: Disaster Relief and the Origins of the American Welfare State* (Chicago: University of Chicago Press, 2013). More generally, see also Theda Skocpol, *Protecting Soldiers and Mothers: The Political Origins of Social Policy in the United States* (Cambridge, Mass.: Harvard University Press, 1992).

5. Howard, 203–204.

6. Howard was writing soon after the San Francisco Earthquake of 1906 to which President Roosevelt responded quickly and Congress appropriated $2.5 million. Steve Kroll-Smith, *Recovering Inequality: Hurricane Katrina, the San Francisco Earthquake of 1906, and the Aftermath of Disaster* (Austin: University of Texas Press, 2018), 90, 138.

7. Howard, 203–204.

8. "Gen. Howard's View: Interview with the Distinguished Military Commander," *Atchison (Kansas) Daily Globe*, August 30, 1897, 3.

9. Peter J. Parish, *The North and the Nation in the Era of the Civil War*, ed. Adam I. P. Smith and Susan-Mary Grant (New York: Fordham University Press, 2003); Susan-Mary Grant, "The Charter of Its Birthright: The Civil War and American Nationalism," in *Legacy of Disunion: The Enduring Significance of the American Civil War*, ed. Susan-Mary Grant and Peter Parish (Baton Rouge: Louisiana State University Press, 2003), 188–206.

10. Francesca Morgan, *Women and Patriotism in Jim Crow America* (Chapel Hill: University of North Carolina Press, 2005); Melina Lawson, *Patriot Fires: Forging a New American Nationalism in the Civil War North* (Lawrence: University of Kansas Press, 2002); Cecilia Elizabeth O'Leary, *To Die For: The Paradox of American Patriotism* (Princeton, N.J.: Princeton University Press, 1999); Jeanne Attie, *Patriotic Toil: Northern Women and the American Civil War* (Ithaca, N.Y.: Cornell University Press, 1998).

11. Julia F. Irwin, *Making the World Safe: The American Red Cross and a Nation's Humanitarian Awakening* (New York: Oxford University Press, 2013), 1–12, 209–212.

12. For a nuanced analysis of the American press before the war, see Bonnie M. Miller, *From Liberation to Conquest: The Visual and Popular Cultures of the Spanish-American War* (Amherst: University of Massachusetts Press, 2011), 19–54.

13. William T. McKinley, *Message of the President of the United States, Communicated to the Two Houses of Congress, on the Relations of the United States to Spain* (Washington: Government Printing Office, 1898), 11.

14. John A. Carpenter, *Sword and Olive Branch: Oliver Otis Howard, with an Introduction by Paul A. Cimbala* (1964; New York: Fordham University Press, 1999), 285.

15. O. O. Howard, *Fighting for Humanity; or, Camp and Quarter-Deck* (London: F. T. Neely, 1898).

16. Tony Smith begins his influential survey of America's "global mission" to spread democracy with the occupation of the Philippines, but the origins could be traced back

to the "humanitarian nationalism" of Reconstruction. Tony Smith, *America's Mission: The United States and the Worldwide Struggle for Democracy* (Princeton, N.J.: Princeton University Press, 1994).

17. Florence Howe Hall, *The Story of the Battle Hymn of the Republic* (New York: Harper, 1916), 88–94. John Stauffer, *Battle Hymn of the Republic: A Biography of the Song that Marches On* (New York: Oxford University Press, 2013).

18. Notable among the many biographies are Elaine Showalter, *The Civil Wars of Julia Ward Howe* (New York: Simon and Schuster, 2016), and Valarie H. Ziegler, *Diva Julia: the Public Romance and Private Agony of Julia Ward Howe* (Harrisburg: Trinity Press International, 2003).

19. Dedication in Julia Ward Howe, *From the Oak to the Olive: A Plain Record of a Pleasant Journey* (Boston: Lee and Shepard, 1868).

20. Julia Ward Howe, *Reminiscences: 1819–1898* (Boston: Houghton Mifflin, 1898), 171. On Samuel, see James W. Trent, *The Manliest Man: Samuel Gridley Howe and the Contours of Nineteenth-Century American Reform* (Amherst: University of Massachusetts Press, 2012).

21. S. G. Howe, *A Letter to Mrs.____, and the Other Loyal Women: Touching the Matter of Contributions for the Army and Other Matters Connected to the War* (Boston: Ticknor & Fields, 1862), 19.

22. Matthew Furrow, "Samuel Gridley Howe, the Black Population of Canada West, and the Racial Ideology of the 'Blueprint for Radical Reconstruction,'" *Journal of American History* 97, no. 2 (2010), 344–370.

23. S. G. Howe, *Report to the Freedmen's Inquiry Commission. The Refugees from Slavery in Canada West* (Boston: Wright & Potter, 1864; reprint, New York: Arno Press, 1969).

24. "American Freedmen's Inquiry Commission Final Report," in *The War of the Rebellion: A Compilation of Official Records*, ed. Fred C. Ainsworth and Joseph W. Kelly, series 2, vol. 4 (Washington: Government Printing Office, 1900), 381.

25. Ibid., 382.

26. Furrow, 369.

27. Julia Ward Howe, *Woman and the Suffrage*, n.p., [1909?]. Nineteenth-Century Collections Online, http://tinyurl.galegroup.com/tinyurl/BSAMn3. Accessed June 30, 2019.

28. Journal, Sept. 10, 1865, reproduced in Laura E. Richards and Maud Howe Elliott, *Julia Ward Howe, 1819–1910*, vol. 1 (Boston: Houghton Mifflin, 1915), 229–231.

29. Several scholars have noted the influence of racial climate theory on Samuel Gridley Howe's thought, particularly through his correspondence with Louis Agassiz. See Nicolas Guyatt, "America's Conservatory: Race, Reconstruction, and the Santo Domingo Debate," *Journal of American History* 97, no. 4 (2011), 987–88; and George M. Frederickson, *The Black Image in the White Mind: The Debate on Afro-American Character and Destiny, 1817–1914* (Middletown, CT: Wesleyan University Press, 1971), 160–163.

30. David Prior, "'Crete the Opening Wedge': Nationalism and International Affairs in Postbellum America," *Journal of Social History* 42 (Summer 2009), 861, 872–873. Prior broadens his canvas in *Between Freedom and Progress: The Lost World of Reconstruction Politics* (Baton Rouge: Louisiana State University Press, 2019). For the larger

international context that demonstrates the ways in which the Howes' perspective resonated in Europe see Don H. Doyle, *The Cause of All Nations: An International History of the Civil War* (New York: Basic Books, 2015); Trent, *Manliest Man*, 248–249.

31. Samuel Gridley Howe, *Letters and Journals of Samuel Gridley Howe*, vol. 2, ed. Laura E. Richards, with notes by F. B. Sanborn (Boston: D. Estes, 1909), 539.

32. Laura E. Richards and Maud Howe Elliott, *Julia Ward Howe, 1819–1910*, vol. 2 (Boston: Houghton Mifflin, 1915).

33. Arman J. Kirakossian, Introduction to *The Armenian Massacres, 1894–1896: U.S. Media Testimony*, ed. Arman J. Kirakossian (Detroit: Wayne State University Press, 2004), 29; Karine V. Walther, *Sacred Interests: The United States and the Islamic World, 1821–1921* (Chapel Hill: University of North Carolina Press), 241–242.

34. "United Friends of Armenia," *Woman's Journal*, June 2, 1894, 170. Nineteenth-Century Collections Online, http://tinyurl.galegroup.com/tinyurl/8iKNT6. Accessed May 8, 2018.

35. Ibid.

36. Ibid.

37. Richards and Elliott, *Julia Ward Howe*, 189–191.

38. Peter Balakian, *The Burning Tigris: The Armenian Genocide and America's Response* (New York: HarperCollins, 2003), 63.

39. Both Abbott and Strong were influenced by evolutionary theories and used the phrase "Anglo-Saxon" frequently, which has led to their being labeled "social Darwinists." Dorothea Muller, "Josiah Strong and American Nationalism: A Reevaluation," *Journal of American History* 53, no. 3 (1966), 492–494.

40. Lyman Abbott, *Reminiscences* (Boston: Houghton Mifflin, 1915).

41. Ibid., 239. Eric Foner, *Reconstruction: America's Unfinished Revolution 1863–1877* (New York: Harper & Row, 1988).

42. Ira V. Brown, "Lyman Abbott and Freedmen's Aid, 1865–1869," *Journal of Southern History* 15, no. 1 (1949), 28.

43. Abbott, *Reminiscences*, 272.

44. Lyman Abbott, "The Armenian Question," *Outlook* (December 1896), reprinted in Kirakossian, *The Armenian Massacres*, 230.

45. Ibid., 231.

46. Ibid., 231–232.

47. Historians have linked overseas Christian missions and their networks to the rise of American internationalism and the establishment of an overseas empire. See Ian Tyrrell, *Reforming the World: The Creation of America's World Empire* (Princeton, N.J.: Princeton University Press, 2010), and Andrew Preston, *Sword of the Spirit, Shield of Faith: Religion in American War and Diplomacy* (New York: Random House, 2012).

48. Ann Marie Wilson, "In the Name of God, Civilization, and Humanity: The United States and the Armenian Massacres of the 1890s," *Le Mouvement Social*, no. 227 (April–June 2009), 27–44.

49. E. L. Godkin, "The Armenian Trouble," *The Nation* 60 (January 1895), 44. Reprinted in The *Armenian Massacres 1894–1896: U.S. Media Testimony*, ed. Arman J. Kirakossian (Detroit: Wayne State University Press, 2004), 53–55.

50. "Miss Barton's Testimony," *Chicago Tribune*, March 26, 1866, 2.
51. Stephen Oates, *A Woman of Valor: Clara Barton and the Civil War* (New York: Free Press, 1994), 365–366; Elizabeth Brown Pryor, *Clara Barton: Professional Angel* (Philadelphia: University of Pennsylvania Press, 1987), 148–150.
52. Clara Barton, *The Red Cross in Peace and War* (Washington, D.C.: American Historical Press, 1899), 36, 60–61, 68.
53. Foster Rhea Dulles, *The American Red Cross, A History* (New York: Harper and Bros, 1950), 29–41.
54. Barton, *Red Cross*, 183.
55. Ibid., 277. Barton mentions Howe's hospitality in "Clara Barton and Cubans," *Macon (Georgia) Telegraph*, November 5, 1896, 4.
56. Balakian, 78–80. Barton, *Red Cross*, 278–280.
57. "Aid for Armenia," *Outlook* (February–May 1896).
58. Dulles, *The American Red Cross*, 443–448; Pryor, *Clara Barton*, 302–307.
59. Merle Curti, *American Philanthropy Abroad* (New Brunswick, N.J.: Rutgers University Press, 1963), 133; and Balakian, 73.
60. Willard B. Gatewood Jr., *Black Americans and the White Man's Burden, 1898–1903* (Urbana: University of Illinois Press, 1975), 16.
61. Ada Ferrer, *Insurgent Cuba: Race, Nation, and Revolution, 1868–1898* (Chapel Hill: University of North Carolina Press, 1999), 195–202.
62. Quoted in Dulles, *The American Red Cross*, 42.
63. "Clara Barton to Go: Will Relieve the Sick and Suffering in Cuba," *Denver Evening Post*, February 1897, 1; Barton, *Red Cross*, 517.
64. Dulles, *The American Red Cross*, 443–448; Pryor, *Clara Barton*, 302–307.
65. Julia Ward Howe, "Miss Howe's Appeal," *Boston Daily Advertiser*, August 20, 1897; 8. Evangelina Betancourt Cosio y Cisneros, *The Story of Evangelina Cisneros as Told by Herself*, introduction by Julian Hawthorne (New York: Continental, 1898), 39–40, 48; Miller, *From Liberation to Conquest*, 42–47.
66. Julia Ward Howe to Clara Barton, March 31, 1897, Clara Barton Papers: General Correspondence, 1838–1912. MSS11973, box: 71; Microfilm reel: 57. Library of Congress, Washington, D.C.; http://hdl.loc.gov/loc.mss/ms005010.mss11973.0298
67. Quoted in Pryor, *Clara Barton*, 303.
68. Abbott, *Reminiscences*, 437. For a description of the speech and its impact see Mark Zwonitzer, *The Statesman and the Storyteller: John Hay, Mark Twain, and the Rise of American Imperialism* (Chapel Hill: University of North Carolina Press, 2016), 258–260.
69. "Wants Cuba Annexed: Senator Gallinger Addresses the Senate on the Cuban Question," *Butte (Montana) Weekly Miner*, March 24, 1898, 1.
70. "The Red Cross in Cuba, By Clara Barton as Interviewed by Elbert E. Baldwin," *Outlook* (April 9, 1898), 911. Another article highlighting the misery witnessed by Barton is Edward W. Abbey, "Cuba and Miss Barton," *Evangelist*, March 3, 1898, 3–4. For a discussion of the scholarly estimates, see John Lawrence Tone, *War and Genocide in Cuba, 1895–1898* (Chapel Hill: University of North Carolina Press, 2006), 209–223; Louis A. Perez, *The War of 1898: The United States and Cuba in History and Historiography* (Chapel Hill: University of North Carolina Press, 1998).

71. "It Is a Hell: Condition of Cuba under Spanish Rule. Senator Proctor Tells the Senate What He Observed," *Los Angeles Times*, March 18, 1898. Proctor's speech was reprinted in Barton, *Red Cross*, 531–539.

72. Lyman Abbott, "The Meaning of the War," *Plymouth Morning Pulpit*, May 31, 1893, 3–4; Benjamin T. Wetzel, "Onward Christian Soldiers: Lyman Abbott's Justification of the Spanish-American War," *Journal of Church and State* 54, no. 3 (2012), 410.

73. Lyman Abbott, "The Duty and Destiny of America," published under the title "An Awakened Nation," *Atchison (Kansas) Daily Globe*, June 10, 1898, 6. Oliver O. Howard also strongly approved of the intervention. See "Gen. Howard on the War: He Thinks Armed Intervention in Cuba Is a Righteous Course," *Atchison (Kansas) Daily Globe*, May 7, 1898, 1. Reprinted from the *Boston Herald*.

74. Abbott, *Reminiscences*, 438.

75. Lyman Abbott, *Rights of Man: A Study in Twentieth-Century Problems* (Boston: Houghton, Mifflin, 1902), 356–357.

76. Julia Ward Howe, "The Uses of Victory," *Christian Register*, September 22, 1898, 1069–1071.

77. Zwonitzer, *Statesman and Storyteller*, 276.

78. The resolution was proposed by Moorfield Storey. See "Opposition to 'Imperialism,'" *Friends Intelligencer: A Religious and Family Journal* 55 (June 1898), 477.

79. See Fitzhugh Brundage, Introduction to *Remembering Reconstruction: Struggles over the Meaning of America's Most Turbulent Era*, ed. Carole Emberton and Bruce E. Baker (Baton Rouge: Louisiana University Press, 2017), 4; and K. Stephen Prince, "Jim Crow Memory: Southern White Supremacists and the Regional Politics of Remembrance," in *Remembering Reconstruction: Struggles over the Meaning of America's Most Turbulent Era*, ed. Carole Emberton and Bruce E. Baker (Baton Rouge: Louisiana University Press, 2017), 20–27.

80. E. L. Godkin, editorial, *The Nation*, January 13, 1898, 23.

81. Moorfield Storey, "Nothing to Excuse Our Intervention: President's Speech at the Meeting of the Massachusetts Reform Club, April 8, 1898," *Advocate of Peace* 60 (May 1898), 114.

82. Michael Patrick Cullinane, *Liberty and American Anti-Imperialism, 1898–1909* (New York: Palgrave Macmillan, 2012). The "Mugwump" commonality among anti-imperialists is described in Robert Beisner, *Twelve against Empire: The Anti-Imperialists, 1898–1900* (New York: McGraw-Hill, 1968).

83. McKinley, *Message of the President*, 11–12.

84. Carl Schurz, "The Future of Cuba," *Harper's Weekly*, April 1898, 292.

85. Ibid.

86. Carl Schurz, "The Philanthropic Policy," *Harper's Weekly*, April 1898, 339. See also Alejandro de la Fuente and Matthew Casey, "Race and the Suffrage Controversy in Cuba, 1898–1901," in *Colonial Crucible: Empire in the Making of the Modern American State*, ed. Alfred W. McCoy and Francisco A. Scarano (Madison: University of Wisconsin Press, 2009), 224–226.

87. "Gen. Howard's View: Interview with the Distinguished Military Commander," *Atchison (Kansas) Daily Globe*, August 30, 1897, 3, reprinted from the *New York Telegram*.

"Gen. Howard on the War," *Atchison (Kansas) Daily Globe*, May 7, 1898, 3, reprinted from the *Boston Herald*.

88. "General Howard Likes the Cubans," *Morning Oregonian* (Portland, Oregon), September 6, 1898, 4.

89. Oliver O. Howard, "The Cuban Insurgents: Their Defects and Merits," *The Outlook* (August 20, 1898), 975.

90. For instance, see Howard's speech on Christian love to freedpeople in 1866 in Howard, *Autobiography*, 324–328.

91. Daniel J. Sharfstein, *Thunder in the Mountains: Chief Joseph, Oliver Otis Howard, and the Nez Perce War* (New York: W. W. Norton, 2017), 476–481; John A. Carpenter, *Sword and Olive Branch: Oliver Otis Howard* (Pittsburgh: University of Pittsburgh Press, 1964), 268.

92. Ibid., 975.

93. "Gen. Howard on the War: He Thinks Armed Intervention in Cuba Is a Righteous Course," *Atchison (Kansas) Daily Globe*, May 7, 1898, 4. Reprinted from the Boston Herald.

94. Howard, "The Cuban Insurgents," 973–975.

95. William McKinley, "Benevolent Assimilation Proclamation," in Julian W. Richards, *A Handbook of the Spanish-American War of 1898 and the Philippine Insurrection* (Cedar Rapids: Republican Trading Company, 1899), 24–26.

96. Amy Kaplan, *The Anarchy of Empire in the Making of U.S. Culture* (Cambridge, Mass.: Harvard University Press, 2005), 3. On the endurance of legal ambiguities surrounding citizenship in the colonies following the Insular Cases, see Sam Erman, *Almost Citizens: Puerto Rico, the U.S. Constitution, and Empire* (New York: Cambridge University Press, 2018), and "Citizens of Empire: Puerto Rico, Status, and Constitutional Change," *California Law Review* 102, no. 5 (2014), 1181–1242.

97. Paul Kramer examines the nuances of benevolent assimilation in *The Blood of Government: Race, Empire, the United States, and the Philippines* (Chapel Hill: University of North Carolina Press, 2006). See also Stuart Creighton Miller, *Benevolent Assimilation: The American Conquest of the Philippines, 1899–1903* (New Haven, Conn.: Yale University Press, 1982).

98. Barton, *Red Cross*, 406.

99. "The Red Cross in Cuba: Something about the American National Society's Noble Work," *Los Angeles Times*, March 21, 1898, 9; Clara Barton, "Our Work and Observations in Cuba," *North American Review* (May 1898), 552–559. Irwin, *Making the World Safe*, 27.

100. Irwin, *Making the World Safe*, 28–29, 35–36, 42, 67–68; Marian Moser Jones, *The Red Cross from Clara Barton to the New Deal* (Baltimore: Johns Hopkins University Press, 2013).

101. Howard quotes this line from the song as the heading to chapter 8. See *Fighting for Humanity*, 43.

102. The "Star-Spangled Banner" was not adopted as the national anthem until 1931. John Stauffer and Benjamin Soskis, *The Battle Hymn of the Republic: A Biography of the Song That Marches On* (New York: Oxford University Press, 2013), 146–148.

103. Mark Twain, *Mark Twain's Weapons of Satire: Anti-Imperialist Writings of the Philippine-American War*, ed. Jim Zwick (Syracuse, N.Y.: Syracuse University Press,

1992), 40–41; Florence Howe Hall, *The Story of the Battle Hymn of the Republic* (New York: Harper, 1916), 88–94.

104. Zwonitzer, *The Statesman and the Storyteller*, 423.

105. M. Howe Elliott, "Julia Ward Howe," *The Outlook*, October 1, 1904, 294; Wilson, "In the Name of God," 42.

106. Abbott, *Rights of Man*, 226.

107. Ibid., 228.

108. Abbott, *Reminiscences*, 438.

109. Abbott, *Rights of Man*, 277.

110. For the Wilsonian connection to liberal interventionists such as Abbott, see Preston, *Sword of the Spirit, Shield of Faith*, 249.

111. Howard, *Autobiography*, 573.

112. Sharfstein, *Thunder in the Mountains*, 453–454.

113. Frederick Chamberlin, *The Blow from Behind, or Some Features of the Anti-Imperialist Movement* (Boston: Lee and Shepard, 1903), 146.

114. Chamberlin, *Blow from Behind*, 146–147.

115. Rebecca Scott, *Degrees of Freedom: Louisiana and Cuba after Slavery* (Cambridge, Mass.: Belknap Press of Harvard University Press, 2005), 205–207.

7

Connected Lives

Albert Beveridge, Benjamin Tillman, and the Grand Army of the Republic

David V. Holtby

How did Reconstruction shape imperialism? One answer lies in the interconnected life stories that stretched from the Civil War through the Spanish-American War. This essay begins with the political lessons a son took from his father's misfortunes. Albert J. Beveridge (1862–1927) was three years old when his father, Thomas H. Beveridge, a Union officer, resumed farming in Ohio in 1865.[1] For the next thirty years the elder Beveridge's life oscillated between limited financial success and bankruptcies. After his death in 1895 his scant possessions went to pay debts. Four years later, Albert Beveridge entered the U.S. Senate, an ambitious and unbridled imperialist.

Beveridge understood Union veterans' hardships, and in 1898 he reassured the 305,000 members of the Grand Army of the Republic (GAR) that an American empire would bring opportunity to men who, like his father, never gained a toehold in the unstable postbellum economy.[2] But he also knew Union veterans desired to see again America's military prowess, and so their shared imperialism reflected both economic anxieties and martial spirit. The GAR also saw in imperialism the culmination of an expanded federal state that would honor pledges to care for crippled and disabled veterans through tariff revenue. Finally, the GAR viewed empire-building as a continuation of their wartime-conferred destiny—to be patriot-sentinels watching over and safeguarding a united Republic. To the GAR, an expansive, imperial America signified a patriotic, unified nation.

The GAR rallied to imperialism largely because its members equated martial valor with national greatness—and that alarmed Southern white supremacists.[3] South Carolina's Democratic senator Benjamin R. Tillman (1847–1918) led their opposition.[4] He argued in Senate debates and during the 1900 presidential campaign that intervention abroad would bring renewed military presence at home, ushering in a revived Reconstruction with U.S. soldiers aligned with African Americans throughout the South. And yet Beveridge and Tillman also shared a belief in the superiority of white Anglo-Americans. During the imperial crisis this racism divided them, with Beveridge's support for a muscular federal government and Tillman's states'-rights philosophy precluding recognition of their shared values. Yet Southern white service in the War with Spain also fueled a drive for reconciliation among Southern and Northern whites. Beveridge ultimately embraced this trend, while the GAR expressed reservations about it. Even later in life Beveridge found his views shifting in ways that aligned him more closely with the "Lost Cause" politics of men like Tillman and their later-day apologists.[5] Beveridge, the GAR, and Tillman typified their era's cross-currents.

The GAR originated in Decatur, Illinois, in April 1866 and began recruiting Union army and navy veterans from nearby states. From the outset the GAR received a warm welcome among Republicans, who saw veterans as a potential voting bloc.[6] Likewise, from its founding the GAR positioned itself close to the levers of political power. Every Republican president from Grant to McKinley was a member of the GAR. On the national stage, Sen. John A. Logan (R-IL) exemplified a veteran-in-politics—a distinguished and battle-tested Union major general who represented Illinois in Congress. Logan's three years as head of the fraternal organization (1868–1870) that would soon become the GAR overlapped with his two terms in the House of Representatives. He was beginning his third term in the Senate when he died in late December 1886. Throughout his time in the Senate he chaired the Committee on Military Affairs, from which he aided veterans and their widows.[7] His 1884 vice-presidential candidacy bespoke respect for his tireless work as the veterans' voice in Congress.[8] His prominence was again honored two years later when he lay in state in the U.S. Capitol's Rotunda, with his casket on President Lincoln's iconic funeral bier.[9]

Logan's political activities on behalf of the GAR illustrate two entwined goals: expanding the federal government's power and securing benefits for Union veterans. The GAR sought government aid for veterans whose physical and mental health had deteriorated due to the Civil War. Their appeal aligned "with the enhancement of the power of the national state in Reconstruction and the 'moral capital' . . . accumulated via the end of slavery."[10] The GAR embraced both tenets—expanding federal authority and expending "moral capital" to aid impaired veterans.[11] They poured moral fervor into their cause when lobbying. In this approach the GAR was not alone. Several grassroots movements fueled by moral righteousness occurred concurrently in the late nineteenth century, including women's suffrage, temperance reform, and—less remembered—benefits for Union veterans. In the successful implementation of the GAR's program of reform, the protective tariff came to sustain disability benefits to Union veterans, which then evolved into pensions for aged and infirm veterans. The GAR also supported its members as patriot-sentinels, especially in the late 1880s amid recurring incidents of white Southerners glorifying the Confederacy, which in turn fed a resurgence of GAR martial spirit. Opposing the GAR veterans were Democrats who favored a limited central government, including many Southern whites who still favored the principle of states' rights. Their political philosophy viewed with alarm an increased federal presence, and during the 1880s Democrats began attacking veterans' benefits and the tariffs funding these.[12]

The national head of the GAR made a transformative decision in 1878 when he committed the organization to becoming a zealous advocate for pension legislation. When the GAR began lobbying Congress in 1878–1879, the move coincided with congressional attention to a major piece of disability legislation—the Arrears Act. The Arrears Act acknowledged that the war's health impacts could be debilitating years later, so it allowed veterans with "newly discovered Civil War–related disabilities to sign up and receive [money] in one lump sum,"[13] retroactive from 1865. Bipartisan support existed for passage of the Arrears Act in 1879, legislation Theda Skocpol describes as an early step in implementing social welfare.[14]

Coinciding with increased lobbying on behalf of Union veterans were two changes in America's political culture that augmented the GAR's voice. First, more GAR leaders were being elected to Congress, especially in the 1890s.[15] Second, equilibrium at the ballot box produced divided government in Washington between 1880 and 1896.[16] As a result, the vote of veterans could tip the scales in elections, and the political clout of the GAR increased dramatically between 1880 and 1900. By 1885 Union veterans constituted almost 15 percent of males of voting age in five key Northern states—New York, Pennsylvania, Ohio, Indiana, and Illinois. Among these veterans about one in six received government payments.[17] By 1890 fully 10 percent of all eligible voters in the North were veterans.[18] Logan's second term in the Senate, beginning in 1879, coincided with the GAR's membership starting to increase significantly— rising from 44,752[19] until reaching its apex at about one-third of Union veterans alive in 1890,[20] or 409,489 members. Both all-Black and integrated posts existed, with more than 200 Black posts in twenty-four states and Washington, D.C., and more than 450 integrated posts in nineteen states and one Canadian province.[21]

Bipartisan momentum was with the GAR through the mid-1880s. Both political parties included support for Union soldiers' pensions in their 1884 presidential election platforms.[22] A bipartisan bill providing pensions for disabled veterans as well as payments to widows and minors passed in the House and Senate early in 1887.²³ Then bipartisanship unraveled when the bill reached the White House where Grover Cleveland, the first Democrat to be elected president after the Civil War (1885-1889), vetoed it.²⁴ President Cleveland believed the bill an "unjust discrimination" because it excluded nonveterans facing circumstances similar to indigent Union veterans, stressing as well—and inaccurately—that it threatened fiscal ruin for the federal government.²⁵ GAR leaders and members went into a rage over what they regarded as misguided fiscal tightfistedness.²⁶ They complained that the loss of the pensions to the disabled meant many tens of thousands of Union veterans in poorhouses would soon be joined by "thousands of others."²⁷ Cleveland lost his reelection bid to Benjamin Harrison (1889–1893), a GAR member from Indiana, who signed the landmark Dependent and Disability Pension Act on June 27, 1890. This bill capped the GAR's decade-long campaign to claim the full measure of the government's wartime commitments to care for infirm veterans, widows, and minor children. Cleveland, of course, was down but not out, and would return the electoral punch to Harrison in 1892, charging that Harrison's administration paid out funds to Union soldiers in a reckless, corrupt fashion.²⁸

As James Marten has noted, the words "Civil War veteran" represented "a social construction with multiple meanings and uses."²⁹ Such a characterization provides insight into the GAR's activities beginning in the mid-1880s. Increasingly the organization struck a firm posture against glorification of the Confederacy and its leaders. This new emphasis marked the GAR's transition as a special interest—expanding their role from lobbyists in Congress to include broader national issues dominating the public square. A generation after Appomattox, new threats to unity prompted them to begin protesting Southern activities deemed defiant and insolent. In doing so the GAR further cemented its support for Republicans and took public positions on issues of the day, precursor steps to their embrace of imperialism.

The GAR began evolving into an organization of patriot-sentinels beginning in the mid-1880s. A rising tide of white Southern pride in Confederate soldiers, living and dead, precipitated the GAR's vigilance. The unveiling of pro-Confederate statues throughout the South elicited sharp denunciations in the GAR's *National Tribune*. They condemned these monuments as "the exaltation of treason" that glorified men who fought "to perpetuate slavery and destroy the Government."³⁰ Similarly when Confederate-leaning histories appeared in textbooks in the mid-1880s, the GAR denounced them and their publishers.³¹ In mid-June 1887 the army's adjutant general, R. C. Drum, acting with Cleveland's approval, but not the War Department's, informed the governors of Southern states that about

600 Confederate battle flags would be returned. The outcry forced Cleveland to rescind Drum's authorization within a day.[32] The GAR fumed that "the Veterans' blood boils over the proposed return of the Rebel flags."[33]

The GAR waded into the battle flag controversy on the side of Republicans, and for the first time they entered a public fray not tied to protective tariffs. A year later they came out in favor of two additional political issues: to take over Cuba and restrict Italian immigration.[34] But one public issue dominated the GAR's attention, so much so that they became the vanguard of "the cult of the flag."[35] The organization made reverence for the stars and stripes a litmus test of loyalty and true nationalism. To promote greater public respect for the flag, especially among immigrants, the GAR pushed for creation of Flag Day. In addition, at its national encampment in August 1889, the GAR posts voted to place a flag in every public school lacking one and proposed training a new generation of citizen-soldiers through military drill at public schools.[36] Building on the efforts of John A. Logan beginning in 1868, for nearly sixty years the GAR lobbied for what became known as Memorial Day.[37] But commemorating the war's dead took a subversive turn in the South. In 1894 one GAR member in Richmond, Virginia, described the Decoration Day celebrations as a "recrudescence of Rebellion" in which speakers proclaimed "the South was right" and "rebel flags" predominated.[38]

On a humid mid-September evening in 1898, GAR members gathered to escort local attorney Albert J. Beveridge from his home to the Indiana Republican party convention. Beveridge's keynote address, "The March of the Flag," offered an imperialistic message that electrified the several thousand attendees. The recent defeat of Spain, he argued, empowered the United States to exercise dominion over Spain's former colonies. Beveridge stressed the economic necessity of empire, of controlling new markets, especially in the Far East, for the bounty of Indiana's and America's farmers and businesses. It was "high duty" and would "please God" to "occupy new markets for what our farmers raise, our factories make, our merchants sell."[39]

Seizing the high ground, Beveridge began with six references to how God willed territorial expansion and invoked God and His guidance eight times in his final paragraph.[40] The Lord abundantly bestowed His favor upon the nation, Beveridge argued, through American exceptionalism.[41] But Beveridge also drew on worldly references. He cast a grand vision of empire-building and commerce merging to advance the nation's purposes. "There are so many real things to be done—canals to be dug, railways to be laid, forests to be felled, . . . markets to be won, ships to be launched, peoples to be saved, civilization to be proclaimed."[42] Thus did territorial conquest and commercial exploitation rhetorically morph into transplanting American institutions and values to uplift peoples deemed backward. Beveridge looked across the Pacific Ocean to the Far East, to "Asia, to the trade of whose hundreds of millions American merchants, manufacturers, farmers have as good [a] right as those of Germany or France or Russia or England."[43] Destiny propelled America's empire-building, and he beseeched his audience, "Will you remember that we do but what our fathers did—we pitch the tents of liberty farther westward, farther southward—we only continue the march of the flag."[44]

Beveridge sought to leapfrog other men vying to be Indiana's new U.S. senator, which Indiana's upcoming Republican-controlled legislature would appoint in January 1899. An early imperialist, he had first espoused imperialism in 1890, at age twenty-eight, before the Indianapolis Literary Club. It was inauspicious. His call for "an imperial national policy" to promote entry into markets in the Far East failed to impress the city's leading men.[45] Eight years later attitudes had shifted, following four years of economic depression punctuated with labor strife and social unrest. A warm welcome greeted his address at Boston's Middlesex Club in April 1898. Invited to mark the seventy-sixth birthday of the late president Ulysses S. Grant, his speech came just days after the U.S. declaration of war against Spain. That evening—before U.S. forces fired shots in the Caribbean—Beveridge declared that the late president, though stymied by opposition (as discussed by Andre Fleche and Gregg French in this volume), "had the instinct of Empire" in his designs on the Dominican Republic and Cuba.[46] Grant's ideas also provided Beveridge with a commercial rationale. He reminded his audience that Grant had said, "Our commerce should be encouraged; American ship-building and carrying capacity increased, and foreign markets sought."[47] Beveridge brought his listeners to their feet when he thundered, "The trade of the world must and shall be ours."[48] The obscure Beveridge used Grant to create a lineage for his ideas and an entrée to the national stage. Newspapers nationwide took notice, and Beveridge rode a crest of national enthusiasm for imperial expansion. He confided to one of his closest friends in May 1898 that "the commercial extension of the Republic has been my dream since boyhood," adding "out here in the [Mid-] West the young men are for it almost to a man—I mean the full-blooded young men."[49]

Everywhere in America, economic instability as well as relentless, transformative processes driven by urbanization, immigration, and technology shaped the prevailing climate of opinion. The result for America in the 1890s, as one historian described it, was to put the country in "a state of upset."[50] Richard Hofstadter concluded that "the entire episode [of empire building from 1898 to 1900] is indeed an instructive case study in the dynamics of national mood." [51] Tumult in the North caught Hofstadter's attention because various crises coalesced to test Americans' resolve. Disputes with Italy and Chile precipitated saber-rattling in 1891, with war nearly resulting from the latter incident. No sooner had these confrontations dissolved than domestic turmoil roiled people's lives. The Panic of 1893 and the ensuing four-year depression brought on widespread unemployment and reduced wages, spawning labor strife and strikes.[52] Populist Jacob S. Coxey headed a caravan of unemployed men marching on Washington, D.C., in 1894. They called for "a giant public works project"—half-a-billion dollars to fund road construction and create jobs.[53] Coxey grasped what the GAR understood: that only the federal government had the wherewithal to undertake large-scale commitments that benefited the public.[54] But such an enlarged scope of the federal government alarmed Democratic politicians and alienated some Republicans, including the GAR, who saw Coxey's army as a band of rabble-rousers.

Against this background of economic turmoil, as Hofstadter suggested, Republican politicians— most prominently Albert J. Beveridge—used calls for empire "to divert the public mind from the grave internal discontents."[55] Indeed, in his September "March of the Flag" speech in Indiana, Beveridge made an intergenerational appeal when he intoned "we do but what our fathers did," but also recast the meaning of marching and planting the flag. The Union veterans' legacy of preserving the nation was ever-present, but they confronted new challenges in economic and social upheaval. Many Union veterans did, as the GAR had pointed out, face life in Northern poorhouses. "The March of the Flag" gave voice to a bright day dawning and writ large aspirations to leave behind decades of hardship so well known to Beveridge's listeners. (For a discussion of how domestic tensions shaped American foreign affairs and expansionism two decades earlier, see Gregg French's chapter in this volume.)

His speech was also the culmination of his life experiences, which wedded political engagement with economic hardship. Albert J. Beveridge was a cradle Republican raised into the party by his father and well familiar with the GAR and its politics. His father was a long-time GAR member, and his father-in-law was a prominent GAR leader in Indiana who spearheaded construction (1887–1902) of a 284-foot-tall obelisk as a GAR memorial in Indianapolis.[56] Beveridge had an acute sense of his own economic condition, as he conveyed in an unpublished account of his life from about 1868 to 1889.[57] It is a fragmentary literature of witness, recounting his childhood, college life, two years in a southwest Kansas cow town, and the beginning of his legal career in Indianapolis. He is unflinching in describing the family's poverty brought on through his father's postwar reversals. Thomas H. Beveridge, between 1866 and his death in 1895, endured economic hardships like those buffeting many veterans. In the fifteen years prior to volunteering and becoming an officer in the Ohio infantry, he farmed successfully, doubled his land holdings to more than 215 acres valued at $4,000, and acquired personal property worth $1,100. But by 1869 he had lost everything in foreclosure proceedings brought on when he was unable to repay bank notes he had co-signed for men he commanded. In the 1870s Thomas Beveridge moved his family several times, settling finally in Indiana, but new attempts at farming and construction resulted in further bankruptcies.

His failures as a farmer most often arose from misfortune beyond his control. He dealt with too much or too little rain and railroad rates that "absorbed the profits of a season's toil."[58] He began construction contracting in the mid-1870s during a depression. Thomas Beveridge's final thirty years align with interpretations of masculinity that historians have recently identified as two archetypes in the postbellum decades. One scholar writes of the "Self-Made Man and the Broken Man,"[59] and the other identifies a broadly held belief that "a man had to achieve a competence,"[60] meaning earn a living, support a family, and be an asset in the community. The dichotomy between self-made and broken encapsulates the contrasting experiences of Thomas Beveridge's prewar and postwar life. His westward relocations and embarking on new enterprises were in search of a competence that he never fully regained.

His son's life, though, followed a different trajectory. Albert seemed to personify the Republican vision of upward mobility through skill and sweat, much as his father's life embodied its blind spots. Thomas introduced Albert to politics early in life by attending local political rallies and encouraged him to emulate Abraham Lincoln. That suggestion proved prescient. Some of Albert's affinities to Lincoln were coincidental, such as each moving to southern Indiana, but others were consequential and even decisive. Both read voraciously, became well acquainted with manual labor in their youth, and grew up in poverty. What is more, both immersed themselves in an oratorical culture, honed the gift of a marvelous memory, and excelled at public speaking.[61] And both embraced the ideology of free labor,[62] which promised rewards for the self-reliant, hardworking, and virtuous. These traits dovetailed with Lincoln's and Beveridge's aspirations, and both grabbed the rung labeled law on the ladder of life and used it to climb into politics. Their successes reinforced a belief in progress. Just as Lincoln's adult life "both embraced and symbolized the opportunity, achievement, and progress that a competence represented,"[63] so, too, did Beveridge's.

In his late teens, several local, influential men became aware of Albert's oratorical skill and recruited him to speak at rural temperance rallies, with one assisting him with college expenses. While at college Beveridge worked at a variety of jobs, never slept more than four hours a night, continued his regime of solitary practice of orations, excelled in the classroom, and accumulated honors and prize money each year in debate and speech competitions. In the fall of 1884, at the beginning of his senior year, he became a local stump speaker on behalf of Republicans, including for the losing presidential ticket of James G. Blaine and John A. Logan. Also in his senior year, he began to socialize with Katherine Langsdale, the daughter of Col. George J. Langsdale, one of Indiana's most powerful Republican leaders, and married her in 1887, the same year he was admitted to the Indiana bar.

His family life embodied the contradictions of the Republican Party's vision of the future in the Gilded Age, and this gave him a special ability to speak within the party across generations. "The March of the Flag," in particular, hit on a common desire of Union veterans, anxious fathers, and aspiring young men to improve their lives. In January 1899 the newly seated Republican majority in the Indiana legislature selected Beveridge as U.S. senator, his rapid rise in the party stemming largely from the speech. Three hundred thousand copies were printed and distributed as the principal Republican campaign document for Indiana, Iowa, and other states.[64] Beveridge tapped into the martial enthusiasm emanating from the GAR and its patriot-sentinels. The GAR had embraced intervention in Cuba in 1888 and again in 1896, when the Indiana state commander at the state's annual meeting denounced "the Spanish Government in its attempts to still popular liberty in Cuba" and expressed solidarity with "that [country's] struggling people."[65] "The March of the Flag" speech deftly merged the GAR's patriotic "cult of the flag" with imperialism. As one historian noted, "The culmination of the Grand Army's patriotic crusade was the war with Spain in 1898, an event greeted in the order with unrestrained enthusiasm."[66]

The mid-term election of 1898—the one that gave the Indiana legislature its Republican majority—brought to national politics a new voice and cause, Albert J. Beveridge and empire-building. As one scholar observed, Beveridge "alone, among Republican orators, took imperialism as his theme in the campaign of 1898."[67] Beveridge was now ahead of the curve. Territorial expansion, as Hofstadter posited, alleviated what he termed the "psychic crisis" of the 1890s. Young people yearning for adventure clamored for imperialism,[68] and within the GAR nostalgia for military prowess surged.[69] The domestic economic turmoil of the mid-1890s seemed to beg for this kind of solution. Beveridge offered certainty in unsettling times in "The March of the Flag"—patriotism cum imperialism would bring territorial expansion and be an economic boon. Beveridge helped formulate a Republican defense of empire that, between 1898 and 1900, became one part of an intense political debate driven forward by the rapidity of the war and looming questions about Spain's former colonies.[70]

The U.S. Senate received the Treaty of Paris ending the war with Spain on January 6, 1899. In the treaty, the United States agreed to pay Spain twenty million dollars to acquire the Philippines, and Spain agreed to cede the islands of Cuba, Puerto Rico, and Guam to the United States as reparations.[71] The Treaty of Paris was devoid of specifics on a colonial policy and "remained silent on citizenship, voting rights, and future statehood," with Congress left to deal with these issues.[72] The U.S. Senate approved the treaty by a vote of 57 to 27 on February 6, 1899. But the vote tally, a mere one "aye" more than the two-thirds majority required, signaled that imperialism remained a divisive issue. Debates about its merits persisted for another twenty months—through the 1900 presidential election.[73] There, the Democratic Party platform regarded "imperialism as the paramount issue of the campaign."[74]

One Southern Democratic senator in particular had a guiding hand in that declaration—Sen. Ben R. Tillman of South Carolina.[75] Tillman grew up in the first generation to embrace a postwar racist ideology that celebrated Confederate valor and persecuted Southern freedpeople and their descendants, all while proclaiming that the Civil War had not been about slavery. White supremacists targeted two inseparable foes: the federal government and the Fourteenth and Fifteenth Amendments, which in concert "severed the legal ties between whiteness and citizenship."[76] For more than forty years Tillman tirelessly urged resubjugating African Americans by repealing these two amendments. These additions to the Constitution, in Tillman's mind, showered precious privileges on uneducated ex-slaves, and in doing so unleashed twin nightmares—citizenship and voting rights for African Americans. To curb the impact of the Fourteenth and Fifteenth Amendments, Jim Crow laws hammered segregation into place, while literacy tests and poll taxes, as well as intimidation and violence, blocked African American men's voting rights. (For more on Tillman and the nexus of violence in the Carolinas and U.S. rhetoric about freeing Cuba, see DJ Polite's chapter in this volume.) White supremacists and segregationists such as Tillman quickly made the Democratic Party in the South a political vehicle for their racist ideology. In doing so they forged systemic racism through legislation, ordinances, regulations, and court decisions.

An ardent white supremacist and segregationist, Tillman regarded the Fourteenth and Fifteenth Amendments as sustaining a pernicious political order thrust on white Southerners.[77] These amendments, he believed, "gave the slaves of the South not only self-government, but they forced on the white men of the South, at the point of a bayonet, the rule and domination of those ex-slaves."[78] Tillman and his allies saw alarming parallels between Reconstruction, allegedly a time of unwarranted and excessive government and military presence, and the imposition of American military rule, particularly in the Philippines. Much as Beveridge channeled the anxieties of Northern Republicans in the Gilded Age, so too did Tillman represent the tortured Lost Cause ideology of Jim Crow white Southerners.

Two weeks into formal debate on the treaty Tillman had a particularly testy exchange with Minnesota Republican senator Knute Nelson (1843–1923), a Civil War veteran. At the end of their verbal parrying, an exasperated Nelson said: "I fear that the Senator [Tillman] is so possessed with all the conditions that grew out of that institution [slavery], that he hardly [can] see clear on this matter of the Philippine Islands or the matter of territorial acquisitions. . . . He is all the time looking at these questions in the light of the problems that they had in the South since the days of the civil war."[79] Tillman's retort crystallized his racist, white-supremacist beliefs borne forth as a Democratic political ideology since Reconstruction:[80] "You are undertaking to annex and make a component part of this Government islands inhabited by ten millions of the colored races, one-half or more of whom are barbarians of the lowest type. It is to the injection into the body politic of the United States of that vitiated blood, that debased and ignorant people that we object."[81] Nelson grounded his comments in the need to look ahead and create a colonial policy. Tillman remained firmly anchored in the past. He saw imperialism as a reenactment of all that was abhorrent in Reconstruction. He dreaded that imperialism amounted to Reconstruction writ large. As a legal scholar recently noted in appraising the South's reaction to imperialism, "A federal government that could rule its islands as colonies was perilously close to one that could re-impose Reconstruction on the South."[82]

Both proponents and opponents in debating the administration of the Philippines laced their positions with racism and a firm conviction that Filipinos were incapable of self-government. Likewise, both sides rejected that, in the phrase of that era, "the Constitution follows the flag."[83] That is, statehood and all the rights it conferred—most notably citizenship and voting—were not extended to Filipinos. Despite Republican assurances of second-class status for Filipinos, Southern Democrats were wary of Republican promises. White supremacist, segregationist ideology had settled into intransigence.[84] Senator Orville H. Platt of Connecticut (1827–1905), in setting forth the Republicans' pro-imperialist position, sought to soften resistance, encourage trust, and restore interparty goodwill.[85] He hoped to silence "the voice of timidity and distrust," convince opponents to ignore "carping critics," and promote "faith in the Government, faith in the future."[86] His appeal could not scale the Democrat's tall wall of fear and hostility.

Albert J. Beveridge had to watch from the sidelines during the Senate's Philippine debates preceding adjournment in early March 1899. He entered the 56th Congress in December 1899, after having traveled to the Philippines to assess conditions firsthand—followed by visits to China, Russia, and Japan.[87] Upon his return in August he began writing a major speech on American policy in the Philippines, which would take nearly two hours to deliver on January 9, 1900.[88] He gave a firm nod to commercial benefits, but his main message to his colleagues was that the "natives are ignorant," which meant they were "incapable of self-rule," and that therefore God ordained the United States to take over the Philippines and to carry out "our saving, regenerating, uplifting work."[89] He asserted that annexing the Philippines was neither a partisan matter nor even a "question of constitutional power. It is elemental. It is racial."[90]

Tillman offered a Democratic rejoinder to Beveridge on January 29, 1900. His speech lasted nearly as long Beveridge's and disputed his colleague's statements. This speech also marked a turning point in Tillman's tactics. Tillman said he "never intended to obtrude my views upon the Senate, but, to content myself with an occasional foray into the *mêlée*, . . . to perform a little guerrilla warfare."[91] Now, in December 1899, he introduced Senate Resolution 34, in which he stated that the "Federal Government has no power to rule over colonial dependences . . . [not] intended for future states" as well as that commerce could not be based upon "a policy of imperialism."[92] His proposal was eventually voted down, but in his speech in late January he elaborated on key points to the Democrat's anti-imperialism. Tillman claimed that the inevitable consequence of imperialism was "familiarizing our citizens to uphold a despotic and a military government," and such acceptance of "despotism propped by bayonets" would soon "make us look on quietly in one part of the country while the other is being despotically governed by military rule."[93] Imperialism, in his view, presented an existential threat because military rule "will be brought back to improve [read: overthrow] our own boasted self-government."[94]

Tillman knew white Southerners would understand that military control in the Philippines cast a foreboding shadow, and newspapers in the South, such as the *Memphis Commercial-Appeal* contended that imperialism threatened "the preservation of its [Southern] civilization, its ideals, its white supremacy, its laws, its institutions."[95] Tillman's perspective informed the party's 1900 platform, which warned "the American people that imperialism abroad will lead quickly and inevitably to despotism at home."[96] William Jennings Bryan, the Democrats' presidential candidate, echoed the platform in his acceptance speech and "devoted himself exclusively to [the] issue of Imperialism," warning that "we cannot repudiate the principle of self-government in the Philippines without weakening that principle here."[97] There were of course nonracist grounds on which to worry over imperialism's implications for democracy, but it was Tillman who drove the issue forward.

Beveridge and Tillman served as poles in the imperial debate, with their contrasting sectional experiences and partisan perspectives informing national politics. The Republican Party printed and distributed more than a million copies of Beveridge's Senate address to use as a campaign pamphlet to help reelect William McKinley.[98] Tillman, besides helping write his party's platform, also read the six-page document at the Democratic convention in Kansas City in early July 1900. He was relentless in depicting imperialism as an imminent threat, and his claims became darker as the election drew closer. A few weeks before the election he declared that imperialism ought to evoke "dread" of "despotic methods" among all Americans.[99] Tillman's article played to people's paranoia, which had been a staple of Reconstruction-era politics in which, as historian Mark W. Summers has noted, "fear, not trust, . . . bred a dangerous kind of politics."[100]

But it must not be forgotten that racism was a national phenomenon. The rants of Northern imperialists such as Albert J. Beveridge matched those of white supremacists such as Ben R. Tillman during Senate debates in 1899 and 1900. After Beveridge's reelection in 1904, he largely dropped his racist comments during Senate debates,[101] while Tillman raged on, including endorsing lynching during a Senate speech in 1907.[102] There was, moreover, an important difference between a racism that condescended to uplift the backward in the name of humanity and one that feared contamination and misrule by the same. Still, that common racism laid the groundwork for Beveridge's ultimate embrace of the very same "Lost Cause" interpretation of the Civil War that Tillman espoused and the GAR had so vociferously condemned.

Beveridge and Tillman were ardent racists as evidenced in their Senate debates. For its part, white GAR members had a complicated relationship with

African American members. Tillman claimed that "scores of times . . . men who wear the GAR button . . . crowd around me" to "express their approval of my utterances" condemning racial equality.[103] But Tillman simplified a complex picture. Existing alongside more than 450 GAR integrated posts were segregationist practices, including separate hotels and social settings for African Americans at annual GAR national encampments.[104] What is more, as historian Barbara Gannon has cogently noted, "For most northern veterans, segregation and other civil rights violations were not pressing issues." Loathing secessionist slaveholders did not in and of itself require a commitment to equal rights.[105] Undoubtedly the GAR membership represented a continuum of opinions on race relations. Many shared with Abraham Lincoln conflicted thoughts that had bedeviled him in the 1850s.[106] If African Americans were freed, he asked, would they be "politically and socially, our equals? My own feelings will not admit of this; and if mine would, we well know that those of the great mass of white people will not." He believed this resistance to equality to be "a universal feeling," one that "can not be safely disregarded."[107] Nearly fifty years later much of the GAR membership was likely able to reconcile to, and perhaps was untroubled by, *Plessy v. Ferguson*, even as they resisted Lost Cause celebrations of alleged Confederate nobility.

Beveridge's nationalism was his bedrock belief, grounded in a united, indivisible America—"The Nation, The Nation, always the Nation," he repeatedly proclaimed.[108] The purest display of nationalism, in this view, occurred through military service to the nation. Here, however, his celebration of martial fervor for the nation could merge with his racism to lead him in a new direction. When Southerners took up arms in the war against Spain, Beveridge and many Republicans deemed it proof of their fidelity to a united America.[109] White Southerners, this thinking went, had redeemed themselves through military conquests in Cuba and the Philippines. Calls for reconciliation swept the country. President McKinley became an early and prominent proponent. As the first president of the twentieth century, he recognized an opportunity to lead the nation's healing. He was "an inveterate conciliator" for whom sectional reconciliation was an "explicit war aim" in 1898.[110] In December 1898 he praised the sacrifices and courage of Southern volunteer soldiers and sailors, which enabled "the magic healing which has closed ancient wounds and effaced their scars."[111] The president returned to this theme of reconciliation in his second inaugural address in early March 1901. He proudly proclaimed: "We are reunited. Sectionalism has disappeared. Division on public questions can no longer be traced by the war maps of 1861."[112]

Beveridge eagerly seized upon reconciliation as a nationalist message of reunification. In an address on the battlefield of Shiloh, Tennessee, in early Spring

1903 he praised the South for its contributions in the war with Spain, urged all alive to "be tolerant of the views of the heroes of the other side [in the Civil War]," appealed for "charitable forgiveness on both sides," and enshrined Nation and American as the embodiment of reconciliation.[113] His remarks added more distance in his growing separation from the GAR.[114]

For its part, the GAR was careful not to let the currents of reconciliation pull them too far from their pride in their earlier accomplishments—and here we can see the generational rift between them and Beveridge.[115] They remained, as Caroline Janney has explained, unreformed nationalists who "refused to forget that they had been both righteous and victorious." But they realized the tide of history flowed away from them, and that "their cause was being diluted if not wholly forgotten"[116] among those promoting reconciliation. In reaction the GAR attempted to be a bulwark against the growing popularity of reconciliation and the concomitant acceptance of the kind of Lost Cause narrative peddled by postbellum Southern white supremacists. They urged Southern whites in 1901 to heed the advice of a former Confederate officer—"to forget the past and live for the future," accept what "had gradually dawned on him that States' Rights was a myth," and stop trying to "whitewash the Rebellion over."[117]

A great irony of imperialism emerged in the war with Spain. Military service afforded the South an opportunity to prove loyalty to the Republic and in turn accept the olive branch of reconciliation—all on terms Tillman had advocated through white supremacy and segregation. Gone forever was the "peculiar institution" of slavery, replaced after war against Spain by a "peculiar" national unity and memory. The "Recrudescence of Rebellion," as a GAR member described Richmond's Decoration Day 1894, became the dominant leitmotif in an ascendant Lost Cause after 1900. The lives and words of Albert J. Beveridge, the veterans of the Grand Army of the Republic, and Benjamin R. Tillman remained connected—albeit in shifting ways. Imperialism, once feared by Southern Democrats as a revived attempt to change the South, in fact opened the way for their triumph.

Perhaps the greatest transformation came in Beveridge himself, who went on to have a distinguished career as a historian of the Civil War era. Two months before he died in 1927, Beveridge was nearly finished with the second of a projected four-volume biography of his childhood hero Abraham Lincoln.[118] But his years of research and writing shattered his hero-worship. He no longer accepted as true his childhood's lessons about the South and the Civil War. As historian John Braeman explains, "He discovered evidence that called into question the legends propagated by Republican bloody-shirt orators of his youth."[119] Beveridge felt deceived, telling one close friend that "everything he was taught was in fact just the other way around."[120] To another good friend—Democratic author and arch-racist Claude G. Bowers[121] (1878–1958)—he complained that "I was taken regularly to old fashioned political rallies where orators indulged in the most shameless misrepresentations of men, measures, and motives of the twenty years before. I believed all the things that were told me . . . until I began going back to the original sources."[122]

Beveridge rejected Union shibboleths that Lincoln was an anti-slavery crusader of Republican legend. Moreover, Beveridge joined the South in blaming abolitionists for the Civil War. In casting aside childhood memories, he became that most unexpected of Republicans—a sympathizer with the Lost Cause. Five years after Beveridge's death Bowers published *Beveridge and the Progressive Era* (1932). This biography sold a reported 100,000 copies but had none of the white-hot furor found in Bower's earlier political histories, most particularly his fanciful and deeply racist narrative of Reconstruction, *The Tragic Era: The Revolution after Lincoln* (1929).[123] In Bowers and Beveridge we see the vagary of memory: a Democratic propagandist for the Lost Cause celebrating the life of a Republican who spent his early career tied to the GAR and its Won Cause.

Notes

1. See John Braeman, *Albert J. Beveridge: American Nationalist* (Chicago: University of Chicago Press, 1971); David V. Holtby, *Forty-Seventh Star: New Mexico's Struggle for Statehood* (Norman: University of Oklahoma Press, 2012), 39–66, 220–240; and Claude G. Bowers, *Beveridge and the Progressive Era* (New York: Literary Guild, 1932).

2. See Stuart McConnell, *Glorious Contentment: The Grand Army of the Republic, 1865–1900* (Chapel Hill: University of North Carolina Press, 1992); Barbara A. Gannon, *The Won Cause: Black and White Comradeship in the Grand Army of the Republic*, Civil War America (Chapel Hill: University of North Carolina Press, 2011); Barbara A. Gannon, "'They Call Themselves Veterans': Civil War and Spanish War Veterans and the Complexities of Veteranhood," *Journal of the Civil War Era* 5, no. 4 (2015), 528–550; and Caroline E. Janney, *Remembering the Civil War: Reunion and the Limits of Reconciliation*, The Littlefield History of the Civil War (Chapel Hill: University of North Carolina Press, 2013). Also see Wallace Evans Davies, *Patriotism on Parade: The Story of Veterans' and Hereditary Organizations in America, 1783–1900*, Harvard Historical Studies, vol. 66 (Cambridge, Mass.: Harvard University Press, 1955); and Mary R. Dearing, *Veterans in Politics: The Story of the G.A.R.* (Baton Rouge: Louisiana State University Press, 1952), which is tendentiously anti-GAR.

3. Davies, *Patriotism on Parade*, 336.

4. Stephen Kantrowitz, *Ben Tillman and the Reconstruction of White Supremacy*, The Fred W. Morrison Series in Southern Studies (Chapel Hill: University of North Carolina Press, 2000).

5. Barbara A. Gannon, *Americans Remember Their Civil War*, Reflections on the Civil War Era (Santa Barbara, Calif.: Praeger, 2017). This book is a recent historiographic survey.

6. The GAR's official weekly, the *National Tribune* (hereafter cited as *NT*), is included in the Library of Congress's Chronicling America: Historic American Newspapers, https://www.lc.gov/chroniclingamerica/lccn/sn2016187. Albert A. Smith Jr., *The Grand Army of the Republic and Kindred Societies: A Guide to Resources in the General Collections of the Library of Congress*, https://www.loc.gov/rr/main/gar, lists sources published from 1866 into the 1950s.

7. Mrs. [Mary Logan] John A. Logan, *Reminiscences of a Soldier's Life: An Autobiography*, foreword by John Y. Simon (1913; Carbondale: Southern Illinois University Press, 1997), 214–227, 243–246, 265–266, 371–432, discusses his and her work in the GAR on behalf of Union veterans. Dearing, *Veterans in Politics* is a jaundiced view of Logan but traces his activities in detail.

8. "A Soldiers' Ticket," *NT*, June 12, 1884, 1 [article]; "A Soldiers' Ticket," ibid., 4 [editorial]

9. "His Last Review," *NT*, January 6, 1887, 1.

10. Eric Foner, "Introduction to the 2014 Anniversary Edition," in *Reconstruction: America's Unfinished Revolution, 1863–1877*, updated ed. (New York: HarperCollins, 2014), xxxix.

11. Only recently have Civil War historians begun to interrogate the psychological impact of the war. See Brian Matthew Jordan, *Marching Home: Union Veterans and Their Unending Civil War* (New York: Liveright, 2014); Michael C. C. Adams, *Living Hell: The Dark Side of the Civil War* (Baltimore: Johns Hopkins University Press, 2014). Each book examines in great detail the war's psychological impact, a topic introduced in Drew Gilpin Faust, *This Republic of Suffering: Death and the American Civil War* (New York: Alfred A. Knopf, 2008). See also Lesley J. Gordon, *A Broken Regiment: The 16th Connecticut's Civil War*, Conflicting Worlds (Baton Rouge: Louisiana State University Press, 2014); James Marten, *Sing Not War: The Lives of Union and Confederate Veterans in Gilded Age America*, Civil War America (Chapel Hill: University of North Carolina Press, 2011); and Gannon, *The Won Cause*, especially 131–139.

12. "Our Protection Platform," *NT*, March 31, 1887, 4.

13. Theda Skocpol, *Protecting Soldiers and Mothers: The Political Origins of Social Policy in the United States* (Cambridge, Mass.: Harvard University Press, 1992), 110.

14. Ibid., 110–111, 102–130.

15. Davies, *Patriotism on Parade*, 196.

16. Donald L. McMurry, "The Political Significance of the Pension Question," *Mississippi Valley Historical Review* 9, no. 1 (1922), 19.

17. Skocpol, *Protecting Soldiers and Mothers*, 109, table 2.

18. McConnell, *Glorious Contentment*, 116.

19. [GAR] *Journal of the Thirtieth National Encampment of the Grand Army of the Republic*, St. Paul, Minn., September 2–4, 1896 (Indianapolis: Wm. B. Burford, Printer and Binder, 1896), 81, providing membership numbers 1878–1896.

20. McConnell, *Glorious Contentment*, 54.

21. Gannon, *The Won Cause*, 39, Appendixes 1, 2.

22. Heather Cox Richardson, *West from Appomattox: The Reconstruction of America after the Civil War* (New Haven, Conn.: Yale University Press, 2007), 211.

23. "Let Us Have United Action!" *NT*, March 20, 1884, 4.

24. Skocpol, *Protecting Soldiers and Mothers*, 102–130, positions the GAR within the Republican Party's "Triumph of Patronage Democracy" in the final three decades of the nineteenth century.

25. Quotation in "Pensions Vetoed," *New York Herald*, February 12, 1887, 2. Skocpol, *Protecting Soldiers and Mothers*, 125–126.

26. See, e.g., "Pensions: The Duty of the Government to the Veterans," *NT*, October 27, 1887, 4, and "Let the Nation Pay Its Debts," *NT*, November 3, 1887, 4.

27. "The New Pension Bill," *NT*, June 16, 1887, 4.

28. On the political conflict, see *Jordan, Marching Home*. Mark Twain added to the vitriol, railing against the venality, absence of "moral courage," and utter cowardice the GAR exhibited in allowing "purchasing [of] civic virtue"; quoted and discussed in *Mark Twain in Eruption: Hitherto Unpublished Pages about Men and Events*, ed. Bernard De Voto (New York: Harper & Brothers, 1940), 69, 66, 70.

29. Marten, *Sing Not War*, 30.

30. "Halt!" *NT*, November 3, 1887, 4; "As To Those Monuments," ibid.

31. "A Bit of History," *NT*, April 14, 1887, 4. W. E. B. Du Bois, *Black Reconstruction in America, 1860–1880*, introduction by David Levering Lewis (1935; New York: Free Press, 1998), 713, 725, highlights (among other agents) biased school textbooks.

32. Representative newspapers' reactions include "The Battle Flags Saved," *New York Times*, June 17, 1887, 1; "Drum Is the Scapegoat," *Chicago Daily Tribune*, June 18, 1889, 2. See also John M. Coski, *The Confederate Battle Flag* (Cambridge, Mass.: Harvard University Press, 2009), 67–69; Janney, *Remembering the Civil War*, 174–175.

33. Veterans' reactions included "A Loyal Blizzard," *NT*, June 23, 1887, 1 (quoted), 1–2, and "No Ill-Will," *NT*, June 30, 1887, 4. A counterpoint is presented in David W. Blight, *Race and Reconciliation: The Civil War in American Memory* (Cambridge, Mass.: Belknap Press of Harvard University Press, 2001), 244–251, with late nineteenth-century writer Ambrose Bierce, a Union veteran, arguing, "Give back the foolish flag whose bearers fell" (249) as a gesture promoting reconciliation.

34. "The Way to Get Cuba," *NT*, August 2, 1888, 4; "Undesirable Immigrants," ibid. See also the political cartoon "An Impending Danger," *NT*, August 9, 1888, 1.

35. Davies, *Patriotism on Parade*, 218.

36. Ibid., 340.

37. "Decoration Day," *New York Times*, May 29, 1869, 1; "Under Arlington's Trees," *Washington Post*, May 30, 1879, 1; "A Scrap of History," *NT*, 2 June 24, 1882, 4. Nicholas W. Sacco, "The Grand Army of the Republic, the Indianapolis 500, and the Struggle for Memorial Day in Indiana, 1868–1923," *Indiana Magazine of History* 111, no. 4 (2015), 349–380.

38. "Recrudescence of Rebellion," *NT*, June 14, 1894, 4.

39. "The March of the Flag," September 16, 1898, 47–57, in Albert J. Beveridge, *The Meaning of the Times and Other Speeches* (Indianapolis: Bobbs-Merrill, 1908), 48. Braeman, *Beveridge*, 26–29. Holtby, *Forty-Seventh Star*, 41–44.

40. "The March," in Beveridge, *The Meaning*, 47.
41. On such rhetoric, see Edward J. Blum, *Reforging the White Republic: Race, Religion, and American Nationalism, 1865–1898*, updated ed. (2005; Baton Rouge: Louisiana State University Press, 2015), 212.
42. "The March" in Beveridge, *The Meaning*, 56.
43. Ibid., 54.
44. Ibid., 50.
45. Beveridge to Perkins, May 3, 1898, Albert J. Beveridge Papers, Box 275, Library of Congress, Manuscripts Division, Washington, D.C.
46. "Grant, The Practical," 36–47, in Beveridge, *The Meaning*, 42. Eric T. L. Love, *Race Over Empire: Racism and U.S. Imperialism, 1865–1900* (Chapel Hill: University of North Carolina Press, 2004), 27–72. For additional context on Grant's expansionism, see Mark W. Summers, *The Ordeal of the Reunion: A New History of Reconstruction*, Civil War America (Chapel Hill: University of North Carolina Press, 2014), 204–227.
47. "Grant," in Beveridge, *The Meaning*, 42.
48. Ibid., 41.
49. Beveridge to Perkins, May 3, 1898, Albert J. Beveridge Papers, Box 275, Library of Congress, Manuscripts Division, Washington, D.C.
50. Ernest R. May, *Imperial Democracy: The Emergence of America as a Great Power* (New York: Harper Torchbooks, 1973), 268.
51. Richard Hofstadter, "Cuba, the Philippines, and Manifest Destiny," 145–187, in Richard Hofstadter, *The Paranoid Style in American Politics and Other Essays* (Cambridge, Mass.: Harvard University Press, 1964), 147.
52. Richardson, *West from Appomattox*, 285.
53. Richard White, *The Republic for Which It Stands: The United States During Reconstruction and the Gilded Age, 1865–1896*, The Oxford History of the United States (New York: Oxford University Press, 2017), 804.
54. Ibid., 807–808.
55. Hofstadter, "Cuba, the Philippines," 152. The same interpretation is advanced in Robert Dallek, "National Mood and American Foreign Policy: A Suggestive Essay," *American Quarterly* 34, no. 4 (1982), 340–342.
56. "Death Finally Seizes George J. Langsdale," *Indianapolis Journal*, December 28, 1903, 10. Today the Soldiers and Sailors Memorial honors Indiana veterans from all wars prior to World War I. See www.indianawarmemorials.org.
57. "Notes and Manuscript of Autobiography [Undated]," Albert J. Beveridge Papers, Box 324, Library of Congress, Manuscripts Division, Washington, D.C.
58. Bowers, *Beveridge*, 5.
59. Scott A. Sandage, "The Gaze of Success: Failed Men and the Sentimental Marketplace, 1873–1893," in *Sentimental Men: Masculinity and the Politics of Affect in American Culture*, ed. Mary Chapman and Glenn Hendler (Berkeley: University of California Press, 1999), 184. See also Scott A. Sandage, *Born Losers: A History of Failure in America* (Cambridge, Mass.: Harvard University Press, 2006).
60. White, *The Republic*, 137, 136–140.

61. On oral culture and its influential role in Lincoln's life, see Ferenc Morton Szasz, *Abraham Lincoln and Robert Burns: Connected Lives and Legends* (Carbondale: Southern Illinois University Press, 2008), 54–55.

62. The classic study is Eric Foner, *Free Soil, Free Labor, Free Men: The Ideology of the Republican Party before the Civil War* (1970; New York: Oxford University Press, 1995). See especially the new introduction, "The Idea of Free Labor in Nineteenth-Century America," x–xxxiv.

63. White, *The Republic*, 138.

64. Holtby, *Forty-Seventh Star*, 42–43.

65. Quoted in Gannon, "'They Call Themselves,'" 528.

66. McConnell, *Glorious Contentment*, 233. Also see the *National Tribune*, which provided extensive and enthusiastic support for the war. It advertised in its May 5, 1898 masthead that "The best history of the War with Spain will be found in the *National Tribune*, from week to week." The brevity of the war limited contemporary military narratives, but in 1903 the paper ran a series of detailed accounts of the war—e.g., "The Manilla Campaign," August 20, 1903, 1. Typical of their partisan articles in 1898 are these: "A Week of War," *NT*, May 5, 1898, 1; "Commodore George Dewey," *NT*, May 5, 1898, 1, which highlighted his four years of naval duty during the Civil War; and "Our Victory in the Philippines," *NT*, May 5, 1898, 4. "What Shall We Do with the Philippines?" *NT*, May 12, 1898, 4, posited that the 5,000 troops sent to the Philippines "will be more than a conquering army. It will be a redeeming, peace-making, civilizing force." "As to the Philippines," *NT*, May 19,1898, 4, predicted "a very large and profitable market for our products." A paean to the U.S political and military leaders of the war appeared in "The Cincinnati National Encampment," *NT*, September 15, 1898, 4.

67. Andy Doolen, *Fugitive Empire: Locating Early American Imperialism* (Minneapolis: University of Minnesota Press, 2005), xv.

68. Amy Kaplan, "Romancing the Empire: The Embodiment of American Masculinity in the Popular Historical Novels of the 1890s," *American Literary History* 2, no. 4 (1990), 660. Reprinted in Amy Kaplan, *The Anarchy of Empire in the Making of U.S. Culture* (Cambridge, Mass.: Harvard University Press, 2002), 92–120. Also see Jesse Alemán, introduction to *Empire and the Literature of Sensation: An Anthology of Nineteenth-Century Popular Fiction*, ed. Jesse Alemán and Shelly Streeby (New Brunswick, N.J.: Rutgers University Press, 2007), xiii–xxx.

69. Hofstadter, "Cuba, the Philippines," 152.

70. James Brádley Thayer, "Our New Possessions," *Harvard Law Review* 12, no. 7 (1899), makes repeated references to reporting on public opinion and discussion of imperialism found in contemporary journalism.

71. Vest, *Congressional Record—Senate*, 55th Cong, 3rd Session, March 1, 1899, 2608.

72. Sam Erman, "'The Constitutional Lion in the Path': The Reconstruction Constitution as a Restraint on Empire," *Southern California Law Review* 91, no. 6 (2018), 1211.

73. Love, *Race Over Empire*, 186–195 summarizes Senate debates between early December 1898 and mid-February 1899.

74. Republican [Party] National Committee, *Republican Campaign Text-Book, 1900* (Philadelphia: Press of Dunlap Printing Company, 1900), 427. Ibid., 426–430, reproduced the Democratic Party's entire 1900 platform.

75. Kantrowitz, *Ben Tillman*.

76. Edward J. Blum and Paul Harvey, *The Color of Christ: The Son of God and the Saga of Race in America* (Chapel Hill: University of North Carolina Press, 2012), 122.

77. Kantrowitz, *Ben Tillman*, 198–242, 262–263. In Tillman's racist rants, he freely acknowledged his part in the murder of five blacks in July 1876; see Benjamin R. Tillman, *The Struggles of 1876: How South Carolina Was Delivered from Carpet-Bag and Negro Rule: Speech at the Red-Shirt Re-Union at Anderson* (Anderson, S.C.: n.p., 1909), 14–39. C. Vann Woodward, *The Burden of Southern History*, 3rd ed. (Baton Rouge: Louisiana State University Press, 1993), 89–107, critically assesses the North, Reconstruction, and Black civil and voting rights.

78. Tillman, *Congressional Record—Senate*, 55th Congress, 3rd Session, January 20, 1899, 837.

79. Nelson, ibid., 837; see also their verbal jousting in ibid., 835–836.

80. Kantrowitz, *Ben Tillman*, 262–264.

81. Nelson/Tillman, *Congressional Record—Senate*, 55th Congress, 3rd Session, January 20, 1899, 837.

82. Erman, "'The Constitutional Lion,'" 1220. See also Sam Erman, *Almost Citizens: Puerto Rico, the U.S. Constitution, and Empire*, Studies in Legal History (New York: Cambridge University Press, 2018). I am indebted to Professor Erman for bringing his publications to my attention.

83. Kal Raustiala, *Does the Constitution Follow the Flag? The Evolution of Territoriality in American Law* (New York: Oxford University Press, 2009), 72–81.

84. See, e.g., "Speech of Senator Tillman," *Chicago Daily Tribune*, July 21, 1899, 2, for his unyielding assertion of racial superiority.

85. Platt, *Congressional Record—Senate*, 55th Congress, 3rd Session, December 19, 1898, 287–297.

86. Ibid., 297.

87. Braeman, *Albert J. Beveridge*, 42–46.

88. Beveridge, *Congressional Record—Senate*, 56th Congress, 1st Session, January 9, 1900, 704–712.

89. Ibid., 708–709.

90. Ibid., 711.

91. Tillman, *Congressional Record—Senate*, 55th Congress, 3rd Session, February 7, 1899, 1529.

92. Tillman, *Congressional Record—Senate*, 56th Congress, 1st Session, December 18, 1899, 564, Resolution 34. In addition, three Southern Democratic senators had introduced resolutions opposing annexation in the 55th Congress: Missouri Democrat George C. Vest, *Congressional Record—Senate*, 55th Congress, 3rd Session, December 6, 1898, 20, Resolution 191; Georgia's Augustus Bacon, *Congressional Record—Senate*, 55th Congress, 3rd Session, January 11, 1899, 561, Resolution 211; Louisiana's Samuel McEnery,

Congressional Record—Senate, 55th Congress, 3rd Session, February 7, 1899, 1534, Resolution 240. All three were voted down. Democratic intraparty conflicts over imperialism are discussed in Richard E. Welch Jr., *Response to Imperialism: The United States and the Philippine-American War, 1898–1902* (Chapel Hill: University of North Carolina Press, 1979), 61–67.

93. Tillman, *Congressional Record—Senate*, 56th Congress, 1st Session, January 29, 1900, 1262, 1255–1263.

94. Ibid., 1262.

95. Quoted in "Consent of the Governed," *Washington Post*, August 27, 1900, 6.

96. Republican [Party], *Republican Campaign Text-Book*, 427.

97. "Mr. Bryan's Speech of Acceptance," *New York Times*, August 9, 1900, 8.

98. Braeman, *Albert J. Beveridge*, 46.

99. B. R. Tillman, "Causes of Southern Opposition to Imperialism," *North American Review* 171, no. 527 (1900), 445

100. Mark W. Summers, *A Dangerous Stir: Fear, Paranoia, and the Making of Reconstruction*, Civil War America (Chapel Hill: University of North Carolina Press, 2009), 272.

101. Holtby, *Forty-Seventh Star*, 41, in discussing Beveridge as chair of the Senate's Committee on Territories (1901–1911), notes, "For Beveridge, promoting colonialism in the Philippines and postponing statehood for New Mexico and Arizona grew out of the same principle: hold each in a dependent status until the United States could uplift the peoples living there." In his oversight of statehood, Beveridge changed the referent of "uplifting" after 1904, shifting from adding more Euro-Americans settlers to rooting out corruption.

102. See, e.g., Tillman, "The Race Problem," *Congressional Record—Senate*, 59th Congress, 2nd Session, January 12, 1907, 1030–1041 in which he justifies lynching Blacks (p. 1041) and catalogs white supremacists' attitudes.

103. Tillman, *The Struggles of 1876*, 12.

104. See, for example, C. W. De Mond, "Report of the Committee on Colored Troops," 56, in *Report of the Officers and Chairman of Committees of the Thirty-Fourth National Encampment G.A.R.*, Chicago, August 26–30, 1900 (Chicago: Dean Bros. Blank Book and Printing Co., 1901). William E. Cummings, "Pomp, Pandemonium, and Paramours: The [Louisville] G.A.R. Convention of 1895," *Register of the Kentucky Historical Society* 81, no. 3 (1983), 283–86, refers to "paramours" encountered in segregated brothels in Louisville, Kentucky.

105. Gannon, *The Won Cause*, 170, 163–177.

106. Eric Foner, *The Fiery Trial: Abraham Lincoln and American Slavery* (New York: W. W. Norton, 2010), 61–72., in which he describes Lincoln's Peoria Speech of October 16, 1854, as an expression of his "own uncertainty" (67) as he struggled to develop his "antislavery ideas" into a "coherent antislavery ideology" (62). Equality was the dilemma.

107. Quoted in Foner, *The Fiery Trial*, 67.

108. See, e.g., Beveridge, "School and Nation," December 9, 1903, 234–243, in *The Meaning of the Times*, 240, and Beveridge, "The Voice of the North to the Soul of the South," April 6, 1903, 218–224; see 222 where he equates Nation and American. The full-

est account of his views is John Braeman's biography of Albert J. Beveridge, which has as its subtitle *American Nationalist*.

109. "Are They Dissatisfied?" *The Nation*, July 14, 1887, 27, is an early public endorsement of reconciliation. In surveying a reunion at Gettysburg, *The Nation* hailed comradery between soldiers from both sides and pronounced that "the soldiers of the 'lost cause' are as loyal to the Union as those of the cause which won. . . . The flag of the nation is the banner to which the South as well as the North is now devoted."

110. Blight, *Race and Reunion*, 351.

111. "Atlanta's Peace Jubilee Is Ended," *Atlanta Constitution*, December 16, 1898, 1; McKinley's speech marked his return to Atlanta thirty-five years after he, as a Union major, had been part of General Sherman's campaign through Georgia and Atlanta.

112. "President's Address," *New York Times*, March 5, 1901, 1.

113. Beveridge, "The Voice of the North," 219–222.

114. See, "Message of Republicanism and Democracy to Young Men," September 1902, Albert J. Beveridge Papers, Box 298, Library of Congress, Manuscripts Division, Washington, D.C. In praising young men as the party's lifeblood, he seemed to dismiss the GAR in comparison to young men, who "look upon the Nation as they look upon themselves—masterful with the vitality of youth—and not as an old man who has lived his day and totters to its end."

115. Janney, *Remembering the Civil War*, 160–231 assesses reconciliation in the North and South, with special attention to Union veterans and the GAR as well as to slavery, race, and reconciliation in the period 1880s to early 1900s.

116. Ibid., 270–271 (both quotations).

117. "A Hero in Gray," *NT*, October 17, 1901, 2.

118. Albert J. Beveridge, *Abraham Lincoln*, 2 vols. (Boston: Houghton Mifflin, 1928).

119. John Braeman, "Albert J. Beveridge and Demythologizing Lincoln," *Journal of Abraham Lincoln* 25, no. 2 (2004), 16.

120. Ibid.

121. Oliver Knight, "Claude G. Bowers, Historian," *Indiana Magazine of History* 52, no. 3 (1956).

122. Claude G. Bowers, "The Lincoln of Fact," *Virginia Quarterly Review* 5, no. 2 (1929), 265.

123. Claude G. Bowers, *The Tragic Era: The Revolution after Lincoln* (Cambridge, Mass.: Houghton Mifflin, 1929).

8

The Lynching of Frazier Baker

Violence from Reconstruction to Empire

DJ Polite

On the night of February 21, 1898, in a wooden frame building on the outskirts of Lake City, South Carolina, the Baker family went to bed in their home, which also served as a local post office. The William McKinley administration had appointed Frazier Baker, an African American, as the federal postmaster of this predominantly white town. The Baker family had received threats from white citizens who openly disapproved of his appointment. Local whites lamented the elevation of an African American to a position of authority. In preceding weeks, white vigilantes had burned down the first post office, shot at Baker's African American assistant, and made threats against Baker's life. Now, around 1 a.m. on this chilly night, Frazier and his wife, Lavinia, awoke to find their rear wall ablaze. Frazier and his wife took on the double task of waking and protecting their six children, while also putting out the blaze with the few water jugs around the home. As the fire spread, and the water in their home ran low, Frazier told his eldest son, Lincoln, to run and cry for help. But as Lincoln opened the front door, shots rang out from the attackers lined outside. Dragging his son back in the home to safety, Frazier frantically paced the living room, attempting to find a way out for him and his family. He turned to Lavinia and told her they might as well die running. Backlit by the flames and an easy target, the attackers shot Frazier, who died in front of his family. As the rest of the Baker family fled, Lavinia's hand was shot through, killing the two-year-old baby, Julia, in her arms. Lavinia, standing in the flames with a dead husband and child, managed to usher her remaining children—Rosa, Lincoln, Cora, Sarah, and Millie—into nearby bushes as the bodies of Frazier and the baby burned along with their home. They hid and waited until the assailants dispersed and local African Americans opened their homes to provide sanctuary.[1]

The lynching of the Baker family is not a new tale. Rather, it is part of a long history of racist violence against African Americans that occurred across the

South, and especially in South Carolina, after the Civil War. South Carolina was the site of the infamous Ku Klux Klan trials from 1871 to 1872, in which the federal government seemed to promise protection from the terrorist organization. Yet by 1876 South Carolina was every bit as violent, as evinced by the Hamburg and Ellenton "riots," more aptly called massacres. Occurring during a gubernatorial and presidential election, these massacres showed the violent measures that racist whites took to cement all-white local control. But in addition to racist violence 1898 presented another challenge. Days before the lynching of the Bakers, the U.S.S. *Maine* exploded in Havana Harbor, bringing calls for military intervention in Spain's wars with its colonies. The *Maine* was most likely not attacked, exploding instead by accident. Nonetheless, the calls for war spread.[2]

The lynching and the start of Spanish-American War are not just contemporaneous. The sinking of the *Maine* and the lynching of the Baker family demonstrate the connections between the spread of U.S. empire and the solidification of local white control in the U.S. South. But how exactly did racial violence in the Carolinas and the rise of Jim Crow influence debates surrounding the Spanish-American War? Political actors both nationally and within South Carolina recognized the hypocrisy of promoting freedom and liberty in Cuba while African Americans were being lynched for exercising voting rights. The discussions over empire and territorial acquisition at the end of the nineteenth century were, in part, framed by racial violence and disfranchisement in the U.S. South. Further, the racial violence in the Carolinas could not be divorced from memories of Reconstruction. The history of violence during and since Reconstruction was tied to this lynching and heightened the stakes of defining the boundaries of political inclusion. Repeatedly, political actors blurred the lines between the fall of Reconstruction and 1898, linking local racial violence to the question of U.S. expansion.

The congressional debate over the 1898 Treaty of Paris showed that the memories of the U.S. Civil War and Reconstruction weighed on Carolinians' stances on American empire. As South Carolina Senators Ben Tillman and John McLaurin debated imperial expansion, they embarked on a multipronged fight. Their stated positions on territorial expansion were couched in discussions and reinterpretations of racial violence since Reconstruction. Repeatedly in discussing the Treaty, they and others mentioned the 1876 massacres in Ellenton and Hamburg together with the 1898 lynching of Frazier Baker. As discussions over the treaty advanced, further violence in Phoenix, South Carolina, and Wilmington, North Carolina, brought more national attention to the Carolinas. The past and the present blurred together as they contested new definitions of the "ambiguous status of the United States as a nation, a republic, and an empire."[3] The result of this debate was a strengthening of both local Jim Crow and overseas empire. Even as Tillman and his colleagues spoke against annexation of new imperial territories, racial violence in the Carolinas buttressed two pillars of political exploitation, Jim Crow and empire.[4]

Connecting the racist violence in Lake City to questions about state, nation, and empire adds nuance to our understanding of why the United States undertook an imperial stance at the turn of the twentieth century. There has been rich discussion of the driving forces behind pro-imperialist sentiment.[5] Similarly, scholars have noted how economics, partisanship, a belief in federalism, and racism drove much of the anti-imperialist forces.[6] This chapter pulls on a thread that is present in earlier literature—that the Southern region's particular history during and after Reconstruction offered a contradictory basis from which to proceed on the imperial question. From the perspective of South Carolina, Lake City provided a moment to reconsider the legacies of Reconstruction and Redemption. Using those memories proved central to how racist white Southerners approached the question of violence, territorial expansion, and local white political power.[7]

For Southern conservatives with memories of Reconstruction, white supremacy needed to be secured at home before empire could be extended. During Reconstruction, federal occupation infringed on white supremacy. After the experience of Reconstruction, a key component of white supremacy was the exclusion of nonwhites from political power (even if a minority of whites also suffered). Invested in white supremacy, white Southerners, seemingly anti-imperialist, also invested political and ideological energies on the connections between empire and racial violence. The threat of federal intervention in response to the lynching of Frazier Baker, and the Jim Crow racial hierarchy more generally, was likened and linked to federal occupation during Reconstruction. To Southern white supremacists, the battle for the proper political order needed to start at home. They must first control themselves, their land, their government, before imposing imperial control on other people. Racial domination elsewhere, on other people abroad, was uncertain if white Southern local control was absent or restrained. Southern white anti-imperialism was often conditional. Once they were confident of the place of white supremacy at home, they could warm to occupation. Empire could only extend from a firm white supremacist political foundation at home.

While the United States grappled with questions of Jim Crow and empire, it also had to come to terms with the lynching of an African American federal postmaster in South Carolina. The lynching of Frazier Baker and his family attracted attention from politicians and media from across the nation. Although some state and national figures condemned the lynching, others painted the violence as a predictable outcome of having an African American in a position of political authority. In South Carolina, the *Dispatch* in Lexington called it one of the worst events in the state in years. Governor William Ellerbe initially refused comment, then offered a reward for the apprehension of the lynching party.[8] The *Newberry Herald and News* labeled the lynching "one of the most horrible deeds that has ever taken place in a civilized community."[9] However, even if condemning the lynching, some remained broadly ambivalent about its causes. The *Dispatch* condemned the actions of the unnamed white assailants but also blamed President William McKinley and the state Republican party for appointing an African American as postmaster in Lake City.[10] Many of these publications and writers believed the lynching would bring national scorn to the state of South Carolina. The scorn did indeed come, and it was influenced by reactions to the explosion of the U.S.S. *Maine* in Havana Harbor.

The lynching of the Bakers battled for national headlines and attention with the wartime furor arising from the alleged attack on the U.S.S. *Maine*. The sinking of the *Maine* occurred only a week before the lynching and instigated increased public calls for war with Spain in the name of freedom and democracy. Those calls for freedom and democracy abroad stood in stark contrast to the lynching in South Carolina. This tension was noted in several publications that explicitly linked the sinking and the lynching. Within South Carolina, one headline read "A Crime More Deplorable than the Loss of a 1000 Men in War," with the article stating that "we would have preferred to see [South Carolina] lose a thousand sons in battle than to have to record such a coward's crime as that which stains her today."[11] While the lynching diminished the United States' moral legitimacy on the questions of freedom and democracy, it was "cowardice" that stained the country. Domestic lynchings revealed an unsettled racial order, and the nation needed to act resolutely to shed its cowardice and restore racial order.

The theme of the lynching as a stain on a democracy preparing for war recurred often, but the nature of that "stain" was not consistent. The *New York Tribune* stated that this "savage" crime was done by white American men, not "by Spanish soldiery against Cuban rebels." The next day, the *Tribune* stated that the United States "had better not preach humanity to the rest of the world" while actions such as that in Lake City occurred unchallenged.[12] The *Washington Bee*, an African American newspaper, detailed the cold-blooded murder for their readers and called it a disgrace to the U.S. Constitution. The *Bee* lamented that this lynching occurred "while the country is all afire over the results with Spain." This sentiment was widespread as several African American newspapers noted that the United States as a nation would lose support from the African American community if the assailants were left unpunished and the African American community unprotected.[13] Here, we see a divergence in how deep the stain went.

Broadly, white Americans framed the lynching as a surface stain that could be easily addressed whereas African Americans presented it as a moral failing with deep and broad roots. Whether in the case of the South Carolina newspaper that labeled the lynching as an act of cowardice or the *Tribune* that posited the lynching as an act of "savagery," each of these were accusations lobbed against the individuals that committed the lynching. Their acts did indeed shame the nation, but as individual failings that were not representative of the nation. From the perspective of the African Americans, the "disgrace" was not just the occurrence of the lynching but how indicative it was of the widespread lack of protection of the African American community. As the U.S. contemplated war with Spain, the inability to protect innocent citizens at home was a disgrace to the Constitution and the principle of equal protection. The idea of the scope and meaning of racial violence also hearkened back to South Carolina's history of bloodshed over the racial boundaries of political power following emancipation and Confederate defeat in the Civil War.

Condemnations of the Lake City lynching brought the memory of Reconstruction into that contemporary moment, with both local and international political implications. The *New York Tribune* reminded its readership that South Carolina had attacked the authority of the federal government before at Fort Sumter, triggering the Civil War. It argued that perhaps South Carolina needed to be reminded "that the United States Government is not to be trifled with."[14] The *New York Times* concurred that the assailants should be brought to justice. Each of these were demonstrations that positioned the lynching in Lake City as outside the character of the wider U.S. nation. By saying that South Carolina needed to be reminded of what occurred after Fort Sumter, the implication was that the lynching was a Southern aberration. It was an event particular to South Carolina, and to a South Carolina that was clinging to a far-off racist past that the U.S. nation had vanquished. With rhetorical bluster, the U.S. nation could distance its present extension into foreign affairs by positioning the lynching of Frazier Baker as separate and distinct—a remnant of its past. However, these calls for the U.S. federal government to intervene in the Lake City case were not easily ignored.

The fact that Lake City was being linked to a longer history of racist violence only increased pressure to react decisively, raising the stakes for those concerned with the nexus of race and political power. U.S. federal officials were pressed to react to such a flagrant attack on federal power, with civil rights advocates concerned with African American political inclusion leading the charge. Anti-lynching advocate Ida B. Wells-Barnett repeatedly exhorted the McKinley administration to provide aid to the Baker family and take control of the investigation. She also worked with Representative George White (R-NC), the only African American left in Congress, to demand indemnities be given to the Baker family.[15] White put forward a resolution to that effect in the House of Representatives, proposing as well a joint congressional committee to investigate the lynching. Meanwhile, Senator William Ernest Mason (R-IL), introduced a similar resolution in the Senate. As Senate Committee Chairman on Post Offices, Mason took a special interest in the case. These resolutions resulted in pushback from South Carolina's prominent politicians; the threat of federal intervention was no longer rhetorical.

The possibility of U.S. federal intervention in South Carolina troubled many white Southerners as a stark reminder of Reconstruction, a period they hoped had passed. South Carolina politicians such as Senator John McLaurin (D-SC) likened a federal investigation of the Frazier lynching to the presence of federal troops during Reconstruction. In early March McLaurin claimed, "Public sentiment is behind our State officers in forcing them to make every effort to secure the arrest and punishment of the perpetrators of this crime."[16] The message was that the state would handle its own affairs, and the federal government should stay far away. From McLaurin's standpoint, the idea of federal officials coming into the state of South Carolina to administer justice, especially to uphold Black political power, looked too much like Reconstruction. Federal officials did indeed take control of the investigation, as a federal district attorney and postal inspectors conducted a fourteen-month investigation. This investigation continued in the background as Congress discussed the Spanish-American war and debated the parameters of annexation—another powerful and divisive issue.[17]

In South Carolina, the lynching of the Bakers was not just about a postmaster, but rather broader questions of who could exercise political power and the limits of that power. The 1895 South Carolina State Constitution effectively disfranchised South Carolina's African American population. But the fact that Frazier Baker had occupied the federal position of postmaster was a visible reminder that African American political participation had not been extinguished and that a brief period of fuller Black citizenship was just over the state's shoulder. The ensuing debates over how to deal with the lynching were not just debates about a single event in 1898. The impact of the lynching could not be isolated to that moment.

Rhetoric tied the lynching to the state's history of racial violence against African American political mobilization since the Civil War. For some, federal handling of the investigation was an echo of military occupation during Reconstruction to ensure that South Carolina respected federal authority. Even if the intention was not long-term occupation, the implication was that the federal government held ultimate authority and would bring the rogue region to heel. Those who decried federal intervention or interference defended their ability to effectively oppress those within their borders on their own terms, specifically African Americans. Such claims about sovereignty, political control, and the delineation of racial and political borders segued easily into others about the War with Spain and the potential annexation of new imperial territories from Spain.

As white supremacist Southern politicians engaged in the imperial debate, they understood that the future of white segregationist politics was at stake. They sought a firmer definition of who would wield political power and where. With the federal investigation underway, white racists within South Carolina believed that further threat of federal involvement was a demonstration that their political supremacy was not firm. In effect, they themselves were held in an inferior position in a political hierarchy. From their own standpoint then, the annexation debates were an opportunity to not only draw the boundaries of the nation but also to lift themselves to a position of true racial supremacy. Debates over empire could establish Jim Crow and cement all-white local control of South Carolina.

Senator Benjamin Ryan Tillman (D-SC) is an archetype of white supremacist politics and a representative example of a strand of Southern anti-imperialism rooted in staunch racism. Tillman served as governor of the state before serving as U.S. senator from 1895 to 1918. As the state's governor, Tillman was intentional about South Carolina's disfranchisement laws being for the explicit purpose of "white supremacy."[18] His racist rhetoric and fearmongering demonstrate the ways in which Southern racism and intransigence toward the acquisition of new territories went hand in hand. In discussing his approach to the imperial debate, one of his biographers stated, "Tillman used the experience of white Southerners since emancipation to argue against bringing still more nonwhite races into uneasy coexistence with whites jealous of their own racial supremacy."[19] Tillman's words and actions must be understood within a context in which the Baker lynching was central to the debate on empire. He opposed annexation not only based on exclusion of so-called racial inferiors from national politics. Rather, Tillman also focused on firmly entrenching the exclusion of what he saw as racial inferiors at home, as he and his contemporaries saw fit. His anti-imperial views were tied to local white supremacist political concerns in his own state.

Senator Tillman expressed his sentiments toward war with Spain through rhetoric that linked the local lynching to the international arena. Only a month after Congress discussed resolutions to take control of the Lake City investigation, South Carolina papers printed Tillman's approach to the Spanish-American War. He was explicitly pro-war, yet anti-annexation. Tillman advocated for the United States to aid the Cuban people with achieving independence. But he wanted to ensure that the United States did not claim Spain's colonies postwar. He criticized President McKinley's "hesitating policy" in regard to answering the apparent Spanish attack on the *Maine*.[20] Tillman blamed Spain for its treatment of the Cubans, and also Wall Street businesses that held financial interests on the island, particularly in sugar. Yet he was not an advocate of the Cubans as equals. Tillman believed they were racially inferior. In fact, for him, the Spanish were also racially inferior.[21] Despite his pro-war jingoism, his main concern was back home in South Carolina. Domestic concerns were never far from his lips.

Tillman's speeches in 1898 reveal that first and foremost he was open to annexation as long as white Anglo-Saxon supremacy was its stated political foundation. Tillman criticized the possible annexation of Hawaii, and local papers understood this to be based on white supremacy. As a vocal and ardent white supremacist, Tillman said that he did not object to annexation, so long as only Anglo-Saxons participated in the government. Tillman insisted that absolute anti-imperialism was not his stance. Expansion into Hawaii was an adequate position to hold, given that the sugar interests did not hurt his state, and that Anglo-Saxons excluded the native populations from the political process. Tillman was not unique in adhering to a worldview in which a belief in Anglo-Saxon superiority and expansion went hand in hand.[22] However, the Baker lynching and the threat of federal intervention unsettled Anglo-Saxon supremacy in South Carolina.

Tillman was incapable of separating international events from the lynching of the Baker family in Lake City. Starting with condemnation of Hawaiian annexation, he pivoted to criticizing the possible annexation of the other islands of the Pacific and Caribbean. He noted the islands of Puerto Rico, Cuba, and the Philippines were already populated "with the races for which we have no affinity or liking." The potential inclusion of what Tillman considered inferior races was not the sole issue. He continued, "We have already one perplexing and harassing problem right here at home."[23] That perplexing problem was whether whites in South Carolina would be forced to share even limited political control with African Americans. To that end, Tillman made international concerns local. But could he make his local concerns into an international issue? The Spanish-American War presented the opportunity to do so as African Americans across the country saw participation in the war as an opportunity to make greater claims to rights.

The McKinley administration called for African American volunteers in the buildup for war, and the African American community answered affirmatively. When in April of 1898 President William McKinley called for 125,000 African American volunteers for the war effort, broadly speaking, the call was answered as several communities nationwide set out to fill the quota. The rationale for the inclusion of African Americans in military service was mixed, including legislation that indicated a belief that African Americans might be more immune to tropical diseases. African Americans were not recruited under the belief of their standing as equal members of American society. Nor were they seen to be equal members of the U.S. military, afforded the same authority or gravitas. That much was clear when the African American troops came to Florida as part of the mobilization.[24]

Much like events in South Carolina, the Tampa "riot" of June 1898 brought into sharp relief the tension of wartime mobilization and white unease at seeing African Americans serve. Florida had the closest port to Cuba and thus became the rallying point for entire regiments from across the nation. African Americans of the 24th and 25th Infantry and the 9th and 10th Cavalry were among the troops that gathered. These Black troops, known as "Buffalo soldiers" were largely renowned for their fighting out in the U.S. West against Native American tribes. In many cases, this made them some of the more experienced groups heading to Cuba. However, their experience did not entail respect and authority in Tampa, as their mere presence unsettled racial mores. That much was clear one night when a white soldier from Ohio grabbed a local African American toddler. Holding the child upside down, the soldier issued a marksman challenge to see if anyone could shoot a hole through the child's sleeve. The child was unharmed, but the news of this vile game reached the African American regiments. The result was a night of violence, as the African American troops sought vengeance for this unfathomable offense.[25] White and Black South Carolinians grappled with the meaning and possibility of African Americans serving in the U.S. military abroad as a reflection of power, opportunity, and rights at home. African American soldiers, with experience and authority, potentially taking justice into their own hands, made a shocking sight for the nation's white supremacists, especially those in the U.S. South. After the Tampa riots, one white South Carolina editor suggested that the African American soldiers be sent "to the Philippines where it would be 'kill dick, kill devil' between them and the Malays."[26]

The experience in Tampa reinforced the belief that armed African American troops were a threat to a white supremacist racial order. In South Carolina, this belief held, as Governor Ellerbe refused altogether to arm Black troops. Even as South Carolina on the whole struggled to meet quotas for volunteer recruitment, the state disarmed African American militiamen and shipped their weapons to Columbia, South Carolina, for use by white volunteers. African Americans still found their way from South Carolina to Cuba as laborers. Blocked from participation as soldiers, these Black laborers said that "they were happy to be leaving Charleston" for greater personal freedom and economic opportunity in the Caribbean island. What is more, the Spanish-American War brought African Americans from across the nation, armed with rifles and wrapped in the U.S. military uniform, across state and international lines on their way from the U.S. West to Cuba. The lines between federal authority, state sovereignty, and imperial strength blurred. This was just the opportunity to project local concerns of white supremacist control outward.[27]

Tillman crafted a critique based on memories of federal military presence during Reconstruction to meld local concerns with the issue of U.S. imperialism. He frequently used the image of "carpetbaggery" to understand U.S. federal action at home and abroad. While federal investigators had been dispatched to Lake City, the White House considered military intervention in Cuba. The issue with military intervention in Cuba was whether the United States needed to recognize the independence of Cuba as a sovereign nation. In response to the McKinley administration's advocating a strategy of "intervention without recognition" in the territories, Tillman likened this to the condition of the South after the Civil War when the "country was overrun with carpetbaggers."[28] Tillman and local newspapers' reference to the carpetbaggers in their "country" is not to be overlooked. Tillman, thirty years after Reconstruction, still considered the U.S. South to be its own entity, occupied by a foreign power and foreign element during the period of Reconstruction. The U.S. federal government was the foreign entity exercising its authority over local whites. Meanwhile, African Americans, despite their citizenship status, were, along with carpetbaggers, a foreign element. Their inclusion in the political system diluted local white political power.

The carpetbagger theme shaped criticism of McKinley's policies by Tillman and several local South Carolina newspapers. Tillman critiqued calls for the

United States to occupy Spanish island territories until they were pacified. He questioned who would define pacification, "the carpet-baggers who will be left in charge of the government until they have grown rich from plundering those impoverished Cubans?" His primary concern was not about the political liberties of the Cuban people. He continued, "South Carolina was left by a foreign element in charge of her government, and they, too, remained here until 'pacification' was accomplished. Didn't they?"[29] Tillman clearly demonstrated a deep distrust of the "federal government" as not of the U.S. South. It was also hyperbole to suggest that the U.S. South or the region's most ardent white supremacists had at all been "pacified." He also evoked that imagery to criticize the calls for federal intervention in South Carolina's Lake City lynching and solidify the local power of white supremacy. When the white mob murdered the Baker family, it was an expression of the violence of boundary making—of how groups use force to define themselves against others—at home and abroad.

Throughout the imperial debate, Tillman sought to protect his state's practice of white supremacy from "foreign" or "alien" intervention. Who constituted these foreign and alien elements was flexible. By midsummer of 1898, Tillman was engaged in a vigorous debate on the possible annexation of Hawaii, along with the Caribbean and Pacific islands under Spanish control. The underlying focus of his rhetoric revealed that one issue at stake was the question of racial fitness for U.S. democracy. A people whose perceived racial debilitation was permanent could not be incorporated into the polity.

The connections between racial identity and fitness for democratic government or citizenship were frequently discussed in political circles (as they had been a few decades earlier during the proposed annexation of the Dominican Republic, as Christina Davidson and Gregg French show in their chapters in this volume).[30] One example is the distinction between Tillman and one of his Southern Democrat colleagues, former Confederate major general William Bate (D-TN). Bate referred to blood to frame the Pacific Islanders and Cubans as racially inferior to U.S Americans. On the annexation of Hawaii, Bate remarked that any negotiations with native Hawaiians were questionable, because for him the Hawaiians were of "doubtful authority." The Hawaiians were illegitimate negotiators. When pressed on how annexation of Hawaii would be different from the annexation of Texas, Bate posited that in the case of Texas, "She was blood of our blood. She was our kith and kin."[31] In a similar way Tillman disparaged Cubans as an ambiguously "colored" populace of dubious racial mixture. For Tillman, these Cubans were "aliens in blood" along with their culture, language, thought, and feeling. More to the point, he stated, "They have had the virus of Spanish misgovernment injected into their blood and bone."[32] For Bate and Tillman, there was an issue with the "blood" of these populations, whether Hawaiians or Cubans.

Bate understood blood as a repository of intelligence, governmental fitness, and a lineage, whereas Tillman believed blood was a source of cultural contagion. Bate imagined Texas as another majority white Southern state. Only as a majority white state could Texas be "kith of our kin" in a biological sense. The idea of blood relationship to those in Texas, inclusive of Native Americans, was a dubious claim. However, Bate remarked that the Senate needed to consider natural causes. What drew Native Americans, inhabitants of Texas, and U.S. citizens together was their shared environment, not a universal claim to Anglo-Saxon whiteness or shared European lineage. This shared environment in North America, a "new world," helped develop their fitness for "civilization" and democracy. Even by 1898, Bate was invested in a view of Manifest Destiny that held the nation together as a whole.[33]

Tillman was less forgiving in his invocation of blood. The environment had little bearing on whether the Cubans were "fit" for democracy. It did not matter that Cuba had a substantial population of people of European descent. Their Spanish heritage and racial mixture was an insurmountable inherited contagion carried in their blood. Bate adhered to a vision where race was at least partially determined and shaped by environment. Tillman was a race determinist who viewed race as an unchanging and unalterable fact. The foreign and the alien could not be incorporated. They must be kept at bay, particularly from the political system, in order to define the borders of political inclusion. These "foreign elements" would be excluded from the political system either ideologically or violently. Whether in discourse or in post offices, the blood of the other was the mortar to erect stronger borders between the nation and the territories, or the federal government and local white politics.

The possibility of territorial annexation and the federal investigation of the white mob in Lake City reinforced Tillman's fear of the permeability of the nation's and his state's borders. After local officials in Lake City proved unable, or unwilling, to find the assailants of the Baker family, federal officials did indeed take over the case. Abial Lathrop, a federal U.S. attorney from Charleston, was provided with resources to investigate; the resources included two postal investigators and a private detective. After additional requests, Lathrop was given the ability to remove potential witnesses from Lake City, under government protection.[34] By late June, two days before Tillman was haranguing about the "blood" and alien nature of the people from the Philippines and the Caribbean, deputy marshals arrested several men for being part of the Baker lynching party. As if to underscore the link between the lynching and the Spanish-American War in the minds of local South Carolinians, four of the men arrested were apprehended at Camp Fitzhugh Lee while training for war with Spain. The U.S. marshal sent for the arrest was confronted by Captain Davis, who refused to allow any arrests unless he received written instruction from the Secretary of War to do so. Here, the lines and jurisdiction between state, nation, and empire were anything but clear.[35]

The federal arrest on a South Carolina base of white men volunteering for war, because of their lynching of a Black man, actively blurred lines among the local, the national, and the international. When Tillman remarked that a "foreign element" had been left in charge of South Carolina's government during Reconstruction, he rhetorically positioned the federal government as alien to his region. Now, the federal government seemingly took control of local South Carolina affairs for the sake of African American political power. The presence of U.S. marshals on a South Carolina base, apprehending white South Carolina volunteers, was difficult to dissociate from Reconstruction memory. If the Spanish-American War provided a period to negotiate the political borders between state, nation, and empire, then the Lake City lynching and its political aftermath muddied the waters. For Tillman, the alien and the foreign were indeed legion and coming from multiple directions. If there was meant to be a clear racial hierarchy of political power, racist white South Carolinians were being excluded or pushed down the hierarchy by the federal government. If the Spanish-American War was meant to bring reunion to the regions, or between the imagined "white" regions of the nation, Lake City and empire were proving to be impediments.

The November elections of 1898 brought more national scrutiny to the Carolinas as racist whites engaged in murder and local coups. In Phoenix, South Carolina, a local Republican family challenged provisions in the 1895 state constitution that disfranchised African American men. Local white Democrats not only repressed this challenge, but lynched and murdered at least eight African Americans in the town for good measure. Meanwhile, whites in Wilmington, North Carolina, executed a coup d'etat against African American local government. Led by former Confederate generals, racist whites not only forced elite African Americans from power but stole their property, turning African American citizens into refugees. Lake City brought the initial focus of the federal government to the Carolinas. Phoenix and its bloodshed increased the Carolinas' notoriety for violence on behalf of local all-white political power. The Wilmington attack, one of the most notorious race massacres in U.S. history, underlined that the Carolinas were no home for African American democratic participation. Starting with Lake City in February, the bloodshed of 1898 marked the boundaries of political control in the Carolinas.[36]

In response to these massacres, Tillman measured several threats to local white supremacy in his state. On one hand, he feared the influence of the federal government in state politics as the U.S. South was in the process of enacting Jim Crow legislation. On the other hand, he encouraged the violence that led up to the Wilmington riots. As a reported 1,000 mounted men participated in a rally in Charlotte, North Carolina, Tillman egged on violence with reference to white supremacist outrage surrounding an African American editor, Alexander Manly. As Tillman remarked, "In South Carolina no Negro editor could slander the white women of the state as that Wilmington Negro did," and that as punishment Manly should be food for "catfish at the bottom of the Cape Fear river." His insistence that bloodshed was an option to enforce the boundaries of local political white supremacy threatened to erase the boundaries between local control and federal power and in fact imperiled the political apartheid white supremacists were building.[37]

Media attention only increased political scrutiny. Whether from Newberry, Lancaster, Keowee, Yorkville, Anderson, or Sumter, South Carolina newspapers printed stories about the "race wars" and "bloodshed" in Phoenix and linked them with the events of Wilmington on their front pages.[38] The news of massacres, coups, and murders in the Carolinas spread beyond the region. In Atlanta, Washington, D.C., and New York, the events of Phoenix and Wilmington were linked together. The upheaval in Wilmington brought calls for federal intervention to aid the newly displaced African American community. The *Washington Post* conjectured that South Carolina caused President McKinley and his Cabinet the most concern. It was South Carolina where the situation was "much more serious" than Wilmington since it was where "Federal officials have been driven from their posts of duty," a clear reference to the events in Lake City. Whether this was true of the McKinley administration or not, from the perspective of the *Washington Post*, South Carolina was of dire political concern.[39]

In Wilmington, the crisis was a local matter, as the African Americans were displaced solely from municipal seats. In South Carolina, Frazier Baker had been a representative of the federal government. South Carolina events raised a question of political authority. The difficulty to investigate and then arrest Frazier Baker's murderers added gravity to events in South Carolina. The Lake City trial had yet to begin when the bloodshed in Phoenix specifically challenged another election, one with federal implications. The *Post* posited that if United States Marshals could not bring order, McKinley should send federal troops. That

Figure 8-1. "Civilization Begins at Home," *Literary Digest*, November 26, 1898, 625, https://archive.org/details/literarydigest17newy/page/625/mode/1up.

threat circulated in the minds of more than paranoid white supremacists like Tillman. The power of the federal government overseas was undermined if the U.S. South's racist vigilantes flouted federal authority at home.[40]

After the violence during the November elections, the connections and tensions between local Southern violence and international empire were palpable. The *New York World* and *Literary Digest* printed the poignant political cartoon, "Civilization Begins at Home," at the end of November 1898 (see Figure 8-1). In it, President William McKinley eyes a map of the Philippines, which was soon to become a U.S. territory, while a figure representing Justice pulls back the curtain to reveal a lynching scene in America's backyard. The Wilmington and Phoenix massacres, occurring in early November, no doubt weighed heavily on the artist's and readers' minds.[41] The assertion of "Civilization Begins at Home" that the United States could not provide civilization to the colonies while lynchings were rampant was echoed in the U.S. Congress. Senator William E. Mason (R-IL), who had advocated for federal control of the Lake City lynching investigation, was a clear and vocal critic of further annexation. He explicitly tied imperial expansion to the events in the Carolinas since Lake City. Mason criticized the idea that the people of the Philippines were incapable of self-governance. The events in Lake City, Phoenix, and Wilmington had demonstrated a return to a darker era. He protested, asking of American imperial rule, "Shall we send special instructors to teach them how to kill postmasters, their wives and children, if their complexion does not suit the populace?" He pressed on, asking his colleagues, "Shall we teach them, as they do in North and South Carolina, how the mobs can run the towns and kill the people?"[42] The memory of Reconstruction, the racial violence and rise of Jim Crow, and overseas imperial annexation had coalesced into a vicious crucible in the Carolinas. Others saw those connections as well, but used them as a lesson on the merits of extending the benefits and levers of white supremacy down to local levels.

To sustain the foundation of Jim Crow in his state, Tillman reached back to Reconstruction, and out toward empire. A week after the election-day massacres, he remarked that these killings were lamentable but justifiable given the "trials" of Southern white men during Reconstruction. Tillman proclaimed that the attention on his state consisted of political and hypocritical attacks from Northern Republicans. He decried those who attacked disfranchisement in the South while ignoring similar disfranchisement in overseas territories. Tillman said in his home county, Edgefield, that the "white men at Phoenix, remembering our own troubles in 1876, were angered by so barefaced and outrageous a travesty on legal voting, and thus the conflict between the races came about."[43] In his logic, attacks on the legal disfranchisement of African American voters urged racial animosity and racial violence in the South.

The interweaving of Reconstruction, with contemporary white supremacist violence and the annexation debate was rhetorically useful for South Carolina's other Senator as well. Senator John McLaurin (D-SC), who contested the federal investigation into the Lake City lynching, imposed the purported wisdom gained from Reconstruction onto the annexation debate. McLaurin cosponsored a resolution written by a former congressman of the Confederacy. The resolution held that the United States had no power to acquire and govern permanent colonies. Defending this resolution, he proclaimed his experience as a South Carolinian made him "peculiarly qualified" to speak on the question of incorporating a "mongrel and semi-barborous [sic] population" into the body politic of the United States. He added, "The experience of the South for the past thirty years with the negro race, is pregnant with lessons of wisdom for our guidance in the Philippines."[44] This wisdom took into account white South Carolina's past "overcoming" Reconstruction through blood in places like Ellenton,

Phoenix, and Lake City.⁴⁵ Although he may not have explicitly invoked each of the above, McLaurin implied that this entire era included lessons to be learned. Nonwhite people could not share governmental power with whites, he suggested, and whites should not have their ability to impose racial hierarchy impeded by an external power.

McLaurin's interpretation linked Reconstruction, Redemption, and the 1898 lynchings and massacres through a singular lens. McLaurin, who had once called himself a "moderate expansionist," declared that if the United States and expansionists were sincere in their overtures to aid the Philippines, then they should pass an amendment to settle the "vexed race and suffrage questions" of the United States. He mockingly asked how annexationists could "advocate a policy for outlying territories, embracing races so nearly akin to the negro, which differs so radically from the policy adopted as to that race in the South."⁴⁶ Following the several attacks on African Americans who dared to exercise political power throughout 1898, McLaurin turned the question on annexation to a larger one of political supremacy. The Filipinos were no more deserving of political power than African Americans. The events in the Carolinas, starting with Lake City, were demonstrations that the acceptable amount of nonwhite political power was zero. That was the precondition for territorial control. Secondarily, the U.S. could extend territorial control only if white South Carolinians could extend and cement their political control over their own "territory." McLaurin's mocking call for an amendment to permanently settle the vexed race and suffrage question in the U.S. nation and empire was a declaration of white supremacy. It was an assertion that the racial violence from Reconstruction to 1898 was the unavoidable effect of intervening in the affairs of the former Confederacy. The federal government had intervened to buttress African Americans during Reconstruction as well as minimally in Lake City in 1898 and had considered further intervention after Phoenix and Wilmington. But if imperialists acquired territories in the Caribbean and the Pacific, while depriving those people of political rights, then the actions being taken in the U.S. South were justified.

This struggle for white supremacist sovereignty left little room for George White (R-NC), the last remaining Black Congressman. George Henry White, the U.S. House representative from Tarboro, North Carolina, had worked with Ida B. Wells-Barnett to bring resolutions addressing the Lake City lynching. He was also in favor of overseas territorial expansion. In a speech in the U.S. House of Representatives, he noted his long support for all previous measures to liberate the Cuban people from Spain. He used his support for the war as an opportunity to speak in Congress about race and political power within the nation and his region. White noted that he was the single African American representative. Pivoting from the international to the domestic, White noted that the peoples in the territories were frequently linked to African Americans in the debate over race, democracy, and citizenship. White continued, "I have heard them referred to as savages, as aliens, as brutes, as vile and vicious and worthless."[47] White objected to those such as McLaurin and Tillman, who linked the peoples of the territories to the African American community, his community. He espoused a pro-American expansionism, yet he criticized the vast disfranchisement rising in the South and the wider system of white supremacy. He had worked with Wells-Barnett to bring justice for the Bakers who were lynched in Lake City. Yet here White contended with the expansion of the U.S. empire's boundaries and the broader language of white supremacy that blurred the lines between the local and the international.

George White was cognizant of how any debate on racial fitness for political power implicitly concerned the African American community. White noted that most South Carolina congressional Democrats had won election without vast voter participation, having relied on voter suppression and disfranchisement of the U.S. South's "negroes." To this point, White accused his white political colleagues, "You have got the idea that any means that will disfranchise him and prevent him from exercising the rights which are given him under the Constitution is legitimate."[48] The overthrow of democratically elected officials in Wilmington added weight and urgency to this assertion. He then pressed on the question of annexation. He called for the United States to take hold of those in Cuba, Puerto Rico, Hawaii, and the Philippine islands. To this he received prolonged applause, but overlooked was his caveat that first the United States must "recognize your citizens at home" and "give them the rights that they are justly entitled to."[49]

On February 7, 1899, Senator Tillman read the text of Rudyard Kipling's "White Man's Burden" on the floor of the U.S. Senate to deliver a diatribe against the embrace of territorial annexation.[50] Tillman often spoke of the need to protect the yeoman white farmer, normally from African Americans. Here, Tillman sought to protect white Southerners from the new threat posed by imperial overseas expansion. After the poem, Tillman stated white Southerners opposed annexation, "not because we are Democrats, but because we understand and realize what it is to have two races side by side that can not mix or mingle without deterioration and injury to both."[51] For Tillman and the white South, the imperial expansionism espoused by Northern Republicans was due to naïveté about the realities of colonialism. Pro-annexationists clearly had not learned the "lessons" of Reconstruction. The U.S. South knew the realities of life under colonial rule, he claimed. The white South had been colonized, stripped of its right to unvarnished white supremacy. Similar to McLaurin, Tillman pointed to the lessons that his white contemporaries in South Carolina had supposedly long learned. White supremacy was and should be the foundation of a functional democracy, and it started at home, wherever white men called home.

The nation needed to embrace the lessons that he and his Southern contemporaries had internalized, that political and social white supremacy should be unambiguously sustained at home and abroad. For Tillman, the United States did not need to avoid expansion altogether, and Tillman welcomed a martial spirit. He valorized the actions of white vigilantes during Reconstruction. Tillman said, "We all rose in our manhood and . . . we took the government away from those people. We have held it ever since and we will hold it for all time."[52] This was a personal claim. He had been one of the participants in the Hamburg Massacre in 1876 in the lead-up to the last election of what can be considered the Reconstruction era. Tillman was accustomed to the federal government, or "the North," condemning his region for upholding white supremacy, and he saw Phoenix, Wilmington, and Lake City as a continuation of history since the close of the Civil War.

Discussions over imperial-annexation and white Southern political violence revealed the intermingled tensions between the local and international. Tillman asked the Senate why "the colored race must be differently treated in the Philippine Islands, Hawaii, and Puerto Rico from what they are treated in our States of Mississippi, Louisiana, Texas, Alabama and South Carolina. If it is good to have white supremacy in the Hawaiian islands, why is it not in my State?" It was a claim that, whether at home or abroad, white supremacy needed to be constructed and enforced in the system. With that in mind, Tillman pushed back against Northern criticisms of Jim Crow. He said it was duplicitous to "attack my State for having suppressed the negro vote unconstitutionally and unduly, and in a mean, dishonest way turn around and enact a provision in the act creating the Territory of Hawaii which is less liberal than we have enacted." Over and again, the debate melded questions of local white control with imperial ramifications.

The Treaty of Paris passed the U.S. Senate in early February of 1899 by the margin of only two votes, despite the pushback and the concerns of several senators. Tillman (D-SC) voted in the negative. With such a thin margin, the positive vote of John McLaurin (D-SC) was a crucial swing vote. Earlier works noted that McLaurin was swayed to vote in favor of the expansion, despite his own anti-annexation sentiments.[53] His vote was gained by being granted political patronage by the Republican McKinley administration, specifically in the form of selecting federal positions within the state of South Carolina. McLaurin, who served on the Committee of Claims and the Committee on Indian Affairs, was given the power to select all the postmasters of his state, a role completely outside of his committee responsibilities. This occurred as the charged assailants of Frazier Baker's family in Lake City still awaited trial. For all of Tillman's bluster, it was McLaurin who convinced the federal government to cede power in his state, at the expense of the Baker family.

From the standpoint of white supremacists in South Carolina, the lynching of Frazier Baker's family did not actually result in the coming of federal troops, but rather greater political power in exchange for a vote in favor of imperial expansion. This article began with a description of the terror that fell upon not just the Fraziers, but African Americans in the surrounding community. For all the attention given to that case and the subsequent racial massacres in the Carolinas, the federal government did not come to uphold the political power of African Americans in the South. Despite claims that these acts besmirched the image of the United States and insulted the authority of the federal government as it attempted to criticize the Spanish, the McKinley administration relented.

After Phoenix, despite brief mentions that federal intervention might come to instill order, it did not arrive. The displaced African Americans from Wilmington lost their homes and did not receive recompense. And George White and his impassioned plea to recognize the African American citizen at home? By 1902, he was no longer a member of Congress and no other African American served for several decades. Two months after the passage of the Treaty of Paris, the eleven accused stood trial in Charleston for the murder of the Bakers. Despite several witnesses testifying, the case ended in a mistrial with all eleven walking free. The case was not retried. If anything, the imperial annexation debate added extra leverage for those such as McLaurin to shore up local control and white supremacy in the state. In essence, one of the crucial votes in favor of imperial expansion was bought and paid for at the expense of African American lives and political power in the Carolinas.[54]

The Jim Crow–era argument over imperial expansion in 1898 offered white politicians in South Carolina leverage to reconsider their place in the nation since Reconstruction. Likewise, it gave the U.S. an opportunity to reconsider the shape and character of the nation, at home and in the world. This was not the first, nor would it be the last, U.S. imperial expansion from a political or economic standpoint. The United States had long operated as an empire. The year 1898 simply provided a checkpoint to legally and ideologically determine the borders of the nation and the rights of citizenship. If overseas expansion and the war with Spain were going to be the vehicles of reunion for Northern and Southern whites, that reunion would have to be negotiated. There were those in the nation who saw the violence in locales such as Lake City, Phoenix, and Wilmington as continuations of a white rebellious spirit that had a decades-long history. These events were a reminder that white racial reactionaries in South Carolina had not repented. South Carolina senators John McLaurin and Benjamin Tillman insinuated that they had little to repent for in that thirty-year history. Nor did they want the massacres of African Americans that they had cheered on to prompt a federal response that would, in their view, place the white U.S. South in the position of a colonial territory, subject to alien, federal control.

If Americans were going to reassess their status as a nation, republic, and empire, the South's white supremacists would not let them do so at the expense of their political power. Rather, if the U.S. embraced empire, it would need the acquiescence of the white U.S. South. This acquiescence came first with a further integration of white Southern political concerns into the national and imperial apparatus. Second, this acquiescence came with ceding greater political sovereignty, power, and authority to the rising Jim Crow South. Last, the memory of Reconstruction continued to be a potent rhetorical tool to impose white Southern concerns not only domestically, but on the U.S. empire.

Carolina politicians had learned that using the negative memory of Reconstruction could indeed shape the nation as republic and empire at the turn of the twentieth century. The disfranchisement of African Americans in the South continued for at least a half century more. Likewise, disfranchisement of nonwhite peoples had expanded to the new territories who were not granted statehood. Criticisms of Reconstruction could be repeatedly used to shape or influence U.S. imperial policy. Just months after the passage of the Treaty of Paris and the end of the Lake City trials, newly acquired Puerto Rico was hit by the San Ciriaco Hurricane. As the island dealt with the devastation of that August 1899 storm, which ravaged the coffee and sugar plantations as well as homes of the island, Tillman attacked efforts to offer aid to Puerto Rico. He stated, "If you start another freedmen's bureau on a small scale in Puerto Rico with this money . . . I warn you that your efforts to rehabilitate that island and put it on its feet will be unsuccessful."[55] White South Carolinians would not be forced to buttress the political and financial burden of those who were written outside of the U.S. political system. Nor would the white South couch their concerns in deference to the federal government or the U.S. nation. If anything, "Reconstruction" would be used as a slur to shame the U.S. nation to buckle to the white U.S. South's concerns.

Notes

1. David Carter, "Outraged Justice: The Lynching of Postmaster Frazier Baker in Lake City, South Carolina, 1897–1899," (Honors thesis, University of North Carolina at Chapel Hill, 1992); David Carter, "'No Painted Apache Ever Did Anything Half So Wanton, or Cannibal in Darkest Africa Ever Acted Upon a More Fiendish Impulse': Newspaper Reactions to the 1898 Lynching of Postmaster Frazier Baker in Lake City, South Carolina, on the Eve of the Spanish-American War," paper presented at the Media and Civil Rights Symposium, University of South Carolina, March 23, 2012; Terence Finnegan, *A Deed So Accursed: Lynching in Mississippi and South Carolina, 1881–1940* (Charlottesville: University of Virginia Press, 2013).

2. Hyman George Rickover, *How the Battleship Maine Was Destroyed* (Washington, D.C.: Naval History Division, Department of the Navy, 1976); Edward J. Marolda, ed., *Theodore Roosevelt, the U.S. Navy, and the Spanish-American War*, 1st ed (New York: Palgrave, 2001).

3. Amy Kaplan, *The Anarchy of Empire in the Making of U.S. Culture* (Cambridge, Mass.: Harvard University Press, 2005), 1. Kaplan claims that the idea of the "nation at home" domestically is linked to broader movements of empire, drawing heavily on literary discourse. This article builds on that assertion and applies that framework to political discourse.

4. Frank Andre Guridy, *Forging Diaspora: Afro-Cubans and African Americans in a World of Empire and Jim Crow,* Envisioning Cuba (Chapel Hill: University of North Carolina Press, 2010).

5. Kristin L. Hoganson, *Fighting for American Manhood: How Gender Politics Provoked the Spanish-American and Philippine-American Wars*, Yale Historical Publications (New Haven, Conn.: Yale University Press, 1998); William Appleman Williams, *The Tragedy of American Diplomacy*, 50th anniv. ed. (New York: W. W. Norton, 2009); Walter LaFeber, *The New Empire: An Interpretation of American Expansion, 1860–1898*, 35th anniv. ed., Cornell Paperbacks (Ithaca, N.Y: Cornell University Press, 1998); Philip Sheldon Foner, *The Spanish-Cuban-American War and the Birth of American Imperialism, 1895–1902*, Modern Reader (New York: Monthly Review Press, 1972); Howard Wayne Morgan, *America's Road to Empire: The War with Spain and Overseas Expansion* (New York: Alfred A. Knopf, 1965); John L. Offner, *An Unwanted War: The Diplomacy of the United States and Spain over Cuba, 1895–1898* (Chapel Hill: University of North Carolina Press, 1992); Richard Hofstadter, *The Paranoid Style in American Politics: And Other Essays* (New York: Vintage Books, 1967).

6. E. Berkeley Tompkins, *Anti-Imperialism in the United States: The Great Debate, 1890–1920* (Philadelphia: University of Pennsylvania Press, 1970); Eric Tyrone Lowery Love, *Race over Empire: Racism and U.S. Imperialism, 1865–1900* (Chapel Hill: University of North Carolina Press, 2004); Paul A. Kramer, *The Blood of Government: Race, Empire, the United States, and the Philippines* (Chapel Hill: University of North Carolina Press,

2006); Edwina Smith, "Southerners on Empire: Southern Senators and Imperialism, 1898–1899," *Mississippi Quarterly* 31, no. 1 (1977).

7. Matthew Karp, *This Vast Southern Empire: Slaveholders at the Helm of American Foreign Policy* (Cambridge, Mass.: Harvard University Press, 2016); Stephen David Kantrowitz, *Ben Tillman and the Reconstruction of White Supremacy*, The Fred W. Morrison Series in Southern Studies (Chapel Hill: University of North Carolina Press, 2000); Tennant S. McWilliams, *The New South Faces the World: Foreign Affairs and the Southern Sense of Self, 1877–1950* (Tuscaloosa: University of Alabama Press, 2007); Smith, "Southerners on Empire: Southern Senators and Imperialism, 1898–1899"; Christopher Lasch, "The Anti-Imperialists, the Philippines, and the Inequality of Man," *Journal of Southern History* 24, no. 3 (1958), 319–331; Tennant S. McWilliams, "The Lure of Empire: Southern Interest in the Caribbean, 1877–1900," *Mississippi Quarterly* 29, no. 1 (1975).

8. "Yesterday, a Mob of Unknown Parties Shot and Killed F. B. Baker," *Dispatch* (Lexington, S.C.), February 23, 1898; "Governor Offers Reward: $500 for Conviction of the Murderers and Prosecution Instituted," *Lancaster (S.C.) Ledger*, February 26, 1898.

9. "The Results of Hannaism: A Horrible Crime Caused by the Appointment of a Negro Postmaster in a White Community," *Newberry (S.C.) Herald and News*, February 25, 1898.

10. "Yesterday, a Mob of Unknown Parties Shot and Killed F. B. Baker," *Dispatch*, February 26, 1898.

11. "The Lake City Horror: A Crime More Deplorable Than the Loss of a Thousand Men in War," *Washington Post*, March 3, 1898, quoting *The State* (Columbia, S.C.).

12. "Humanity in South Carolina," *New York Tribune*, February 24, 1898; "Punishment for Baker's Assassins," *New York Tribune*, February 25, 1898.

13. "Democratic Negroes Please Read" and "The South's Pretended Friendship," *Washington Bee*, February 26, 1898. For more examples consult George P. Marks, *The Black Press Views American Imperialism (1898–1900)*, The American Negro, His History and Literature (New York: Arno Press, 1971).

14. "Punishment for Baker's Assassins," *New York Tribune*, February 25, 1898.

15. For discussions on Ida B. Wells's work in Washington, D.C., on behalf of the Bakers, consult Carter, "Outraged Justice"; Trichita Chestnut, "Lynching: Ida B. Wells-Barnett and the Outrage over the Frazier Baker Murder" (National Archives, Fall 2008).

16. "Lake City Investigation Resolution," *Congressional Record* 55th Congress, 2nd Session, March 3rd, 1898, S2406.

17. John L. Dart, *The Famous Trial of the Eight Men Indicted for the Lynching of Frazier B. Baker and His Baby: Late U.S. Postmaster at Lake City, S.C.: in the U.S. Circuit Court, at Charleston, S.C., April 10–22, 1899*, 1899, 47.

18. Benjamin Tillman, February 18, 1895, State of South Carolina Executive Chamber, Benjamin R. Tillman Papers, South Caroliniana Library, Columbia, S.C.

19. Kantrowitz, *Ben Tillman and the Reconstruction of White Supremacy*, 264.

20. "Tillman for War-Makes a Red Hot Speech in Favor of the Independence of Cuba," *Dispatch*, April 20, 1898; "Tillman Wants Cuba Free from Spain and Wall Street," *Manning (S.C.) Times*, April 20, 1898.

21. Kantrowitz, *Ben Tillman and the Reconstruction of White Supremacy*.

22. Reginald Horsman, *Race and Manifest Destiny: The Origins of American Racial Anglo-Saxonism* (Cambridge, Mass.: Harvard University Press, 1994).

23. "White Supremacy—The Burden of Senator Tillman's Speech on Annexation of Hawaii," *Lexington Dispatch*, July 6, 1898.

24. Willard B. Gatewood, *Black Americans and the White Man's Burden, 1898–1903*, Blacks in the New World (Urbana: University of Illinois Press, 1975). On the "Buffalo Soldiers" consult Ron Field and Richard Hook, *Buffalo Soldiers, 1892–1918* (Oxford: Osprey, 2005); Brian McAllister Linn, *Guardians of Empire: The U.S. Army and the Pacific, 1902–1940* (Chapel Hill: University of North Carolina Press, 1998).

25. Gary R. Mormino, "Tampa's Splendid Little War: Local History and the Cuban War of Independence," *OAH Magazine of History* 12, no. 3 (1998), 37–42; Willard B. Gatewood, "Black Americans and the Quest for Empire, 1898–1903," *Journal of Southern History* 38, no. 4 (1972), 545–566; Willard B. Gatewood, "Negro Troops in Florida, 1898," *Florida Historical Quarterly* 49, no. 1 (1970), 1–15.

26. "Fit for Halter," *The State*, June 13, 1898.

27. *The State*, July 27, 1898; George Brown Tindall, *South Carolina Negroes, 1877–1900*, Southern Classics Series (Columbia: University of South Carolina Press, 1952), 286–288.

28. "Tillman Wants Cuba Free from Spain and Wall Street," *Manning Times*, April 20, 1898.

29. "Tillman Wants Cuba Free from Spain and Wall Street," *Manning Times*, July 6, 1898.

30. Kramer, *The Blood of Government*; Ariela Julie Gross, *What Blood Won't Tell: A History of Race on Trial in America* (Cambridge, Mass: Harvard University Press, 2010).

31. Senator William Bate, speaking on H. Res. 259, *Congressional Record* 55th Congress, 2nd Session, June 30, 1898, S6519.

32. Tillman, speaking on H. Res. 259, *Congressional Record* 55th Congress, 2nd Session, June 30, 1898, S6531.

33. Horsman, *Race and Manifest Destiny*.

34. Abial Lathrop to Attorney General, April 18, 1898, DOJ, year file 177431898, box 1047 A, file 3463198, folder 172; Abial Lathrop to Attorney General, June 25, 1898; Abial Lathrop to Attorney General, 2 July 1898.

35. "Murderers in Camp," *Lancaster Ledger*, July 2, 1898, 2; "Camp Fitzhugh Lee," *County Record* (Kingstree, S.C.), July 7, 1898, 1.

36. Tom Henderson Wells, "The Phoenix Election Riot," *Phylon* 31, no. 1 (1970), 58–69; Daniel Levinson Wilk, "The Phoenix Riot and the Memories of Greenwood County," *Southern Cultures* 8, no. 4 (2002); Jeffrey Crow and Robert Durden, *Maverick Republican in the Old North State: A Political Biography of Daniel L. Russell* (Baton Rouge: Louisiana State University Press, 1977); H. Leon Prather, *We Have Taken a City: The Wilmington Racial Massacre and Coup of 1898* (Cranbury, N.J.: Associated University Press, 1984); Glenda Elizabeth Gilmore, *Gender and Jim Crow: Women and the Politics of White Supremacy in North Carolina, 1896–1920*, Gender & American Culture (Chapel Hill: University of North Carolina Press, 1996); David S. Cecelski and Timothy B. Tyson, eds., *Democracy Betrayed: The Wilmington Race Riot of 1898 and Its Legacy* (Chapel Hill: University of North Carolina Press, 1998).

37. "Scraps and Facts," *Yorkville (S.C.) Enquirer*, November 9, 1898, 2.

38. "Two More Killed: Hunting and Shooting of Negroes Continues in Greenwood" and "Blood and Riot: Five Negroes and Two White Men Killed at Wilmington," *Newberry (S.C.) Herald and News*, November 15, 1898; "Race War in Greenwood: Bloodshed and an All Day Fight over the Election," and "Bloodiest Day Ever Known in the City of Wilmington, N.C.," *Lancaster Ledger*, November 12, 1898, 1; "Talk with 'Red' Tolbert: Man Responsible for the Greenwood Trouble Gives His Side," and "Cause of the Trouble: This Is Why Ten Negroes Were Killed in Wilmington," *Yorkville Enquirer*, November 16, 1898, 1; "The Race Riot in Greenwood," and "McKinley Cabinet Gave Them Some Attention," *The Watchman and Southron* (Sumter, S.C.), November 16, 1898, 1; "Bloody Riot: Highly Respected White Man Murdered at Phoenix, S.C.," and "Blood and Riot at Wilmington," *Anderson Intelligencer*, November 16, 1898.

39. "Cause of Carolina Race Riots" *Atlanta Constitution*, November 11, 1898; "The Carolina Race Riots," *New York Times*, November 12, 1898; "To Send Federal Aid," *Washington Post*, November 12, 1898.

40. Lewis L. Gould, *The Presidency of William McKinley*, American Presidency Series (Lawrence: Regents Press of Kansas, 1980); John L. Offner, "McKinley and the Spanish-American War," *Presidential Studies Quarterly* 34, no. 1 (2004), 50–61; David F. Trask, *The War with Spain in 1898* (Lincoln: University of Nebraska Press, 1996). A further discussion of the tension between African American protest for Wilmington to the McKinley administration can be found in Cecelski and Tyson, *Democracy Betrayed*.

41. "Civilization Begins at Home," *New York World*, reprinted in *Literary Digest*, November 26, 1898.

42. Senator Mason, S533.

43. "A Talk with Tillman: What He Has to Say about the Phoenix Riots," *Newberry Herald and News*, November 18, 1898, 1.

44. Senator McLaurin on Senate Resolution 191, *Congressional Record*, January 13, 1899, S639.

45. Mark M. Smith, "'All Is Not Quiet in Our Hellish County': Facts, Fiction, Politics, and Race: The Ellenton Riot of 1876," *South Carolina Historical Magazine* 95, no. 2 (1994).

46. McLaurin on SR 191, S639.

47. White on HR 11022, January 26, 1899.

48. White, January 26, 1899.

49. White, January 26, 1899.

50. Senator Benjamin Tillman, speaking on House Resolution 259, *Congressional Record*, 55th Congress, 3rd Session (February 7, 1899), S6530.

51. Tillman, speaking on Senate Res. 240, *Congressional Record* 55th Congress, 3rd Session (February 7, 1899), S1532.

52. Tillman, speaking on Senate Res. 240, S1532.

53. E. Berkeley Tompkins, *Anti-Imperialism in the United States*, 195; Love, *Race over Empire*, 194.

54. Cecelski and Tyson, *Democracy Betrayed*; David Carter, "Outraged Justice."

55. Tillman, speaking on H.R. 9080, S6522.

9

"The Same Patriotism... as Any Other Americans"

Reconstruction, Imperialism, and the Evolution of Mormon Patriotism

Reilly Ben Hatch

In March 1899, *Harper's Weekly* ran an article on the Utah volunteer units engaged against Filipino freedom fighters. The writer praised the Utahns' fortitude, saying that they were "most valuable" to the armed forces in the Philippines and noted their bravery, efficiency, and commitment. Though clearly impressed with the actions of the Utahns, the author suggested that their military conduct was a surprising feature, given that "two-thirds of the men in the batteries are Mormons," who were commanded by the grandson of Brigham Young, no less. "While Mormon leaders in Utah may be showing disregard for American sentiment by upholding the continued practice of polygamy and by interfering in the affairs of the State," the article reads, "the Utah artillery at Manila is demonstrating that, religion aside, the same patriotism animates Mormons as any other Americans."[1] This statement encapsulated the complicated relationship between the American state and the Mormon people at the turn of the twentieth century, one influenced by Reconstruction politics and American imperial projects.

For decades, the United States government had been preoccupied with the "Mormon question" for two primary reasons: the Mormon practice of polygamy and the intrusion of ecclesiastical leadership in territorial and state politics. Territorial, state, and federal governments had attempted to curb these divergent customs for decades, but Mormons were largely able to circumvent these attempts, at least until the 1880s. Then, building on an initial series of legislative and administrative actions in the 1860s and 1870s, the Republican-dominated Congress passed several acts that empowered the federal government to jail church leaders and escheat church properties and assets. Mormon leaders, many of whom lived in hiding, officially suspended the practice of polygamy in 1890 and affiliated with national political parties thereafter. Still, even with the public abandonment of polygamy and theocratic government, the Church of Jesus Christ of Latter-day Saints (the official name of the organization) lingered on the edge of mainstream American society.[2] The advent of the Spanish-American War gave Mormons the chance to recast themselves as patriotic, "normal" Americans and to publicly prove that they were worthy of trust and acceptance as citizens of the United States.

Or so the story usually goes. Scholars of Mormon history have frequently referred to the 1890s as the beginning of a "transition" period for the LDS church, when Mormons—having shed themselves of polygamy and theocratic tendencies—emerged from their isolationism and claimed American identity without reservations. Thomas Alexander explained that Mormons in the 1890s "began groping for a new paradigm that would save essential characteristics of their religious tradition, provide sufficient political stability to preserve the interests of the church, and allow them to live in peace with other Americans."[3] Klaus Hansen likewise argued that between 1890 and 1910, Mormons not only began to act increasingly American but also began to think like Americans.[4] David Bigler gave the paradigm shift a definitive date, arguing that by 1896, the year of Utah statehood, the Mormon struggle against the intervention of federal government was over.[5]

This essay challenges the narrative that Mormon patriotism surged in the 1890s solely as a method by which Mormons attempted to gain legitimacy in the eyes of their fellow Americans. That church members sought wider acceptance post-statehood is not questioned here, but their motivations to do so are. Mormons had always firmly believed that the American form of government was superior to all others save the ultimate kingdom of God and that the spread of the former would hasten the latter. Residual pressures of Reconstruction politics certainly led to exaggerated displays of loyalty during American imperialist wars, but a complex and distinctive form of Mormon patriotism predated the changes that came with the 1890 Manifesto that officially ended plural marriage in the LDS church. This essay connects the nationalistic zeal of the 1890s to early Mormon ideas of American exceptionalism and shows how the Spanish-American War served as a curative that solidified that patriotism as an essential component of Mormon identity.

American imperial projects, however, also brought to light many tensions within Mormonism's conception of the American state, and the evolution of these tensions within the church was evident in whether and how to engage in the Spanish-American War and American imperialism. This essay explores how the church responded to American imperial policy at the end of the nineteenth century, with an emphasis on the questions that violence and race posed to Mormon servicemen in the Philippines and church leadership in Utah. Even though Mormons boldly claimed to be ultra-patriots and servants of the nation, they maintained a higher loyalty to divine law, which commanded them to abstain from warfare when possible and to honor the liberty of all peoples. These commitments were tested, and ultimately set aside, during Mormon involvement in the Spanish-American War, setting a precedent for Mormon political life during the twentieth century.[6]

Reactions to the Spanish-American War and imperialism were grounded in Mormon theology regarding North and South America, based primarily on teachings from the Book of Mormon. Joseph Smith, Mormonism's founder, referred to the book as "an account of the former inhabitants of this continent, and the source from whence they sprang," claiming that "the fulness [sic] of the everlasting Gospel was contained in it, as delivered by the Savior to the ancient inhabitants."[7] As such, the text itself contains numerous references to the divine role of the land, both historically and prophetically. The Book of Mormon argues that God designated the Americas as a "promised land," intending them to be lands of freedom for any peoples that made them their home, provided they followed his commandments.[8] One author in the book stated "this land is consecrated unto him whom [God] shall bring," and "it shall be a land of liberty unto them."[9] This promise included the American nation that would arise in the New World, an event that the Book of Mormon explained as being part of God's plan of gathering the House of Israel before the second coming of Jesus Christ.[10] The Book of Mormon takes specific interest in the freedom of religion, claiming that it is the right of all to "worship God according to their desires," in this land of liberty.[11] This was especially attractive to Mormons who had been widely mocked and persecuted through much of the nineteenth century because of their beliefs.

Early church leaders mirrored the Book of Mormon's reverence for America. Joseph Smith, speaking prophetically, stated that the American continents would be "free unto all of whatsoever nation, kindred, tongue, or people they may be" and later specified that the founders of the United States were divinely inspired and chosen by God to establish a government in which a restored version of Jesus Christ's church could flourish.[12] George A. Smith, a Mormon apostle and cousin of Joseph, claimed that God prompted the American Revolution to establish a nation that guaranteed the freedom of religion, thus ensuring the survival of the Mormon faith. "There is no nation under heaven among whom the kingdom of God could have been established and rolled forth with as little opposition as it has received in the United States," Smith stated.[13] Orson Hyde, another member of the twelve apostles, likewise argued that only "after this government became fully established, and had time to command the respect of all nations," could the restoration of Christ's true church eventuate.[14] Church leaders particularly praised the Declaration of Independence and the United States Constitution. Joseph Smith stated that God "established the Constitution of this land, by the hands of wise men whom [he] raised up unto this very purpose."[15] Smith even went so far as to equate the Constitution with scripture, saying "that God is true; that the Constitution of the United States is true; that the Bible is true; that the Book of Mormon is true . . . that Christ is true."[16] Smith was not alone in his praise of the American founding documents. Apostle Parley P. Pratt remarked that "the Constitution of American Liberty, was certainly dictated by the spirit of wisdom, by a spirit of unparalleled liberality, and by a spirit of political utility," implying divine management in the creation of the document.[17]

Between the teachings of the Book of Mormon and the statements of church leaders—whom Mormons held to be prophets speaking on behalf of deity—it is clear that early nineteenth-century Mormons considered America, both the continent and the nation, to be divinely favored. Mormonism was not the only Christian sect in America to believe this, but no other church embraced a doctrine in which America filled such an important role for God's plans in the past, present, and future. They believed themselves patriotic citizens of the United States and supporters of the Constitution, and, by living their religion, they fulfilled the will of God and the will of the founding fathers simultaneously. The image of Mormons as model Americans, however, was not widely held by non-Mormons.

Even before Joseph Smith officially organized a church in 1830—known then simply as the Church of Christ—followers of Mormonism faced opposition to their faith.[18] The Protestant minister Finis Ewing wrote in 1831 that "the Mormons are the common enemies of mankind, and ought to be destroyed"; many Americans shared his sentiment, religious and nonreligious alike, and the Mormons gradually moved from state to state to find a place where they could live their religion unobstructed.[19] Although they always moved on when compelled to do so, the persecutions Mormons faced inculcated a resentment against the state and federal governments that failed to guarantee their right to religious freedom. As the harassments became more severe, that bitterness grew. Joseph Smith himself openly chastised the government for failing to protect Mormon rights, but he was careful to lay the blame at the feet of misguided or lazy civil servants, never at the nation itself and certainly not at the Constitution or the legacy of the founding fathers. "I am the greatest advocate of the Constitution of the United States there is on the earth," he asserted, but he also made it clear that his loyalty to the

American government only extended as far as it aligned with God's will.[20] "If the authorities that are on the earth will not sustain us in our rights, nor give us that protection which the laws and constitution of the United States, and of this State, guarantee unto us," Smith proclaimed, "then we will claim them from a higher power—from Heaven—yea, from God Almighty."[21] Whatever his motivations, statements such as these further alienated the Mormon people from mainstream American society, casting them as disloyal separatists and dangerous fanatics who would rebel against the United States if their religious convictions called for such action. These fears partially contributed to Smith's murder in 1844.[22]

Faced with intensifying persecution and threats, a majority of the Mormon people rallied under the leadership of Brigham Young and sought isolation from the American state. They migrated west, eventually settling in the Salt Lake Valley, far from the borders of the American nation that they still loved but now considered corrupted and misguided.[23] To many non-Mormons, this departure was a confirmation of Mormon separatist tendencies, but to Mormons themselves, the exodus to Utah was neither treasonous nor separatist. Rather, distance from federal power allowed Mormons to live their religion according to the dictates of their collective conscience, a constitutional right that corrupt officials had denied them. "When we left . . . the United States—what did we leave for?" apostle John Taylor asked a crowd at the Salt Lake Tabernacle in 1865. "Was it because its constitution was not one of the best that was ever framed? No. Was it because the laws of the United States, or of the States where we sojourned, were not good? No. Why was it? It was because there was not sufficient virtue found in the Executive to sustain their own laws."[24] If anyone was treasonous, Taylor argued, it was the government that neglected the Mormons and left them to their persecutors in Ohio, Missouri, Illinois, and now Utah.[25]

Although many Americans believed the Mormon colony in Utah to be thoroughly un-American, Mormons continued to view themselves as patriotic citizens of the United States. In fact, many church leaders claimed to be living the democratic principles of the nation more faithfully than their non-Mormon counterparts. Facing the threat of federal troops marching to Utah in 1857 by the order of President James Buchanan, John Taylor told his audience at the Salt Lake Tabernacle that by staying true to their religious beliefs—which included polygamy—"you are patriots, standing by your rights and opposing the wrong which affects all lovers of freedom as well as you. . . . You are standing by the Declaration of Independence, and sustaining the Constitution which was given by the inspiration of God; and you are the only people in the United States this time that are doing it."[26] George A. Smith similarly remarked on Mormons' superior regard for the Constitution during an Independence Day celebration in Salt Lake City in 1861, mere days before the First Battle of Bull Run in Virginia. He contrasted Mormon social and religious cohesion to the contentious state of affairs in the Eastern states, saying that "we are at the present time the only people in the United States that are willing to be governed by the Constitution, and to grant to all men the same liberties that we ourselves enjoy." The rest of the country, he continued, "pretend to honor the Constitution," but their determination to engage in a civil war proved that desire false.[27]

While the Mormons in Utah stayed clear of combat and destruction in the Civil War, they were unable to avoid its political aftermath. As Eric Foner has stated, the tasks of postwar economic recovery, the abolition of slavery, the attempted integration of Blacks into American society, and the reconstruction of the Southern states for readmission into the Union led to a more centralized, activist-oriented federal government.[28] Aside from direct Reconstruction policies in the South, the federal government expanded its role in national affairs and increasingly turned its attention outward and exerted its influence on the lives of American individuals.[29] This was especially true for the Mormons of Utah. Having been politically marginalized since the early days of the church, Mormons faced even greater scrutiny from the newly established Republican party, whose platform proudly asserted its intention to "prohibit in the Territories those twin relics of barbarism, polygamy and slavery."[30]

With the advent of the Civil War, Republicans in Congress—who no longer had to face the opposition of proslavery Democrats who supported popular sovereignty in the western territories—began legislating against Mormon polygamy as early as 1862 when they passed the Morrill Anti-Bigamy act, but the war left that law unfunded and unobserved.[31] Still, Republicans who generally considered the reconstruction of Southern states and the outlawing of polygamy as a unified process, continued to push for action against Mormons. Their opportunity came at the end of Southern Reconstruction. Anti-Mormonism, which had been championed primarily by Republicans, took on a "bipartisan and national character" in the mid-1870s, and both Republicans and Democrats from readmitted Southern states focused their attention and resources on Mormon Utah, ushering in what Sarah Barringer Gordon has called a "second Reconstruction."[32]

The Poland Act, which essentially reinforced the Morrill Anti-Bigamy Act by giving it teeth, marked the first victory for anti-polygamy lawmakers in Washington. The U.S. Attorney in Utah could now prosecute polygamous Mormons; however, church leaders could not be tried for marriages ex post facto, wives could not be forced to testify against their husbands, and records of marriages that had been officiated in the Endowment House remained confidential. Mormons defied the Poland and Morrill Acts, proclaiming that they were within their rights under the Free Exercise Clause of the First Amendment. In response, Congress tightened the pressure on the LDS church by passing the Edmunds Act in 1882 and the Edmunds-Tucker Act in 1887. These laws made it illegal to cohabitate with more than one spouse, bypassing the sticky subject of confidential temple marriages. Those found guilty could not only be fined and jailed, but they were also prohibited from voting, sitting on a jury, or holding public office. The Edmunds-Tucker Act also allowed for the disenfranchisement of women entirely (Utah women had legally been voting since 1870), the replacement of probate court judges with federally appointed judges, and, most notably, the disincorporation and seizure of church assets.[33]

Mormons were furious. They argued that the Constitution protected their right to engage in plural marriage. As such, church leaders in the 1880s continued to defy the Edmunds law, citing a higher loyalty to divine law. George Q. Cannon, a counselor in the First Presidency of the church, made it clear that Mormons would continue to choose God and religious freedom over the laws of a corrupt government, saying in 1882: "I expect we shall continue to contend for liberty . . . despite the Edmunds' law, despite the Poland law, despite the law of '62, or any other law that may be made in violation of the Constitution, and of the Bill of Rights."[34] But faced with the imprisonment of church leaders and the loss of church property, it seemed that Congress had finally tightened the screws on the Mormons sufficiently, and Wilford Woodruff, who became president of the church in 1889 after the death of Taylor, issued the manifesto in 1890 that officially suspended polygamy in the LDS church. Congress restored the church corporation and its assets three years later, and granted Utah statehood—for which it had petitioned since 1849—three years after that. Mormons remained popular targets of the press and novelists, and they still faced hostility from other religious groups, but their church, their community, and their belief system (minus polygamy) were largely intact.

With polygamy suspended, Mormon leaders could focus their efforts on public relations, and the war with Spain seemed to be a perfect opportunity to curry favor with non-Mormons. Here, only two years after statehood, Utah had the chance to manifest its loyalty to a nation that still regarded Mormon patriotism with skepticism. An enthusiastic and prompt response to a call for volunteers—which would surely accompany a declaration of war—would greatly enhance the Mormon image. But Mormons, though dedicated Americans, still answered to a higher authority, one that spoke through appointed ministers by revelation.

Thus, church members eagerly awaited the counsel of their leaders at the April 1898 general conference, which took place only two weeks before Congress declared war.[35]

However, the general authorities of the church were initially disunited on the subject of war. After all, Jesus Christ had taught his followers to be peacemakers and to shun violence.[36] As D. Michael Quinn has pointed out, before the Spanish-American War Mormons had engaged in "selective pacifism," the right to participate or not participate in any given conflict, at the discretion of the church president.[37] But, as previously discussed, Mormon doctrine also espoused loyalty to the nation in war and in peace, especially if the outcome of war would be the freedom of oppressed peoples. This moral dilemma is clearly present in many of the speakers at the general conference, such as Francis M. Lyman. "We should be peacemakers," the apostle urged his audience before quoting Christ's Beatitudes. "We want peace. We should preach peace, teach peace, pray for it, live for it, and do everything on earth for peace that is honorable before we engage in war." He added, however, that Latter-day Saints "love our country" and that "the government of our country will find as generous a response from this State as from any other state in the Union."[38] Although Lyman supported civic accountability, his seemed to have been, in the case of war at least, a reluctant loyalty.

Matthias Cowley and Brigham Young Jr. also made clear their disappointment in the prospect of war but in stronger terms. Mormons were not only commanded to be peacemakers, but their Zion-like community was also meant to serve as refuge for those who sought shelter from war. "War will be poured out upon the nations of the earth," Cowley said of the tumults that would precede the coming of Christ, "and it shall come to pass among the wicked that every man that will not take up his sword against his neighbor must needs flee unto Zion for safety." He added that in those turbulent days, "the [Latter-day Saints] shall be the only people that shall not be at war one with another."[39] If Mormons fully supported the war effort and sent their young men to fight it, they would compromise their pacifistic identity and their status as an asylum from worldly mayhem. Young seemed to endorse Cowley's comments, praying that members of the church would choose the things of God (peace and order) over things of the world (war and chaos).[40]

Peacemaking, however, was not as simple as a refusal to fight. As Francis Lyman mentioned, Mormons had a civic responsibility to aid the war effort if called to do so by the American government, but they were also mandated by God to refrain from violence. On the verge of war with Spain, Mormons found themselves with two seemingly contradictory commandments to observe. While apostles Lyman, Young, and Cowley spoke of the virtue of pacifism, apostles John Henry Smith, Franklin D. Richards, and George Q. Cannon, reminded the Saints of the sacred nature of the creation of the American republic and their duty as American citizens. Smith openly praised the policies of the McKinley administration and reminded the Saints of their responsibility to the mission of the United States, saying, "all of us feel within our souls a determination to stand for the principles of right, and sustain our government in every proposition of liberty, justice and mercy."[41]

The key to balancing the obligations to God and nation was to temper the willingness to serve with a reluctance to kill. War was justified if undertaken in national defense, if previous efforts in compromise had failed, and if fundamental liberties (especially the freedom of religion) were at stake. An eagerness for war, however, could only be viewed as sinful. Franklin D. Richards worried that the nations of the world had become "anxious for the opportunity" of going to war.[42] He admonished the congregation to avoid such bellicosity. It seems that when war was presented to Mormons, who could no longer realistically practice "selective pacifism" and who could no longer evade military service, the attitude with which they approached the impending conflict mattered a great deal for how they rationalized their participation.

George Q. Cannon expounded this complex concept when he counseled young Mormon men to avoid getting "filled with the spirit of war and be[ing] eager for the conflict." He then qualified his own statement by rhetorically asking the congregation: "Is it not our duty to defend our country and our flag?" To Cannon, the answer was an obvious yes. He assured his listeners—Mormon and non-Mormon alike—that "the day will come, or is here now, that if this people called Latter-day Saints should be required to go to defend their country and its institutions, their homes and their religion, and the rights of their fellowmen, there would be an almost universal response in favor of that."[43] Cannon encouraged the Mormon people to support the nation with enthusiasm, but to engage in war-making with a sour reluctance.

Though plenty had been said on the subject, the church's stance on war remained ambiguous. Still to speak, however, was the president of the church, Wilford Woodruff. In his closing remarks, Woodruff commended all who had spoken, but he did not explicitly outline a course of action for the church. Instead, he defaulted to the long Mormon tradition of praising the founding fathers of the United States, calling them "the best spirits the God of heaven could find on the face of the earth," and stating that their endeavors were "inspired of the Lord." He then veered from the topic altogether and ended his address with a call for personal obedience to Christ's teachings. Though he clearly put a premium on the value of patriotism, Woodruff, as head of the LDS church, left the subject vague.[44]

Congress officially declared war less than two weeks after the conference adjourned, and the federal government issued a call for volunteers that included two batteries and one cavalry unit from Utah composed of over four hundred men. Newspapers across the state, pro- and anti-Mormon, printed headlines dripping with patriotism and buoyant assurances that Utah's men would speedily volunteer.[45] But before Mormon men could illustrate their willingness to enlist, the situation was muddled even further by the apostle Brigham Young Jr., who spoke in the Salt Lake Tabernacle the morning after the call for volunteers was received in Utah. Among other things Young "advised the young men of Zion to show their patriotism to the nation by tilling the soil and getting from it that which would sustain those who had been legitimately called to the front to defend the [nation]."[46] This, he argued, would be a better use of LDS resources and manpower than "rushing foreward [sic] pell mell to engage in shedding the blood of their fellowmen."[47] Young ended his remarks by saying that Mormons should manifest their patriotism by being "true to their God," and not "throw themselves into the chasm that had been dug by uninspired men."[48]

The backlash to Young's remarks was immediate. An editorial in the *Salt Lake Tribune* "hotly resented" the speech, calling it "dastardly and unworthy of anyone except a mischief-maker and sneak."[49] The *Salt Lake Herald* echoed the *Tribune*. Edited by Charles W. Penrose—who had been the editor of the *Deseret News* for many years and who would later be called to serve as an apostle of the church—the *Herald*, which had a long history of defending church leaders, took a surprisingly harsh tone against the son of Brigham Young. "The sentiments expressed by the apostle are not in harmony with the doctrines and teachings of the Mormon church," the article said, expressing doubt about Young's apostolic role, at least in this particular instance. "The Mormon people who reside in Utah and the United States are part and parcel of this great nation," the *Herald* continued; "they claim the protection of its flag; they love the freedom which it guarantees, and, if need be, they must lay down their lives in the defense of both."[50] The editorials also worried that Young's remarks would taint the state's reputation in the union, "throwing distrust on Utah's good faith and patriotism," as well as "disgrace . . . against the Mormon people."[51] Their fears turned out to be legitimate, with newspapers across the country wondering if Young's opinions were "reflections upon the patriotism" of the Mormon people.[52]

Realizing the confusion resulting from the conference and Young's subsequent speech, Wilford Woodruff ordered the apostle to meet with him the day after his tabernacle address. Young's brother Willard and nephew Richard, West Point graduates and members of the Utah National Guard who were expected to lead the Utah volunteer units, also attended. Willard and Richard expressed their disappointment with Brigham, claiming that his comments hindered their recruiting efforts, and that his stance was "diametrically opposed to the views they entertained and the mission in which they expected to be engaged."[53] Brigham defended his words, but he was firmly instructed by Woodruff that "Utah should stand by the government in the present crisis and that our young men should be ready to serve their country when called upon," and added that it was "bad policy for any of our leading men to take a stand not in harmony with the government." Woodruff ended the meeting by instructing Willard and Richard Young to proceed with their recruitment of volunteer soldiers: "Brethren, you have my mind; go ahead and do your duty, and God bless you."[54]

Woodruff then asked the *Deseret News*, the official organ of the LDS church, to immediately publish an editorial repudiating all accusations of disloyalty on the part of the Mormon people. Drawing on teachings that had existed in the LDS church since its creation, the church-approved article pointed out that "patriotism is not only a matter of practice and instinct—it is an essential feature of [Mormons'] religion, a part of their very life." Though Mormons are "not lovers of war nor given to bloodthirstiness," the article read, "they are nevertheless firmly and steadfastly with and for Our Country in every just cause—and he but poorly knows their heart and spirit who utters a word or harbors a thought that they are lacking in any element of the purest, staunchest and most enduring loyalty."[55] Woodruff personally reinforced this sentiment in a public letter to Governor Heber Wells, in which he called on the members of the church to "respond with alacrity to this call which is made upon our state."[56] Thus, the official stance of the Church of Jesus Christ of Latter-day Saints was made clear. With the backing of the president of the church, Mormon men were expected to fill the quota given by the federal government and enthusiastically support the foreign policy of the United States as loyal citizens were expected to do.

The response was immediate. Within a day of Woodruff's open letter, over three hundred men had joined the volunteer ranks, the majority of them Mormon.[57] Woodruff was pleased, expressing in a personal conversation that he wished that there would be "enough Mormon boys in the Utah organization to make of it a Mormon organization" entirely.[58] Communities across the state threw enlistment parties, often with church support. The small village of Gunnison in central Utah, for example, held a "war meeting" in the local chapel, conducted by the local Mormon bishop. The Relief Society, the female auxiliary of the church, attended the meeting and provided decorations. Following a number of speeches given by civil, religious, and military leaders, thirteen young men walked to the pulpit and announced their intention to enlist. After minutes of raucous cheering, the choir and congregation sang "America," while the fresh volunteers "grasped each other's hands."[59] Similar scenes occurred in Vernal, Ogden, Manti, and Provo, and within three days the quota was filled to excess.[60] Forgotten, it would seem, were the years of animosity between the Mormons and the federal government, drowned out by patriotic hymns accompanied by church organs.

Mass enlistment for the Spanish-American War was not exclusive to Mormons, of course, but the motivation of the volunteers made Mormon enlistment unique. As previously discussed, Mormon doctrine espoused a loyalty to the American nation, but only insomuch as it harmonized with God's plans. This was a difficult binary to balance, which may have been part of the reason that so many Mormon men waited for clear direction from the church officials before enlisting. Some still sought guidance even after Woodruff's letter. One example is Willard Call, a young man from Bountiful, Utah, who had recently returned from a mission in England. Feeling the desire to "[follow] old glory into foreign territory," but unsure if he should leave his family, Call and his wife, Adelaide, went to Salt Lake City to ask the advice of the prophet on the matter. Woodruff did not say whether or not it was Call's duty to enlist, since the young man would leave small children and a pregnant wife behind, but he did assure him that "if you go, you will go with our blessings and the blessings of the Lord will attend you." Call decided to enlist, and the next day he received a blessing in which Woodruff promised that "his blood would not be spilled in battle and that . . . he would return safely to his family."[61] This episode is illustrative of the inherent complexity in Mormon patriotism, a patriotism that, despite its vibrancy, needed the approval of God's appointed mouthpiece. This applied to Mormon women as much as men. In a later sketch of Adelaide's life, Willard Call wrote, "When the flag of our country had been insulted by the Dons of Spain and her husband volunteered to go in its defense, she asked only to be made sure that the servants of the Lord approved."[62]

Although many Mormons proudly asserted their patriotism, many outside the church—and some inside—were still skeptical of LDS motivations. An editorial in Utah's *Springville Independent* voiced this concern. "Why is it necessary," the writer asked, "when the national and State [sic] governments call for troops, to have the sanction of an ecclesiastical organization in order to get them?" Though it agreed that church leaders eventually supported the "right side of the question," it labeled Mormon patriotism "decidedly un-American," saying that "a man who allows his patriotism to ebb and flow at the command of another is false to his God, his country and himself."[63] The *Salt Lake Herald*—staffed mostly by Mormon writers and editors—took a similar approach when it bluntly asked, "What's wrong with Utah?" The writer was pleased that President Woodruff called on Latter-day Saints to enlist but lamented that his counsel was necessary. "Do the men to whom this letter will most strongly appeal wish to have it said of them that they responded to their country's call only when bidden to do so by their religious leaders?" the article asked. The *Herald* further contended that the most upsetting outcome of the situation was the inevitable distrust of the rest of the nation. The memories of the Edmunds and Edmunds-Tucker Acts were still fresh in the minds of Utah Mormons, along with years of suspicion and persecution. Now, after a forced reconstruction of the state by the federal government and the abandonment of practices that had been so central to Mormon life for decades before the manifesto, Mormons were finally in a position to transition from social others to typical—or even exemplary—American citizens. The war could serve as a catalyst to that transition, but hesitancy might squander their chance. "A disgrace will be put upon [Utah] if the volunteering is not prompted by a desire to serve the country," the *Herald* concluded.[64] So, although it is true that Mormons eventually filled their quotas in a timely fashion, it seems that the majority of the volunteers first needed the go-ahead from their church leaders, reflecting the Mormon tension between national and religious loyalties, and the continuing authority of the church hierarchy in the daily life of Mormons.

Although it appears that Mormons genuinely supported the war effort based on a keen sense of duty, involvement in the war with Spain also gave members of the church opportunities to accomplish their own objectives, such as missionary work. As can be seen from some of the doctrinal discourse mentioned above, Mormons were a missionary-minded people from the beginning, gaining many converts within the church's first seventy years. Many church leaders suggested that the war itself offered an opportunity to accelerate proselytizing efforts. J. Golden Kimball, a Seventy—or traveling minister—of the church, indicated at the October conference of 1898 that the "time to thrust in the sickle," was optimal, since "the Lord has softened the hearts of the children of men towards this people."[65] The show of patriotism by the LDS church in the wake of the war, Kimball argued, made America and the world more prepared to receive Mormonism's message.

The war also expanded the geographical reach of Mormon missionaries. Church leaders believed that Spain's colonies would ultimately benefit from a combination of American religious liberty and Mormon proselytizing after the war, as Franklin D. Richards explained in the October 1898 conference. "Wars are a necessary concomitant to this latter-day work," he said. Conflict, he alleged, had the ability to shake up the customs of nations and open up missionary fields, as had been done in the American Revolution and Civil War. The same principle applied to the current war, Richards implied. "These wars have to occur to loosen up the bonds of governments that are so tight and strong against religious liberty," Richards clearly stated. He then concluded by equating the work of the war and the work of LDS missionaries when he prophesied that "these wars are going to be as necessary to the progress of liberty in this dispensation as are the labors of our Elders."66 Just as Mormon missionary efforts in Hawaii had benefited from American political and military influence in those islands, missionary efforts could find success by piggybacking on American imperialism in the Philippines and in Cuba.67

The First Presidency consequently called two Utah volunteer soldiers to be missionaries while overseas. George A. Seaman and Willard Call—both volunteer corporals, though Seaman was later promoted to second lieutenant—accepted the call to be Elders before they embarked, making them the first Mormon missionaries to labor in the Philippines.68 Although their mandate included preaching to the locals, the primary assignment of these two missionaries was to preserve the piety of the Mormon volunteers who would be so far from home and far from the voice of priesthood leadership. Captain Richard W. Young, who was in command of Utah units in the Philippines, instructed them "to hunt out the L. D. S. members in our organizations and draw them together in a spiritual way and keep their membership and activities alive."69 Upon arrival in the Philippines and after the Utah batteries assisted in the capture of the city of Manila from the Spanish, Seaman and Call began organizing weekly meetings for all LDS servicemen, with an open invitation to all others who were interested. The meetings consisted of a short session of Bible study, followed by a lecture of general interest.70 A Spanish-speaking Mormon volunteer offered classes in the language, giving "an inducement for [non-Mormons] to join [the meetings]."71 Several did indeed apply for membership and were welcomed enthusiastically, but the focus of the first Philippine mission remained the fortification of Mormon believers over the conversion of others. "We hope by assiduous labor," Seaman wrote from the Philippines to the editors of the *Improvement Era*, a church-published periodical, "to do some good by diverting the minds of some from gaming and other idle practices, that are so apt to accompany the ease and laziness of barrack life, and shall seek to center them upon more holy things."[72]

Attending religious meetings, of course, was not the primary activity of the Utahns in the Philippines. In fact, the Utah batteries frequently found themselves in the fiercest combat on Luzon—first against the Spanish, then against Filipino freedom fighters—because they were the only units that had up-to-date artillery pieces.[73] As such, they had the opportunity to match their conduct with contemporary Americans' expectations of battlefield bravery and win praise for their actions from non-Mormons. Captain Frank Jennings commented that all other troops in the Philippines spoke of the Utah boys with the "highest praise and love" and "look upon them as a band of dauntless heroes." He then added that their actions on the battlefield positively influenced the reputation of the entire state, providing an "inestimable" service for Utah in the eyes of the American people.[74]

Though Jennings may have exaggerated the lofty praises by the non-Utah units, he was correct in saying that the war exploits of the batteries brought accolades to the Mormon people by association. Various news outlets across the country applauded the performance of Utah's volunteers, like the previously mentioned *Harper's Weekly* article and the *National Tribune* in the nation's capital. Even C. C. Goodwin, the editor of the *Salt Lake Tribune*, who rarely spoke positively of the LDS church, had nothing but praise for Utah's troops, the majority of whom were Mormon.[75] But Joseph Pulitzer's *New York World* perhaps gratified the people of Utah best when it summarized not only the military feats accomplished by Utah's sons, but the changing attitude of the nation toward Mormons generally:

> Our latest state has borne its share in adding to the glory of the nation. In the battle of Malate the Utah light artillery, whose guns were dragged through deep mud to send shrapnel into the Spaniards' ranks, showed itself deserving of all honor. Utah has had its troubles in the past, but when she sends such a contribution to the nation we wipe out the memory of all troubles.[76]

This is exactly what most Mormons were craving to hear. A major newspaper in the nation's largest city, with perhaps the largest circulation of any daily at the time, had said that the actions of Utah's soldiers had essentially absolved Mormons of any past unpleasantness between the religious sect and the American nation. This was the outcome church leaders and Utah journalists had hoped for when the volunteers first marched off for the Philippines.

While the evidence presented here suggests that Mormons were almost monolithically united in their support of the war and in praise of their servicemen, discussions of the aftermath of the war were not nearly as united, especially regarding the annexation of new territories and the potential of American imperialism. Expansion held particular significance for Mormons because it related strongly to the advancement of the church. Early Mormon documents reveal the reciprocally beneficial relationship between the expansion of the United States and the expansion of the kingdom of God.

Joseph Smith and other early church leaders considered the Constitution the "palladium of liberty"; as such, it ensured the freedom of religion to its citizens, which allowed Latter-day Saints to "claim the privilege of worshipping Almighty God according to the dictates of our own conscience, and allow all men the same privilege, let them worship how, where, or what they may."[77] An extension of American borders meant an extension of American liberties, which cleared a path for the eventual kingdom of God that would attend the Second Coming of Jesus Christ and his subsequent millennial reign. Speaking at an Independence Day celebration in 1854, Orson Hyde claimed that God assisted the American Revolution "to open and prepare the way for the Church and kingdom of God to be established on the western hemisphere, for the redemption of Israel and the salvation of the world."[78] Thus, the stone that would fill the whole earth may have been cut without hands, but its paths would be made straight by the American Constitution.[79]

Mormon expansionist thought can be traced back to Smith, who had argued that "the whole of America is Zion itself from north to south," and prophesied that both continents would eventually be unified under the same government, both earthly and heavenly.[80] Territorial expansion was a major component of Smith's platform during his 1844 campaign for the presidency of the United States, in which he argued for liberal annexation policies. "When a neighboring realm petitioned to join the union of the sons of liberty," Smith promised, "my voice would be, come: yea, come, Texas; come Mexico; come Canada; and come all the world — let us be brethren, let us be one great family, and let there be a universal peace."[81] Smith clearly imagined a United States that was not only an empire of liberty, but a forerunner of the kingdom of God.

Orson Hyde perhaps explained that forerunner role best in proto-Turnerian terms. "The United States," Hyde stated at an Independence Day celebration in 1853, "should therefore be regarded by the Latter-day Church as the men that fell the timber and clear the land, removing every obstacle in the way of ploughing and the sowing of seed." The freedom of religion, in other words, allowed for Mormon missionary efforts. "Remember, that whatever land or country falls under the Government of the United States," Hyde continued, "there you may go and preach the Gospel, and not be thrust into prison for it as you now are in many countries." Thus American expansion lubricated the gears of the millennial machine that would usher in "fullness of times" and culminate in the Second Coming.[82] Hyde concluded his address with a flourish, brazenly calling for specific territorial acquisitions that were politically topical:

> Spain must give up Cuba; England, Canada; and the United States of America must hold, as her dependencies, every country on the Western Continent. . . . We have recently had a liberal slice off from Mexico, but the whole loaf must come. The north must give up, and the south keep not back, while the islands are waiting for thy law. The voice of God, through American policy, with loud and thrilling notes, cries, Come unto me, all ye ends of the earth . . . and regale yourselves under the tree of liberty, whose branches are rapidly extending, and whose fruit is rich and desirable, and whose leaves are for the healing of the nations.[83]

Not all Mormons agreed with these policies, however. Parley P. Pratt believed that all nations could find refuge in the America's sphere of influence, but unlike Smith and Hyde, he believed that territorial acquisition was not necessarily desirable. "The influence of our institutions, the pattern we set, the working of these institutions, and their influence abroad will bring about the same results precisely," he said, "whether it is particularly by annexation or not."[84] It is clear from this evidence that American expansion held a special place in the beliefs of many early church leaders. Those sentiments, however, seemed to have become more convoluted by the time of the Spanish-American War, possibly because church leaders were far less vocal in their opinions of imperialism than their predecessors had been. Instead of being dispensed over the pulpit, the subjects of imperialism and annexation were discussed and debated in the press.

Utah newspapers had been publishing articles concerning the hypothetical annexations of Mexico, Canada, Hawaii, and Cuba for many years prior to the war of 1898. These stories were more like "what if" essays than real debates over policy.[85] But after the successful campaign against Spain, the United States had to officially decide what to do with its new possessions in Cuba, Puerto Rico, Guam, and the Philippines. Following the numerous articles printed by Utah newspapers on the subject reveals a noteworthy pattern: periodicals were pro- or anti-imperialism based more on political party affiliation than church influence.

The Democratic *Salt Lake Herald*, for example, was one of the most outspoken opponents of "the new imperialism," calling it the "silliest sort of sentimental rot."[86] It believed that "imperialism for the United States is disaster for the United States" and would "inevitably [lead] to the destruction of free institutions and the substitution of the institutions of tyranny."[87]

This sort of discourse could be expected of a Democratic newspaper in 1898, but it diverged sharply with the rhetoric being printed in the *Deseret News* at the same time. The *Herald* was almost entirely LDS, and many of the editors were prominent Mormons who frequently defended the church. The *Deseret News*, though not officially owned by the LDS church at the beginning of the war, acted as its journalistic voice. It was also owned and operated at the time by the Cannon family, who were prominent Republicans. So while Mormon writers at the *Herald* vehemently condemned imperialism, other Mormon writers at the *Deseret News* championed the American acquisition of Spain's old colonies, often using religious language. "He who fails to see in the miraculous victory of Manila the hand of Providence pointing out the destiny of the great American Republic and its duty toward less-fortunately situated fellow beings," the *Deseret News* asserted, "is not capable of reading the signs of the times."[88] It added on another occasion that "a power superior to that of man led the host of the United States on to victory," making it the "destiny of the United States to extend protection and the blessings of a free government to the races inhabiting those colonies."[89] These are just a few examples of numerous back-and-forth arguments between the Republican and Democratic newspapers of Utah. Smaller papers like the *Logan Journal*, the *Ogden Standard*, the *Wasatch Wave*, and the *Springville Republican* similarly broke down along party lines, even though Mormons owned and operated them. And so when it came to imperialism and annexation, it seemed that Mormon journalists tended to affiliate with their political party more than their religion.

Mormon servicemen in the Philippines also debated the morality of imperialism. The war against Spain made sense to many of the volunteers, like Stephen Bjarnson, an Icelandic convert from Spanish Fork, because Spain had been "depriving their subjects of a blessing which God bestowed upon all mankind—liberty and freedom."[90] A military occupation of the Filipino people, however, was more ethically complicated for these men of religion. Willard Call, who had been ordained a missionary before leaving Utah, was one who saw no value in colonizing the Philippines. "I had some sympathy for the Philipino [sic]," he wrote in his diary, "for he was fighting for his country, his home and his family, and it matters not how ignorant he might be, or how much better an American Protectorate might be for him." Consequently, Call and several of his companions requested and were granted an early discharge, returning home nine months before their unit was relieved.⁹¹

Other volunteers opposed occupation for more practical reasons: They simply wanted to go home. George Seaman, the other ordained missionary, wrote a letter to George Albert Smith about one month prior to the beginning of hostilities between American troops and Filipino freedom fighters. In it, he expressed his hope that all disagreements could be solved diplomatically, for "though I enlisted for war, the less of it I see the better satisfied I am."⁹² George Pruce Simpson, a Mormon serving with the Idaho infantry unit in the Philippines, voiced his frustration in racialized language common among U.S. troops, telling his wife that "if we have to stay here and fight these niggars [sic] another year, there will not half of us get back alive."⁹³ He prayed that he would be back with his wife soon, "never to part again, through my patriotism at any rate."⁹⁴ David Davis, a private in Battery B, meanwhile lamented in a letter to his parents that "there have been too many good Americans lay down there [sic] lives, which already is more than the Islands are worth."⁹⁵

Other Mormon men, however, agreed with American imperial policy in the Philippines. Captain Edgar Wedgewood of Provo wrote home to his wife that he believed the war was "necessary, justified, and morally right," and that if the Americans had demanded the disarmament of all Filipinos from the moment they landed, much trouble could have been avoided.⁹⁶ Albert Allen, a lieutenant in the regular infantry, assured Utah reporters that soldiers in the Philippines had a "very poor opinion" of anti-imperialist literature that had been distributed among them.⁹⁷ Isaac Russell, a private from Salt Lake City, based his support for a continuing war on a deep hatred for the Filipino people. In a lengthy letter to his anti-imperialist brother, Russell argued that the average Filipino—whom he referred to as a "stinking, garlicky, washed-once-last-year-and-wont-wash-again, lazy brute of a naygur [sic]"—was incapable of governing himself, and coercive American guidance was necessary for their progression. It was the soldiers' duty "to hold the Philippines and reduce them to law and order," because "no government could be established in the Philippines with any native race at its head."⁹⁸ These differences of opinion among LDS servicemen, along with the divisive rhetoric of the Utah newspapers, illustrate the tensions within Mormonism's outlook of American imperialism. Though nearly all church leaders had endorsed American expansion in theory, the messy application of expansionist policy muddied the waters in fact.

At the heart of this tension was the issue of race, as indicated by these soldiers' letters. Although some argued the necessity of continued American influence in the Philippines because of the ineptitude of the local population, others argued that Filipino inferiority was precisely the reason that the United States should disengage from further involvement. Whether critical or supportive of imperialism, Mormon servicemen seem to have fully embraced the racialized arguments of both sides of the national debate.[99] (See, for example, David Holtby's discussion of racism and the views of Albert Beveridge and Benjamin Tillman in his chapter in this volume.) Additionally, it is clear from these statements that Mormons in the Philippines clearly identified as white. Although this may seem unremarkable to modern readers, it was significant at the end of the nineteenth century. As Paul Reeve has pointed out, Mormons were often characterized as nonwhite by white American Protestants, even while Mormons themselves emphatically claimed whiteness.[100] Although Reeve's argument is worth consideration, it is clear that Mormon soldiers did not face the same level of discrimination as Filipinos, or even the Black soldiers that they served alongside. In fact, they took an active role in reinforcing a racial hierarchy that privileged whites, a category in which they included themselves. Mormon soldiers almost unanimously wrote about Filipinos with disdain, and they frequently referred to the local population in racial epithets that had traditionally been directed at African Americans back in the States, as was common in other white units. Although some Mormons sympathized with the insurgents' cause, none of them saw Filipinos as potential equals. And so although Mormon soldiers shared some similarities with other "dispossessed Americans striving to share more equitably in the rights and privileges of first-class citizenship," such as African American servicemen in the Philippines, they never had to face the dilemma of serving as "spokesmen abroad among 'colored people' for a country which made color a badge of inferiority," the way Black troops did. Mormons never had to doubt their status as full and equal citizens after aiding the war effort.[101]

For all the complexity of Mormonism's relationship to imperialism and racism, members of the church unvaryingly supported their men in uniform. Mormon newspapers eagerly reported on the activities of the volunteer units and praised them unashamedly. When the troops returned at the end of August 1899, the citizens of Utah threw an elaborate celebration, complete with parades, speeches, choirs, and a massive triumphal arch in downtown Salt Lake City, across the street from the Mormon temple. Though the festivities were certainly dedicated to honoring the service of the volunteers, they also served as another public display of Mormon patriotism and solidarity, demonstrating to the rest of the United States that, as *Harper's Weekly* had said, "the same patriotism animates Mormons as any other Americans."[102]

Mormons continued to manifest their patriotism after the war, and for the most part the American nation slowly began to accept their offerings. Thus, although the Mormon people did indeed undergo a transformation at the end of the nineteenth century, those changes were less revolutionary than they were evolutionary. Mormonism's distinctive form of patriotism—one that balanced loyalty to God with loyalty to country—survived Utah's political Reconstruction, largely because the Spanish-American War showed how those loyalties could be congruent, at least after the suspension of polygamy. Additionally, the war clarified the tensions that had existed within Mormon patriotism prior to the manifesto by giving Mormons real-life experience on how to balance peacemaking and warfare, how to negotiate loyalty to the Constitution and loyalty to the elected government, and how to claim the freedom of religion while respecting the power of the state. Although their conflicts with the federal government were not over, Reconstruction and the war with Spain helped put the church on the path to American normalcy in the twentieth century.

Notes

1. "Mormons at Manila," *Harper's Weekly*, March 25, 1899, 237.
2. The fact that many Mormons continued to practice polygamy in secret without church approval further alienated Mormons from the mainstream.
3. Thomas G. Alexander, *Mormonism in Transition: A History of the Latter-day Saints, 1890–1930* (Urbana: University of Illinois Press, 1996), 14.
4. Klaus J. Hansen, *Mormonism and the American Experience* (Chicago: University of Chicago Press, 1981), 206.
5. David L. Bigler, *Forgotten Kingdom: The Mormon Theocracy in the American West, 1847–1896* (Logan: Utah State University Press, 1998), 362.
6. For a full exploration of Mormonism's relationship with violence and the state, see Patrick Q. Mason, "Disciplinary Democracy: Mormon Violence and the Construction of the State," in *Reconstruction in Mormon America*, ed. Clyde A. Milner II and Brian Q. Cannon (Norman: University of Oklahoma Press, 2019), 88–110.
7. *The Pearl of Great Price*, trans. Joseph Smith Jr. (Salt Lake City: The Church of Jesus Christ of Latter-day Saints, 1981), Joseph Smith History 1:34.
8. *The Book of Mormon*, trans. Joseph Smith Jr. (Salt Lake City: The Church of Jesus Christ of Latter-day Saints, 1981), 1 Nephi 17:13; 1 Nephi 2:20. Hereafter *BofM*.
9. *BofM*, 2 Nephi 1:7; Ether 2:7, 12.
10. *BofM*, 2 Nephi 10:10–11.
11. *BofM*, Alma 43:9.
12. *The Doctrine and Covenants of The Church of Jesus Christ of Latter-day Saints* (Salt Lake City: The Church of Jesus Christ of Latter-day Saints, 1981), 10:51. Hereafter *D&C*.
13. George A. Smith quoted in *Journal of Discourses* (Liverpool: Asa Calkin, 1859), 6:364. Hereafter *JD*.

14. Orson Hyde, *JD*, 7:107

15. *D&C*, 101:80.

16. Joseph Fielding Smith, ed., *Teachings of the Prophet Joseph Smith* (Salt Lake City: Deseret Book, 1976), 147–148.

17. Parley P. Pratt, *JD*, 1:137.

18. For detailed accounts of the various persecutions endured by Mormons in the antebellum United States, see Spencer J. Fluhman, *"A Peculiar People": Anti-Mormonism and the Making of Religion in Nineteenth-Century America* (Chapel Hill: University of North Carolina Press, 2014); Stephen C. LeSueur, *The 1838 Mormon War in Missouri* (Columbia: University of Missouri Press, 1987); Leonard J. Arrington and Davis Bitton, *The Mormon Experience: A History of the Latter-day Saints* (New York: Alfred A. Knopf, 1979), chaps. 3–5; Richard Lyman Bushman, *Joseph Smith: Rough Stone Rolling: A Cultural Biography of Mormonism's Founder* (New York: Vintage, 2007).

19. Finis Ewing, quoted in Hubert Howe Bancroft, *History of Utah* (San Francisco: History Company, 1889), 100.

20. Joseph Fielding Smith, ed., *Teachings of the Prophet Joseph Smith*, 326.

21. Joseph Smith, *JD*, 2:163.

22. The Mormon political threat was by no means the only reason for Smith's murder; see Bushman, *Joseph Smith: Rough Stone Rolling*.

23. Their existence outside of the American nation was short-lived. The Mexican-American War began only months after the first wagon trains left Nauvoo, and the Treaty of Guadalupe Hidalgo—which ceded the majority of what is now the American West, including Utah—was signed less than a year after the vanguard company of Mormon pioneers arrived in the Salt Lake Valley.

24. John Taylor, *JD*, 11:90.

25. John Taylor, *JD*, 5:156.

26. John Taylor, *JD*, 5:156.

27. George A. Smith, *JD*, 8:360.

28. Eric Foner, *Reconstruction: America's Unfinished Revolution, 1863–1877* (New York: Harper and Row, 1988).

29. David Prior, "Civilization, Republic, Nation: Contested Keywords, Northern Republicans, and the Forgotten Reconstruction of Mormon Utah," *Civil War History* 56, no. 3 (2010), 285.

30. Republican platform of 1856 quoted in E. B. Long, *The Saints and the Union: Utah Territory during the Civil War* (Urbana: University of Illinois Press, 1981), 9; see also Benjamin E. Park, "Joseph Smith's Kingdom of God: The Council of Fifty and the Mormon Challenge to American Democratic Politics," *Church History* 87, no. 4 (2018), 1029–1055.

31. See Brent M. Rogers, *Unpopular Sovereignty: Mormons and the Federal Management of Early Utah Territory* (Lincoln: University of Nebraska Press, 2017).

32. Patrick Q. Mason, "Opposition to Polygamy in the Postbellum South," *Journal of Southern History* 76, no. 3 (2010), 547; Sarah Barringer Gordon, *The Mormon Question: Polygamy and Constitutional Conflict in Nineteenth-Century America* (Chapel Hill: University of North Carolina Press, 2002), 144.

33. For more information on Utah's Reconstruction, see Christine Talbot, *A Foreign Kingdom: Mormons and Polygamy in American Political Culture, 1852–1890* (Urbana: University of Illinois Press, 2013); Richard D. Poll, "The Political Reconstruction of Utah Territory, 1866–1890," *Pacific Historical Review* 27, no. 2 (1958), 111–126; Gustive O. Larson, *The "Americanization" of Utah for Statehood* (San Marino, Calif.: Huntington Library, 1971); Sarah Barringer Gordon, *The Mormon Question: Polygamy and Constitutional Conflict in Nineteenth-Century America* (Chapel Hill: University of North Carolina Press, 2002); and Edward Leo Lyman, *Political Deliverance: The Mormon Quest for Utah Statehood* (Urbana: University of Illinois Press, 1986).

34. George Q. Cannon, *JD*, 24:43.

35. Beginning in 1830, the LDS church has held regular yearly meetings in which the membership gathers to hear discourses from church leadership. Beginning in 1840, the meeting was held biannually, in April and October, with only a few exceptions in its long history. After its completion, conferences were held in the Salt Lake City Tabernacle, which seated thousands of spectators, and transcriptions of the speeches were published in *Deseret News*. Conference talks are a vital part of LDS documentary history since they addressed important church doctrine and policy and because they were widely heard and read.

36. Mason, "Disciplinary Democracy," 104.

37. D. Michael Quinn, "The Mormon Church and the Spanish-American War: An End to Selective Pacifism," *Pacific Historical Review* 43, no. 3 (1974), 342.

38. Francis M. Lyman, "Conference Report April 1898," 58. Hereafter CR.

39. Matthias F. Cowley, CR April 1898, 25.

40. Brigham Young Jr., CR April 1898, 27.

41. John Henry Smith, CR April 1898, 56.

42. Franklin D. Richards, CR April 1898, 81.

43. George Q. Cannon, CR April 1898, 87–88.

44. Wilford Woodruff, CR April 1898, 89–90.

45. "Will Serve the Nation," *Salt Lake Tribune*, May 1, 1898; "Patriotism," *Provo Enquirer*, January 5, 1897; "Still Patriotic," *Logan Journal*, February 26, 1898; "Full of War Spirit," *Salt Lake Tribune*, March 9, 1898; "This, That, and the Other," *Lehi Banner*, April 5, 1898; "All Ready for the Call to War," *Salt Lake Herald*, April 22, 1898.

46. "Services at the Tabernacle," *Deseret Evening News*, April 25, 1898.

47. *Journal History of the Church of Jesus Christ of Latter-day Saints*, April 24, 1898, 2, Church History Library, Salt Lake City, Utah.

48. "Services at the Tabernacle," *Deseret Evening News*, April 25, 1898.

49. "Apostle Young Repudiated," *Salt Lake Tribune*, April 26, 1898.

50. "Apostle Young's Advice," *Salt Lake Herald*, April 26, 1898.

51. "Apostle Young Repudiated," *Salt Lake Tribune*, April 26, 1898.

52. "Mormon Churchmen at Odds," *Evening Star*, April 29, 1898. See also "Saints Urged to Enlist," *Topeka State Journal*, April 29, 1898; "Sensation in Salt Lake," *Santa Fe New Mexican*, April 29, 1898; untitled article, *Wichita Daily Eagle*, April 30, 1898.

53. *Journal History*, April 25, 1898, 2.

54. *Journal History*, April 26, 1898, 2–3.

55. "No Disloyalty Here," *Deseret Evening News*, April 25, 1898.

56. "President Woodruff to Governor Wells," *Salt Lake Herald*, April 29, 1898.

57. "The Volunteer Corps," *Deseret Evening News*, April 30, 1898.

58. Lowell E. Call, "Latter-day Saint Servicemen in the Philippine Islands: A Historical Study of Their Religious Activities and Influences Resulting in the Official Organization of the Church of Jesus Christ of Latter-day Saints in the Philippines," (master's thesis, Brigham Young University, 1955), 84.

59. "Gunnison's Patriotism," *Deseret Evening News*, May 3, 1898.

60. "Patriotism in Utah," *Deseret Evening News*, May 2, 1898.

61. Call, "Latter-day Saint Servicemen," 84–85.

62. Ibid., 85.

63. "Young Repudiated," *The Independent*, May 5, 1898.

64. "What's Wrong with Utah?" *Salt Lake Herald*, April 29, 1898.

65. J. Golden Kimball, CR October 1898, 17.

66. Franklin D. Richards, CR October 1898, 32–33.

67. For a recent discussion of Mormon missionizing in Hawaii and its colonial and racial implications, see Hokulani K. Aikau, *A Chosen People, A Promised Land: Mormonism and Race in Hawai'i* (Minneapolis: University of Minnesota Press, 2012).

68. Call, *Latter-day Saint Servicemen*, 85.

69. Ibid., 88.

70. George A. Seaman, "The 'Far East' Improvement Association," *Improvement Era* 2, no. 2 (1898), 153.

71. Ibid., 154.

72. Ibid.

73. The Utah batteries fought at Malate, Santa Mesa, Malabon, Quingua, Bag Bag, and San Fernando, along with various other skirmishes. Charles R. Mabey, *The Utah Batteries: A History* (Salt Lake City: Daily Reporters, 1900), 15.

74. "Capt. Jennings Returns Home," *Deseret Evening News*, August 5, 1898.

75. James I. Mangum, "The Spanish-American and Philippine Wars," in *Nineteenth-Century Saints at War*, ed. Robert C. Freeman (Provo, UT: Religious Studies Center, Brigham Young University, 2007).

76. The *World* article was reprinted in B. H. Roberts, "Progress of the War between Spain and the United States of America," *Improvement Era* 2, no. 2 (1898), 131.

77. Article of Faith, 11

78. Orson Hyde, *JD*, 6:367.

79. This is an allusion to Nebuchadnezzar II's dream as recorded in the Bible in Daniel 2:31–45, in which a giant idol made of several different materials is smashed to pieces by a giant rolling stone that is "cut without hands" and gains in size until it fills the whole earth. The idol, according to Daniel, represents the great empires of the earth, and the stone represents the coming Kingdom of God. Many Mormons believed that the LDS church was the fulfillment of that prophecy.

80. Joseph Fielding Smith, ed., *Teachings of the Prophet Joseph Smith*, 362.

81. Joseph Smith, *General Smith's Views of the Power and Policy of the Government of the United States* (Nauvoo, Ill.: John Taylor, 1844), 7–8.

82. Ephesians 1:10.
83. Orson Hyde, *JD*, 7:107.
84. Parley P. Pratt, *JD*, 1:137.
85. "Annexation of Mexico," *Salt Lake Herald*, January 6, 1880; "Annexation of the Sandwiches," *Salt Lake Herald*, October 16, 1889; "Cuba and Canada," *Salt Lake Herald*, May 15, 1889; "The Spirit of Annexation," *Deseret Evening News*, December 24, 1888; "Hawaiian Annexation," *Deseret Evening News*, June 22, 1892.
86. "The Philippines," *Salt Lake Herald*, July 3, 1898.
87. "The New Imperialism," *Salt Lake Herald*, May 22, 1898.
88. "After the War," *Deseret Evening News*, July 2, 1898.
89. "As to Annexation," *Deseret Evening News*, September 3, 1898.
90. Call, *Latter-day Saint Servicemen*, 86.
91. Call, *Latter-day Saint Servicemen*, 98.
92. Letter, George A. Seaman, December 8, 1898, George Albert Smith Papers, Marriott Library, University of Utah, https://collections.lib.utah.edu/details?id=853353.
93. For additional racial thinking among American troops in the war, see Anti-Imperialist League, *Soldiers' Letters: Being Materials for the History of a War of Criminal Aggression* (Boston: Rockwell and Churchill, 1899).
94. Letter, George Pruce Simpson, May 8, 1899, folder 1, Lucy Coila Workman Papers, Marriott Library, University of Utah.
95. Letter, David J. Davis, April 9, 1899, reel 1, David J. Davis collection, 1886–1911, Church History Library, Salt Lake City, Utah.
96. Letter, Edgar A. Wedgewood, February 18, 1899, Edgar A. Wedgewood Letters, MSS 1001, L. Tom Perry Special Collections, Harold B. Lee Library, Brigham Young University.
97. Scrapbook, Box 1, Albert C. Allen Papers, Marriott Library, University of Utah.
98. Letter, Isaac K. Russell, March 5, 1900, Box1, Folder 7, Isaac K. Russell Papers, Marriott Library, University of Utah.
99. See Charles Quince, *Resistance to the Spanish-American and Philippine Wars: Anti-Imperialism and the Role of the Press, 1895–1902* (Jefferson, N.C.: McFarland, 2017), 51–52, 60–63, 133.
100. W. Paul Reeve, *Religion of a Different Color: Race and the Mormon Struggle for Whiteness* (New York: Oxford University Press, 2015). See also Max Perry Mueller, *Race and the Making of the Mormon People* (Chapel Hill: University of North Carolina Press, 2017).
101. For more information on the experience of Black soldiers in the Spanish-American and Philippine-American Wars, see Willard B. Gatewood Jr., *"Smoked Yankees" and the Struggle for Empire: Letters from Negro Soldiers, 1898–1902* (Fayetteville: University of Arkansas Press, 1987), 18; Willard B. Gatewood Jr., *Black Americans and the White Man's Burden, 1898–1903* (Urbana: University of Illinois Press, 1975); and Cynthia Marasigan, "Between the Devil and the Deep Sea: Ambivalence, Violence, and African American Soldiers in the Philippine-American War and Its Aftermath" (PhD diss., University of Michigan, 2010).
102. "Mormons at Manila," *Harper's Weekly*, March 25, 1899, 237.

10

Schooling "New-Caught, Sullen Peoples"

Illustrating Race in U.S. Empire

Brian Shott

Historians of the United States are familiar with *American Progress*, John Gast's 1872 oil painting of Lady Liberty floating East to West across the continent (see Figure 10-1), bringing light and civilization to the U.S. frontier: She trails telegraph wires behind her and scatters Native Americans and dangerous wildlife in front. The painting is a surefire PowerPoint addition to a lecture on Westward expansion, for it vividly portrays the notion of Manifest Destiny, the belief that the United States' fate and benevolent duty was to settle the continent.

As scholarship on race and empire has advanced, another image is popping up on history blogs, in classrooms, and in scholarly monographs: "School Begins," an 1899 color drawing by Louis Dalrymple (see Figure 10-2) and published in *Puck*, a popular weekly news magazine of the time. In the cartoon, Uncle Sam as schoolmaster threatens to discipline four young students, representing Cuba, Puerto Rico, Hawaii, and the Philippines, should they fail to learn their lessons in civilization. A trenchant depiction of U.S. imperial ideology, its racial constructions, and even its internal contradictions, "School Begins" is often described as representative of a new, turn-of-the-century Manifest Destiny—a racially charged outward push for imperial possessions in the Caribbean and the Pacific. This interpretation is not incorrect, per se, and is bolstered by a large amount of "race and empire" or "cultures of U.S. imperialism" scholarship in the fields of history, American studies, and literature. But the cartoon and others like it differ markedly from earlier, more optimistic images of continental conquest such as Gast's. Rather than portraying a simple call for uplift by a supposedly superior race and culture, the cartoon performs a more cautious, but perhaps just as malicious, reckoning with the tensions and contradictions within American imperial rhetoric—and it places the classroom at the center of the quest to resolve those conflicts.

Figure 10-1. John Gast, "American Progress," 1872. Prints and Photographs Division, Library of Congress, https://www.loc.gov/pictures/resource/ppmsca.09855/. The piece shows Lady Liberty moving west across the American landscape.

Figure 10-2. Louis Dalrymple, "School Begins," *Puck*, January 25, 1899, centerfold. Prints and Photographs Division, Library of Congress, https://www.loc.gov/pictures/resource/ppmsca.28668/. The piece depicts four recent island possessions of the United States as unruly schoolchildren.

Louis Dalrymple was born in Cambridge, Illinois, sometime around 1866 (sources show varying birthdates), of Scottish parentage. He studied at the Philadelphia Academy of Fine Arts in 1883, and then worked for some of the biggest illustrated presses of the time, including *Puck* and *Judge*, and newspapers including the New York *Daily Graphic*, the *St. Louis Post-Dispatch*, and the *Chicago Tribune*. Toward the end of his life he traveled frequently and worked sporadically. He died in his late thirties or early forties in a sanitarium, of venereal disease. The New York *World* reports that Dalrymple was found roaming the streets of Manhattan shirtless and screaming at children a few weeks before his death on December 27, 1905.[1]

Puck was founded in 1876 by Joseph Keppler, an Austrian immigrant who came to the United States in 1867. After two unsuccessful attempts to start German-language magazines in St. Louis, Keppler moved to New York and started the German-language *Puck* in 1876 and a more popular English edition the following year. Thomas Nast in *Harper's Weekly* had by then paved the way for caricature as a powerful and even feared tool of reformers and politicians. As industrial production grew and craftwork and a producerist mentality declined nationally, *Puck's* illustrators combined the scandalous urban political drama of the late nineteenth century with a growing middle-class focus on leisure and entertainment.[2] *Puck* became the first regularly published humor magazine in the United States; *Judge* and *Life* were its main competitors. Historian Ian Gordon describes *Puck's* politics as independent Democratic; *Judge* sided more frequently with the Republican Party.[3]

Keppler hired Dalrymple in 1886, at the age of twenty. Author Richard S. West says that Keppler had "high hopes" for his protégé, calling him a "born caricaturist." West calls Dalrymple's early work for *Puck* "unrefined" yet charming, with a "light-handed comic tone." But according to West, Dalrymple's weaknesses as an artist dogged his drawings, which became "just plain sloppy."[4] Contemporary observers were more generous, though most felt Dalrymple didn't possess the talent of Keppler or Frederick Opper, a pioneer of the comic strip form and an illustrator for *Puck* for eighteen years. Dalrymple took over as lead cartoonist after Keppler's death in 1894.

Whatever Dalrymple's level of talent, the venue for his drawings had great influence. In today's image-saturated culture it may be hard to grasp the power that nineteenth-century illustrated magazines such as *Puck, Judge,* and *Life*—and before them *Harper's Weekly* and *Frank Leslie's Illustrated News*—wielded in distilling political, ideological, and moral positions for the American populace. Some scholars suggest that *Puck* and *Judge* in particular may have been more influential in the late 1800s than all daily newspapers combined, though such impact of course is difficult to quantify and measure.[5] Each magazine accompanied its articles with pen-and-ink and watercolor drawings, including color front covers and centerfold cartoons.

Cartoonists of the time put in visual form the major news of the day, and the first three years of the Philippine-American War (1899–1902) counted as a top story. Illustrators drew Uncle Sam alongside England's John Bull and figures representing other European powers—America had "joined the big boys" in imperial adventuring. In April 1898, about a year before the cartoon's appearance, the United States declared war on Spain. The sinking of the U.S.S. *Maine* in Havana's harbor, from an explosion many at the time ascribed to Spanish sabotage, plus agitation for war among the U.S. public and "yellow" press, led President William McKinley to declare war on Spain, ostensibly to help Cubans gain their independence. The next month, U.S. warships led by Admiral George Dewey sailed to Spain's longtime colony in Southeast Asia, destroyed the Spanish fleet in Manila Bay, and prepared to attack Spanish ground forces in Manila. McKinley claimed that in response to this rash move he had struggled to find the Philippines on a map and said he later prayed to God for guidance on what to do with America's new possessions. His solution was "benevolent assimilation," which he described as official U.S. policy toward the Philippines in December of 1898, after the Treaty of Paris earlier that year ended the Spanish-American War (the United States would pay Spain $20 million for the possession of Guam, Puerto Rico, and the Philippines; the Senate ratified the treaty in February of 1899). McKinley instructed military officers to win the respect of Filipinos by "assuring them in every possible way that full measure of individual rights and liberties which is the heritage of free peoples."[6] Cartoonists responded with images of Uncle Sam or President McKinley as schoolmasters, adoptive parents, or disciplinarians bringing their new, wayward children—Hawaii (annexed separately in 1898), Cuba, Puerto Rico, and the Philippines—into the American fold.

Filipinos who had been revolting against Spanish rule were allies with the United States for a time. After Spanish surrender, however, a tense standoff between U.S. troops and Filipino rebels outside Manila exploded into fighting on February 4, 1899, and the United States began battling Filipino revolutionaries on the archipelago in a brutal war that would kill 4,165 U.S. troops and as many as 20,000 Filipino fighters and lead to the deaths of up to 750,000 civilians.[7] As many as 6,000 African American troops would support U.S. aims in the Philippines, fighting in six all-Black military regiments led by white officers. President Theodore Roosevelt would declare fighting over on July 4, 1902, although armed resistance to the United States would continue until 1913, particularly on southern islands. Before he was captured in 1901, Emilio Aguinaldo, Philippine rebel leader and president of the First Philippine Republic (January 1899 to April 1901), appeared in many political cartoons. The Filipino figure in "School Begins" is probably meant to represent him.

"School Begins" appeared in the January 25, 1899, issue of *Puck*, during that standoff between Filipinos and U.S. troops and Senate debate over ratification of the Treaty of Paris. Dalrymple depicts a headmaster, Uncle Sam, in a kind of expansive one-room schoolhouse, teaching a course in American civilization to four dark, disheveled children representing America's new possessions.[8] "Now children, you've got to learn these lessons, whether you want to or not," Sam tells his students. "But just take a look at the class ahead of you, and remember that, in a little while, you will feel as glad to be here as they are!" Behind these four new pupils sit the "class ahead": older children with the names of U.S. states (California and Texas), territories (New Mexico and Arizona), and the district of Alaska. All are orderly and, with the exception of Alaska, light-skinned. (Dalrymple appears to gloss over racial tensions in these areas; Anglo-Americans in New Mexico and Arizona in particular viewed Hispanics as unprepared for citizenship.)[9] Behind this scene appear three other prominent figures: a Chinese child, poised outside the doorway of the schoolhouse; a Native American, sitting just within the room, his speller held upside-down; and an African American, smiling and washing windows on a ladder several feet in the air.

On the classroom's blackboard are written three consecutive points: "The consent of the governed is a good thing in theory, but very rare in fact"; "England has governed her colonies whether they consented or not. By not waiting for their consent, she has greatly advanced the world's civilization"; and, "The U.S. must govern its new territories with or without their consent until they can govern themselves." As if to drive home the point further, a placard above and adjacent to the door proclaims, "The Confederate states refused their consent to be governed, but the Union was preserved without their consent."

How is "School Begins" being interpreted in today's high school and college classrooms? An exhaustive quantitative analysis is beyond the scope of this essay, but blogs, syllabi, and recently published books that reproduce the image reveal several tendencies of interpretation. The website "The Struggle for Puerto Rican Autonomy," a part of the digital Omeka network, a project of the Roy Rosenzweig Center for History and New Media, George Mason University, and the Corporation for Digital Scholarship, describes the cartoon as promoting the acceptance of the "White Man's Burden" and, in reference to the whitened class behind the darker children, an "assimilationist attitude which continues today."[10] Many other analyses, some student commentaries, and syllabi stress the outward push or missionary zeal of racialized notions of civilization present in the cartoon.[11]

One monograph, Susan-Mary Grant's *A Concise History of the United States* (2012), reproduces "School Begins" amid a more nuanced discussion of U.S. imperialism. Within a chapter on late-nineteenth-century expansion that explores the writings of evangelist Josiah Strong, Grant writes that the clergyman, in his book *Expansion: Under New World-Conditions* (1900), posited abroad "what was essentially a 'war without end' paradigm for the United States" that "appealed to the social reformer and the soldier alike."[12] Grant sees an essentially defensive position in the missionary zeal of reformers like Strong, who imagined a "danger of contagion from abroad" that must be controlled proactively, by going out into the world to save souls.[13] It is within this framework that Grant discusses "School Begins."

This complex view of the relationship between white racial nationalisms and imperialism recalls Eric T. L. Love's 2004 study of early U.S. imperial efforts. Love's book was fairly well received and is frequently cited, though often in passing, as a counterexample to studies stressing white supremacy's imperial push. Love claimed that, especially in congressional debate over annexation of the Philippines, white supremacist notions were used primarily and most effectively by anti-imperialists, not expansionists.[14] (Several decades before him, the historian Christopher Lasch, in one of his first published journal articles, found much the same.)[15] Those opposed to annexation raised again and again the specter of inassimilable, alien others reaching the country's shores from its new possessions. Love claims that all the way to the turn of the century, white supremacist attitudes shared by both imperialists and anti-imperialists consistently inhibited expansion; imperialists in Congress, he argued, mentioned race as little as possible in debates about annexation of Hawaii, the Dominican Republic, and the Philippines.

Love's sources tended to be diplomatic and congressional, and some reviewers criticized him for downplaying a pro-expansionist "white man's burden" manifest in the nation at large without drawing on material that might have revealed just such a phenomenon.[16] Social and cultural historians, for their part, have examined fiction, art, advertising, plays, and world's fairs, but often exclude political or diplomatic sources. Such studies, which Paul Kramer labels a "cultures of United States imperialism" strain of scholarship, sometimes make broad claims about a cultural push toward the possession of colonies abroad as constituting a new, turn-of-the-century moment when social Darwinist philosophies and religiously inspired notions of Manifest Destiny and racial uplift worked together to push America outward toward the "uncivilized" world.[17] Though such scholarship may acknowledge that many anti-imperialists played the race card with more vigor than imperialists, the overall effect still can be to downplay many Americans' racially based misgivings about "expansion."

Much in the cartoon does support "cultures of U.S. imperialism" scholarship, and the strength of such scholarship likely accounts for teachers' and scholars' use of "School Begins" as an example of racialized justification of U.S. imperialism. The work of American studies scholars on world's fairs in the United States, in particular, likely paved the way for the later work of scholars of cultures of U.S. imperialism and helps reveal a kind of pedagogy of civilization and progress tying education to imperial power that recalls Dalrymple's sketched classroom. Scholars have noted that Francis Bellamy's "Pledge of Allegiance" helped put flags in U.S. schools in time for the 1893 World's Columbian Exposition in Chicago celebrating the 400th anniversary of Columbus's arrival in America. Frederick Jackson Turner's first presentation of his frontier thesis—in which he linked American democracy and individualism to westward expansion—at the American Historical Association meeting was purposely held in conjunction with the exposition. Robert Rydell believes that world's fairs emphasized white supremacy as a "utopian agency" that "muted class divisions among whites, providing them with a shared national purpose."[18] In the Midway section of the Chicago world's fair, science and entertainment merged: "Evolution, ethnology, and popular amusements interlocked," as anthropologists sought to create, in the words of Smithsonian Institution administrator G. Brown Goode, who was called on to arrange and classify the Midway exhibits, "an illustrated encyclopedia of civilization."[19] Although Japan was given prime placement in the exposition and seen as a nation making rapid moral and industrial progress, China was a different story. The country sent no commissioner to Chicago in protest of the Chinese Exclusion Act of 1882. Embarrassed fair organizers quickly employed Chinese Americans to set up a small exhibit.[20] Dalrymple's school, too, seems uncertain about whether it will admit a Chinese student.

Historian Richard Slotkin has examined the educative function of another late-nineteenth-century cultural production, Buffalo Bill's "Wild West" shows, which were a hugely popular commercial entertainment from 1883 to 1916 (Buffalo Bill, in fact, set up a show next to the 1893 Chicago World's Fair). Flyers and posters promoting the show consistently promised its educational value and historical accuracy, not just its ability to entertain. Slotkin traces changes in the Wild West shows as they evolved to conflate the frontier myth with the new era of imperial expansion. In 1899, show organizers replaced "Custer's Last Fight" against Plains Indians with the famous "Battle of San Juan Hill" of the Spanish-American War.[21] The Native American figure in "School Begins" may represent more than simply the notion of enduring Indian savagery; his outlier status could suggest his perceived uselessness to the continued expression of American vigor. After decisive military defeats of most Native American tribes and the announced closure of the frontier, the white man's new burden, and opportunity to exercise his virtuous traits, lay outside the continental United States, and cultural productions shifted concurrently.

Yet as Love and other scholars have noted, annexation and war were still controversial. Although they could not stop the occupation of Cuba and the annexation of Hawaii, Puerto Rico, and the Philippines, anti-imperialists were a strong voice in Congress and in popular culture. Many Americans who were opposed to the taking of foreign territories thought that the United States was reneging on its republican traditions of self-government for all. Many more, out of a mix of racism and anxiety over potential competition for jobs, opposed "expansion" because they feared immigration from the newly acquired territories. Surely, these anti-imperialists argued, constitutional rights must travel with the American flag, and thus newly made, nonwhite citizens abroad might come to the United States and damage its traditions and culture or take jobs and drive down wages.

Such misgivings were enough to cause a significant minority of commentators at the time to interpret Rudyard Kipling's poem "The White Man's Burden"—printed in *McClure's* and republished in newspapers less than two weeks after Dalrymple's cartoon ran in *Puck*, and subtitled "The United States in the Philippines"—as a *critique* of imperialism, not its justification. The short, dark poem, which was a cultural phenomenon in its own right, contains at least one reversal, whereby the colonizer seems to be enslaved and serving the colonized.[22]

Could "School Begins" be an *anti-imperialist* cartoon in this fashion? Perhaps Dalrymple asks us to see the dark, unruly children as obviously unlikely to whiten, soften, and civilize to join the "class ahead." Why would the United States seek a different kind of "Negro Problem" or more inassimilable brown people holding their spellers upside down? Dalrymple, in this reading, would have us take the text on the blackboard—"The consent of the governed is a good thing in theory, but very rare in fact"; or, on the placard, "The Confederate states refused their consent to be governed, but the Union was preserved without their consent"—ironically, as pro-imperialist propaganda. Here, the cartoon exposes the harsh, absurd, anti-democratic Realpolitik at the heart of the expansionist project. In this interpretation, the cartoon would take the position of republican anti-imperialism (or what historian Fabian Hilfrich calls constitutional anti-imperialism), expressed in the racist mores of the day.²³

This stark a revision seems untenable. Dalrymple penned many straightforwardly pro-expansionist centerfolds for *Puck*.²⁴ Yet he does depict real tensions and potential contradictions in "School Begins." A profile of Dalrymple and other "humorists" in the British publication the *Strand* quotes Dalrymple as describing the *Puck* centerfold as the "political lesson of the week," which may imply that sometimes the cartoonist strove to capture multiple perspectives from events of the previous days, rather than push one focused, ideological take. In fact, the texts on the blackboard and placard mirror arguments over expansion among different factions in Congress; Dalrymple is surely drawing on these debates. Politicians repeatedly brought the Civil War and Reconstruction into debates about the United States' new imperial role. Hilfrich finds that imperialists "claimed that the Civil War had been fought solely to save the Union and that its enduring mandate consisted of advancing reconciliation between the sections, which had been sealed by the war against Spain." These imperialists cast overseas expansion as the "inescapable destiny of the 'completed' union."²⁵ One anti-imperialist view, such as the one espoused by Mark Twain, typically admitted that while ending slavery may not have been the original purpose of the Civil War, consent of the governed had perfected American democracy and neglecting that high purpose overseas would only weaken the nation at home.²⁶ By contrast, many other anti-imperialists, typically but not exclusively Southern and white, repeatedly noted that imperialists spoke *against* racial or cultural equality in their zeal for expansion but had pushed just such a thing on the South. These Southerners argued against expansion by saying that they had long known that other races were incapable of self-government, and that they were busy correcting the outrages of Reconstruction by disenfranchising Southern Blacks.²⁷ Dalrymple's "School Begins" seems to nod toward this complex political and rhetorical field while remaining a pro-expansion effort. Politicians of the time called for tax-supported, government-supervised public schools in Hawaii, the Caribbean, and the Philippines, but few supported African American education in the South; they engaged in lengthy discussions about when to give voting rights to new, nonwhite colonial subjects amid aggressive disenfranchisement of Blacks at home. Such moves, as literary scholar Peter Schmidt explains, "were justified using the rhetoric of carefully controlled tutelage and uplift—Progressivism's supposedly rational response to the alleged limitation of a people's character and culture."²⁸

The term "Jim Crow colonialism" may help describe the relationship between segregation at home and U.S. imperial efforts. Some scholars have used the term to describe racial divisions in labor and social spheres transplanted to U.S. colonies and interests in the Caribbean basin—as, for example, with enforced segregation in the construction of the Panama Canal.[29] But Schmidt's definition is more complex and perhaps useful. Schmidt calls an article by Progressive Charles Denby titled "What Shall We Do with the Philippines?" and published in a leading Progressive journal in March 1899, a succinct summation of Jim Crow colonialism. Denby writes in the journal,

> We, who are a trifle progressive, are called "imperialists," because we are not going to allow the poor Filipinos to vote. Probably we are not going to allow them to vote until we are satisfied they can vote intelligently; but, just as certainly, when the time comes that the islanders are qualified to exercise the right of suffrage they will get it. In all human probability they will secure it sooner than some of the negro population in some of the Southern States. Gentlemen of the South, gentlemen of Dixie—some of us imperialists do not blame you at all for taking all possible legal measures to protect your cherished rights. Will you not forgive us, if we pursue the same policy with regard to a new and untried race?[30]

Contradictions in foreign and domestic social policies would be smoothed over by emphasizing an ongoing process of tutoring to gain civil rights.

In this way "School Begins" evokes Paul Kramer's concept of "calibrated colonialism" in the Philippines, which entailed "criteria by which Filipinos would be recognized as having the capacity to responsibly exercise power in the colonial state."[31] These benchmarks of progress were continually readjusted, making freedom promised but "endlessly deferred." The United States continually assessed the Filipinos' capacity, "identifying key social, cultural, and intellectual milestones" on the road toward full civilization but "constantly mark[ed] tragic insufficiency in the present."[32] Uncle Sam's book, "First Lesson's in Self-Government," may spell out these benchmarks. The cartoon's four children, and Uncle Sam's reassurance that they will soon feel fortunate to be enrolled in his course on civilization, represent Dalrymple's depiction of "benevolent assimilation." As Vicente Rafael puts it, "Colonization as assimilation was deemed a moral imperative, as wayward native children cut off from their Spanish fathers and desired by other European powers would now be adopted and protected by the compassionate embrace of the United States."[33] Rafael's conception of "white love" captures the (tough) "love" Uncle Sam must show to his new wayward, youthful charges. But Uncle Sam's wooden rod, and the folklore about sadistic schoolmasters it evokes, remains as an allusion to the very real violence inherent in the imperial project. Dalrymple was not alone in choosing the classroom to describe U.S. expansion; another cartoonist depicted a wild Filipino rebel labeled "Aguinaldo" fleeing a pack of anthropomorphized free schools bringing "civilization." Still another drew a classroom scene with Aguinaldo in the corner in a dunce cap.[34]

All this makes the schoolhouse far more than an offhand metaphor for the U.S. imperial project. Its central conceit was to be the space and policy that would resolve the tensions between the perceived failures of Reconstruction and the push and pull of white racial fantasies with respect to expansion. In fact, Dalrymple's iconic, one-room schoolhouse was at the heart of a debate on education in the late-nineteenth century led by Progressives. During the industrial boom of the Gilded Age, according to historian of education Jonathan Zimmerman, "poets started to celebrate the one-room school as the locus of America's lost rural simplicity."[35] Yet in the late 1890s and the early twentieth century, many Progressives wanted to close its doors. To reformers, modern society demanded not just forest conservation, prohibition, and food inspection, but school consolidation. Education officials distributed postcards depicting dilapidated one-room schoolhouses as the "Old Way," along with the alternative: shiny, multistory buildings ("The New Way").[36] In "School Begins," the school's ceilings are lofty; a huge flag stretches up into the air, and a tall glass window also disappears out of the frame. In the background, a giant alcove holds rows of students. The architecture likewise suggests grandiosity and perhaps hearkens back to the fabled birthplace of democracy, ancient Greece, in the vaguely Doric columns of the doorframe and the large, blocky threshold at the doorsill. Instead of a ramshackle Little Red Schoolhouse, Dalrymple's creation seems a kind of hybrid between visions of a modern, industrialized education system and simpler, more agrarian one-room instruction. This may reflect tensions between descriptions of the U.S. imperial project as representing and requiring modern ideas and technologies and the reality of America's new Asian possession, decidedly agrarian and allegedly locked in time.

As schools transformed to prepare students to take positions in a rapidly industrializing America, this domestic struggle over modernization was in close and sometimes contentious conversation with imperial interests.[37] Educational efforts in the Philippines, in fact, swung between vocational efforts to prepare Filipinos for productive labor and a classical education designed to make Filipinos into democrats unbeholden to the Filipino elite. The first general superintendent of the Philippines, Fred Atkinson, held the position from 1900 to 1902 and sought to design education in the Philippines around the educational programs of Black educator and ex-slave Booker T. Washington. Atkinson wrote to Washington and visited both the Hampton and Tuskegee institutes before traveling to the Philippines. "We should heed the lesson taught us in our reconstruction period when we started to educate the negro" and implement an agricultural and vocational education specifically modeled after Tuskegee, he wrote to the Philippine Commission, the U.S. colonial government in the islands, arguing against an academic or literary curriculum for Filipinos.[38] But this approach was scrapped by the next superintendent, David Barrows, who from 1903 to 1909 emphasized academic education in order to create "not a proletariat," but an educated "peasant proprietor," resembling Jefferson's independent yeomanry.[39] The next superintendent, Frank White, shifted education back to a vocational basis.[40]

U.S. teachers themselves often resisted the commission's educational efforts and emphasis. In the same way that Black soldiers in the Philippines imagined and occasionally found employment opportunities unavailable to them at home, African American teachers might, as Sarah Steinbock-Pratt has argued, use their position to "disrupt the linking of civilization and modernity with whiteness."[41] Black teachers consistently claimed American identity abroad and capitalized on white Americans' insistence to Filipinos that race would not be a barrier to their participation in social, economic, and political life under U.S. tutelage.[42] Meanwhile, Filipino students in America (*pensionados*, who began arriving in the early 1900s) started their own publications, including U.C. Berkeley's *Filipino Students' Magazine*, which advocated for better treatment for the Philippines.[43]

Viewers of "School Begins" would likely see the African American figure as aligned with popular conceptions of Booker T. Washington's industrial (meaning vocational, agricultural, and teacher-training) Tuskegee program. This window washer's bucket may even recall Washington's often repeated phrase, "Cast down your bucket where you are," part of the Tuskegee educator's emphasis on practical professions for African Americans over academic education or political agitation against segregation. The industrial and vocational education model of Hampton/Tuskegee influenced U.S. colonial policymakers in Puerto Rico and in the Philippines; U.S. policymakers and educators debated which "race," Filipinos or African Americans, needed more vocational versus academic training.[44]

Washington's Tuskegee program always had an imperial pedigree. The Hampton Normal and Agricultural Institute, which Washington attended as a young man and upon which he modeled Tuskegee, was founded in 1868 by Samuel C. Armstrong. Armstrong, the son of Hawaiian missionary parents, led African American troop regiments in the Civil War and died in 1893. He wrote that "from 1820 to 1860, the distinctively missionary period, there was worked out in the Hawaiian Islands the problem of the emancipation, enfranchisement, and Christian civilization of a dark-skinned Polynesian people in many respects like the negro race."[45] Historian Gary Okihiro notes that an 1882 letter from Hawaii's Bureau of Immigration to Armstrong, which asked the famed educator about the feasibility of Black labor on Hawaii, reveals that "the ideas of native education and servile labor for the ostensible uplift of subject races migrated between island and continent, and a seed first cultivated in Hawai'i and transplanted in the American South had found its way back, full circle, to the Islands."[46]

That uplift efforts abroad were in dialogue with perceived racial "problems" at home does not seem lost on Dalrymple, who along with the African American child added as outliers in Uncle Sam's civilizational classroom Native American and Chinese figures. The assault on African American rights after Reconstruction is well known to historians; despite the Fourteenth and Fifteenth amendments, Southern white supremacists used state and local ordinances that, along with terrorist and mob violence, steadily disenfranchised African Americans. In Louisiana in 1896, for example, 130,000 African Americans were still registered to vote; just eight years later in 1904, only 1,300 were.[47] But scholarly work in the last decade has emphasized overlapping, multiracial struggles for American belonging following the Civil War.[48] State ratification of the Reconstruction amendments was contested for several years, and Western politicians defeated several racially egalitarian proposals by Radical Republicans. Debate around African American rights and Chinese exclusion were sometimes in dialogue. Supporters of Chinese exclusion might argue that the nation did not need another "problem" race like African Americans. Or in arguing for Black civil rights, the Chinese could be used as a foil, as in Associate Justice John Marshall Harlan's dissenting opinion in *Plessy v. Ferguson*, where he asked how the Supreme Court could allow the Chinese, a race "so different from our own" that it was denied citizenship, to ride with whites on train cars while excluding African Americans, many of whom had fought to preserve the Union.[49]

Like African Americans, Chinese in America had by the turn of the century also suffered civil rights victories and defeats. In 1868, signed along with the Fourteenth Amendment, the Burlingame Treaty was strongly antiracist, protecting Chinese workers on the West Coast, where they were discriminated against by the Irish and other manual laborers worried about low-wage competition. Anti-Chinese forces eventually gained the upper hand, and by 1882 had passed the Chinese Exclusion Act, which drastically restricted Chinese immigration to America. In historian Alexander Saxton's view, the earlier defeat of Senator

Charles Sumner's hopes for naturalization of the Chinese in 1870 had "predicted the abandoning of Reconstruction" for African Americans; the end of Reconstruction, in turn, "would seal the fate of the Chinese in the West."[50]

Educators may be tempted to use the Chinese student in "School Begins" as an example of anti-Chinese racism and the Exclusion Act, the first legislation in the United States to restrict immigration for a specific nationality. Some contemporary analyses of the cartoon describe the Chinese figure as drawn with ridicule. But this is not the disease-ridden Chinese figure in "A Statue for Our Harbor" printed in San Francisco's *Wasp* magazine, or even the disheveled and disorderly front-row students in Darlymple's classroom.[51] Instead, a well-kempt, curious student is poised at the schoolhouse door. Dalrymple may be nodding to an ongoing debate about the Chinese that, by 1899, still contained pro-Chinese voices. Historian Lon Kurashige, in fact, has focused on the strength and persistence of pro-Chinese sentiment among commentators throughout the latter half of the nineteenth century. Kurashige flips the success story of anti-Chinese organizing and asks why it took until 1882 to pass an exclusion act (that still contained exceptions to exclusion), when robust Chinese immigration to the United States had begun several decades earlier. By the turn of the century some Western intellectuals saw Chinese entrepreneurialism as vital to the development of Southeast Asia. Planters on Hawaii sought an exemption to Chinese exclusion, believing the Chinese worker to be a virtual automaton.[52] And as Paul Kramer has shown, many American politicians and merchants were more interested in a "filter" to Chinese immigration that let some desired classes of Chinese in, rather than complete exclusion.[53]

Empire's challenge to national and racial constructions appeared in the illustrated pages of the late-nineteenth-century periodical press in many drawings not authored by Dalrymple. In a fashion similar to race scientists' struggles to describe the purported origins of the "Malay race" in the heterogeneous islands of the Philippines, cartoonists of the time were flummoxed about how to depict "the Filipino." Illustrators sometimes gave Filipinos the stereotypical marks of savagery in much the same way they drew American Indians; at other times the dark skin, white eyes, kinky hair, and large lips of minstrelsy identified them. One example is a color cartoon that appeared in *Judge* in 1899. Uncle Sam is a barber; his scissors, with blades named "civilization" and "education," have just been used to give a trim to two figures representing Hawaii and Puerto Rico, both caricatured to look African American. "You're next," Uncle Sam shouts to a figure representing the Philippines, whose hair and clothing resemble Native American stereotypes.[54]

Booker T. Washington was attuned to the new racial constructions and hierarchies that empire catalyzed. Addressing a Brooklyn audience in early 1903, Washington almost appears to be speaking about cartoonists and their race humor:

> Just now the Filipino seems to be going through the interesting process of being carefully examined. If he can produce hair that is long enough and nose and feet that are small enough, I think the Filipino will be designated and treated as a white man; otherwise he will be assigned to my race. If I were to consider the question purely from a selfish standpoint, I should urge that our new subjects be classed as Negroes; but if I were to consider unselfishly the peace of mind of the Filipino himself, I should hope that he ... will not struggle through all future generations considered and looked upon as a problem, instead of a man.[55]

Washington probably feared images such as that in Figure 10-3, which visually dissolves the romantic racialism of the antislavery novel *Uncle Tom's Cabin* and repurposes it into a cynical kind of advocacy for strategies of racial containment and transformation abroad. Published in *Judge* about two weeks after "School Begins" appeared in *Puck*, "Our New Topsy" recalls the well-meaning enslaved girl from Harriet Beecher Stowe's immensely popular novel, published in 1852. In Stowe's novel, Eva, the angelic daughter of a slave owner, treats Topsy with kindness and love, transforming her self-hatred and wicked ways, which Stowe blamed on the institution of slavery, not biology. But the Topsy of popular culture, the one commonly performed on stage in the popular "Tom shows" of the nineteenth century, was often an unchangeable wild child played for laughs; this is the Topsy of Figure 10-3. A put-upon and feminized Uncle Sam (dressed as "Miss Feeley," Stowe's abolitionist Northerner whose ambiguous feelings toward African Americans the novel exposed) is tormented by Topsy-like, Iloilo-based Filipino rebel leader Emilio Aguinaldo. "I's so awful wicked there cain't nobody do nothin' with me," Aguinaldo-as-Topsy declares. Stowe's novel, despite its own stereotyping of African Americans, expressed a strong egalitarian vision; that vision has faded.[56]

But Booker T. Washington also saw the possibility that American empire could scramble racial logics in ways that might benefit African Americans. In 1900, he described for readers of *Century* magazine how, for Black Cubans, "In only a few instances [was] the color-line drawn." Would the United States, Washington asked, now import its own inegalitarian racial regime into the island?

Figure 10-3. Victor Gillam, "Our New Topsy," *Judge*, November 7, 1899, cover. Philippine rebel leader Emilio Aguinaldo is portrayed as the enslaved Topsy from Harriet Beecher Stowe's *Uncle Tom's Cabin*.

"Certainly it will place [the United States] in an awkward position to have gone to war to free a people from Spanish cruelty" only to "treat a large proportion of the population worse than did even Spain herself, simply on account of color." To Washington, a U.S. encounter with Cuba's fainter color line might highlight and unsettle sharply drawn racial segregation at home.[57] Black troops fighting in the Philippines and possibly staying in the islands after the war might also complicate U.S. imperialism. "If the American flag remains in the Philippines, Afro-Americans will have to be drafted to hold it up," wrote T. Thomas Fortune, a militant journalist and friend of Booker T. Washington, upon returning from a visit to the islands.[58] Several regiments of Black troops would fight in the Philippines; they wrote home to the Black press with a variety of opinions, ranging from enjoyment and pride about their service to bitter condemnations of white soldiers and their racism toward Filipinos.[59]

Dalrymple's cartoon, of course, could not predict in 1899 the tensions and solidarities that would develop between Black civilians and troops and Filipinos in the Philippines; nor do we see a direct portrayal of the interrelated nature of Black, Chinese, and Native American racialization in the image in the form of engagement of the representative figures with each other. One cartoon that does come closer to foreshadowing the complex field of race and empire in the late-nineteenth century is "The Reconstruction Policy of Congress, as illustrated in California," a letter sheet printed in 1867 by the Democratic Party to attack California Republican gubernatorial candidate George C. Gorham, a supporter of Black male suffrage (see Figure 10-4). Stacked on Gorham's shoulders in the illustration are, from the bottom, an African American, a Chinese man, and a "Digger" Indian. Racist tropes are present in both the form, dress, and speech of all three nonwhite men in the human stack. The African American figure says that he is obliged to "carry dese brudders," for there is "no stinkshun ob race or culler any more." The Chinese man declares Gorham a "belly good man," for "he say chinaman vo-tee all same melican man." The Native American is the most inarticulate and excited: "Ingen vote! Plenty whisky all time. Gorham big ingin." A stern Uncle Sam implores Gorham to "read the history of his country" to "learn that this ballot box was dedicated to the white race, alone."[60] White racism is strong and obvious in this Reconstruction-era cartoon. But as with "School Begins," white supremacist notions reveal isolationist impulses: To buttress their arguments about Black inferiority, Democrats needed to associate African Americans with the foreign cultures of Chinese immigrants and Native Americans.

Did white racism stay the hand of U.S. imperialism as much or more than it empowered and guided it? Why, Eric T. L. Love asks, did the powerful United States not annex all of tiny Panama to build a canal? For Love, the answer was that many Americans wanted to avoid "the entanglements of race." But such questions are difficult to answer with certainty. The tendency of many contemporary U.S. historians to pounce on any argument they view as relying on, even unconsciously, U.S. exceptionalism,[61] may make scholars of race and empire reluctant to fully explore the isolationist impulses of white supremacy. Some have done so, of course. Historian Ann K. Ziker hears strong strains of the race-based anti-imperialist position of the late-nineteenth century persisting well after World War II, in the debate over Hawaiian statehood. Southern segregationists repeatedly referred to Hawaii as home to a "mongrel" population that would threaten the U.S. mainland; some even went so far as to argue for full independence for the territory.[62] The racism involved in the "birther" controversy surrounding Hawaiian native

Figure 10-4. "The Reconstruction Policy of Congress, as illustrated in California," letter sheet, 1867. Artist unknown. Library of Congress, Prints and Photographs Division, https://www.loc.gov/pictures/item/2008661701/. The letter sheet attacks California Republican gubernatorial candidate George C. Gorham for threatening racial hierarchies.

Barack Obama's presidential campaign, and the white nationalist impulses of many of the conspiracy theory's leading proponents, gains new valence here.

Of course, racist fears of national contagion can sometimes exist within imperial arguments and actions, as Susan-Mary Grant showed in her examination of Josiah Strong's defensive missionary approach. But even when white Americans settled abroad, and especially when they viewed their stay as temporary, racism's more unvarnished forms could inhibit American interests. The white soldier press in Manila was a thorn in the side of U.S. imperialists in the Philippines; its virulent anti-Filipino racism led these journals to oppose "Filipinization," the paternalistic U.S. government policy of appointing Filipinos to local government positions.[63]

At the turn of the century, racism granted imperialism a kind of paternalistic gloss but also simultaneously provided intellectual and emotional power to anti-imperialists. Education—mainly unequal and racist educational uplift strategies—was a key way that the nation quelled the potential for a renewal of sectional conflict among whites and smoothed over what Gary Gerstle describes as America's contradictory mix of racial and civic nationalism.[64] It was the schoolhouse—figuratively in the sketches of cartoonists, but quite literally in the policies of U.S. colonial officials—that would attempt to resolve tensions between liberal notions of self-government and fantasies of racial supremacy. It would provide, many hoped, a careful system of tutelage and control for those deemed not yet ready for full citizenship. Cartoonists such as Louis Dalrymple recognized this strategy, seeing the classroom as key to America's imperial efforts and to its continuing social and political challenges at home.

Schools made citizens, but for those regarded as not quite American, citizenship was, as Helen H. Jun has argued, "a narrow discursive field within which differently racialized groups [were] forced to negotiate their exclusion in relationship to others."[65] Many of the cartoons examined in this essay show an uncanny awareness of this powerful field and its polyvalent racial ideologies. Cartoonists expected their readers to be familiar with the political "lesson of the week" in some complexity and contentiousness; scholars must not underestimate nineteenth-century Americans' capacity for self-satire and doubt. Dalrymple, for one, seemed to instinctively know that the question of who was in and who was out of Uncle Sam's schoolhouse—and under what conditions—would trouble the nation for years to come.

Notes

The quotation in the title is from Rudyard Kipling, "The White Man's Burden," originally printed in *McClure's*, February 1899.

1. "Louis Dalrymple, Cartoonist, Dead," *The World* (New York), December 28, 1905, 9.
2. Ian Gordon, *Comic Strips and Consumer Culture, 1890–1945* (Washington, D.C.: Smithsonian Institution Press, 2002), 16–17.
3. Ibid., 175n5.
4. Richard S. West, *Satire on Stone: The Political Cartoons of Joseph Keppler* (Urbana: University of Illinois Press, 1988), 323.
5. Stephen Hess and Sandy Northrop, *Drawn and Quartered: The History of American Political Cartoons* (Montgomery, Ala.: Elliott & Clark Publishing, 1996), 65, in Abe Ignacio et al., *The Forbidden Book: The Philippine-American War in Political Cartoons* (San Francisco: Eastwind Books of Berkeley, 2004), 3.
6. William McKinley to the Secretary of War, December 21, 1898. Quoted in Paul Kramer, *The Blood of Government: Race, Empire, the United States, and the Philippines* (Chapel Hill: University of North Carolina Press, 2006), 110.
7. Mortality figures, which for Filipino civilians include death from conditions created or exacerbated by war, such as disease, come from Michael H. Hunt and Steven I. Levine, *Arc of Empire: America's Wars in Asia From the Philippines to Vietnam* (Chapel Hill: University of North Carolina Press, 2012), 57–58.
8. Maurice Horn puts Dalrymple's birth in 1861. See Maurice Horn, ed., *The World Encyclopedia of Cartoons* (New York: Gale Research, 1980), 183.
9. See David Holtby, *Forty-Seventh Star: New Mexico's Struggle for Statehood* (Norman: University of Oklahoma Press, 2012), 39–66.
10. Available at http://aguilo79.omeka.net/exhibits/show/interpretation-of-political-ca/what-do-these-images-mean-/school-begins.
11. See, for example, the blog Becoming America, "Fall Semester 1 with Prof. Robert Hannigan," which links "School Begins" to Social Darwinism in U.S. foreign policy (accessed at http://becomingamerica.edublogs.org/tag/school-begins/); Brian Kundinger, *Brown Journal of History* 7 (2013), 7–10, who sees the cartoon as an example of the United States' embrace of a "civilizing mission" in its foreign policy (https://blogs.brown.edu/bjh/files/2014/05/BrownJournalofHistory2013.pdf); Ellen Sebring, "Civilization and Barbarism: Cartoon Commentary and the 'White Man's Burden' (1898–1902)," MIT Visualizing Cultures (https://visualizingcultures.mit.edu/civilization_and_barbarism/cb_essay.pdf); and "School Begins" described as an example of "the dark history of education as a tool of settler colonialism and cultural destruction" (https://ratical.org/ratville/SchoolBegins.html). None of these interpretations is incorrect in seeing racism as powering turn-of-the-century U.S. imperialism; they simply fail to see much tension or nuance in the cartoon or explore racism's full and complex relationship to U.S. foreign policy. At another website, a blog entry titled "The Interesting Role of *Puck* in 'School Begins,'" from a student at Albion College, describes the "racial bias" in the image as something "used to legitimize the rise in imperialism within Europe and the United States"; see https://herweyernewberry.wordpress.com/2015/09/16/the-interesting-role-of-puck-in-school-begins/

12. Susan-Mary Grant, *A Concise History of the United States of America* (Cambridge: Cambridge University Press, 2012), 258.

13. Ibid., 259.

14. Eric T. L. Love, *Race over Empire: Racism and U.S. Imperialism, 1865–1900* (Chapel Hill: University of North Carolina Press, 2004).

15. Christopher Lasch, "The Anti-Imperialists, the Philippines, and the Inequality of Man," *Journal of Southern History* 24, no. 3 (1958), 319–331.

16. See, for example, Janet M. Davis, "A Smaller, Purer America," *Journal of the Gilded Age and Progressive Era* 5, no. 1 (2006), 74–76; and Frank Schumacher, *Amerikastudien / American Studies* 51, no. 4 (2006), 610–612.

17. See Paul Kramer, "Power and Connection: Imperial Histories of the United States in the World," *American Historical Review* 116, no. 5 (2011), 1348–1391.

18. Robert Rydell, *All the World's a Fair: Visions of Empire at American International Expositions, 1876–1917* (Chicago: University of Chicago Press, 1987), 237.

19. Ibid., 45.

20. Ibid., 49–50.

21. Richard Slotkin, "Buffalo Bill's 'Wild West' and the Mythologization of the American Empire," in *Cultures of United States Imperialism*, ed. Amy Kaplan and Donald E. Pease (Durham, N.C.: Duke University Press, 1994), 175–176.

22. Gretchen Murphy discusses the cultural impact of Kipling's poem in *Shadowing the White Man's Burden: U.S. Imperialism and the Problem of the Color Line* (New York: New York University Press, 2010).

23. See Fabian Hilfrich, *Debating American Exceptionalism: Empire and Democracy in the Wake of the Spanish-American War* (New York: Palgrave Macmillan, 2012).

24. See, for example, Dalrymple's cartoons for *Puck* on September 28, 1898; October 4, 1899; March 8, 1899. Reprinted in Abe Ignacio et al., *The Forbidden Book*, 29, 34, 125.

25. Hilfrich, *Debating American Exceptionalism*, 120.

26. Ibid., 126.

27. Ibid., 66.

28. Peter Schmidt, *Sitting in Darkness: New South Fiction, Education, and the Rise of Jim Crow Colonialism* (Jackson: University Press of Mississippi, 2008), 99–100.

29. See Michael L. Conniff, *Black Labor on a White Canal: Panama, 1904–1981* (Pittsburgh: University of Pittsburgh Press, 1985).

30. Charles Denby, "What Shall We Do with the Philippines?" *Forum* 27 (March 1899), 48. Schmidt discusses Denby's article in *Sitting in Darkness*, 104.

31. Kramer, *The Blood of Government*, 191.

32. Ibid., 192.

33. Vicente L. Rafael, *White Love and Other Events in Filipino History* (Durham, N.C.: Duke University Press, 2000), 21.

34. Grant Hamilton, "The Filipino's Bugaboo," *Judge*, August 5, 1899; W. A. Rodgers, "Uncle Sam's New Class in the Art of Self-Government," *Harper's Weekly*, August 27, 1898.

35. Jonathan Zimmerman, *Small Wonder: The Little Red Schoolhouse in History and Memory* (New Haven, Conn.: Yale University Press, 2009), 3.

36. Ibid., 80–81.

37. Michael B. Katz details how reformers prepared a tractable labor pool for the industrializing era in *Irony of Early School Reform: Educational Innovation in Mid-Nineteenth Century Massachusetts* (Cambridge, Mass.: Harvard University Press, 1968).

38. Glenn May, *Social Engineering in the Philippines: The Aims, Execution, and Impact of American Colonial Policy, 1900–1913* (Westport, Conn.: Greenwood Press, 1980), 93.

39. Ibid., 98.

40. Ibid., 115.

41. Sarah Steinbock-Pratt, "A Great Army of Instruction: American Teachers and the Negotiation of Empire in the Philippines," (PhD diss., University of Texas at Austin, 2013), viii.

42. Ibid., 267.

43. See Lawrence Lawcock, "Filipino Students in the United States and the Philippine Independence Movement, 1900–1935" (PhD diss., University of Michigan, 2001); Paul Kramer, "Is the World Our Campus? International Students and U.S. Global Power in the Long Twentieth Century," *Diplomatic History* 33, no. 5 (2009), 775–806; and Barbara M. Posadas, and Roland L. Guyotte, "Unintentional Immigrants: Chicago's Filipino Foreign Students Become Settlers, 1900–1941," *Journal of American Ethnic History* 9, no. 2 (1990), 26–48.

44. See Matthew J. Hetrick, "Liberia College and Transatlantic Ideologies of Race and Education," in *Reconstruction in a Globalizing World*, ed. David Prior (New York: Fordham University Press, 2018), 50–73; Jose-Manuel Navarro, *Creating Tropical Yankees: Social Science Textbooks and U.S. Ideological Control in Puerto Rico, 1898–1908* (New York: Routledge, 2002); and Anne Paulet, "To Change the World: The Use of American Indian Education in the Philippines," *History of Education Quarterly* 47, no. 2 (2007), 173–202. Also see Solsiree del Moral, *Negotiating Empire: The Cultural Politics of Schools in Puerto Rico, 1898–1952* (Madison: University of Wisconsin Press, 2013).

45. Edwin A. Start, *New England Magazine* 6, no. 4 (1892), 444, quoted in Gary Y. Okihiro, *Island World: A History of Hawaii and the United States* (Berkeley: University of California Press, 2008), 105–106.

46. Okihiro, *Island World*, 134.

47. C. Vann Woodward, *The Strange Career of Jim Crow* (Oxford: Oxford University Press, 2002), 85.

48. See, for example, Joshua Paddison, *American Heathens: Religion, Race, and Reconstruction in California* (Berkeley: University of California Press, 2012), and Joshua Paddison, "Race, Religion, and Naturalization: How the West Shaped Citizenship Debates in the Reconstruction Congress," in *Civil War Wests: Testing the Limits of the United* States, ed. Aron Arenson and Andrew R. Graybill Smith (Berkeley: University of California Press, 2015), 181–201; Helen H. Jun, *Race for Citizenship: Black Orientalism and Asian Uplift from Pre-Emancipation to Neoliberal America* (New York: NYU Press, 2011); and Barbara Young Welke, *Law and the Borders of Belonging in the Long Nineteenth Century United States* (New York: Cambridge University Press, 2010).

49. Jun discusses Harlan's decision in *Race for Citizenship*, 15–16.

50. Alexander Saxton, *The Indispensable Enemy* (Berkeley: University of California Press, 1975), 105. For California's debate around the 1870 act and ratification of the

Fourteenth and Fifteenth amendments, which revolved tightly around race, religion, and "heathenism," see Paddison, "Race, Religion, and Naturalization," 192–195; Paddison, *American Heathens*, chap. 1; and Jun, *Race for Citizenship*.

51. See George Frederick Keller, "A Statue for Our Harbor," *The Wasp*, November 11, 1881.

52. Lon Kurashige, *Two Faces of Exclusion: The Untold History of Anti-Asian Racism in the United States* (Chapel Hill: University of North Carolina Press, 2016).

53. Paul Kramer, "Imperial Openings: Civilization, Exemption, and the Geopolitics of Mobility in the History of Chinese Exclusion, 1868–1910," *Journal of the Gilded Age and Progressive Era* 14, no. 3 (2015), 317–345.

54. For a reproduction of the cartoon, see Ignacio et al., *The Forbidden Book*, 73.

55. Booker T. Washington, speech to Brooklyn Institute of Arts and Sciences, February 22, 1903. In Louis R. Harlan and Raymond Smock, *Booker T. Washington Papers* (Urbana: University of Illinois Press, 1977), 7:85–97.

56. Meg Wesling discusses "Our New Topsy" in *Empire's Proxy: American Literature and U.S. Imperialism in the Philippines* (New York: New York University Press, 2011), 69–80. Robin Bernstein's *Racial Innocence: Performing American Childhood from Slavery to Civil Right* (New York: New York University Press, 2011) contains an excellent discussion of *Uncle Tom's Cabin*.

57. Booker T. Washington, "Signs of Progress among the Negroes," *Century Magazine* (January 1900), 472–478. Available at www.unz.org/Pub/Century-1900jan-00472.

58. T. Thomas Fortune, "The Filipino," part 1, *Voice of the Negro* (March 1904), 97.

59. Willard B. Gatewood, *Smoked Yankees and the Struggle for Empire: Letters From Negro Soldiers, 1898–1902* (Urbana: University of Illinois Press, 1971). For a fascinating and detailed look at Black soldiering in the Philippines, including the possibility that the U.S. military exploited Black-Filipino solidarity, see Cynthia Marasigan, "Between the Devil and the Deep Sea: Ambivalence, Violence, and African American Soldiers in the Philippine-American War and Its Aftermath" (PhD diss., University of Michigan, 2010).

60. Image from Library of Congress, https://www.loc.gov/pictures/resource/cph.3a04618/.z

61. See Paul A. Kramer, "How Not to Write the History of U.S. Empire," *Diplomatic History* 42, no. 5 (2018), 911–931, and Daniel Immerwahr, "Writing the History of the Greater United States: A Response to Paul Kramer," *Diplomatic History* 43, no. 2 (2019), 397–403.

62. Ann K. Ziker, "Segregationists Confront American Empire: The Conservative White South and the Question of Hawaiian Statehood, 1947–1959," *Pacific Historical Review* 76, no. 3 (2007), 439–466. Hawaii achieved statehood in 1959.

63. See Brian Shott, *Mediating America: Black and Irish Press and the Struggle for Citizenship, 1870–1914* (Philadelphia: Temple University Press, 2019), chap. 3.

64. Gary Gerstle, *American Crucible: Race and Nation in the Twentieth Century* (Princeton, N.J.: Princeton University Press, 2001).

65. Helen H. Jun, "Black Orientalism: Nineteenth-Century Narratives of Race and U.S. Citizenship," *American Quarterly* 58, no. 4 (2006), 1049.

11

An Empire of Reconstructions

Cuba and the Transformation of American Military Occupation

Justin F. Jackson

In 1910, Robert Lee Bullard, a U.S. Army lieutenant colonel, declared that the American soldier as traditional "war-maker" had, over the last fifty years, adopted a new role: that of "peacemaker and peace-preserver." Appearing in an essay titled "Military Pacification" in the *Journal of the Military Service Institution*, addressed to its readership of professionalizing Progressive-era officers, Bullard's retrospective on the army's pacifying function since the Civil War mixed historical, political, and sociological observations. It was also partly autobiographical, as Bullard located his authority on this subject in personal experiences of war and occupation. Born William Robert in 1861, this Alabama native stressed that he had matured "under Southern Reconstruction." Immersed in the Lost Cause, Bullard, at his five-year-old baptism, had asked his parents, owners of a small cotton plantation recently divested of their few slaves, to rename him after the Confederacy's beloved general. Graduating from West Point in 1885, Bullard pursued Apaches in the New Mexico and Arizona territories. Between 1899 and 1904, in the Philippines, he fought insurgents on Luzon and Muslim rebels on Mindanao. Two years later, as an intelligence officer, he joined the Army of Cuban Pacification during the island's second U.S. occupation.[1]

Bullard drew on this lengthy career to define pacification and its challenges, and to dictate rules for conducting it. He foregrounded elements of Americans' liberal political traditions and values, such as the need to secure the consent of the governed and protect freedom of speech and political association. He also warned that pacification elicited opposition: domestic critics in the metropole (Copperheads and anti-imperialists) and violent "secret societies" in zones of occupation (the Ku Klux Klan and Katipunan). Bullard urged caution, recommending that commanders avoid "passionate" measures, lest they inflame resistance. As examples, he pointed to Reconstruction-era lawmaking, including the Fourteenth Amendment and Enforcement and Civil Rights Acts, and compared these to counterinsurgency practices in the Philippines: "burnings, rough usage, and [the] water cure." Looking to freed people, Bullard also rejected as futile Americans' enlightened interest in educating the occupied. Generally, he abjured attempts to upend long-standing laws and customs in societies under occupation, be they foreign or domestic.[2]

Such opinions obviously reflected Bullard's paternal racism as a white Southerner, as did his judgment of Reconstruction as the single "badly conducted pacification" in U.S. history. Events in Cuba, Puerto Rico, and the Philippines had shown, in his mind, the folly of idealistic Americans' "assumption that all races and peoples have the genius of self-government." For Bullard, this fallacy first became evident in the multiracial democracy of the postbellum South, when Northerners placed "the negro, a race that had never in all history given the least proof of governing power," in "high government," only "to see him ruin it." Bullard warned fellow officers (all white, in a segregated army), not to ignore the "inferiority" of the occupied. With the freed slave, just like the Native American or Muslim Moro of the Philippines, he argued, white American soldiers had "expected too much of him, were disappointed, and becoming impatient and disgusted made altogether a poor job of his management." Indeed, the lieutenant colonel touted his own abilities to manage the darker races of the world, in the war and after it. Having commanded highly disciplined Black Alabama volunteers stateside in 1898, during the conflict with Spain, he nevertheless now rejected using nonwhite troops for military pacification. Despite evidence to the contrary, he insisted that Cubans and Filipinos had resented African American troops' presence. "However wrong," he apologized, looking to the apparent lessons of Reconstruction, "race prejudice" was a stubborn "fact." It "irrupts like a volcano," wrote Bullard, "if we attempt to ignore or suppress it."[3]

Bullard's essay evoked more than just the enduring power of white supremacy in the United States, linking its late-nineteenth-century progress there to American power abroad in the early twentieth century. It also connected episodes in U.S. military government that scholars usually treat separately. Of course, historians have tied Reconstruction to U.S. overseas empire since at least the 1930s, when W. E. B. Du Bois published *Black Reconstruction in America*. In this pathbreaking revisionist book, Du Bois argued that the failure to fully enfranchise emancipated slaves with land and votes had ensured that white-owned monopoly capital in the United States would join European colonialism in oppressing unfree peoples of color worldwide.[4] Historians today, perhaps wary of drawing overly schematic causal or effective ties between Reconstruction and empire, have extended Du Bois's allusions to Reconstruction's global context and implications by mapping its international and transnational dimensions. Among others, David Prior has argued that Reconstruction was part and parcel of profound transnational political and social changes in a globalizing nineteenth-century world; even the term "reconstruction," he notes, had conceptual origins in European precedents and transatlantic connections. According to Prior, reconstruction had two predominant transatlantic meanings, especially in the wake of the 1848 revolutions—the reconstitution of vanquished polities in new and "modern" nation-states and empires, and fundamental transformations of social order advocated by socialists and other radicals. Alternatively, Andrew Zimmerman capaciously defines reconstruction as a "contested set of global political and economic processes" that reflected and intersected with political and social struggles beyond North America, across the late nineteenth-century globe. For Zimmerman, Reconstruction in the U.S. South, and its aftermath in the era of Jim Crow, represented only one instance of a worldwide clash between elite and popular classes over the terms of a great transition in agricultural societies from slavery and serfdom to new kinds of unfree labor, forever altering the global countryside. Its consequences included intensified colonial-capitalist exploitation of African and Asian labor, often by techniques modeled explicitly on whites' control of Black peasants and proletarians in the post-Reconstruction South.[5]

Scholars have enriched the literature on Reconstruction by employing comparative methods and expanding its temporal and spatial scope. Comparative histories have juxtaposed Reconstruction in the U.S. South with different post-emancipation agrarian societies, from the Caribbean to Russia and Italy, in order to compare transitions from slavery and serfdom to freedom, and their politics and political economy. Especially close to the United States in geographical and temporal proximity, for comparative purposes, has been Cuba, where Spanish colonial authorities confronted by armed independence movements between the 1860s and 1890s fully abolished slavery by 1886. Rebecca Scott has studied the politics of race, citizenship, and labor in Louisiana and Cuba, examining them as comparable and connected post-slavery sugar-producing societies. In both, newly free African-descended peoples struggled against white supremacist plantocracies to attain economic livelihoods, civil rights, and political power. Gregory Downs has linked the revolutionary and coercive "bloody constitutionalism" of the Civil War and Reconstruction eras to armed republican and antislavery revolt in Cuba in the same decades.[6] Syntheses of late nineteenth- and early twentieth-century U.S. history have also extended Reconstruction beyond both 1877 and Northern and Southern states, beginning with Heather Cox Richardson's contention that Reconstruction also involved the North American West. Steven Hahn writes of "imperial reconstructions" in which a powerful new federal state, remade by the Civil War and the conquest of the West, invaded the tropics in 1898 amid Americans' growing impetus for industrial, commercial, and cultural expansion.⁷

This essay builds on this scholarship to argue that the War of 1898 and postwar occupation in Cuba represented a pivotal event in the *longue-durée* history of reconstruction, conceived here as an imperial mode of U.S. military policy and foreign relations. Americans' global war against Spain that year reoriented outward into a twentieth-century world of empires a historical phenomenon and discourse of "reconstruction" that Americans heretofore understood as an internal and specifically national process of political and social reconstitution within North America. This conflict and its aftermath signaled the start of Americans' turn toward making reconstruction a recurrent and familiar repertoire in U.S. foreign relations, as many saw armed intervention and military rule as a legitimate means to restructure distant polities and societies. It can hardly be denied that 1898's most significant immediate consequence was the United States' new status as a globe-spanning archipelagic empire, of island colonies and neo-colonies strung along the Tropic of Cancer.⁸ The destruction of the U.S.S. *Maine* in Havana's harbor in February that year precipitated simultaneous U.S. interventions in anticolonial revolutions in Cuba and the Philippines, sealed Spain's defeat, and robbed that declining power of its remaining possessions. It also prompted U.S. military occupations in these islands and Puerto Rico and Guam. The United States incorporated Hawai'i, annexed Puerto Rico and the Philippines as colonies, and, by 1902, made Cuba a neocolonial protectorate, a nominally independent republic subordinated to U.S. military power and North Americans' economic and cultural influence.

Whether or not Americans and the peoples whom they now supervised endorsed this new empire, they often perceived and described its soldiers' mission as reconstruction. Reconstruction as a militarized historical legacy, national ideology, political institution, and social fact thus inflected discussions of various U.S. military regimes abroad after 1898. Some Americans embraced imperial military reconstruction abroad as an expression of their exceptional nation's redemptive civilizing mission overseas. For others, military government in the tropics obscured the imperial realities of U.S. power, refashioning pacification as a benevolent tutelary exercise in nation-building, undertaken by a model anticolonial republican metropole. Yet, as Natalie Ring has shown, Americans with divergent opinions about Reconstruction in the South and their nation's new empire in 1898 often used the language and legacies of reconstruction to mediate the postwar U.S. occupation of Cuba.⁹

Above all, this new empire of armed reconstruction emerged from the crucible of the 1898 war in Cuba and its legacy. Little studied by historians in the United States today, the U.S. occupation of this island became an experiential vehicle by which Americans and Cubans both appropriated histories of militarized reconstructions in their respective nations, and infused them with a new global content in the age of high imperialism. As a result, reconstruction understood not as pacification, per se, but as military government, began shaping the perception of Americans and allies abroad that warfare in the twentieth century would exceed the problems of battlefield victory. Of course, military occupations in modern world history preceded the Union Army's rule over the Confederate South. Before U.S. military governments were imposed on French Louisiana, Spanish Florida, and the southwestern territories seized in the war with Mexico, Europeans already considered military occupation a distinct phenomenon. Beginning in the 1790s, with the French Revolutionary and Napoleonic wars, various national and international laws stipulated that belligerent occupants might exercise the powers of government over foreign territories, without necessarily asserting true or lasting sovereignty over their populations. Yet the first U.S. occupation of Cuba was significant for underscoring that foreign reconstruction undertaken by the United States would entail more than just the guarantees of peace and state-building in war-torn societies. It would also involve remaking foreign economies according to the particular interests, technologies, and knowledges of Americans and their elite local partners, and global capital at large..[10]

Reconstruction as a historical phenomenon thus cannot be separated from ideas of "wartime" and "postwar," which, as Mary Dudziak has shown, have their own history. Traditionally, wartime has denoted a finite period of constitutional emergency in which the powers of the national state have expanded temporarily (or, in some ways, permanently), and civil liberties have been permissibly curtailed. By the same token, "postwar" has been that unit of time in which many Americans accepted their government's right to use military power and rule to reconstruct other nations, states, and societies—if only as a provisional measure warranted by extraordinary emergency conditions. Indeed, in his book *After Appomattox*, Gregory Downs contends that Radical Republicans and their Black and white allies in the South only extended new legal rights and protections to the freed people, and defended them, as long as the U.S. Army occupied the former Confederate states. Cubans' and Americans' perception of U.S. military rule in Cuba after 1898 as reconstruction thus flowed from their knowledge and experience of their two polities' protracted internal wars and postwar eras: in the United States, the Civil War and Union occupation of former Confederate territory; in Cuba, the Ten Years' War, its first armed independence struggle, between 1868 and 1878, and the next year, the short-lived Guerra Chiquita, and their aftermaths.[11] Between these two postbellum societies, reconstruction as military occupation evolved into a durable institutional expression of U.S. empire. Through it, Americans commanding central-state power, centered in the federal government in Washington, D.C., would repeatedly attempt to remake the twentieth-century world in their own image.

Of course, as case studies for military reconstruction, these two societies' substantial differences resist comparison. The South at the end of Civil War combat was a vast internal territory of some 750,000 square miles in area, populated by roughly 9 million people. The island of Cuba, much smaller at 42,000 square miles, and inhabited in 1898 by an estimated 1.5 million, arguably represented a less formidable challenge to the effective use of U.S. power. Perhaps most important, in the U.S. South, constitutional law and tradition often limited the scope of federal military authority. In Cuba however, American generals enjoyed a much greater sway over political, social, and economic life, constrained mostly by treaties, executive branch orders, and, to a lesser degree, congressional statute. Most in the United States recognized that Reconstruction in the South was, at minimum, a process for politically reintegrating the rebel states into the federal union, even as they fought bitterly about how to restructure Southern labor, politics, and racial relations. Yet most Americans agreed that military victory and cultural superiority over Spain and its fading empire awarded the United States only a temporary formal sovereignty in Cuba. Accordingly, after 1898, few Americans seemed concerned for Cubans' rights to self-government. Most accepted as an imperative necessity the injury to Cuban nationhood imposed by military occupation and the Platt Amendment, which, among other things, authorized future U.S. invasions to preserve North American life and property. Compared to Reconstruction in the U.S. South, over which Radical Republicans in Congress seized power from the executive branch, imperial administration in Cuba shifted the locus of national policymaking from Congress to the White House. Beginning that year, U.S. Army officers, responsible primarily to the War Department, and Presidents William McKinley and Theodore Roosevelt ruled the nation's new tropical periphery with day-to-day autonomy from Congress.[12]

Yet the occupations of the former Confederacy and insurgent Cuba may be compared profitably along thematic lines. Both societies experienced military regimes, imposed by a metropolitan federal state in Washington, D.C. In both cases, those regimes were meant to neutralize rebel armies and dispense humanitarian aid, rehabilitate and transform economies, and reconstitute polities and relations with the United States. As Bullard's observations suggested, the politics of race in these two post-emancipation societies also determined how differently Americans and Cubans conducted military reconstruction and understood its purposes, possibilities, and meanings. Therefore, this essay compares sequentially and thematically separate but parallel histories of the politics of pacification and humanitarian relief, economic recovery and development, and state-building in these two occupied societies.

The U.S. Army's institutional importance in the South prefigured its imperial contribution a few decades later in Cuba. Months after civil war erupted, Union soldiers occupied Confederate territory and asserted civil authority. Military occupation immediately affected Southern society, as Union troops offered safety to enslaved African Americans and loyal white Southerners. The army's power over Southern space gradually spurred military emancipation and eroded the social order—resting on racialized chattel slavery, plantations, and hierarchy—that the Confederacy existed to defend. First in areas of northern Virginia during 1861, and then the next year in Louisiana and the border state of Tennessee, Union generals offered escaping slaves refuge. Although some Union officers satisfied owners' demands to return fugitives, others declared them confiscated rebel property, or "contraband of war," and utilized their labor for their own purposes. Soon Congress barred Union forces from returning slaves, and ordered them to free any Confederate-owned slaves present in Union-occupied territory. Building on these congressional Confiscation Acts, President Abraham Lincoln's 1863 Emancipation Proclamation further advanced antislavery Republicans' agenda by declaring free all three million slaves in as yet unoccupied Confederate territory and authorizing Black volunteers' enlistment in the U.S. Army. This weakened rebel armies and a Southern economy dependent on enslaved labor. Ultimately, only constitutional revision, and not any temporary war measure, would permanently end slavery. Still, Northern soldiers, Black and white, henceforth waged war as a crusade to end human bondage in America.[13]

In the South, as in Cuba, the U.S. Army enacted conflicting policies, radical in some regards, reactionary in others. Commanders promoted ideals of free labor and racial egalitarianism even as they simultaneously sought to restore the plantation economy, often in concert with white landowners. Union Army officers paid wages to freed people, taught them literacy, enlisted them by the thousands, and forwarded these new soldiers' demands for equal pay (which Congress eventually granted). On the other hand, U.S. military authorities frustrated freedpeople's desire for immediate freedom and equality. They paid Black soldiers less, relegated them to manual labor, punished alleged insubordination harshly, and executed them more frequently than white troops for the same infractions. Events in Louisiana illustrated the apparent contradictions of army practices. As early as 1862, in occupied New Orleans, General Benjamin F. Butler sought to nurture Unionist politics by distributing confiscated beef and sugar to residents, cleaning its streets, creating jobs for the unemployed, and fighting yellow fever. Yet nearby, in the lucrative sugar districts lining the Mississippi River, Butler and then General Nathaniel P. Banks compelled tens of thousands of freed people to return to planters' estates under wage contracts imposed and enforced by the army. Elsewhere in the South, U.S. officers followed suit, pushing freedmen and women to resume work on cotton and rice plantations under terms set by the army and white landowners. Predicated on war-making and military occupation, Reconstruction emerged as an exigency of the Union efforts to subdue the Confederacy and manage fugitives entering their lines.[14]

The authority of the U.S. Army over civil government in former Confederate states persisted once conventional war ceased, as "the only agency of the federal government that could have policed the South," in one historian's words. Union generals arrested Confederate officials, prevented state legislatures from meeting, voided legislation passed since secession, and vacated local offices. Many Republicans in Congress and the War Department believed that a legal state of war remained after the summer of 1865, sustaining the extraordinary powers that the Lincoln administration had invoked and authorizing the military's continuing control of civil affairs in rebel territory. They held that as long as Union soldiers occupied the South and monopolized local governments and courts, and Congress set the conditions under which new states would be recognized and readmitted to the federal union, belligerent conditions endured. The army thus furnished radical Republicans the physical force they required to reintegrate Southern states into the federal union and reorder Southern society. Absent the presence and pressure of a much reduced but still tangible U.S. army of occupation after April 1865, recalcitrant Southern whites would not likely have reconstituted loyal state governments on terms set by Northerners. Even less probable would have been most reconstituted states' ratification, over the next four years, of Republican-generated constitutional amendments that abolished slavery and granted civil rights to African American men and safeguarded their vote. Admittedly, a small U.S. garrison force mandated to pacify an immense region of roughly 9 million people, 3.5 million of whom were former slaves, and dispersed in some 334 posts by late summer 1865, exercised only a "patchwork sovereignty." From most white Southerners' perspective, however, the U.S. Army's control over civil life in the South represented *imperium in imperio*—a sovereign military power seizing public authority from the citizens of a conquered nation on behalf of a metropolitan federal government dominated by Republican Northerners.[15]

Despite Andrew Johnson's personal career with military rule, the policies of this white supremacist president inflamed Southern whites' resistance to U.S. Army control over civil government and its practical ability to aid freed people. Assuming that office with Lincoln's assassination in April 1865, Johnson the next month declared that former Confederate states could reenter the union on terms slightly harsher than those delineated by Lincoln in late 1863. Lincoln's so called "ten percent plan," resting on his wartime powers, specified that military governors would call state constitutional conventions when no less than 10 percent of the state's 1860 electorate had sworn oaths of loyalty. These white male electorates would exclude high-ranking civil and military Confederate officials. New state constitutions would have to outlaw slavery before Congress would seat their representatives. Johnson followed this essential structure, but added requirements that senior Confederate officials and wealthy Southerners apply to him individually for pardons. If Johnson avoided martial rule by allowing defeated white Southerners to establish provisional state governments, he understood its utility, having himself reconstructed a Confederate state under Lincoln's plan. In early 1862, Lincoln had appointed him Tennessee's military governor, and Johnson used that power to craft a new state constitution abolishing slavery, approved with the votes of "unconditional Unionists." By June 1865, loyalist conventions in Union-occupied areas of the border states and Confederate periphery had established "reconstructed" governments in western and northern Virginia, Maryland, Arkansas, Louisiana, and Missouri with new constitutions abolishing slavery. By the war's end, these were the only Southern states that had representatives—all Republicans—in Congress; that body recognized no other reconstructed former Confederate states, except for a new state enabled by U.S. Army occupation, West Virginia.[16]

Presidential Reconstruction initially saw Northern troops continue their ambivalent role. By the summer of 1865, Union commanders had overseen the emancipation of some 2.75 million slaves in the Southern interior and, in some cases, defended African Americans' claims to equal civil rights. Yet Johnson's administration blunted the radical potential of U.S. soldiers' presence in the South. In former Confederate states yet to be readmitted under Johnson's terms, whites wrote new state constitutions. To all except the wealthiest rebels, his government offered amnesty, pardons, and restoration of all properties (other than former slaves). Johnson also required white Southern men to swear loyalty and support for the Thirteenth Amendment, enacted by Congress in January 1865. Yet the president consistently refused Radical Republican demands that the rehabilitated Southern states be required to enfranchise the freedmen. His leniency, including rapid pardons for rich Southerners, ensured that new provisional state governments, dominated by Southern Whigs purportedly more loyal to the Union, did little more than abolish slavery in barely revised constitutions. Encouraged by Johnson, white Southerners' resistance to Union rule dovetailed with planters' attempts to restore labor discipline among African Americans.[17]

Southern whites' resentment of occupation foreshadowed the actions of Cuban elites who, by turns, accommodated and opposed U.S. rule after 1898. Throughout the South, white landowners sought to coerce African Americans by using civil courts, contracts, and legislative statutes, or so-called Black Codes, to mandate, among other things, that African Americans retain passes and proof of employment. Acting on the belief that "wartime" still held in the South, however, generals in Virginia and South Carolina struck down some of the most extreme of these laws. In a few cases, Johnson actually ordered commanders to refuse to enforce them, for example, by permitting testimony by African Americans in courts. Still, most Southern officials enforced new race-specific state laws until 1866, when Congress passed civil rights legislation. In August 1865, Johnson also palliated Southern white racist backlash by ordering all Black troops removed from the region. Within two years, the army withdrew most African American soldiers from the Southern interior and entire regions of the South altogether, and dissolved Black regiments organized during the Civil War.[18]

Johnson's policies thwarted military occupation's potential agency as a midwife of social and economic revolution, and thus anticipated how U.S. intervention in Cuba only marginally and briefly disrupted prewar class relations and patterns in land tenure there. In January 1865 General William T. Sherman offered small plots of confiscated land to freedmen in coastal Georgia and South Carolina, motivated primarily to reduce the burden of feeding thousands of destitute former slaves. His distribution of some 400,000 acres to nearly 40,000 freed people boosted other former slaves' expectation that the federal government would use military power to ensure their personal and socioeconomic autonomy from former masters and white landowners. Such hopes grew two months later when Republicans in Congress established the Freedmen's Bureau and tasked its agents with both issuing the former slaves food, medicine, and other humanitarian relief, and helping them lease nearly one million acres of confiscated and abandoned Southern lands now under bureau control. Despite Radical efforts, land reform never garnered support from most U.S. congressmen and generals. In late

1865 and 1866, the Freedmen's Bureau, under Johnson's direction and backed by U.S. troops, restored the expropriated properties to white owners. From southeastern Virginia and the coastal Carolinas, through the Georgia low country, to parts of Louisiana and Mississippi (including even former Confederate president Jefferson Davis's estate), former slaves recently settled on lands by Union commanders now faced eviction by the very same army that had freed them. Tens of thousands of African Americans living the Jeffersonian ideal of agrarian independence now had no choice but to return to plantation labor for wages under unfavorable annual contracts. Freedmen received little comfort from army officers who gave them rations to use as collateral in renting or leasing farm properties, against the value of future harvests.[19]

At the same time, the Freedmen's Bureau was largely a creature of U.S. military power. Agents' provision of relief and education, and their attempts to enforce the freedmen's contractual rights in civil and army provost courts, expanded Northern soldiers' contribution to Reconstruction. In microcosm, the Freedmen's Bureau and its institutional genesis and authority, if not its exact politics, prefigured occupation regimes installed by U.S. generals in 1898. Growing out of a commission formed in 1863 by Northern abolitionists under War Department sponsorship, the bureau after 1865 stayed nested within that department, and was funded by it. Union veterans, including bureau chief General Oliver Otis Howard, made up most of its staff. Some 900 agents, tasked with ensuring basic labor and civil rights for Southern African Americans, faced resistance, often armed and violent, from white landowners and employers, local officials, and vigilantes. Indeed, in much of the South, only U.S. Army troops protected Black Southerners and bureau efforts to help them. Nevertheless, soldiers' capacity to affect Southern life diminished throughout the late 1860s, as Congress incrementally reduced the army's size and shifted troops to Texas and the Great Plains to combat the French-backed Mexican Empire, renegade Confederates, and resistant Native Americans. The total number of U.S. Army garrisons and personnel in the South shrank steadily to a skeleton force, and their geographic footprint in its countryside receded. From over one million U.S. troops stationed across over six hundred garrisons in April 1865, occupation forces in the rebel states dwindled over five years to little more than four thousand soldiers at thirty posts (excepting Texas).[20]

Even as Congress reduced the army's Southern front, the advent of congressional Reconstruction reaffirmed the military's vital role in civil government there, prefacing its subsequent purpose in Cuba. Republicans increasingly clashed with President Johnson, assailing him for failing to reap the fruits of victory by ensuring free labor and civil rights for African Americans, and possibly the vote, for Black men. In 1866, when Johnson vetoed Republicans' legislation, including the civil rights bill (which, as historian Michael Vorenberg notes, empowered U.S. troops to enforce it), and another to extend the Freedmen's Bureau, Congress overrode them. The next year, Republicans wrested administrative control over the South from the president and vested it in the U.S. Army by passing the Reconstruction Acts over yet another presidential veto, and implementing them in defiance of Johnson's obstructionism. (This included his public campaign urging voters to refuse to ratify the Fourteenth Amendment, removal of Secretary of War Edwin Stanton, and appointment of more conservative generals in the South, all of which pushed Moderates to endorse Radical calls for impeachment.) Republican Congressmen also passed the Fourteenth Amendment, granting birthright citizenship and barring states from denying due process and equal protection of the law to citizens, and sent it to the states for ratification.[21]

These measures rested on Radical Republicans' assumption that a continuing state of war authorized the U.S. Army to establish biracial democracy in the South. It also created a military-administrative regime, empowered to establish civil government, the likes of which reappeared in Cuba. The Reconstruction Acts split the former Confederacy (except Tennessee) into five military districts commanded by U.S. generals who were to register voters, including African American men. This electorate was to vote for delegations sent to state constitutional conventions, the membership of which included newly enfranchised freedmen. Congress required new state governments to ratify the Fourteenth Amendment and extend the suffrage to African American men before it would recognize them and seat their representatives and senators in Washington. Between 1868 and 1871, U.S. Army officers directing this process in each of the former Confederate states, backed by the votes of 600,000 Black men registered under military supervision, created new states governed by Black-white Republican coalitions. The Fifteenth Amendment, ratified in 1870, sought to permanently protect the voting rights originally extended under Military Reconstruction by barring these new states from denying any male citizen the ballot on the basis of race or previous condition of servitude.[22]

Johnson shared white Democratic opinions that continued martial law posed a threat to republican liberties and states' rights, and he tried blunting Military Reconstruction's radicalism. He appointed generals whom he knew would not interfere too much with white supremacist civil officeholders, removed generals who checked Southern white officials, and sent them suspect legal opinions, drafted by his attorney general, denying Congress's power to extend civil authority in the South to the U.S. military. In fact, most generals did little beyond reconstituting the Southern state governments. Only rarely did they remove racist white officials or challenge discriminatory local and state courts that violated the new federal laws and constitutional amendments. Yet U.S. generals did exercise police powers when they arrested and tried men in provost courts and military commissions, and confined them in military jails. In some military districts, army commanders desegregated public transportation and took steps to protect Black laborers and tenants from employers and landowners. By creating new state governments initially controlled by biracial Republicans, military rule also ensured the political conditions needed to enable newly reconstructed states to form the majority of states required to ratify the Fourteenth and Fifteenth Amendments. Military government in the South thus contributed to the constitutional architecture on which African Americans' freedoms would forever rest—even if white-supremacist terror and "Redemption" of Southern states to white Democratic control soon tragically allowed white Southerners to practically nullify them until the 1950s.[23]

Ultimately, the transfer of Southern state-level political power from generals to civilians after 1867 eased the reversal of Reconstruction's achievements. Perhaps inevitably, the termination of war powers and the transition to civil rule neutered the U.S. Army's power to intervene in Southern life. As rebel states rejoined the Union, Democrats in the North and South and a growing number of Northern Republicans (and even some Southern Republicans) hesitated to renew military coercion. Inexorably, as wartime in the South gave way to peacetime, pressure mounted to honor the constitutional tradition that soldiers defer to local civilian authorities in domestic conditions of peace. Facing rising terrorism against Southern Black and white Republicans at the hands of white supremacist paramilitaries, Congress beginning in 1870 passed several Enforcement Bills that temporarily authorized regular troops to maintain public order and uphold new federal civil and voting rights. Yet President Ulysses Grant and Democratic and Liberal Republicans eager to "have peace" preferred not to deploy soldiers to administer federal law in readmitted states. The year 1871 proved the last for real U.S. military authority in the South, when Congress finalized Georgia's reentry. The army's gradual retreat from the South thus hastened the triumph of "Redemption" and "home rule"; one after another, state governments there fell to white-supremacist Democratic control. As the 1873 recession helped Democrats rob Northern Republicans of their majority in the U.S. House of Representatives, and turned their attention to mounting class conflict in the industrializing North, concerns about working-class radicalism shaded views of freedmen's desire for economic equality. By 1877, the few U.S. troops still in the South virtually disappeared from public view, as one element of a compromise between Democrats and Republicans which secured the victory of Rutherford B. Hayes, the latter party's presidential candidate in the previous year's contested election.[24]

By supporting the freedpeople's rights, martial rule over the conquered Confederacy had altered Southern society and enabled national and state constitutional reformation. Together, war, military occupation, and the struggles of former slaves and their white allies had ended slavery and established new freedoms for African Americans. Yet Southern white intransigence converged with Americans' traditional opposition to large, expensive, and potentially tyrannical standing armies. Northern Republicans' willingness to concede Southern white Democrats' allegations of corruption and incompetence in new biracial, Republican-led state governments also confounded Reconstruction and its promise. With the failure of land reform and Democrats' capture of state capitals, whites reduced Black Southerners to a sharecropping peasantry and agricultural proletariat effectively disenfranchised in Southern politics and society. White-supremacist elites maintained an iron grip over the South's political economy, as white landowners, businessmen, and entrepreneurs worked with Northern capital to establish a New South of dynamic industrial development that kept African Americans segregated to the economic margins. By the 1890s, of course, a discriminatory "Jim Crow" regime of state and local laws, upheld by U.S. Supreme Court decisions, instantiated racial segregation in every dimension of Southern life, including poll taxes and other voting laws that sharply curtailed Black political power. White Southerners used their voting bloc's influence in the national Democratic Party and, beginning in the 1930s, the New Deal coalition, to bend national politics and policies to their interest in maintaining African American subordination. Only the civil rights activism of the "Second Reconstruction" in the 1950s and 1960s resurrected the original constitutional guarantees of political and legal equality wrought by the nation's militarized "second founding" in the Civil War and Reconstruction eras.[25]

While many Americans in 1898 shared Robert Lee Bullard's view that Reconstruction in the South had been a failure, or worse, they also understood the U.S. occupation imposed that year on Cuba as an exercise in reconstruction. For them, the term evoked striking similarities between the postbellum United States and Cuba, the most urgent of which, for Washington policymakers and American generals, was the presence of armed insurgents requiring pacification. Unlike

Confederate veterans, of course, Cuban separatists' Army of Liberation had not been the United States' enemy, but its friend, as both forces in the summer of 1898 waged war on Spain. Yet just as the wartime alliance between Northern white Unionists and Southern African Americans frayed during Reconstruction, the U.S.-Cuban military partnership quickly devolved into mutual suspicion and antagonism. Racist U.S. soldiers encountering insurgents and their mostly Afro-Cuban ranks in eastern Cuba during the joint campaign that seized Santiago dismissed the rebels as a ragtag army incapable of victory, much less national self-rule. Following President William McKinley's orders, American commanders angered Cuban separatists by refusing to recognize their provisional government. Indeed, for months after victory at Santiago, insurgent generals kept some 50,000 troops in the field. Anxious to prevent annexation, they also wanted to influence postwar politics and pressure civilian Cuban leaders and the U.S. government for pay that the nationalist junta had promised them during the war. Americans in Cuba and beyond continued to endorse annexation even though the Teller Amendment, passed by Congress in April 1898, officially prohibited it. In response, Cuban *independentistas* sought to demonstrate their capacity for civilization and self-rule before skeptical Americans. Simultaneously, they condemned the occupation, especially when the Treaty of Paris (December 1898) transferred authority over the island to the United States without Cubans' consent.[26]

For the occupiers, challenges of humanitarian crisis, economic recovery, and public health intersected with the problem of insurgent demobilization. In war-ravaged Oriente during late 1898, General Leonard Wood, the region's military governor, considered measures to mollify the roughly 11,000 insurgents near Santiago and spur agricultural revival. Much like Northern antislavery Republicans and pragmatic Union generals in the South, such as William T. Sherman, who had been eager to make freedpeople self-sufficient, Wood briefly pondered land redistribution. Giving public and private lands to Cuban veterans, nearly all of humble origins and destitute at war's end, would have fulfilled their wartime hopes for social and economic reform. Some in eastern Cuba might have also found it a familiar imperial gesture, after Spanish authorities in the 1880s distributed some public lands in the region to former insurgents.[27] Yet Wood ultimately followed the conservative example of post–Civil War officials who embraced a coercive labor policy instead of land reform, and compelled land-poor Cubans to resurrect agriculture as proletarian wage earners.

Yet Wood's strategy differed from that employed by the Union Army in the wartime South. His approach centered not so much on reviving the few large plantations in Oriente but on leveraging his soldiers' temporary control over vital foodstuffs to mobilize civilian and veteran Cuban labor for public works. In Oriente, the sugar industry and immense latifundia so typifying central Cuba were less developed, and small farms predominated. But the war had inflicted its greatest damage here, for the longest duration, so here subsistence staples had become especially scarce. Wood's access to food imports thus allowed him, if briefly, to tie relief to compulsion in ways that the Union Army and Freedmen's Bureau never had. In September 1898, Wood's army informed starving insurgents near Santiago that they would no longer receive American rations until their regiments disbanded or they began working for the Yankees on various public projects. Simultaneously, U.S. commanders told civilians that they, too, would no longer be issued army rations gratis, and that all able-bodied male Cuban civilians would have to toil for the Americans if they wished to eat U.S. foodstuffs. To forestall hunger, thousands of Cuban men labored for U.S. soldiers in various ways, ranging from cleaning streets and homes, which the Yankees considered a sanitary measure against yellow fever and other diseases, to repairing and building city streets and rural highways.[28] Wood used emergency public works and ration restriction to immunize the U.S. occupation of Oriente, relieve civilian suffering, and demobilize insurgents. They became the coercive germ of his broader efforts to revive the agricultural economy.

Not unlike Andrew Johnson's move to incorporate moderate former rebels in new state governments, General Wood tried to appease Cuban nationalists by appointing them to offices in municipal and provincial civil governments. Similarly, this process had a conservative tenor that reflected the same elitist and racist pretensions among white Americans that informed "redemption" and the rise of Jim Crow. Often contemptuous of Cubans, whom he stigmatized for both Latin and African ancestry, Wood favored wealthier, whiter, and more Americanized Cuban men for these positions. Many of his appointees were educated professionals—planters, businessmen, and expatriates—who had visited the United States, and admired its culture. At the local level, the Americans also largely maintained the Spanish colonial legal codes. U.S. commanders largely left prewar administrative structures intact, much as Johnson's provisional state governments had (aside from acknowledging the federally mandated abolition of slavery).[29]

Wood further secured nationalists' cooperation by organizing an all-Cuban paramilitary force, the Rural Guard, and furnishing it with horses and guns. Composed largely of former insurgents, these men policed the island's easternmost countryside, ruthlessly pursuing Cubans, including fellow veterans, who resorted to social banditry. By the summer of 1899, after many U.S. Army officers adopted policies modeled, in the words of one fawning American journalist, on General Wood's "plan of reconstruction," their military government neutralized the insurgent threat by partially satisfying Cuban soldiers' demands for back pay. By July, the Americans had distributed $3 million to the Liberation Army's rank and file, handing each veteran $75 in exchange for his guns. This sum was far less than that which many Cubans believed a poor *campesino* needed to revive or start a farm. Americans knew these payments would cost less to the United States than rebellion, especially while counterparts in the Philippines struggled to suppress the same.[30]

The *veteranos'* payouts alluded to larger problems of economic policy. U.S. military authorities and Cubans invoked the language of reconstruction when describing the occupation's efforts to rehabilitate and transform the island's economy. If field operations, a Union blockade, and slave resistance and emancipation had hobbled Confederate agriculture, war likewise devastated a Cuban agricultural industry dependent on export. Three years of war took an awful toll, particularly on the large estates and small farms that grew sugar and tobacco. By 1898, the sugar industry had suffered the effects of the first independence war, fought between 1868 and 1878, the abolition of slavery, and recession and expanding international competition, mostly in beets. In 1895, to prosecute the new war for independence, insurgents imposed a moratorium on sugar cultivation, expanded the ban the next year, and torched the estates of those who defied it. In turn, Spanish forces under General Valeriano Weyler inaugurated a policy of *reconcentracion*, meant to limit rebels' ability to live off the countryside, by relocating the rural civilians who supported them. The policy hurt sugar production, concentrated in the island's central provinces, tobacco in western provinces, and cattle ranching in the east. Between insurgent casualties, the many more civilians who died from disease and starvation, and reduced births, Cuba's population during the war declined from 1.8 million to under 1.5 million. At war's end, plantations lay prostrate, with labor dispersed and concentrated in cities, nearly all livestock dead, and most sugar mills ruined or needing repair. Yankee officials estimated that the war destroyed two-thirds of Cuba's wealth, including by slashing land values. With little capital and potential collateral left, credit was unavailable to the poorest Cubans who needed it most to be able to purchase seed, livestock, and tools. Many planters, already indebted before the war, sold their properties. (On similar capital scarcities in the postbellum U.S. South, see Adrian Brettle's chapter on conservative Virginians in this volume.) Letters and petitions from desperate Cuban cultivators and impoverished municipalities deluged American military authorities, urging them to aid the "reconstructions" of farms and towns. They requested direct government assistance in addition to the rations, medical care, sanitation, and public works jobs that U.S. Army officers dispensed to Cubans, many of them *reconcentrados* and veterans in garrisoned cities and towns.[31]

Similar to their predecessors in the U.S. South, American commanders in Cuba were anxious to revive Cuban agriculture so they could end expensive relief efforts. After the Civil War, most Republicans in Congress and Freedmen's Bureau officials preferred to aid freedpeople only long enough to put them on a footing by which they could then support themselves. White U.S. Army officers in Cuba shared their racism and bourgeois Protestant morals as they feared that continuous and unconditional public assistance might promote poor Cubans' "dependency" on the state, and discourage labor. Like Union Army commanders who had been eager to revive the Southern cotton industry, the McKinley administration saw stimulating agricultural exports as crucial to Cuba's prosperity, and thus, its political stability. Reviving the sugar industry and other cash crops, they believed, would promote social order by shifting veterans and refugees from crowded cities to the countryside, where labor was scarce and in high demand. Increased trade would raise the insular customs revenues that the U.S. military regime in Havana wanted to finance Cuba's governance and reduce the need for federal appropriations. Like European colonial contemporaries, American generals, Congress, and McKinley's administration wanted empire on the cheap. Yet unlike some Radical Republicans after the Civil War who advocated direct relief for freedpeople, most U.S. Army officers in Cuba sanctioned only indirect forms of economic aid for struggling Cubans.[32]

Policy divisions frustrating united action also existed among U.S. commanders in Cuba, just as they had within the Union Army and Republican-dominated Congress, and between these bodies and the White House. After January 1899, when General John R. Brooke took office as military governor, subordinate generals temporarily improvised their own farm-related measures in their respective provinces. In Oriente, General Wood, a patrician New Englander, reflected the Republicans' Whig tradition and a proto-Progressive and proto-Keynesian political economy as he advocated aiding Cuban cultivators through public works. Wood believed that infrastructural development and public health would spur agricultural exports and individual proprietorship, and he liberally spent provincial customs revenues on sanitation, road building, water works, harbor improvements, and other projects. By contrast, General James Wilson, overseeing the central provinces of Matanzas and Santa Clara, favored the creation of state agricultural banks. A Union veteran who had briefly governed a central Georgia district in 1865, a railroad businessman, and a staunch Republican, Wilson wanted to grant Cubans long-term, low-interest loans no larger than $400. Yet Brooke, directing island-wide policy from Havana, proved relatively conservative. Unlike Wood and Wilson, Brooke hewed closely to a laissez-faire political economy legitimated in the Gilded Age by the Social Darwinism of the likes of Herbert Spencer and William Graham Sumner. Having served in the U.S. Army continuously since 1861, including during Reconstruction, Brooke may have been skeptical about the postwar political efficacy of military rule. In Louisiana in 1874, he had served for one day as its military governor, after armed white supremacist Democrats violently overthrew the state's Republican administration.[33]

By mid-1899, Brooke centralized fiscal authority and other economic policymaking in his office. He rejected Wood's public works and Wilson's agricultural banks, but took only limited steps to forestall economic catastrophe. His administration imposed a two-year moratorium on mortgage and debt collection, eliminated internal trade and export taxes, minimized tariffs on agricultural equipment and supplies, and suspended municipal taxation on ruined or otherwise unproductive properties. Favoring wealthier planters with sufficient collateral to secure credit, however, these measures abandoned tens of thousands of Cubans who desperately needed capital for small-scale farming. By year's end, Brooke, sounding like a Democratic critic of Freedmen's Bureau relief, ordered his troops to stop issuing food to indigent Cubans. The practice, he believed, was "on the verge of encouraging or inducing pauperism." The governor believed his parsimony facilitated Cuba's economic recovery. By October, even as he admitted that food scarcity still plagued some regions, the governor cheered that "in the tobacco and sugar-cane districts the work of reconstruction is proceeding so rapidly as to promise prosperity in the future." Direct financial aid from the state, he fretted, would create a "system of paternalism" that threatened to "destroy the self-respect of the people," and might spark political strife between those who did and did not receive public loans. Confident in the magic of unfettered markets, Brooke declared that capital would flow to Cuba's impecunious farmers through private banks, once economic conditions improved sufficiently.[34]

The failure of land reform in the post–Civil War South condemned millions of freed people to poverty and dependence. Lacking access to property or credit, they relied on white landowners for wages or sharecropped small plots of land, typically sinking into debt as global cotton prices declined. In Cuba after 1898, the military regime's refusal to provide direct material aid to poor Cubans likewise stymied popular aspirations of postwar autonomy. In response, Cubans appropriated and deployed the language of reconstruction to pressure the

Americans to fulfill their stated commitment to rebuild the island's economy. As early as September 1898, the leaders of the Moncada Club, a clandestine separatist organization formed in Santiago during the war, professed to General Wood their willingness to "dedicate all its energy to the reconstruction of the country." Yet by 1899 many Cuban cultivators, officials, and newspapers in Oriente and beyond turned the Americans' talk of reconstruction against Brooke's imperial austerity. A broad-based recovery, they argued, would be impossible without giving the neediest Cuban farmers access to credit that only the state could provide. Indebted Southern whites and Blacks in the capital-poor South had asked for state-level stay laws after the Civil War, only to receive little more than homestead exemptions on debt collection and state subsidies for railroad construction. Cubans, by contrast, sounded like American Populists as they asked the central government in Havana to directly subsidize agriculture.[35]

Cuban officials frequently invoked the word "reconstruction" as they insisted that both private capital and public credit were essential to postwar recovery. In Santa Clara province, where General Wilson organized a civil government under General José Miguel Gómez, an insurgent general and future president, Cuban leaders shared Wilson's interest in direct state financing. In April 1899, Gómez published and circulated "A Plan of Reconstruction," in which he proposed using military government revenues to issue household loans in sums up to $150 to help farmers. Making elaborate calculations, Santa Clara's governor posited that his plan would establish 2,500 new farms in only six months. Cuban civil secretaries supervising national-level departments in Havana also challenged Brooke's miserly policy by endorsing a public agricultural bank. In October, Pablo Desvernine, the secretary of finance, rejected pleas from municipal officials in Santa Clara that they be permitted to grant loans to farmers; given municipalities' poverty, he dismissed the idea as impractical. Yet Desvernine also appealed to General Brooke: "The work of reconstruction," he wrote the military governor, would be "greatly helped and furthered" with only "moderate help" from Havana, in low- or no-interest loans to individuals no greater than $250, repayable in ten years. While Desvernine acknowledged that the war had ruined large landowners, he contended that wealthier Cubans possessed enough collateral and social prestige to acquire credit through mortgages or business partnerships. But "poor farmers," he insisted, "have no hope of obtaining any help unless it be from the bounty of the state." Wood, succeeding Brooke in December 1899, maintained his predecessor's opposition to public largesse. Yet protests grew as Cubans faced expiration of the stay law preventing debt collections. In late 1900, Perfecto Lacosta, Wood's agriculture secretary, condemned the occupation for failing to establish the agricultural banks and other financial institutions that he believed would furnish the "pecuniary resources" necessary for "the work of reconstruction."[36]

The U.S. regime's stinginess rendered the island's economy more vulnerable to foreign capital and accelerated the transfer of land and other agricultural wealth from Cuban to non-Cuban hands. Simply by preventing revolutionaries from carrying out land reforms, the occupation accelerated and exacerbated the concentration of land ownership. In 1896 General Máximo Gómez had signaled his intent to establish an independent republic of small-holding farmers by dividing up and redistributing the *latifundia* on which Spain's colonial wealth had long rested. Yet U.S. policies accelerated the transfer of farmlands. Critical was General Wood's May 1901 decision to allow debt collections, including on mortgages, and establish a four-year term for settling loans. "Nothing has done more to keep money out of the country and prevent reconstruction," Wood wrote at the time, "than the original stay law." Thousands of Cubans throughout the island, both planters and small farmers, had to sell properties. They passed almost entirely to North American companies investing in sugar or fruit production, railroad construction, and land speculators and real estate companies that bought up Cuban lands at depressed prices and sold them high to other foreigners. Estimates varied but suggested that, by 1906, North Americans had acquired some 15 percent of all Cuban landed properties. Others reported that foreign companies had bought some 60 percent of rural farmlands, with another 15 percent held by Spaniards and the remainder left to Cubans.[37]

Foreigners' power expanded beyond sugar to other cash-poor industrial sectors. Investors and migrants from North America—but also Great Britain, France, Germany, and Spain—swarmed Cuba, in a process comparable to the entry into the South of migrants and capital, often from Northern states and Europe, after the Civil War. Foreign capitalists attained more prominent positions in Cuba's economic life than did most so-called "carpetbaggers" in the Reconstruction-era South, and were more akin to Northern capitalists who pursued the New South's promise of economic modernization. They used Cubans' financial weakness and the political framework created by U.S. occupation to make quick profits. Non-native entrepreneurs displaced Cuba's prewar elite by purchasing old family businesses and establishing new corporations in tobacco cultivation and cigar manufacturing, ranching, and iron and copper mining, as well as banking, utilities, retail establishments, transportation, and construction. A 1903 trade treaty with the United States quickened the concentration of Cuban wealth into foreign hands by giving Cuba's sugar and tobacco preferential access to the U.S. mainland and reducing Cuban tariffs on U.S. goods. Cuba became more dependent on North American markets for its exports, and its manufacturers and farmers for imports. By 1911, American investments in Cuba exceeded some $200 million, up from only $50 million in 1897, almost three times the amount of European capital. If credit-poor postbellum Southern whites became ensnared, as contemporaries and scholars suggested, in a "colonial" relationship with the North, the same was all the more true for Cuba in relation to the United States after 1898. Even as Cubans required international investment to revive their war-torn economy, they resented a neocolonial economy that marginalized them within their own nation. Lacking better alternatives, many owners abandoned estates or proprietary enterprises to accept positions as managers and supervisors for foreign-owned companies. Yankees arriving in droves introduced the latest technologies and engineering practices, established agricultural colonies, and promoted English, baseball, tourism, gambling, and other hallmarks of early twentieth-century North American modernity. The two national cultures fused to form a new and hybridized Cuban nationality and identity built on intimate but unequal relations.[38]

Cuba's neocolonial status was also complemented and reinforced by the military regime's political reforms, including attempts to limit ordinary Cubans' participation in self-government. Although Cuban *independentismo* made U.S. annexation impossible, General Wood and Elihu Root, President McKinley's new secretary of war, worked to ensure that the Cuban republic would protect North American interests, especially investments in sugar and ancillary industries. Even as General Brooke and then General Wood supervised a census in the run-up to elections for delegates to a constitutional convention, they balked at the prospect of a popular franchise. With evident anti-Black racism, the two generals warned of a second Haiti if ordinary Cubans were allowed to govern. (For the longer history of ideas within the U.S. concerning Haiti, see Gregg French's and Christina Davidson's chapters in this volume.) They feared that a pro-independence majority of the poor, small farmers, laborers, and veterans, many of them Afro-Cubans, would turn the republic against Americans, foreign investors, and whiter creole elites and Spanish *peninsulares*. Echoing racist narratives about Reconstruction in the United States, many white Americans compared Cubans, and especially Afro-Cubans, to allegedly bumbling former slaves in the postwar U.S. South. Impoverished, uneducated, and with darker skins, both the freed people and freed Cubans were deemed by Yankee generals as incapable of "responsible" republican self-rule. They legitimated Cubans' disenfranchisement by the same metropolitan racist claims of political incapacity now justifying Southern whites' restrictions on Black suffrage in the South.[39]

White U.S. Army commanders shared mainland Americans' fears that poorer Cubans, once in power, would embrace the corruption and partisanship that allegedly ruined multiracial democracy in the South. Ironically, Wood in 1901 sought to alleviate fellow Americans' fears about Cuban politicians' "greed and political avarice" by confirming such dubious analogies. "Havana," he informed one reporter, "is like Washington in the days of Reconstruction after our Civil War," as he implied that its native politicians competed for spoils instead of pursuing the public good. Such commentary reinforced popular narratives that graft and misrule had compromised Reconstruction, and spoke to U.S. military rulers' desire to restrict suffrage for occupied peoples, not expand it, as they had done in 1867. While Wood and Root failed in their efforts to disqualify all Cuban veterans from voting, they did impose severe restrictions on the municipal elections that selected delegates to the constitutional convention in Havana. Defying revolutionaries' cross-racial and civic-nationalist ideology, the military regime required the island's all-male electorate be composed of individuals who were either literate and owned at least $250 in real or personal property or who had served in the Army of Liberation during the war. This excluded two-thirds of Cuba's adult men, and reduced its electorate to 5 percent of Cuba's total population. From Havana, Wood wrote to Root in Washington that their voting rules "met the approval of practically all the best people here." Yet their efforts to stem the popular tide floundered when the pro-independence National Party prevailed at the polls. In 1900, constitutional delegates sent to Havana were decidedly not the "best people" whom Wood and Root desired. They forcefully repudiated the North Americans' anti-democratic impulses by enshrining universal manhood suffrage in the new republican constitution.[40]

Nevertheless, the U.S. occupation narrowed Cubans' democratic aspirations, as General Wood warned the convention that Yankee troops would depart only after it accepted constraints on Cuba's sovereignty. By June 1901, Wood forced its delegates to adopt in the constitution a U.S. congressional amendment drafted by Root and Senator Orville H. Platt. Justified as a measure to safeguard Cuba from European interference, its text exposed the island to repeated U.S. military interventions. It allowed the United States to send gunboats and troops to Cuba whenever its policymakers deemed them necessary to protect "life, property, or individual liberty." The U.S. government could invade to preserve its sanitation measures against yellow fever and contain other epidemiological threats to North

America. The amendment also compelled the Cuban republic to sell or lease land for U.S. naval stations (soon Guantánamo), and barred its officials from contracting excessive debts and making treaties with foreign governments that granted them a colonial or military presence on the island. Despite the failure of annexationism, the Platt Amendment ensured Cuba's subordination well after the first occupation ended in 1902. The neocolonial republic's politics were volatile, propelled in part by growing foreign control of its economy, and the prospect that internal disorder might incite another U.S. invasion and tip the scales against opponents. These conditions prompted future interventions, the next in 1906, as President Theodore Roosevelt, invoking his corollary to the Monroe Doctrine, sent gunboats and troops to quell civil strife over election results. The Army of Cuban Pacification enforced the authority of a Provisional Government led by Charles Magoon, a War Department lawyer specializing in military government, until national elections prompted U.S. soldiers' evacuation in 1909. The Marines returned in 1917, in smaller numbers, in the midst of another civil war, to protect American properties. This proved the final such armed intrusion. President Franklin D. Roosevelt's administration in 1933 and 1934 refused to send troops to secure Cuba's government from popular revolt and adopted a noninterventionist policy in Latin America.[41]

The effects of Cuba's first occupation endured, as U.S. generals, Washington policymakers, and their allies abroad construed the work of U.S. military occupations in western Europe and eastern Asia following two world wars as reconstruction. After President Woodrow Wilson sent Marines into Mexico, Haiti, and the Dominican Republic, his country's vital military contribution to defeating Germany and the Central Powers in World War I also produced an allied military occupation of the Rhineland between 1919 and 1923, through which the United States and its army attempted to influence Europe's postwar reconstruction. For Wilson, the peaceful postwar order secured at Versailles would ensure more than just the creation of new sovereign nations from the ruins of the Austro-Hungarian, German, Russian, and Ottoman empires. To be sure, Wilson, a native Southerner and Democrat, rejected Reconstruction as a misguided radical effort by vengeful Northern Republicans to enfranchise African Americans. The same racist historical sensibility led him to endorse the League of Nations' mandate system of deferred self-government for colonized peoples in Africa and the Middle East. Yet for Europe he embraced postwar political and economic reconstruction as an international exercise in promoting the liberal capitalism he had enshrined in the Fourteen Points. For Wilson and his administration, reconstruction would revive and stabilize western European nations' industrial capitalist economies and state finances, by expanding trade and conducting it on cooperative terms. This, he hoped, would prevent both future intra-European warfare and the spread of Bolshevism beyond a newly socialist Russia.[42]

A policy rubric and rhetoric of reconstruction also infused ambitions among U.S. politicians, officials, and generals after World War II to rehabilitate the economies of western Europe, as U.S. troops occupied Austria and parts of Germany, in addition to Japan and southern Korea. As the Cold War unfolded in the late 1940s, the reconstruction of states and capitalist industry became a central pillar of the grand strategy of containment developed by President Harry S. Truman's administration. Communism's expansion in Europe and beyond was to be halted by combining economic assistance to western Europe and Japan with a military buildup in these regions, in concert with anti-communist allies such as the Philippines, in order to defend American and allied nation's resources and markets. As U.S. foreign policy operationalized modernization theory in the form of development and aid programs, reconstruction served as the bedrock of an American and international lexicon of postwar economic planning and foreign policy. After the Cold War ended and the United States responded to the 2001 terrorist attacks by invading and attempting to transform Iraq and Afghanistan, American leaders again invoked discourses and practices of reconstruction to frame military missions in them. Yet they believed its lineage dated only to the United States' altruistic efforts to rebuild Europe and Asia following the Second World War, the "good occupations" that followed the "good war."[43] From an early twenty-first century perspective, these post–World War II reconstructions seemed not imperial in nature, but successful exercises in nation-building that had strengthened liberal democracy and global capitalism, and helped vanquish international communism. Reconstruction's imperial transmutation in Cuba had all but been forgotten. The nineteenth-century promise of reconstruction as radical social transformation and egalitarian nationalism had been recast in a postcolonial mold, one suited to building nation-states abroad friendly to U.S. interests and global capitalism.

Notes

The author thanks Mark Elliot, Eric Foner, David Prior, and anonymous reviewers for their comments and suggestions.

1. Robert L. Bullard, "Military Pacification," *Journal of the Military Service Institution* 46, no. 163 (1910), 1–3; Katherine Bjork, *Prairie Imperialists: The Indian Country Origins of American Empire* (Philadelphia: University of Pennsylvania Press, 2019), chap. 3, 139–149, 152–162, 182–183, 194–197.

2. Bullard, "Military Pacification," 4–20.

3. Bullard, "Military Pacification," 19–20, 23–24. Many observers in Cuba and the Philippines claimed that Black U.S. soldiers enjoyed friendlier relations with Filipinos than with white American soldiers, given their racism; see Willard B. Gatewood Jr., *Black Americans and the White Man's Burden, 1898–1903* (Urbana: University of Illinois Press, 1975), 42–43, 121–128, 144–145, 215–216, 279–282.

4. W. E. B. Du Bois, *Black Reconstruction in America* (New York: Harcourt, Brace, 1935), 9, 15–16, 30, 632; see also David Prior's Introduction to this volume.

5. David Prior, "Introduction," and "Reconstruction, from Transatlantic Polyseme to Historiographical Quandary," in *Reconstruction in a Globalizing World*, ed. David Prior (New York: Fordham University Press, 2018), 1–20, 172–208; Andrew Zimmerman, "Reconstruction: Transnational History," in *Interpreting American History: Reconstruction*, ed. John David Smith (Kent, Ohio: Kent State University Press, 2016), 171–172; Sven Beckert, *Empire of Cotton: A Global History* (New York: Alfred A. Knopf, 2015); Andrew Zimmerman, *Alabama in Africa: Booker T. Washington, The German Empire and the Globalization of the New South* (Princeton, N.J.: Princeton University Press, 2010). The impact of Booker T. Washington's industrial education movement on Cuba is charted in Frank Andre Guridy, *Forging Diaspora: Afro-Cubans and African-Americans in a World of Empire and Jim Crow* (Chapel Hill: University of North Carolina Press, 2010), esp. chap. 1. On Du Bois's arguments linking Reconstruction and early twentieth-century racial imperialism, see Eric Foner, "*Black Reconstruction*: An Introduction," *South Atlantic Quarterly* 112, no. 3 (2013), 409–419, esp. 414–416; and Moon-Ho Jung, "*Black Reconstruction* and Empire," *South Atlantic Quarterly* 112, no. 3 (2013), 465–471.

6. Eric Foner, *Nothing But Freedom: Emancipation and Its Legacy* (Baton Rouge: Louisiana State University Press, 1983); Peter Kolchin, *Unfree Labor: American Slavery and Russian Serfdom* (Cambridge, Mass.: Harvard University Press, 1983); Steven Hahn, "Class and State in Postemancipation Societies: Southern Planters in Comparative Perspective," *American Historical Review* 95, no. 1 (1990), 75–98; Frederick Cooper, Thomas C. Holt, and Rebecca Scott, eds., *Beyond Slavery: Explorations of Race, Labor, and Citizenship in Post-Emancipation Societies* (Chapel Hill: University of North Carolina Press, 2000); Enrico Dal Lago, *Civil War and Agrarian Unrest: The Confederate South and Southern Italy* (New York: Cambridge University Press, 2018); Rebecca J. Scott, *Degrees of Freedom: Louisiana and Cuba after Slavery* (Cambridge, Mass.: Belknap Press of Harvard University Press, 2005); Gregory P. Downs, *The Second American Revolution: The Civil War Era Struggle over Cuba and the Rebirth of the American Republic* (Chapel Hill: University of North Carolina Press, 2019). One history of postwar U.S. military occupations as nation-building is Jeremi Suri, *Liberty's Surest Guardian: American Nation-Building from the Founders to Obama* (New York: Free Press, 2011).

7. Heather Cox Richardson, *West from Appomattox: The Reconstruction of America after the Civil War* (New Haven, Conn.: Yale University Press, 2007); Steven J. Hahn, *A Nation without Borders: The United States and Its World in an Age of Civil Wars, 1830–1910* (New York: Viking, 2016), 4–6, 485–500. See also *United States Reconstruction across the Americas*, ed. William A. Link (Gainesville: University Press of Florida, 2019).

8. Alfred W. McCoy, Francisco A. Scarano, and Courtney Johnson, "On the Tropic of Cancer: Transitions and Transformations in the U.S. Imperial State," in *Colonial*

Crucible: Empire in the Making of the Modern American State, ed. Alfred W. McCoy and Francisco A. Scarano (Madison: University of Wisconsin Press, 2009), 3–33. The causes of this conflict are not reviewed here; for a brief review of the historiography of the Spanish-American War, see Kristin Hoganson, *Fighting for American Manhood: How Gender Politics Provoked the Spanish-American and Philippine-American Wars* (New Haven, Conn.: Yale University Press, 1998), 7–10, and fn. 14, 210–214.

9. Louis A. Pérez Jr., *The War of 1898: The United States and Cuba in History and Historiography* (Chapel Hill: University of North Carolina Press, 1998); Louis A. Pérez Jr., *Cuba between Empires, 1878–1902* (Pittsburgh: University of Pittsburgh Press, 1983), 59–64, 185–186, 208–210; Julian Go, *American Empire and the Politics of Meaning: Elite Political Cultures in the Philippines and Puerto Rico during U.S. Colonialism* (Durham, N.C.: Duke University Press, 2008). Natalie J. Ring, "A New Reconstruction for the South," in *Remembering Reconstruction: Struggles over the Meaning of America's Most Turbulent Era*, ed. Carole Emberton and Bruce E. Baker (Baton Rouge: Louisiana State University Press, 2017), 184–86.

10. Peter M. R. Stirk, *A History of Military Occupation from 1792 to 1914* (Edinburgh: Edinburgh University Press, 2016), 4–7, 24–25, chap. 3.

11. Mary L. Dudziak, *War Time: An Idea, Its History, Its Consequences* (Oxford: Oxford University Press, 2010); Gregory P. Downs, *After Appomattox: Military Occupation and the Ends of War* (Cambridge, Mass.: Harvard University Press, 2015), 2–6, 12–14, 20–25; Ada Ferrer, *Insurgent Cuba: Race, Nation, and Revolution, 1868–1898* (Chapel Hill: University of North Carolina Press, 1999), 99–110. Other studies of Reconstruction stressing its military dimension include William L. Richter, *The Army in Texas during Reconstruction, 1865–1870* (College Station: Texas A&M University Press, 1987); James K. Hogue, *Uncivil War: Five New Orleans Street Battles and the Rise and Fall of Radical Reconstruction* (Baton Rouge: Louisiana State University Press, 2006); Mark L. Bradley, *Bluecoats and Tar Heels: Soldiers and Civilians in Reconstruction North Carolina* (Lexington: University Press of Kentucky, 2009); Andrew F. Lang, *In the Wake of War: Military Occupation, Emancipation, and Civil War America* (Baton Rouge: Louisiana State University Press, 2017).

12. Downs, *After Appomattox*, 14; Louis A. Pérez Jr., *Cuba in the American Imagination: Metaphor and the Imperial Ethos* (Chapel Hill: University of North Carolina Press, 2008); Colin D. Moore, *American Imperialism and the State, 1893–1921* (Cambridge: Cambridge University Press, 2017), 15–22.

13. Eric Foner, *Reconstruction: America's Unfinished Revolution, 1863–1877* (New York: Harper and Row, 1988), 1–7; Eric Foner, *The Fiery Trial: Abraham Lincoln and American Slavery* (New York: W. W. Norton, 2010), esp. chaps. 5–7; James Oakes, *Freedom National: The Destruction of Slavery in the United States, 1861–1865* (New York: W. W. Norton, 2013), esp. xi–xv, 93–105, 218–223, chap. 7, 317–328, chap. 10; Downs, *Second American Revolution*, 29; Chandra Manning, *What This Cruel War Was Over: Soldiers, Slavery, and the Civil War* (New York: Alfred A. Knopf, 2007); Chandra Manning, *Troubled Refuge: Struggling for Freedom in the Civil War* (New York: Vintage Books, 2016). Oakes makes the case that military emancipation during the war reflected Republicans' bedrock antislavery commitments, contrary to arguments that Lincoln and moderate congressional Republicans attacked slavery only reluctantly as a pragmatic war measure;

for the latter, see, among others, William E. Gienapp, *Abraham Lincoln and Civil War America: A Biography* (New York: Oxford University Press, 2002).

14. Foner, *Reconstruction*, 7–10, 28–30, 50–60; Oakes, *Freedom National*, 218–223, 245–254; Ira Berlin, Joseph P. Reidy, and Leslie S. Rowland, eds., *Freedom's Soldiers: The Black Military Experience* (Cambridge: Cambridge University Press, 1982); Joe Gray Taylor, *Louisiana Reconstructed, 1863–1877* (Baton Rouge: Louisiana State University Press, 1974), 6–7; Peyton McCrary, *Abraham Lincoln and Reconstruction: The Louisiana Experiment* (Princeton, N.J.: Princeton University Press, 1978), 77–78, 82.

15. Joseph G. Dawson III, *Army Generals and Reconstruction: Louisiana, 1862–1877* (Baton Rouge: Louisiana State University Press, 1982), 1; Downs, *After Appomattox*, 12–14, 19–26.

16. Foner, *Reconstruction*, 35–50, 73, 176–184; Eric McKitrick, *Andrew Johnson and Reconstruction* (Chicago: University of Chicago Press, 1960), 134–136; Downs, *After Appomattox*, 2–6, 12–14, 20–25; Mark Wahlgren Summers, *The Ordeal of the Reunion: A New History of the Reconstruction* (Chapel Hill: University of North Carolina, 2014), 1–23.

17. Foner, *Reconstruction*, 181–197; Downs, *After Appomattox*, 41–46.

18. Foner, *Reconstruction*, 198–209; Downs, *After Appomattox*, 52–53, 84–87, 108–110, 143.

19. Foner, *Reconstruction*, 66–71, 158–170; Eric Foner, *Politics and Ideology in the Age of the Civil War* (New York: Oxford University Press, 1980), chap. 7; Downs, *After Appomattox*, 13.

20. Foner, *Reconstruction*, 68–71, 142–158, 164–170; James M. McPherson, *The Struggle for Equality: Abolitionists and the Negro in the Civil War and Reconstruction* (Princeton, N.J.: Princeton University Press, 1964), chap. 8; William S. McFeely, *Yankee Stepfather: General O. O. Howard and the Freedmen* (New Haven, Conn.: Yale University Press, 1968), chap. 4; Downs, *After Appomattox*, 25–28, 46–47, 89, 232.

21. Foner, *Reconstruction*, 243–280, 333–336; Michael Vorenberg, "The 1866 Civil Rights Act and the Beginning of Military Reconstruction," in *The Greatest and Grandest Act: The Civil Rights Act of 1866 from Reconstruction to Today*, ed. Christian G. Samito (Carbondale: Southern Illinois University Press, 2018), 60–88.

22. Foner, *Reconstruction*, 271–280; Downs, *After Appomattox*, chaps. 7–8, 217–219.

23. Downs, *After Appomattox*, 174, 179–203; Downs, *Second American Revolution*, 40–48.

24. Foner, *Reconstruction*, 412–601, passim; Downs, *After Appomattox*, 219–242; Summers, *Ordeal of the Reunion*, 254–272; Heather Cox Richardson, *The Death of Reconstruction: Race, Labor, and Politics in the Post–Civil War North* (Cambridge, Mass.: Harvard University Press, 2001).

25. C. Vann Woodward, *Origins of the New South, 1877–1913* (Baton Rouge: Louisiana State University Press, 1951); C. Vann Woodward, *The Strange Career of Jim Crow* (New York: Oxford University Press, 1955); Ira Katznelson, *Fear Itself: The New Deal and the Origins of Our Time* (New York: W. W. Norton, 2013); Richard M. Valelly, *The Two Reconstructions: The Struggle for Black Enfranchisement* (Chicago: University of Chicago Press, 2004); Eric Foner, *The Second Founding: How the Civil War and Reconstruction Remade the Constitution* (New York: W. W. Norton, 2019), chap. 4. For a careful study of

how Southern lawmakers made the Solid South at the congressional level, and operated it, see David Bateman, Ira Katznelson, and John S. Lapinski, *Southern Nation: Congress and White Supremacy after Reconstruction* (Princeton, N.J.: Princeton University Press, 2018).

26. Richard J. Hinton, "Cuban Reconstruction," *North American Review* 168, no. 506 (1899), 92–102; Franklin Matthews, "The Reconstruction of Cuba," *Harper's Weekly*, February 18, 1899, 181; Pérez, *Cuba between Empires*, 198–210, 217–220, 224–260; Ferrer, *Insurgent Cuba*, 187–192; Louis A. Pérez Jr., *Lords of the Mountain: Social Banditry and Peasant Protest in Cuba, 1878–1918* (Pittsburgh: University of Pittsburgh Press, 1989), 63.

27. Ferrer, *Insurgent Cuba*, 100–101.

28. Pérez, *Lords of the Mountain*, 58–66, 78–88, 112–116; Louis A. Pérez Jr., *Rice in the Time of Sugar: The Political Economy of Food in Cuba* (Chapel Hill: University of North Carolina Press, 2019), 21–22, 62–68; Jack C. Lane, *Armed Progressive: General Leonard Wood* (Lincoln: University of Nebraska Press, 2009), 55–59.

29. Pérez, *Cuba between Empires*, 286–295; Alejandro de la Fuente, *A Nation for All: Race, Inequality, and Politics in Twentieth-Century Cuba* (Chapel Hill: University of North Carolina Press, 2001), 24, 40.

30. Pérez, *Lords of the Mountain*, 87, 116–128; Franklin Matthews, *The New-Born Cuba* (New York: Harper and Bros., 1899), 306.

31. Pérez, *Cuba between Empires*, 18–22, 346–347; John Lawrence Tone, *War and Genocide in Cuba, 1895–1898* (Chapel Hill: University of North Carolina Press, 2006), 57–68, 223; Pérez, *Lords of the Mountain*, 50–51, 58–62; Louis A. Pérez Jr., *On Becoming Cuban: Identity, Nationality, and Culture* (Chapel Hill: University of North Carolina Press, 1999), 101. For Cuban officials who invoked "reconstruction" in their appeals to the U.S. military government for assistance, see, among others, Padro Grinan, "Informe," Santiago de Cuba, June 30, 1900, and Bartoleme Falcon Paz, "Informe," El Cobre, Sept. 29, 1900, both in Box 101, Entry 3, Record Group 140, National Archives and Record Administration [hereafter NARA], College Park, Maryland.

32. De la Fuente, *A Nation for All*, 40–42; Leonard Wood to Russell Alger, September 9, 1898, Box 915, Entry 25, Record Group 94, NARA, Washington, D.C.; Foner, *Reconstruction*, 152–153.

33. David F. Healy, *The United States in Cuba, 1898–1902: Generals, Politicians, and the Search for Policy* (Madison: University of Wisconsin Press, 1963), 51–52, 60, 88–97; Eric Foner, *The Story of American Freedom* (New York: W. W. Norton, 1998), 116–124; Edward G. Longacre, *From Union Stars to Top Hat: A Biography of the Extraordinary General James Harrison Wilson* (Harrisburg, Pa.: Stackpole Books, 1972), chap. 11; Dawson, *Army Generals and Reconstruction*, 168–179, 227–234; Scott, *Degrees of Freedom*, 59–60, 155.

34. Pérez, *Lords of the Mountain*, 68–74; United States War Department, *Annual Reports*, 1899, vol. 1, pt. 6 (Washington, D.C.: GPO, 1900), 9, 12–14.

35. Foner, *Reconstruction*, 212–213, 325–327, 382–385, 392–394; Mariano Gomez to General Lawton, September 17, 1898, Box 2, Entry 1487, Record Group 395, NARA, Washington, D.C.; Pablo Desvernine to John R. Brooke, October 4, 1899, Box 24, Entry 3, Record Group 140, NARA, College Park, Maryland; *Patria*, October 1, 1899; Foner, *Story of American Freedom*, 126–128.

36. Foner, *Reconstruction*, 404–409; Pérez, *Lords of the Mountain*, 68–71; Pérez, *Rice in the Time of Sugar*, 65; "Gobierno Civil de la Provincia de Villaclara. Un plan de reconstruccion. Santa Clara, 1899," Box 11, Entry 1331, Record Group 395, NARA; Pablo Desvernine to John R. Brooke, October 4, 1899, Box 24, Entry 3, Record Group 140, National Archives and Records Administration; U.S. War Dept., *Annual Reports*, 1900, *Military Government of Cuba, Civil Affairs*, vol. 1, pt. 4 (Washington, D.C.: GPO, 1901), 9.

37. Pérez, *Cuba between Empires*, 135–137; Louis A. Pérez Jr., *Cuba under the Platt Amendment, 1902–1934* (Pittsburgh: University of Pittsburgh Press, 1986), 69–72; Leonard Wood to Elihu Root, May 30, 1901, Leonard Wood Papers, Library of Congress, Washington, D.C.

38. Pérez, *Cuba under the Platt Amendment*, 70–77; Pérez, *On Becoming Cuban*, 107–164; Pérez, *Rice in the Time of Sugar*, 66; Woodward, *Origins of the New South*.

39. Pérez, *Cuba under the Platt Amendment*, 34–41; Gary Gerstle, "Race and Nation in the United States, Mexico, and Cuba, 1880–1940," in *Nationalism in the New World*, ed. Don H. Doyle and Marco Antonio Pamplona (Athens: University of Georgia Press, 2006).

40. Alejandro de la Fuente and Matthew Casey, "Race and the Suffrage Controversy in Cuba, 1898–1901," in McCoy and Scarano, *Colonial Crucible*, 220–229; Wood to Elihu Root, February 23, 1900, Box 28, Leonard Wood Papers, Library of Congress, Washington, D.C., quoted ibid; Edward Marshall, "A Talk with General Wood," *Outlook*, July 20, 1901, 673.

41. Pérez, *Cuba under the Platt Amendment*, 41–55, 98–107, 167–170, 324–325; Pérez, *Cuba between Empires*, 323–327.

42. Erez Manela, *The Wilsonian Moment: Self-Determination and the International Origins of Anticolonial Nationalism* (New York: Oxford University Press, 2007), 28–33; Samuel L. Schaffer, "'A Bitter Memory Upon Which Terms of Peace Would Rest,'" in *Remembering Reconstruction*, 203–222.

43. Michael J. Hogan, *The Marshall Plan: America, Britain, and the Reconstruction of Europe, 1947–1952* (New York: Cambridge University Press, 1987); John W. Dower, *Embracing Defeat: Japan in the Wake of World War II* (New York: W. W. Norton, 1999), 23, 80–83, 529; Walter M. Hudson, *Army Diplomacy: American Military Occupation and Foreign Policy after World War II* (Lexington: University Press of Kentucky, 2015), 37–44; Kornel Chang, "Independence without Liberation: Democratization as Decolonization Management in U.S.-Occupied Korea, 1945–1948," *Journal of American History* 107, no. 1 (2020), 77–106; Grant Madsen, *Sovereign Soldiers: How the U.S. Military Transformed the Global Economy after World War II* (Philadelphia: University of Pennsylvania Press, 2018); Colleen Woods, *Freedom Incorporated: Anticommunism and Philippine Independence in the Age of Decolonization* (Ithaca, N.Y.: Cornell University Press, 2020); Suri, *Liberty's Surest Guardian*, 238–258; Susan L. Carruthers, *The Good Occupation: American Soldiers and the Hazards of Peace* (Cambridge, Mass.: Harvard University Press, 2016), 1–5.

Afterword

Rebecca Edwards

In the decades after the U.S. Civil War, who tried to Reconstruct what, and who resisted those Reconstructions? The essays in this volume explore those questions from many angles, through histories that bridge the divide between the immediate postwar years, especially as they unfolded in the former Confederacy, and the era of imperial projects that arose in the war's wake. These authors show that federal officials and military leaders were hardly the only ones advocating Reconstructions, local and global. Buoyed by Emancipation and Union victory, many American thinkers began to imagine what a Greater United States might look like as they struggled over whose vision of the nation would prevail.

Several themes emerge. First, even after the Civil War the eventual geographic shape of the twentieth-century United States was not preordained. After Union victory, many Americans assumed the nation would expand to include most or all of the Western Hemisphere. As the essays by Andre Fleche and Gregg French demonstrate, President Ulysses Grant moved quickly to claim the Dominican Republic, though his aims were thwarted. With slavery gone, Grant saw no impediment to annexing "racially diverse territories" whose residents could eventually become equal citizens of the United States. Expelling Spain was another enticing rationale for U.S. expansion into the Caribbean—one that recurred, of course, two decades later. Though the United States may not have launched occupations of countries such as Haiti until the twentieth century, historians need to reckon more with its nineteenth-century Caribbean *pre*occupations, in multiple senses of the word.

Grant's 1869 annexation proposal was part of a broader, racially inclusive moment in Republican policy—one that did not last long but also should not be too quickly dismissed. Just a year earlier, in 1868, William Seward and Anson Burlingame concluded a treaty that invited Chinese immigrants to enter the United States on an equal basis with other newcomers. The treaty nullified state laws that barred Chinese and affirmed rights of free migration irrespective of race. Grant extended that vision outward, toward an expansive multiracial nation that could include future states in the Caribbean and beyond. In those heady days of 1868 and 1869, when the Fourteenth and Fifteenth Amendment were also moving to ratification, some victorious Unionists proposed even more ambitious projects, which precipitated struggles in Washington. It is notable that Senator Charles Sumner opposed Dominican annexation while at nearly the same moment, in May 1869, he proposed that Great Britain pay for damage wrought by the Liverpool-built C.S.S. *Alabama* by handing over Canada to the United States.

These expansionist proposals, with their complex racial valences, were rooted not only in faith in republican forms of government and confidence in U.S. military might but also in the conviction that America was poised to export its superior "civilization." Christina Davidson shows that African Methodist Episcopal church leaders articulated one such vision. In a distinctive way, A.M.E. missionaries traced the same geographical path that other reformers did, starting with a focus on the former Confederacy and then turning to the Caribbean before launching projects in Africa and other parts of the globe. A.M.E. missionaries simultaneously advanced the goal of Black racial solidarity *and* participated in building U.S. racial empire, though they lacked funding to extend their reach as far as church leaders hoped. The United States' domestic post-Reconstruction order, which left the majority of Southern A.M.E. members impoverished, helped determine which Americans built networks and exercised influence beyond the nation's borders, and which did not have those opportunities.

Mark Elliott also shows how multiple versions of the civilizing mission unfolded between the 1870s and 1890s, laying foundations for later humanitarian interventions. Among the most influential voices of the era was that of Congregationalist Lyman Abbott, who emphasized public schools and Christian churches as instruments of uplift. Theodore Roosevelt famously said that if the U.S. was "morally bound to abandon the Philippines, we were also morally bound to abandon Arizona to the Apaches."[1] Abbott offered the cultural corollary: If the United States was morally obligated to send teachers and Christian missionaries to uplift the Apaches, it must send them to Filipinos as well.

Both Abbott and James Redpath, both born in the early 1830s, shared the outlook of the abolitionist generation of reformers. Redpath was far more nationally prominent before the war, but Abbott also moved in influential circles by the 1860s as the son-in-law to Lincoln's first Vice President Hannibal Hamlin. Other like-minded men of the same generation, such as "The Christian General" O. O. Howard, participated directly in Southern Reconstruction, and their experiences gave a strong military cast to postwar thinking. As Mark Elliott astutely observes, such men were not only familiar with military rule as a context for social change; they conceived of military occupation *as* humanitarianism. The lessons they learned about ex-Confederate intransigence, while they labored in the South, also suggested to them that armed force was essential to progress. The startling issue, of course, is that race trumped nationalism: Many Unionist leaders ultimately allied themselves more with white ex-Confederates rather than with African American Unionist allies. By the 1890s, many such men ended up justifying ex-Confederate resistance to their own work.

A future volume of essays might compare such military leaders' ventures in the South with their experiences in the U.S. West—another location where critical events bridged the eras of the Civil War and imperialism. As Justin Jackson points out, most men who remained in the U.S. Army after Reconstruction went west to conquer Indigenous peoples. General Howard himself, in 1874, forced the surrender of Nez Perce Young Chief Joseph and his people. The "civilization" brought by Union churches and schoolhouses required the brutal removal of people already living in the West. As Jackson points out, federal policies toward Native peoples, combining military conquest with uplift and "reform," built a legal and ideological framework for overseas conquest. Brian Shott is right to suggest that historians explore more deeply the comparisons and contrasts between the U.S. West and the Caribbean. In both places, between 1865 and 1900, U.S. policy, local colonialist agendas, and Indigenous resistance created violent "schoolrooms" for empire. In both, the authority of central governments remained limited and contested.[2]

Though the late 1860s marked a racially inclusive moment in American expansionism, that moment was short-lived. As early as 1870, Republican congressmen from the Pacific states blocked passage of a naturalization act that removed all racial barriers to immigration; instead, Congress extended immigration rights to people of African descent but not to Asians. The road from Emancipation to U.S. occupation of the Philippines was in some sense already open. An influential dialogue had begun between resurgent white supremacists (in this case led by Westerners, not leaders in the defeated South) and white Reconstructionists, including abolitionists, who began to revise or recant their earlier antiracist views.

As Gregg French shows, for example, two of the most influential opponents of Grant's plan to annex the Dominican Republic were Charles Sumner and Grant's own secretary of state, Hamilton Fish. Faced with Dominicans of "every shade and mixture of color"—who had the temerity to own property, no less—Fish decided that the Republic could not be a "desirable acquisition." Two decades later U.S. Generals John Brooke and Leonard Wood viewed Cubans through a similar lens, expressing fears of "a second Haiti." The fact that a Haitian-style uprising had not materialized during the U.S. Civil War did not, apparently, shake a century of deep-seated fears.

Similarly, Lawrence Glickman demonstrates that James Redpath, despite his antebellum fame as an abolitionist, did not follow the logic of that position into antiracist work after Emancipation. Instead, he rather remarkably became an apologist for former Confederate President Jefferson Davis, while also taking up the cause of Irish nationalism and denouncing the British Empire for its oppressions in Egypt. Redpath's Scottish background may help explain his unusual trajectory, but he was not alone among Republican-leaning thinkers in romanticizing white Southerners' rebellion and linking it to other struggles against centralized authority. The careers of Samuel Howe and Julia Ward Howe, who identified with the cause of Greek independence and later denounced the genocide of Armenians in Turkey, also reminds us how normative it was for American thinkers to view events in their own country through a Eurocentric lens, which enabled these Americans to regard themselves as opponents of empire rather than practitioners of it.

At the same time, a younger generation began by the 1890s to view international relations less as a humanitarian project and more as a matter of business. David Holtby demonstrates how Albert Beveridge broke with Republican stalwarts in the Grand Army of the Republic to advocate a "March of the Flag" focused primarily on trade. At a moment of rising nativism in the 1890s, Beveridge praised immigration: Like his contemporary Theodore Roosevelt, he welcomed "virile, man-producing immigrants" who would expand the U.S. population. Yet the shift from Anson Burlingame's multiracial 1869 vision was apparent, since Beveridge focused entirely on European immigrants (while rejecting New Mexico and Arizona statehood because neither territory contained enough people he defined as white). Beveridge hailed the aggressive call to conquest—"Forward!"— as an "Anglo-Saxon impulse" that had begun with Jefferson, "the first Imperialist of the Republic."[3]

We thus learn, in this volume, some of the ways in which some prominent Republicans and reformers changed their minds after the Civil War ended. Others, who continued to fight for racial justice, found themselves superseded by a young generation who counted themselves among what some called the club of "Angry Saxons." At the same time, as early as the mid-1870s Republicans faced serious challenges from resurgent white supremacists in the South. Adrian Brettle shows how ex-Confederate Virginians skipped barely a step after their crushing military defeat, before renewing the push for their prewar economic agenda. At a moment when Burlingame was welcoming Chinese citizens to help build a multiracial society in the United States, former Confederates were reading Charles Dilke's just-published best seller, *Greater Britain*. Undeterred by Dilke's antislavery principles, these Southerners focused on his romanticized racial links between England and the United States and his prediction that Americans would "rul[e] mankind through Anglo Saxon institutions and the English tongue."

The trajectory from 1865 to 1898 hinged, of course, on the national rehabilitation and acceptance of such views, even though Southern white supremacists were not always successful in shaping foreign policy. By the 1890s, men such as Benjamin Tillman openly rejected the inclusion of "barbarians of the lowest type . . . debased and ignorant people" or "mongrel populations" into the American polity, linking racism against foreign peoples to the relentless quest to disfranchise African Americans at home. DJ Polite shows how deeply and skillfully men like Tillman pursued these goals.

Events such as the horrific lynching of South Carolina postmaster Frazier Baker caused some Americans to question how they could "civilize" the world. Of all contemporary American commentators, Mark Twain offered perhaps the most powerful critiques on that subject—though he did not always publish them. Perhaps fear of the wrath of Julia Ward Howe motivated Twain not to publish the line, "mine eyes have seen the orgy of the launching of the Sword." But he also filed away his essay "The United States of Lyncherdom," which he wrote in 1901 after reading about a mob of Texas lynchers who burned their victim alive. Imagining that Americans could witness all at once, one night, the 203 lynchings that had occurred the previous year, Twain proposed to "import American missionaries from China" and send them out to convert lynchers. In a passage Burlingame might have approved had he still been alive, Twain wrote that "the Chinese are universally conceded to be excellent people, honest, honorable, industrious, trustworthy, kind-hearted," but warned that each convert in China "runs a risk of catching our civilization." "We ought to think twice," wrote Twain, "before we encourage a risk like that." "Our country is worse off than China," Twain concluded as he contemplated the horror of lynchings; "O compassionate missionary leave China! Come home and convert these Christians!"[4]

As Twain saw, and as Polite's essay suggests, it was no accident that America's overseas "launching of the sword" coincided with the domestic rise of lynchings and the Tampa and Wilmington violence, as well as the Supreme Court's *Plessy* decision and a broader shift toward disfranchising Black and poor voters in the South. Brian Shott invites us to think of these events on American soil as dimensions of a "Jim Crow colonialism" that arose both at home and abroad. The Jim Crow South, after all, was *not* a product of the 1870s and 1880s, when

African Americans continued to vote in many areas and to mount effective protests against segregation and disfranchisement. Rather, Jim Crow was a product of the 1890s. Viewed from this angle there is not as much difference as one might think between Theodore Roosevelt—who viewed progressivism and imperialism as efforts to impose order, respectively, on economic and diplomatic chaos—and "Pitchfork Ben," who asked, "If it is good to have white supremacy in the Hawaiian Islands, why is it not in my State?" The answer, of course, was that most white Americans—even some former abolitionists—had become comfortable with both.

By the 1890s white supremacists also justified the open murder of an African American postmaster by claiming that his appointment was a form of "carpetbaggery." Cynicism about government, fueled by real corruption as well as perceived overreaches of "big government" and the steady demonization of Southern Republicans (especially Black officeholders), meant white supremacists could insinuate by 1898 that the appointment of a Black postmaster in the white South was a capital offense. The effectiveness of "carpetbaggery" accusations calls attention to the United States' poor record of governance—to the many failures of what Justin Jackson aptly calls the "American way of postwar." After Reconstruction, the federal government proved unable to sustain its experiment in *governance*—in establishing just, effective democracies across the South. Since such experiments had died in Georgia and Mississippi, it is understandable that Americans thought that if governments by and for the people were attempted in Cuba and the Philippines, those too would perish from this earth.

An emphasis on military power at the expense of other governmental capacities had in fact been a hallmark of federal power in the Jacksonian period and arguably a cause of the Civil War itself. A bent toward military occupation, often without successfully translating that occupation into effective post-occupation government, would continue to haunt the United States after 1898 in its overseas exploits. Yet Americans still viewed themselves as triumphant Emancipationists and benevolent Christians with a mission in Armenia and beyond—a path straight to Woodrow Wilson's Fourteen Points and all its many contradictions.

These essays show that there was no single imperial or anti-imperial vision, any more than there had been a united Union or Confederacy. Historians can do more, in essays such as these, to expand our understanding of what we might call "alternative imperialisms," articulated not by leading men such as Theodore Roosevelt and Albert Beveridge but by groups like the A.M.E. Church. Particularly insightful is Reilly Hatch's interpretation of how the Church of Jesus Christ of Latter-day Saints expected U.S. expansion to encompass the whole Western Hemisphere. Mormon leaders identified that project with their own expansionist goals, imagining the future nation and church fused together: As Joseph Smith had said, "The whole of America is Zion." "America," of course, meant not the United States as it is geographically bounded today, but a much broader realm.

Yet the project of conquest looked much uglier up close, even to its proponents. Two idealistic Mormon missionaries, as Hatch shows, enlisted in the U.S. war to subdue the Philippines but came away disillusioned. Even though one of them, Willard Call, thought an "American Protectorate" would be the best outcome for the Philippines, he sympathized with the Filipino guerrilla "fighting for his country, his home, and his family. . . . It matters not how ignorant he might be." Call asked to be discharged and sent home to Utah. George A. Seaman, meanwhile, found a mission in discouraging Mormon soldiers from "gaming and other idle practices" but wrote, "though I enlisted for war, the less of it I see the better satisfied I am." He could have spoken for many an American soldier of other eras, prior and since.

These essays raise many questions for further exploration. How distinctive, for example, were the ideas of women such as Julia Ward Howe and Clara Barton? To what extent did such women see themselves as participants in the Protestant missionary movement, in which women were achieving new peaks of influence by the 1890s? How did these and other female commentators describe the links between the flourishing world of women's club and reform work in the United States and new projects overseas? How did their ideas fit into the broader context of women's patriotic work, in groups such as the Daughters of the American Revolution and the United Daughters of the Confederacy? Historians are now giving sustained attention to the imperial dimensions of domesticity and the gendered dimensions of Reconstruction and imperialism, making this an opportune moment to consider relationships between the two.[5]

We need to know much more about the points of view of those being occupied and ostensibly "Reconstructed": not just the juxtaposed situations of white Southerners and American freedpeople, both subject to U.S. rule, but also Indigenous people in the United States and elsewhere; Dominicans, Cubans, and Filipinos; and all those who fought against, worked in, and accommodated themselves to new imperial orders. They, just like the Reconstructers and occupiers, had complex identities that could pull in opposite directions. Did Cuban commanders and soldiers, for example, exploit ideological differences between former Union soldier Federico Fernández Cavada and ex-Confederate general

Thomas Jordan, when both arrived to fight for Cuban independence? Or was Cavada's Cuban heritage more important to them, in his vigorous defense of Cubans' capacity to rule themselves—while Jordan shared with other *Americanos* in Cuba, whether Unionist or Confederate, a desire to preserve older relationships of property and power and effect revolution "on the cheap"?

W. E. B. DuBois was surely right to call attention to the rising power of global capital in the post–Civil War decades. He insisted, as David Prior notes, that racial conflict be understood in the context of struggles over labor and property. Since the United States, well into the twentieth century, remained deeply dependent on Southern export crops, connections between domestic and global unfree forms of labor stayed at the forefront. Republicans' relentless desire to resurrect export agriculture in the interests of the national economy was thus closely interwoven with the rising objectives of imperialism: the quest to build trade networks, including coaling stations for cross-oceanic shipping routes, as well as to access raw materials and consumer markets.

As Barbara J. Fields has brilliantly argued, the push for export revenues helped produce new forms of racism. During Reconstruction, Republican officials insisted that freedpeople should continue to devote their labor to production of export crops, believing "very genuinely that, in offering the freedmen a chance to become free wage laborers, [federal policymakers] were offering them a wonderful boon. But the freedmen . . . wanted their own land and the right to farm it as they chose. And their choice was likely to disappoint those eager to reconstitute the staple economy: most found bizarre the white folks' preoccupation with growing things no one could eat." Thus, the Reconstructers found themselves frustrated. Fields concludes that what these policymakers "typically experienced—that is to say, the way ideology usually interpreted their experience to them—was that the freedmen had disappointed them by failing to live up to their responsibilities. They were shiftless, were not dependable wage workers, failed to respond like civilized people to wage incentives."[6]

We can compare this to the ways in which U.S. policymakers' optimistic commencement of new economic and political "reform" projects overseas left them disappointed, and "ideology interpreted" that disappointment for them as the racial incapacity of people of color in places the U.S. sought to colonize. Thus we see similar patterns of disillusionment in post–Civil War Reconstruction; in the United States' project of depopulating, repopulating, and incorporating adjacent lands in the West; and in the administration of captured territories. Empire relied on coercive labor rather than land reform, and overseas as well as at home, slavery morphed into new forms of economic disempowerment.

The French historian Ernest Renan said that not only remembering but also "forgetting . . . is a crucial factor in the creation of a nation." Drawing on that insight, Thomas Bender has written that the experience of the U.S. Civil War fused liberalism and nationalism in American ideology, by linking the goals of Emancipation and preservation of the Union, but that afterward the United States "forgot liberalism and remembered nationalism."[7] We can add that the United States "forgot" many other mistakes and misunderstandings, as it launched new, particular forms of aggression that brought control over overseas territories not destined to become states in the Union. Historians perhaps have "forgotten" that William Walker, one of the most famous proslavery filibusters, was shot in Honduras less than two months before Lincoln's election, and that Grant proposed to purchase the Dominican Republic less than eight years later.[8] The history of the Civil War and Reconstruction has traditionally emphasized moments of sharp discontinuity: the firing on Fort Sumter, Emancipation, Lincoln's assassination, the end of Reconstruction. This volume helpfully points us instead to continuities, on a longer and broader scale.

These essays suggest that Reconstruction did not end in 1874, or 1898, or even with the New Deal. Rather, these authors situate the North's treatment of the post–Civil War South in the broad context of Americans' efforts to extend the "influence of our goodly institutions," as leaders of the A.M.E. Church declared. The high ideals and messy realities of attempting to reconstruct people, especially through missions of "uplift" backed by military might, set a long-term trajectory for U.S. internal regional and racial politics. At the same time, the First Reconstruction laid the foundation for U.S. exercise of power around the globe in the twentieth century and beyond. Its influence has not ended yet.

Notes

1. For a powerful meditation on connections between the South and the West, and broader discourses of race and nationalism, see Elliott West, "Reconstructing Race," *Western Historical Quarterly* 34, no. 1 (2003), 6–26. Roosevelt quoted in Walter L. Williams, "United States Indian Policy and the Debate over Philippine Annexation: Implications for the Origins of American Imperialism," *Journal of American History* 66, no. 4 (1980), 825.

2. For further reflections on the U.S. West and the legacies of the Civil War, see Heather Cox Richardson, *West from Appomattox: The Reconstruction of America after the Civil War* (New Haven, Conn.: Yale University Press, 2007), and the essays in *The World the Civil War Made*, ed. Gregory P. Downs and Kate Masur (Chapel Hill: University of North Carolina Press, 2015).

3. Albert Beveridge, Address, September 16, 1898, to an Indiana Republican Meeting, Indianapolis, Library of Congress, nationalhumanitiescenter.org/pds/gilded/empire/text5/beveridge.pdf.

4. The definitive version of Mark Twain's essay, which remained unpublished until after his death, is L. Terry Oggel, "Speaking Out about Race: 'The United States of Lyncherdom' Clemens Really Wrote," in *Prospects: An Annual of American Cultural Studies 25*, ed. Jack Salzman (New York: Cambridge University Press, 2000), 115–158.

5. For some suggestive links see Kristin Hoganson, *Consumers' Imperium: The Global Production of American Domesticity, 1865–1920* (Chapel Hill: University of North Carolina Press, 2007); Catherine Ceniza Choy, *Empire of Care: Nursing and Migration in Filipino American History* (Durham, N.C.: Duke University Press, 2003); Sarah Steinbock-Pratt, *Educating the Empire: American Teachers and Contested Colonization in the Philippines* (Cambridge: Cambridge University Press, 2019); as well as starting points in Karen Cox, *Dixie's Daughters: The United Daughters of the Confederacy and the Preservation of Confederate Culture* (Gainesville: University Press of Florida, 2003); and Carol Faulkner, *Women's Radical Reconstruction: The Freedmen's Aid Movement* (Philadelphia: University of Pennsylvania Press, 2004).

6. Barbara Fields, "Ideology and Race in American History," in *Region, Race, and Reconstruction*, ed. J. Morgan Kousser (New York: Oxford University Press, 1982), 164–166.

7. Thomas Bender, *A Nation among Nations: America's Place in World History* (New York: Hill and Wang, 2006), 179–180.

8. For explorations of this context from other angles see, for example, Thomas Schoonover, "Napoleon Is Coming! Maximilian Is Coming? The International History of the Civil War in the Caribbean Basin," in *The Union, the Confederacy, and the Atlantic Rim*, ed. Robert E. May (West Lafayette, Ind.: Purdue University Press, 1995), 106.

Contributors

Adrian Brettle is a lecturer and the associate director of the Political History and Leadership Program in the School of Historical, Philosophical, and Religious Studies at Arizona State University. He is the author of *Colossal Ambitions: Confederate Planning for a Post–Civil War World* (University of Virginia Press, 2020) and essays in *Civil War History* and the *Journal of Policy History*.

Christina C. Davidson is a postdoctoral research associate at the John C. Danforth Center on Religion and Politics at Washington University in St. Louis and an assistant professor of history at the University of Southern California. She is the author of essays in *Church History* and the *Journal of Africana Religions*, and she is revising her book manuscript, *Converting Hispaniola: Religious Race-Making in the Dominican Americas*.

Rebecca Edwards holds the Eloise Ellery Chair as a professor of history at Vassar College. She is the author of *Angels in the Machinery: Gender in American Party Politics from the Civil War to the Progressive Era* (Oxford University Press, 1997) and *New Spirits: Americans in the "Gilded Age," 1865–1905* (Oxford University Press, 2nd ed., 2010).

Mark Elliott is an associate professor of history at the University of North Carolina, Greensboro, and is the author of *Color-Blind Justice: Albion Tourgée and the Quest for Racial Equality from the Civil War to Plessy v. Ferguson* (Oxford University Press, 2006) and the co-editor of *Undaunted Radical: The Selected Writings and Speeches of Albion W. Tourgée* (Louisiana State University Press, 2010).

Andre M. Fleche is a professor of history at Castleton University and the author of *The Revolution of 1861: The American Civil War in the Age of Nationalist Conflict* (University of North Carolina Press, 2012). His writings have appeared in *Civil War History*, the *Journal of the Civil War Era*, and *A Companion to U.S. Foreign Relations: Colonial Era to the Present*.

Gregg French is an assistant professor at the University Windsor. His current book project, which is under advanced contract with the University of Nebraska Press, will explore U.S.-Spanish relations during the long nineteenth century and how these interactions influenced the creation of the U.S. colonial empire.

Lawrence B. Glickman is the Stephen and Evalyn Milman Professor of American Studies at Cornell University and the author and editor of five books, including *Free Enterprise: An American History* (Yale University Press, 2019) and *Buying Power: A History of Consumer Activism in America* (University of Chicago Press, 2009).

Reilly Ben Hatch is a PhD candidate in history and Russell J. and Dorothy S. Bilinski Fellow at the University of New Mexico, where his dissertation uses the Posey Wars of 1915 and 1923 to examine the relationships between Mormons and Indigenous communities in the context of federal assimilation efforts. He teaches history at Davis High School in Kaysville, Utah. He has published essays in the *Journal of the Southwest* and the *New Mexico Historical Review*.

David V. Holtby is the associate director and editor-in-chief, retired, of University of New Mexico Press. He is the author, most recently, of *Forty-Seventh Star: New Mexico's Struggle for Statehood* (University of Oklahoma Press, 2012) and *Lest We Forget: World War I and New Mexico* (University of Oklahoma Press, 2018).

Justin F. Jackson is an assistant professor of history at Bard College at Simon's Rock, where he is revising his book manuscript, *The Work of Empire: War, Occupation, and the Making of American Colonialisms in Cuba and the Philippines*. His writings have appeared in *Labor: Studies in Working-Class History*, the *International Labor and Working-Class History Review*, and *On Coerced Labor: Work and Compulsion after Slavery* (Brill, 2016).

DJ Polite is a visiting assistant professor of African American studies at the College of Charleston. He earned his PhD in history from the University of South Carolina, where he completed his dissertation, "Democracy, Citizenship, and Puerto Rican Autonomy under the U.S. Jim Crow Empire." His writings have appeared in the *Washington Post*, *Proceedings of the South Carolina Historical Association*, *Black Perspectives*, and *Activist History Review*, among others.

David Prior is an associate professor of history at the University of New Mexico. He is the author of *Between Freedom and Progress: The Lost World of Reconstruction Politics* (Louisiana State University Press, 2019) and the editor of *Reconstruction in a Globalizing World* (Fordham University Press, 2018).

Brian Shott is a historian of the nineteenth-century United States and the author of *Mediating America: Black and Irish Press and the Struggle for Citizenship, 1870–1914* (Temple University Press, 2019) and "Forty Acres and a Carabao: T. Thomas Fortune, Newspapers, and the Pacific's Unstable Color Lines, 1902–03," in the *Journal of the Gilded Age and Progressive Era*.

Index

Abbott, Lyman, 15, 161, 168–69, 172, 174–75, 180–82, 318; and *The Outlook*, 168, 172, 177–78, 181; and *The Results of Emancipation in the United States*, 168–69; and *The Rights of Man* (1902), 181

abolition and emancipation, 1, 5, 6, 16, 21n22, 28–30, 37, 40, 44, 45; and anti-imperialism, 17n1; as benefiting Southern whites, 109; and Britain, 110; and Brazil, 34; in the Caribbean, 111; and Christian missions, 14; in Cuba, 13, 27, 33, 37, 38, 44, 45, 47, 81, 303; and economic conditions, 4, 293; reactions to U.S. abolition abroad, 28–29, 44, 109; southern white reactions to, 9, 11, 116; in the United States, 12, 13, 27, 105, 107, 108, 110, 111, 116, 142, 155, 165, 167, 175, 218, 244, 289, 293–94, 302–3; and U.S. hegemony, 9–10, 13, 164, 317; throughout western hemisphere, 86. *See also* abolitionists; *and individual people, laws, and societies*

abolitionists, 3–4, 30, 87, 88, 137, 142, 155, 167, 172, 206, 278, 297, 318, 319, 322: *See also* Cavada, Federico Fernández; Howe, Julia Ward; Howe, Samuel Gridley; Redpath, James; *and other individuals*

Academy of Music in Brooklyn, 45

Adams, John Quincy, 83

Afghanistan, 311

Africa and Africans: 5, 14, 31, 40, 87, 289, 318; Ashantee and Dahomey, 146; and civilizing missions to, 55–56, 65, 70, 72, 78n106; sub-Saharan, 146. *See also* African Diaspora; *and individual countries and regions*

African Americans: 1, 5, 8, 12, 319; and Afro-Caribbeans, 87, 88; and Afro-Cubans, 3; and Afro-diasporic connections, 55, 58–60, 62, 64, 65, 71–72, 73n16; as Buffalo soldiers, 222–23; as civilizing missionaries, 55, 58, 70, 73n13; and community safety, 218; disenfranchisement of, 137, 142, 144, 215, 219–20, 226, 229, 231, 234, 300; economic aspirations of, 324; equality and political participation of, 1, 2, 6, 7, 15, 27–28, 45, 71, 81, 82, 85, 86, 91, 93, 114, 137–38, 143–44, 166, 200, 215–19, 294, 272, 276, 288, 296, 298, 321, 322; and GAR, 203–4; and gradual emancipation, 142–44; graphic representation of, 17, 145, 149, 268, 275, 276, 280, 281; and Hawaii, 276; as immigrants, 54–78, 86, 141; and Irish peasantry, 151–52, 156; on lynching, 21; and military service, 35, 222–23, 258, 267, 275, 279, 288, 293–94, 296; nationalism from, 56; and New Deal subordination, 300; and Northerners, 13; oppression of, 147–48, 150, 156, 220; and Pacific railroad convention, 116; racial violence against, 214–22, 224–34; and racist interpretations of Reconstruction, 8; and relations with Filipinos, 10, 275, 279–80, 286n59; and James Redpath, 137–45, 147–53; as refugees, 226–27, 233; as Republicans, 2; self-determination of, 55, 58, 60; and sharecropping, 300, 305; in Venezuela, 34; and views of Dominican Republic, 72n4; and views of Haiti, 72n4; and wage contracts, 294, 297; in War of 1898, 222–23. *See also* African diaspora; African Methodist

African Americans (*continued*)
Episcopal (AME) Church; Baker, Frazier; DuBois, W. E. B.; Freedpeople; *and other individuals*
African diaspora, 14, 55, 58, 75n39, 76n62, 80, 82, 84, 87, 88, 90, 289, 302, 318. See also African Methodist Episcopal (AME) Church; Afro-Cubans; Dominican Republic; Haiti
African Methodist Episcopal (AME) Church: 318; African missions of, 14, 55–57, 65–67, 70, 72; and AME Discipline, 78n101; and AME Publishing Department, 68; and Bermuda Annual Conference, 71; and Bethel congregation, 60–61; and Dominican Republic, 55–71; as expansionists, 54–57, 64, 68, 70–72, 322, 325; finances of, 54–55, 56, 57, 58, 60, 65, 66–67, 68–70, 78n106; Freedpeople in, 56, 63, 70; and General Conferences, 57, 62, 63, 67, 70, 74n17; and Haiti (nation), 14, 55–61, 63–66, 68–71; and "Hayti" (Hispaniola), 54, 60, 67; history of, 54–58, 70; and Parent Home and Foreign Missionary Society, 66; and racial "uplift," 55, 58–60, 64; and U.S. Empire, 55–56; and U.S. South, 54, 57; and Women's Home and Foreign Missionary Society, 70. See also *Christian Recorder*; *individual members and other Methodist organizations*
Afro-Caribbeans, 72
Afro-Cubans, 3, 10, 301
Agassiz, Louis, 166
Agromonte, Ignacio, 38–39
Aguinaldo, Emilio, 179, 268, 274, 278, 279
Alabama, 232, 287, 288
Alabama Claims, 46–47, 53n143, 85, 318
Alaska, 2, 268
Alexander, Thomas, 240
Algeria, 169
Allen, Richard, 56
Allen, Woody, 136

Amazon, the, 5
Ambler, Jacob A., 102n80
American Baptist Church, 61
American Colonization Society, 57, 86
American Freedmen's Union Commission, 168
American Historical Association, 270
American Red Cross, 170–74, 180
American Revolution: 14, 82–83, 241, 251, 254; and Declaration of Independence, 242, 243
American Progress (John Gast), 264
American Samaná Bay Company, 60, 64, 75nn39,45
American Women's Aid Society for the Relief of Cuban Women and Children, 45
Anderson, Joseph R., 114, 116, 125
Anglo-Saxons, idea of, 3, 34, 87, 110, 130n27, 143, 144, 186n39, 221, 225, 320, 321. See also evolution, the idea of; racism; white supremacy
Apache, 287, 318
Apostle Philip, 64
Appleman Williams, William, 9
Appomattox, 33, 194
Archer, Edward, 125
Archer, Robert, 125
Arizona, 123, 268, 287, 318, 320
Arkansas, 295; Arkadelphia, 71
Armenia, 4, 15, 161, 167–69, 171–73, 320, 322
Armstrong, Samuel C., 180, 275–76
Arrears Act, 193
Asia, 123, 196, 289, 311
Astwood, Henry C. C.: 67–69, 77n84, 78n114; and *Child's Reporter*, 68
Atkinson, Fred, 274–75
Atlanta, 36
Atlantic, the, 2, 29, 56, 109, 121
Austrian Empire, 110, 310–11

Babcock, Orville E., 87
Báez, Buenaventura, 87

INDEX 331

Baker, Cora, 214
Baker, Frazier, 16, 321, 322; lynching of, 214–21, 224–27, 229–31, 233
Baker, Lavinia, 214
Baker, Lincoln, 214
Baker, Millie, 214
Baker, Rosa, 214
Baker, Sarah, 214
Banks, Nathaniel P., 90, 102n80, 294
Barrows, David, 275
Barton, Clara, 15, 323; and American Red Cross, 161, 164, 170–74, 180; and National Armenian Relief Committee, 171
Bate, William, 224–25
Battle of Bull Run (first), 244
Bellamy, Francis, 270
Beale, Howard K., 8
Beard, Charles, 8
Beard, Mary, 8
Beauregard, Pierre Gustave Toutant, 34, 122
Bedford Forrest, Nathan, 13–14
Beecher Stowe, Harriet, 86–87
Belford Magazine, 153
Bellows, Henry, 170
Bender, Thomas, 325
Berlin, 6
Bermuda, 67
Beveridge, Albert, 15, 16, 191–92, 195–206, 212n101, 258, 320, 322; and "The March of the Flag," 195, 197, 199–200, 320
Bible, the: references to, 59, 64, 76n62, 174, 178, 242, 262n79
Billings, Josh, 141
Bigler, David, 240
Bjarnson, Stephen, 256
Blaine, James G., 199
Blair, Austin, 102n80
Blair, Francis P., Sr., 124
Blight, David, 11, 139
Bowers, Claude G.: and *Beveridge and the Progressive Era* (1929), 206; and *The Tragic Era: The Revolution after Lincoln*, 206

Boyer, Jean-Pierre, 57
Braeman, John, 205, 213n108
Branch, Thomas, 114–15
Brazil: Confederates in, 33; exports from, 86; slavery in, 27, 33–34
Brettle, Adrian, 14, 303, 320–21
British Empire, 6, 15, 31, 33, 46–47, 53n143, 66, 80, 85, 86, 90, 109–11, 119, 124–27, 196, 267, 268, 307, 318, 320, 321; Berwick-on-Tweed, 140; and colonialism, 144, 152, 156; and decentralization, 119; on Egypt, 146–47; and Ireland, 144–48, 152–53; and landlordism, 140, 151–3, 156; and Pax Britannica, 126; and Queen Victoria and Duke of Edinburgh, 145; Scotland, 140. *See also* racism: in British Empire
British Guiana, 67
British Methodist Episcopal Church, 67
British Wesleyan Missionary Society, 61–62
Brooke, John, 304–6, 308, 319
Brown, John, 136, 140–41
Brown, Morris, 61
Bryan, Joseph, 110
Bryan, William Jennings, 203
Buchanan, James, 84, 98n39, 243
Bull, John, 147
Bullard, Robert Lee, 287–88, 293, 300
Burgess, John W., 7
Burlingame, Anson, 276, 317, 320, 321
Butler, Benjamin, 99n47, 294
Butler Simkins, Francis, 8, 23n38
Byrd, Brandon R., 56, 63, 73n13

Cain, Richard H., 67
Calhoun, John C., 83, 124
California, 151: San Diego, 123, 268, 276, 280, 281; San Francisco, 152, 180
Call, Willard, 250, 252, 256–57, 323
Camagüey (Cuba), 37, 38, 40
Canada, 2, 119, 124, 127, 193, 254, 255, 318; Ontario, 165
Cannon, George Q., 245, 247, 256

Caribbean and Caribbean Basin: 15, 55, 56, 61, 67, 70, 110, 111, 196, 317–18; and African Methodist Episcopal Church, 54–78; and Anglophone Caribbean, 61; British imperialism and hegemony in, 80, 85, 110–11; French imperialism in, 110; slavery in, 31, 33; Spanish imperialism in, 1, 79–104; U.S. intervention and influence in, 3, 27–28, 71–72, 79–104, 221, 223–24, 230, 272, 273, 289, 319. *See also individual colonies, countries, and empires*

carpetbaggers, 16, 144, 175, 176, 223–24, 307, 322

Carter, Dan, 106–7

Carvajal, José de, 91

Casserly, Eugene, 101n65

Castelar, Emilio, 91

Catholicism, 31, 42, 46, 58, 59, 61–62, 152

Cavada, Adolfo, 31, 42, 44

Cavada, Emilio, 43

Cavada, Federico Fernández, 162; background on, 42; execution of, 44; and Ten Years' War, 13, 27–32, 42–44, 46, 323–24

Centennial Exhibition, 92–93

Céspedes, Carlos Manuel de, 27, 32, 37–39

Chamberlain, Joseph, 110, 119

Chamberlin, Frederick: and *The Blow from Behind, or Some Features of the Anti-Imperial Movement* (1903), 182

Chattanooga, 36

Chief Joseph, 178

Childs, Matt, 29

Chile, 197

China, 5, 8, 107, 119, 127, 202, 270, 317, 321

Chinese Exclusion Act (1882), 13, 270, 276–77

Chinese immigrants: as contract laborers in Cuba, 31, 37; exclusion of, in United States, 13, 17, 145, 151, 157, 270, 276–77, 317–18, 321; representations of, 268, 276, 277, 280, 281; and Southeast Asia, 277; in Ten Years' War, 37, 39, 40

Christians and Christianity, 2, 13, 55, 59, 65, 68, 142, 166–70, 172, 178–79, 242, 276, 318, 321, 322. *See also* African Methodist Episcopal (AME) Church; Bible, the; Catholicism; Methodists and Methodism; Mormons; Protestants

Christian Recorder, 54–55, 57, 58, 59, 62, 63, 64, 66, 68, 137, 147, 151

Cienfuegos (Cuba), 31

Cinco Villas (Cuba), 42

Cisneros, Evangelina, 173

citizenship. *See* equality

civilization and barbarism: and African Methodist Episcopal Church, 55–56, 59, 70; and anti-imperialism, 80, 82, 201, 203, 321; and China, 321; and civilized world, 166, 171, 173; and Cuba, 43–44, 301; and democracy, 166, 181, 225; and England, 145–47; and Hawaiian Islands, 270, 276; ideas of, 4, 105, 196; and labor, 324; and modernity, 146, 275; and morality, 167; and Mormons, 244; and Philippines, 273, 274; and South, 105, 164, 203, 228–29; and violence, 40, 164, 171, 217, 228; and U.S. influence abroad, 171, 174, 181–82, 195–96, 228, 270, 271, 277, 318, 321; and U.S. West, 264, 319. *See also* Dalrymple, Louis: and "School Begins"; education; racism

Civil Rights Act of 1875, 88, 287

Civil War, 20n13, 252, 322; and civilian atrocities, 20n13; Confederate planners during, 127; and Confederate tactics, 39, 41; and continuities, 325; and Cuba, 27–53; W. E. B. Du Bois on, 6; and empire, 12, 31, 272, 317; and European powers, 31, 79, 82, 85; expansion during, 85, 105; and humanitarianism, 15, 161–62, 169–70; legacies and lessons of, 4, 15, 27–29, 40, 43, 54, 161, 205–6, 216, 244, 325; memory and interpretations of, 46, 81, 107, 109, 138, 163, 205, 215–16, 272; and Mormons, 244; psychological impact of, 207n11; and slavery, 12, 13,

27, 29, 47, 57, 70, 164, 170, 200; and state centralization, 85, 120, 289–90, 322; and veteran disabilities, 193. *See also* abolition and emancipation; Cleveland, Grover; Confederacy, the, and Confederates; Grant, Ulysses S.; Redpath, James; sectionalism and reconciliation; slavery; Union, the; Union veterans; United States military; *and other events and individuals*
Cleveland, Grover, 93, 194–95
Cody, William F. (Buffalo Bill), 270–71
Cold War, 8, 311
Colfax, Schuyler, 113–14
Colorado: Denver, 153
Columbus, Christopher, 77n84, 83, 93, 270
Commonwealth, 153–54
Communism, 311
Confederacy, the, and Confederates, 12, 16, 33, 81, 136, 137, 139, 154–57, 193, 194, 229, 230, 287, 292, 293, 294, 298, 300, 317; agriculture, 303; and American identity, 107, 118; and colonization, 109; and commerce, 107–8, 118–19, 121, 126–27; conception of history, 154; and Confederate War Department, 111; and Cuba, 33, 34–42, 46; and decentralized government, 106, 120, 124–27; defeat of, 27, 30, 106, 108–9, 115, 268, 271; economic determinism of, 111; and emancipation, 105, 107–9, 116; émigrés, 109, 111; and expansionism, 105–6, 107–8, 110–11, 118–19, 120, 123, 124–27, 320; glorification of, 194, 200; ideology of, 107; and mutual expansion, 118; nationalism, 107; navy of, 85; and Northwestern Confederacy, 116; patriotism of, 118; physical destruction in, 107, 111; political rights of, 112–15, 117; and James Redpath, 136–60; and secession and secessionists, 12, 31, 34, 108, 136–37, 139, 154, 204, 294; and Ten Years' War, 35, 39–40. *See also* Jordan, Thomas; Redpath, James; *and other individuals and states*
Confiscation Acts, 293
Congress, 59, 88, 90
Constitution, the, 242, 243–44, 245, 272, 289. *See also* Reconstruction: and constitutional amendments; *and individual amendments*
Cooper Institute, 32
Cooper, William, 136
Copperheads, 116, 287
Costa Rica, 180
Cowley, Matthias, 246
Cox Richardson, Heather, 4, 11, 289
Coxey, Jacob D., 197
Cramer, Alexander J., 94n1
Crete and Cretan independence, 166, 173–74
Cuba, 162–64, 172–80, 183; and Army of Cuban Pacification, 287, 310; and Army of Liberation, 301, 303, 309; and Confederate cause, 39; creole elites in, 89, 296, 308; democratic republic of, 183; and desire to annex, 33, 35, 80, 84–85, 89, 91, 93, 196, 255; economic policy in, 303–8; economy of, 28, 31, 33, 43, 84, 292, 301–8; *long-durée* history of, 290; Matanzas, 304; Oriente, 301–2, 304, 306; patriotism in, 43; in political cartoon, 17, 264; race relations in, 28, 33, 45, 278–79; and race relations in U.S., 34; and Revolution of 1895, 3, 81, 93, 173, 290; and Rural Guard, 302; Santa Clara, 304, 306; and self-rule, 322; and slave rebellions, 84, 85; slavery in, 27–53; and Spanish Empire, 79–104, 267, 279; Spanish loyalists in, 36, 43, 45; U.S. occupations of, 3, 17, 47, 81, 84, 90, 93, 195, 204, 215, 217, 221–25, 230, 252, 287–93, 296–97, 300–311, 323; and U.S. Reconstruction, 28, 79–104. *See also* Cavada, Federico Fernández; Jordan, Thomas; Spanish-American War; Spanish Empire; Ten Years' War

Cuban Junta, 35, 43, 301
Cullen Bryant, William, 32
Cushing, Caleb, 82–83, 92, 99n47

Dalrymple, Louis: life of 264, 266; and "School Begins," 16–17, 264–65, 268–69, 270, 271–72, 273–75, 276, 277, 280, 282
Dana, Charles A., 32, 34
Daniel, John W., 110–11
Danish West Indies, 2
Daughters of the American Revolution, 323
David, Oliver Wilson, 44
Davidson, Christina C., 13–14, 147, 224, 308, 318
Davis, Jefferson, 15, 35, 109, 118, 136–39, 142, 152–57, 320; and 1865 proposals, 124
Davis, Varina, 137, 153
Day, William R., 94
De Bow, James D. B., 110–13; and *De Bow's Review*, 110–11, 114, 116
De Jarnette, Daniel C., 115
democracy, 6, 10, 11, 28, 91
Democrats, 2, 194, 203, 206; conservative alliances with, 15; and Cuban independence, 99n49; factionalism among, 108; and imperialism, 200, 202, 205, 211n92; and Mormons, 244; Northern, 2, 28; and race, 85, 201–2, 224, 280, 300, 305, 320; and Reconstruction, 87, 108, 114, 115, 118, 120, 122, 144, 280, 281, 299–300, 305, 310; and James Redpath, 144; and slavery in Cuba, 33; Southern, 105, 108, 114–15, 117–18, 122, 193, 200–1, 211n92, 226, 231; and state centralization, 120, 197, 298, 299. See also Bryan, William Jennings; Hunter, Robert M. T.; Tillman, Benjamin Ryan; *and other individuals*
Dependent and Disability Pension Act, 194
Deseret News, 248, 249, 256, 261n35
Desvernine, Pablo, 306

Dewey, George, 267
Dickerson, Dennis C., 56
Dickinson, Anna, 141
Dilke, Charles, 109–10, 321; and *Greater Britain* (1868), 110
diplomacy and international law, 32, 39, 40, 45, 46, 53n143, 55, 79, 89, 90, 91, 141, 171, 172, 223. See also *Alabama* Claims; Monroe Doctrine; *Virginius* Affair; *and individual conflicts and treaties*
Dispatch, 217
Dominican Republic, 2, 14, 28, 310; civilization missions in, 55, 58–78; proposed U.S. annexation of, 58–60, 75n39, 80, 84–91, 94, 224, 269, 318, 323; and Spain, 31, 85, 86; and trade with U.S. 86; and U.S. race relations, 88. See also African Methodist Episcopal (AME) Church; Haiti and "Hayti"; Hispaniola; Santo Domingo (city)
Dorce, Solomon G., 68–69, 71, 78n98
Douglass, Frederick, 73n16, 136, 138, 141, 172,
Downs, Gregory P., 29, 106, 289; and *After Appomattox*, 291
Drum, R. C., 194
Du Bois, W. E. B.: and *Black Reconstruction in America* (1935), 5–9, 12, 21n22, 21n25, 22n28, 23n46, 288; on capitalism, 5–6, 324; on colonial enslavement, 12; on empire and imperialism, 5–6; on Reconstruction, 5; on Southern freedpeople, 21n22
Dudziak, Mary, 291

Echols, John, 114
economic conditions and policies: and capital shortages, 106, 111, 112, 116, 119, 303, 305, 306–7, 307–8; and class, 111; and debt peonage, 2, 140; and Dominican Republic annexation, 59; idea of overproduction, 9, 126–27; industrial capitalism, 2–3, 7, 9, 11, 12, 17, 26n63, 60; and internal improvements, 105,

107, 116, 119, 121–23, 124, 127, 197; and popular culture, 266; and racism, 3, 79, 324; and recessions/depressions, 3, 15, 79, 92–93, 108, 111, 112–13, 119–20, 124, 125, 196–98, 299; and South, 4, 7, 105–6, 109, 111–13, 115–16, 119–22, 123; and taxes, 33, 89, 112, 200, 300, 305; and tariffs and trade, 106, 107–8, 116, 119, 124, 125, 126–27, 191–93, 195, 305, 308. *See also* Du Bois, W. E. B.; transcontinental railroads; Virginia and Virginians: economic conditions in

Edison, Thomas, 136
Edmunds Act, 245, 251
Edmunds-Tucker Act, 245, 251
education, 2, 142, 143, 156, 174, 179–81, 288, 297; and AME Missions, 55, 58, 59, 66; and German Empire, 106; and Native Americans, 272, 319; and Progressives, 272, 274; and U.S. colonies, 163, 175, 179–80, 181, 183, 272, 274–75, 319; and U.S. imperialism, 176, 264, 268, 270–71, 273–76, 277, 282, 318; and U.S. South, 2, 6, 26n62, 141, 142, 143, 156, 162, 170, 175, 179–80, 272, 276, 297. *See also* Armstrong, Samuel C.; Dalrymple, Louis: and "School Begins"; Redpath, James; Washington, Booker T.
Edwards, Rebecca, 17
Egypt, 15, 145–47, 157, 320; Alexandria, 146
Ellerbe, William, 217, 223
Elliott, Mark, 15, 60, 75n42, 142, 318–19
Ellis, William, 12
Emancipation Proclamation, 27, 293
empire and imperialism: and colonialism, 8, 31; Confederate imperialism, 14; definitions of, 1, 4, 7, 18n2, 120; as democracy, 120–21; W. E. B. Du Bois on, 5–7; free trade, 105–7, 110, 116, 120, 127; and Great Powers, 126; and Imperial Federation League, 119; and the Union, 15; variants of, 322–23. *See also* Democratics: and imperialism; Du Bois, W. E. B.: on empire and imperialism; Europe: and imperialism; Grand Army of the Republic; racism; Republicans: and free trade imperialism; *and specific colonies and empires*

Enforcement Acts and Bills, 79, 85, 287, 299
English (language), 62, 69
Episcopal Church, 61
equality: and citizenship, 3, 7, 15, 28, 29, 175, 177, 179, 200, 219–20, 223, 231, 233–34, 268, 276, 282, 289, 298; and civil rights and liberty, 1–2, 5, 8, 9, 12, 14, 28, 47, 81, 82, 115, 142, 144, 151, 155, 165, 167–68, 176, 204, 211n77, 219, 273, 276, 291, 293–300; and colonies, 200, 202, 224, 282; in Cuba, 32, 37, 38–39, 47, 51n69, 289; economic, 300; Haiti and Dominican Republic as symbols of, 60; and marriage, 31, 42; and Mormons, 258; social, 28, 37, 38; transatlantic ideas of, 39. *See also* racism; Reconstruction; Redpath, James; *and other individual people and legislative acts*
Europe: and Geneva Accords of 1864, 170; and imperialism, 5–6, 10, 29, 56, 80, 86, 89, 90, 92, 107, 109, 147, 167, 225, 288, 304, 310–11; and revolutions of 1848, 38–39, 289; and U.S. South, 109, 116, 123. *See also individual empires, nations, and people*
Evans, Augusta Jane: and *St. Elmo*, 106, 116
evolution, idea of, 141–42, 143, 144, 146, 168, 181, 186n39, 269–70. *See also* racism: and science/evolution
Ewing, Finis, 242
expansionism, 3, 10, 14, 33, 56, 58, 60, 65, 70–72, 80, 81, 84, 87, 88, 90; and American exceptionalism, 181, 195, 240, 280; as providential, 195–96; and U.S. domestic racial violence, 215–18, 220–24, 226, 228–34. *See also* African Methodist Episcopal (AME) Church; Manifest Destiny; Monroe Doctrine; Reconstruction; *and other events and individuals*

Faber, Christine, 148
Far East, 195–96
Far Left, 8–9
Farnsworth, John F., 46
Fenians, 2
Ferrer, Ada, 28
Fields, Barbara J., 324
Fifteenth Amendment, 1–2, 126, 200–1, 276, 285n50, 298–99, 318
filibusters, 29, 33, 35, 46, 47, 89, 90. *See also* Cavada, Federico Fernández; Jordan, Thomas; López, Narciso; *Virginius* Affair; Walker, William
Filipinos, 163, 176, 178–80, 182, 201–2, 288; racial categorization of, 257–58, 277–78; in U.S., 10, 275. *See also* Philippines, the
Filipino Students' Magazine, 275
Fish, Hamilton, 14, 28, 32, 46, 80, 82, 84–92, 94, 99n47, 319; background of, 86; imperial and racist views of, 80–82, 84–87
Fleche, Andre, 13, 73n12, 86, 162, 196, 317
Flegler, Samuel F., 66
Florida: Spanish, 83, 291; Tampa "riot," 222
Foner, Eric, 5, 13, 244
Forrest, Nathan Bedford, 13, 35, 36, 39
Forsyth, John, 84
Fort Pillow Massacre, 35
Fort Sumter, 218, 227
Fortune, T. Thomas, 279
Fourteen Points, 310
Fourteenth Amendment, 1–2, 28, 126, 200–1, 276, 285n50, 287, 298–99, 318
Fox, Horatio, 32
Freedmen's Aid Society, 162, 168
Freedmen's Bureau, 161–62, 168–69, 234, 296–98, 302–3, 305; and Freedmen's Bureau Bill, 162
Freedmen's Inquiry Commission, 165
freedpeople, 166–67, 200, 288, 291, 293–94, 301, 305, 308; in African Methodist Episcopal Church, 56, 63, 65, 70; in Cuba, 29; and Democrats, 114; in Dominican Republic, 86; W. E. B. DuBois on, 5–7, 21n22; and Ku Klux Klan, 33; in Liberia, 57; and James Redpath, 139; in Ten Years' War, 37, 39, 41; and U.S. Army, 294–300. *See also* African Americans
French (language), 69, 78n98
French Empire, 2, 6, 60, 63, 86, 106, 196, 297; and Franco-Prussian War, 170; and Napoleon III, 110; Napoleonic Wars, 291; Revolutionary War, 291; Versailles, 310
French, Gregg, 14, 28, 53n143, 58, 196, 197, 224, 308, 317, 319
Fry, Joseph, 107

Gannon, Barbara, 13, 204
García, Calixto, 93
Garrison, William Lloyd, 88
Gast, John, 264; and *American Progress*, 264, 265
gender, 151, 163, 170, 323; and abolition, 3; and analysis of empire, 19n10; and Confederacy, 35; and manhood and masculinity, 3–4, 59, 63, 118, 140, 142, 198, 213n114, 232, 309; and nationalism, 163, 164; and racism, 2, 3–4, 278–79, 320; and U.S. chauvinism, 55; and violence, 167; and womanhood and femininity, 3–4, 164, 250, 323; and women's rights and suffrage, 136, 139, 164, 166, 175, 181, 192
George, Henry, 136, 139
Georgia, 141, 296–97, 304–5; Atlanta, 213n111, 227; Savannah, 148
German Empire, 106
Germany, 6, 106, 152, 196, 307, 310, 311
Gerstle, Gary, 282
Gettysburg, 213n109
Ghana, 8
Gilded Age, 4, 12, 16, 199, 201, 274, 305
Glickman, Lawrence, 15, 181, 320
globalization: and trade, 126
Glymph, Thavolia, 148
Godkin, E. L., 169, 175–76

Gómez, José Miguel, 306
Gómez, Máximo, 307
Goode, G. Brown, 270
Goodwin, C. C., 253
Gordon, Ian, 266
Gordon, Sarah Barringer, 244
Gorham, George C., 280
Grand Army of the Republic (GAR), 15–16, 191–213, 320; and *National Tribune*, 194, 210n66; and Won Cause, 206
Grant, Susan-Mary, 269, 282
Grant, Ulysses S., 14, 27, 32, 45–47, 53n143, 80, 81, 84, 85, 92, 94, 114–15, 152, 169, 192, 196, 299; administration of, 44, 46–47, 80, 81, 85, 87, 169, 172; and Dominican annexation, 80, 84–91, 94, 166, 172, 177–78, 196, 317, 318, 319, 325; foreign policy of, 82, 85–86, 89; and "no transfer" resolution of 1811, 81–82; and racial tensions, 82, 86–88, 92, 94. *See also* Cuba; Dominican Republic; Fish, Hamilton
Granville, Jonathas, 57
Great Depression, the, 5–8
Great Plains, the, 297
Greece, 173, 274, 320; Greek Revolution, 165, 167
Greeley, Horace, 117, 140
Green, Duff, 112
Gross, Elijah R., 67, 69
Guáimaro (Cuba), 33, 37, 38
Guam, 200, 255, 267, 290

Hahn, Steven, 11, 289–90
Haiti and "Hayti," 4, 54–78, 308, 310, 317; as Black "Promised Land," 55; and Haitian Episcopal Church, 76n71; and Haitian Revolution, 55, 56; racist views of, 84, 92, 308, 319–20; and sovereignty, 75n39; as a symbol, 73n13; usage of terms, 72n4. *See also* African Methodist Episcopal (AME) Church; French Empire; Port-au-Prince; Spanish Empire

Hamblin, Hannibal, 318
Hamburg Massacre (S.C.), 142, 215, 229, 232
Hamid II (Sultan), and Hamidian massacres, 167, 172
Hamilton, John, 61
Hampton Institute, 275–76
Hansen, Klaus, 240
Harlan, James, 101n65
Harlan, John Marshals, 276
Harper's Weekly, 239, 253, 258, 266
Harrison, Benjamin, 194
Hatch, Reilly Ben, 16, 322–23
Havana (Cuba), 36, 39, 43, 84, 173–74, 215, 217, 267, 290, 304–6, 309
Hawaiian Islands, 1, 3, 17, 127, 177, 221, 223–25, 231–32, 252, 255, 264, 267, 269, 271, 272, 275–76, 277, 280–81, 290, 322
Hayes, Rutherford B., 300
Hays, John, and Open Door of 1899, 119
Hazard, Samuel, 75n47
Heath, Andrew, 120
Hesseltine, William, 8
Hilfrich, Fabian, 272
Hispaniola, 14, 55–60, 62, 64, 66–72. *See also* African Methodist Episcopal (AME) Church; Dominican Republic; Haiti and "Hayti"
Hobsbawm, Eric, 26n63
Hoetink, Harmannus, 61
Hofstadter, Richard, 197, 200
Holguín (Cuba), 36, 37
Holly, James Theodore, 76n71
Holtby, David, 15–16, 212n101, 258, 320
Hope Franklin, John, 8
Hotze, Henry, 124
House Foreign Affairs Committee, 90, 102n80
Howard, Guy, 182–83
Howard, Oliver O., 15, 161–64, 168, 177–82, 297, 318, 319; and *Fighting for Humanity*, 164
Howard University, 64

Howe, Julia Ward, 15, 60, 161, 164–68, 170, 173, 175, 180–81 320, 321, 323; and "Battle Hymn of the Republic, 164–65, 167, 180–81
Howe, Samuel Gridley, 60, 161, 164–66, 172, 320; and Boston Emancipation League, 165
Huntington, Collis Potter, 122
humanitarian nationalism, 161–62, 164, 168–70, 178, 183
humanitarianism, 1, 4, 11, 15, 47, 60, 110, 142, 144, 162–64, 167–74, 177–80, 183, 292, 296, 301–7, 318–19, 320; and humanitarian expansionism, 179
Humphreys, Andrew A., 31
Hunter, Robert M. T., 14, 117–18, 120–21, 123, 125–27; and Morrill Tariff, 125; and race, 120–21; and "Slave Power," 117
Hurst, John, 71, 78n115
Hyde, Orson, 241–42, 254–55

Illinois, 46, 144, 193; Decatur, 192
immigration, 3, 319, 320
India, 5, 15, 145–47, 161
Indian Wars of the 1870s, 182
Indiana, 87, 193–95, 197–99; Indianapolis, 197–98; and Indianapolis Literary Club, 196; and Soldiers and Sailors Memorial, 209n56
Industrial revolution, 126
Insular Cases (1901), 179–80
Iowa, 171, 199
Iraq, 311
Ireland and Irish, 15, 140, 144–48, 150–52, 155–57, 320; and Irish Home Rule, 147; nationalism, 144; as victims of imperialism, 146
Irish Americans: and race, 140, 145, 152, 155
Irish immigrants, 276
Irving, Washington, 84
Irwin, Julia, 163
Islam and Muslims, 169, 172, 287–88
Italy, 6, 197, 289; and Italian immigration, 195

Jackson, Andrew, 83
Jackson, Justin, 17, 319, 322
Jackson, Stonewall, 121
Janney, Caroline, 11, 155, 205
Japan, 180, 202, 270, 311
Jefferson, Thomas, 275, 320
Jennings, Frank, 253
Jew and Hebrew, 140, 143, 148
Jim Crow: 2, 5, 10, 16, 81, 93, 137, 138, 140, 145, 148, 153, 179, 181, 200, 201, 227, 232, 234, 289, 300, 302; and U.S. colonialism, 215–16, 220, 229, 233, 272–73, 321–22. *See also* racism
Johnson, Andrew, 1, 28, 85, 111–12, 170, 295–98, 302; and Amnesty Proclamation of 1865, 111; and civil rights bill, 298
Jordan, Thomas, 13–14, 27–28, 33–43, 45–46; in Cuba, 34–42; on emancipation, 28; and interracial army in Cuba, 35–42; and the Lost Cause, 35, 50n40, 109; racist views of 38, 40–41, 86, 323–24; on slavery and empire, 34, 50n40; and *The South: Its Products, Commerce, and Resources*, 34
Journal of the Military Service Institution, 287
Judd, Norman Buel, 102n80
Jun, Helen H., 282
Jung, Moon-Ho, 5

Kansas, 6, 136, 144, 197
Kant, Immanuel, 166
Katipunan, 287
Kean, Robert Garlick Hill, 111
Kearney, Denis, 151
Kemper, James L., 117–18, 122
Kentucky, 57
Keppler, Joseph, 266
Keynesian, 304
Kimball, J. Golden, 251
Kipling, Rudyard, 271; and "White Man's Burden," 231
Korea, 311

Kramer, Paul, 269, 273, 277
Ku Klux Klan, 33, 35, 169, 215, 287
Kurashige, Lon, 277

Lacosta, Perfecto, 306
Lake City (SC), 16
Lamar, Lucius Q. C., 116, 118–20, 123; and Gold Standard, 119
Langsdale, George J., 199
Langsdale, Katherine, 199
Langston, John Mercer, 76n71
Langtry, Lily, 148
Lasch, Christopher, 269
Las Villas (Cuba), 43
Lathrop, Abial, 225
Latin America: Confederates in, 33–34; U.S. interventionism in, 3, 30, 32, 310. *See also* Spanish Empire; United States, the; *and individual colonies and countries*
Lee, Robert E., 35, 108, 111, 114, 152
Levering Lewis, David, 8
Letcher, John, 14, 112–14, 116–17, 121–22
Liberia, 57, 66, 70
Libertos, 41
Lincoln, Abraham, 1, 31, 32, 87, 112, 120, 124, 153, 165, 176, 192, 198–99, 204–6, 293, 295, 313n13, 318, 325; administration of, 165, 294; and Cuba, 30; and Dominican Republic, 31; and "ten percent plan," 295
Lincoln University, 64
Literary Digest, 228
Little, Lawrence, 55
Liverpool (UK), 109
Locke, David R., 141
Logan, John A., 192–93, 195, 199
London (UK), 6, 34, 124
López, Narciso, 33
Lost Cause, the, 35, 50n40, 107, 109, 136, 139, 192, 201, 203–6, 213n109, 287
Louisiana, 83, 276, 289, 293–94, 297, 305; French, 291; New Orleans, 294
Love, Eric T.L., 269, 271, 280

Lowell, James Russell, 145
Lyman, Francis M., 246
lynching, 203, 214–21, 224–26, 228–31, 233
Lyons, James, 114

Maceo, Antonio, 44
Macy, William R., 98n39
Madison, James, 120, 169
Madrid, 31, 79, 83, 84, 89–91
Magruder, John B., 109
Malaysia, 223
Malcolm, Thomas S., 63, 64
Manifest Destiny, 54, 163, 225, 264, 269–70
Mantilla, António, 99n47
Marchant, H. C., 119
Marten, James, 194
Marxism, 5, 8, 21n23
Maryland, 26n63, 295
Mason, John Y., 84
Mason, William Ernest, 219, 228
Massachusetts: Boston, 166–67, 196
Maury, Matthew Fontaine, 109, 111, 115
McCrae, C. C., 115
McCurry, Stephanie, 106
McGlynn, Edward, and Anti-Poverty Society, 144
McKeon, John, 32–33
McKinley, William, 16, 93, 163, 173–76, 178–80, 182, 192, 203–4, 213n111, 214, 217, 219, 221–23, 227–28, 233, 247, 267, 292, 301, 308; administration of, 16, 81, 94, 304; and Benevolent Assimilation, 176, 179, 267, 273; and Central Cuban Relief Committee, 173; and Teller Amendment, 93
McKivigan, John R., 139, 154
McLaurin, John, 16, 215, 219, 229–34
McWilliams, Tenant, 107
Memorial Day, 195
Memphis Commercial-Appeal, 203
Memphis Daily Appeal, 35, 36
Methodists and Methodism, 54, 57, 62, 63, 65. *See also* African Methodist Episcopal (AME) Church

Mevs, Adolphus H., 68–71, 78n113
Mexico, 180, 291, 310; Confederates in, 33–34; French occupation of, 2, 86, 110; Guaymas, 123; Gulf of, 33; and Benito Juárez, 109; and Maximilian I (emperor), 34, 109, 111, 124; and Mexican-American War, 34; Mexican Empire, 297; revolution in, 29; Sonora, 123; and Zachary Taylor, 32; and transcontinental railroad, 123; and U.S. expansionism, 84, 254, 255; Virginian Confederates in, 109
Michigan, 140
Middle East, 310
Midway Atoll, 2, 270
Miller, Isaac, 61
Minnesota, 201
Miralles, Juan de, 83
missions and missionaries. *See* African Methodist Episcopal (AME) Church; Mormons; *and individual denominations and organizations*
Mississippi, 118, 232, 297; Biloxi, 137; freedom movement in, 142; Greenville, 78n113; River and Valley, 29, 33, 35, 121, 294, 297, 322
Mississippi Clarion-Ledger, 144
Missouri, 295; Kansas City, 203; St. Louis, 122
Mitchell, Margaret, 106
Monroe Doctrine, 2, 85, 310
Monroe, James, 83
Mormons, 4, 16; and assimilation, 239–40, 251, 253, 258–59; and Book of Mormon, 241, 242; and church hierarchy, 239, 240, 246, 250–51; migration of, 242, 243; military service of, 239, 240, 248, 249–50, 253, 256–57, 258, 259, 323; and missionaries, 251–53, 256–57; non-Mormon views of, 242–43, 250–51, 253, 258; and pacifism, 240–41, 246–47, 248, 259; patriotism of, 239, 240–44, 246–47, 248, 249–51, 254, 258–59; and political affiliations, 255–56; and polygamy, 239–40, 243, 244–45, 259; and race, 240–41, 257–58; and Reconstruction of, 16, 239–40, 251, 259; and religious freedom, 241, 242, 245, 252, 254–55, 256; and U.S. expansionism, 240, 241, 254–57, 322–23; and views of U.S. government, 242–44, 245, 248, 254, 259. *See also* Utah; *and individual Mormons and legislative acts*
Morrill Anti-Bigamy Act, 244–45
Morton, Oliver P., 87–88, 101n65
Mossell, Charles W., 65–66, 68, 69, 71, 76nn70,75, 77n97; and *Toussaint L'Ouverture, the Hero of Santo Domingo* (1896), 65
Mossell, Mary Ella, 65–66, 71, 77n97
Munford, George W., 113, 116
Moulton, S. W., 144

Nast, Thomas, 266
Nation, The, 213n109
nationalism, 47, 161–64, 168–70, 180, 183, 204–5. *See also* Confederacy, the, and Confederates: patriotism of; Cuba: patriotism in; humanitarian nationalism; Mormons: patriotism of; North, the, and northerners: and patriotism; Union, the (1861–1865): and patriotism
Native Americans, 2, 178, 222, 225, 288, 297; representations of, 264, 268, 271, 276, 280, 281; in Spanish colonies, 83; and U.S. expansionism, 84, 319, 323; and U.S. military, 4. *See also* Apache; Indian Wars of the 1870s; Nez Perce
nativism, 3, 320
Nebraska, 122
Nelson, Knute, 201
Neutrality Act, 45
New Deal, 300
New Mexico, 88, 123, 268, 287, 320
New York, 6, 32, 35, 37, 45, 60, 86, 89, 117, 125, 146, 156, 167, 171–73, 193, 227; Brooklyn, 168; New York City, 150, 152

INDEX

New York Herald, 36
New York Sunday News, 36
New York Times, 34, 36, 37, 38, 40, 42, 44, 45, 218
New York Tribune, 38, 140, 173, 217, 218
New York World, 228
Newberry Herald and News, 217
Nez Perce, 178
Nicaragua, 84
Nicholas, Sarah, 113
Nightingale, Florence, 168, 170
North, the, and Northerners, 12; capitalist investors, 112–13, 116; class conflict in, 299–300; commercial recovery in, 119; and Confederate economic dependence, 113; on Confederates, 160n72; and humanitarianism, 164; and patriotism, 15, 163; on race and slavery, 13, 43; and racism, 15, 28; reformers, 142; unemployment in, 119. *See also* African Methodist Episcopal (AME) Church; Democrats: Northern; Grand Army of the Republic; Republicans: Northern; sectionalism and reconciliation; *and specific individuals and states*
North America, 124
North American Review, 137, 143, 153
North Carolina, 16, 106, 112, 200, 229, 297; Charlotte, 227; Tarboro, 230; Wilmington massacre, 215, 226–34, 321
Nuevitas (Cuba) 42
Nuremberg, Bavaria, 121

Ohio, 64, 68, 191, 193, 198; Cincinnati, 116
Ohio River, 121
Okihiro, Gary, 276
Onís, Luis de, 83
Onley, Richard, 93
Opper, Frederick, 266
Oregon, 34
Ostend Manifesto, 84, 98n39
Ottoman Empire, 167, 310. *See also* Turkey and Turks

Pacific, the: islands, 224, 230; Ocean, 196, 221; Spanish colonies in, 1
Pacific Islanders, 224
Page, Thomas Nelson, and *Red Rock*, 139
Panama, 3, 30, 273, 280
Paris, 6
Parks, Henry Blanton, and *Africa: The Problem of the New Century* (1899), 70
Parsons, Albert, 11–12
Pasha, Tewfik, 171–72
Patterson, James W., 101n65
Payne, Daniel A., 63
Pennsylvania, 64, 193; Johnstown flood in, 171
Penrose, Charles W., 248
Philadelphia, 44, 56–57, 61, 63, 66, 67
Philippines, the: democratic republic of, 183; Luzon, 182, 287; Mindanao, 287; Muslim Moro of, 288; in political cartoon, 17, 264, 271, 273–74; revolution in, 13; representative government in, 322; San Isidro, 182; and U.S. colonialism, 1, 3, 10, 15, 16, 107, 143, 162–64, 174–76, 179, 182, 200–4, 221, 228–32, 252, 253, 255, 267–68, 269, 271, 273–75, 282, 287–88, 290, 311, 318, 319, 323; and U.S. War with Spain, 253, 267
Phillips, Wendell, 88, 141
Platt Amendment, 292, 310
Platt, Orville H., 202, 309
Plessy v. Ferguson, 204, 276, 321
Poland Act, 244–45
Polite, DJ, 16, 88, 200, 321
Polk, James K., 84
Polo de Barnabé, José, 91–92, 99n47
Pope Leo XIII, 173
Port-au-Prince (Haiti), 55, 61, 63–66, 68–69, 71
Portugal, 180
Postel, Charles, 11
Potomac River, 36
Pratt, Parley P., 242, 255
print culture, 2, 35, 137, 139, 146, 267, 282; and Filipino students in U.S., 275; and

print culture (*continued*)
  foreign news coverage, 36–37, 37–38, 40, 42, 44–45, 90, 91, 92; and illustrated press, 266–67; and Mormons, 245, 248, 249, 250–51, 252–53, 255–56, 258. See also *Christian Recorder*; Dalrymple, Louis; *Deseret News*; Redpath, James: and *Redpath's Illustrated Weekly*; *Salt Lake Herald*; *Salt Lake Tribune*; and other editors, events, and publications
Prior, David, 166, 289, 324
Proctor, Redfield, 174
Progressive Era, the, 4, 287
Protestants: reformers, 167, 169. See also African Methodist Episcopal (AME) Church; Christianity; Mormons; *and individual denominations and organizations*
Pryor, J. B., 35
Puck, 16, 264, 266, 268, 271, 272, 278. See also Dalrymple, Louis: and "School Begins"
Puerto Principe (Cuba), 42
Puerto Rico, 17, 27, 28, 47, 83, 86, 162–63, 174–75, 179, 200, 220, 231–32, 234, 255, 264, 267, 271, 275, 288–89
Pulitzer, Joseph, 253,

Queenstown College (South Africa), 70
Quesada, Manuel de, 38
Quinn, D. Michael, 246

racism: and abolition, 3, 319; in academia, 8; from African Methodist Episcopal Church, 54–78, 76n62; toward Afro-Caribbeans, 80, 82, 87–90, 92; and assimilation vs. contagion, 88, 268–69, 271–72, 273, 282; in British Empire, 145–48; and claims about specific European races, 34, 109–10, 140, 320–21; and climate theories, 30, 87, 105, 165, 166, 176, 185n29, 225; and colonies, 3, 201, 324; and defining categories, 277–79, 281; and Du Bois's imperial thesis in *Black Reconstruction*, 5–9; and idea of docility, 88; as inhibiting expansionism, 3, 17, 19n8, 80, 82, 87, 88–89, 107, 176, 216, 269–70, 271–72, 280–82, 283n11, 319–20, 321; during nineteenth century, 80; and political power, 215–17, 219–21, 223–27, 229–34; racial categories in Latin America, 41–42, 46, 58, 61, 278–79; and racial violence, 214–34; scholarship on, 5, 8; and science/evolution, 165, 269–70, 277; structural or systemic, 142, 201, 203; toward Turks, 169; and U.S. imperialism, 3–4, 12, 17, 55, 264, 269–70, 273–74, 282; and violence, 4, 16, 35, 276, 321. See also Anglo-Saxons; Fish, Hamilton; Jim Crow; Johnson, Andrew; Jordan, Thomas; Ku Klux Klan; Latin America: Confederates in; lynching; South, the, and Southerners: white supremacy in; white supremacy
Rafael, Vicente, 273–74
Ramírez, Dixa, 72n4
Randolph, George W., 108–9, 113
Rawlins, John A., 28, 89
Reconstruction: Acts, 298; and African Americans, 1, 5, 8, 12; backlash against, 147; and class, 111; Congressional, 166, 183; and constitutional amendments, 81, 85, 87, 276, 294, 299; and economic transformation, 3, 8, 92–93, 105, 108, 111–16, 119, 124, 126, 289; historiography of, 4–5, 8–11, 13, 107, 289–91; and imperial expansion, 200–3; and integration, 82, 86, 93; and internationalism, 15, 80; meaning of term, 1, 4, 7, 18n2, 22n28, 244, 290, 291, 300–1, 303–4, 305–7, 310–11, 317, 325; memory of and references to, 16, 175–76, 215–16, 218, 223, 229, 234, 288; and military pacification, 287–88, 290–91, 299–303; Military Reconstruction, 1, 108, 290–300, 303, 306–7, 309, 311; and nationalism, 169; and Panic

of 1873, 119, 197; political legacy of, 15, 27–28, 274, 277, 290; politics of, 27, 28, 80, 81, 82, 85, 86–89, 91, 92–93, 94, 105, 107–8, 111–15, 117–18, 203; Presidential, 112, 295; process of, 108; racial tensions throughout, 80, 82, 85, 86, 88, 90, 92–94; Radical, 113, 117, 122, 136, 142 165; and Reconstruction Committee of the House, 115; and Redemption, 109, 138, 141–43, 153, 216, 230, 299, 302; and religious leaders, 55; revolutionary constitutionalism throughout, 289; "Second," 300; and Senate Judiciary Committee, 115; as a slur, 235; and socialism, 160n67; and taxation, 112; and Ten Years' War, 28–29, 82, 85, 89; transnational dimensions of, 288–89; and U.S. imperialism, 5, 7, 79–104, 108, 272; and U.S. West, 276. *See also* abolition and emancipation; abolitionists; African Americans; Civil War, the; Confederacy and Confederates; Democrats; economic conditions; Grant, Ulysses S.; Howe, Samuel G.; McKinley, William; racism; Republicans; slavery; United States, the; War of 1898; *and individual amendments, historians, laws, politicians, and states*

"The Reconstruction Policy of Congress, as illustrated in California," 280, 281

Redpath, James, 318, 320; as anti-imperialist, 138–40, 145–46, 155; background on, 136–37, 140–41, 144–45; changing views of, 138–39, 141–45, 147–48, 150–55, 157; and *The Crusader of Freedom*, 136; and *The Public life of Capt. John Brown*, 141; on race, 140, 142–46, 151–52, 154–57; as radical, 136, 138–41, 145, 155, 157n5; and Redpath Lyceum Bureau, 141; and *Redpath's Illustrated Weekly*, 145–50, 152–53; and *The Roving Editor: or Talks with Slaves in the Southern States*, 139; and *A Short History of the Confederate States of America*, 137; on slavery, 15, 148, 150–51, 153, 157; as sympathizer of Jefferson Davis, 136–39, 142, 152–57; for women's rights, 136, 139. *See also* Ireland and Irish; Irish Americans

Reeve, Paul, 258

religion, 2, 21n22, 58–60, 62, 168, 181. *See also* African Methodist Episcopal (AME) Church; Catholicism; Christians and Christianity; Islam; Methodists and Methodism; Mormons; Protestants; *and individual denominations and organizations*

Renan, Ernest, 325

Rendón, Francisco, 83

Republicans, 1–2, 3, 7, 12, 28, 81, 82, 87, 88, 114–15, 117; biracial, 298–300; and British Empire, 110, 119; and civil/political rights, 115; and commercialism, 110; and Cuban independence, 45, 99n49; and ex-Confederate politics, 114; and exports, 324; and free labor ideology, 198–99; on free trade imperialism, 124; and high tariff policy, 125; Liberal, 117, 299; and Mormons, 239, 244–45; Northern, 12, 179, 231, 295, 299–300, 310; as protectionist, 108, 126; and race, 1, 85, 317–18, 320; radicals, 87, 105, 114, 136, 172, 291, 294, 296, 298, 304; Southern, 2, 299; and state centralization, 120, 125, 244. *See also* Grand Army of the Republic; Reconstruction; *and individual members*

Richards, Franklin D., 247, 252

Richmond Enquirer, 160n67

Rio de Janeiro, 6

Ring, Natalie, 290

Robertson, Wyndham, 115, 117

Rome, 6

Roosevelt, Franklin D., 310

Roosevelt, Theodore, 180–81, 267–68, 292, 310, 318, 322

Root, Elihu, 308–9

Russia, 6, 15, 34, 161, 171, 180, 196, 202, 289, 310

Ryan, A. C., 51n69
Rydell, Robert, 270

Salt Lake City, 244, 250, 257, 258, 261n35
Salt Lake Herald, 248, 251, 256
Salt Lake Tribune, 248, 253
Samaná Bay and Peninsula, 60–63, 75n47, 86
Sánchez Bregua, José, 79
Santiago de Cuba, 44, 90, 93, 177, 301–2, 306
Santo Domingo (city), 55, 56, 60–65, 67–78, 95n10, 319
Schmidt, Peter, 272–73
Schurz, Carl, 88, 101n65, 175–77, 179
Scott, Rebecca J., 25n53, 28, 41, 289
Scott, Tom, 122
Seaman, George A., 252–53, 257, 323
sectionalism and reconciliation, 2, 3, 11, 14, 16, 80, 82, 84, 91, 94, 105, 107, 118, 119, 122–23, 127, 138–39, 152–53, 155, 157, 176, 192, 203–5, 319
segregation, 2, 200–2, 204–5, 220, 288
Senate Foreign Relations Committee, 82, 84, 87, 88, 101n65. *See also* Fish, Hamilton; Morton, Oliver P.; Sumner, Charles
Serrano, Francisco, 82–83, 92
Seward, William Henry, 10, 30–32, 120, 124, 170–71, 317
Sexton, Jay, 29
Seymour, Horatio, 114
Sheffley, Hugh W., 116
Sheldon, Porter, 102n80
Sheridan, Phil, 44
Sherman, William T., 296, 301
Shott, Brian, 16–17, 88, 143, 319, 321
Sickles, Daniel, 44, 79, 82, 91–93
Siege of Petersburg, 29
Sierra Leone, 70
Silber, Nina, 11
Skocpol, Theda, 193
slavery: in Cuba: 27–31, 33–35, 37–38, 41, 43–45, 47, 81, 89; as "Divine economy," 34; in Haiti, 57; as racial caste system, 153; Reconstruction-era debates on, 47; in the United States, 2, 6, 8, 10, 12, 13, 26n63, 27–31, 34, 37, 43, 84, 109–10, 150–51, 153–54, 157, 165, 192, 194, 200–1, 293–94, 300, 302. *See also* abolition and emancipation; abolitionists; *and individual people and places*
Slotkin, Richard, 270–71
Smith, George Albert, 241, 243–44, 257
Smith, John Henry, 247
Smith, Joseph, 241, 242–43, 254, 255, 323
Social Darwinism, 144, 305
Socialism, 21n23, 154, 160n67, 289
Soulé, Pierre, 84
South, the, and Southerners, 2, 106; commercial expansion of, 123–25; and Cuba, 91; economic collapse in, 111; federal occupation of, 1, 17, 161, 165, 220, 223, 226, 229, 292–94, 296–99, 322; and free trade imperialism, 107; historiography of, 106; humanitarianism in, 15; industrial development of, 113; and masculinity, 118; and national anthem, 181; and the North, 12, 113, 119–20; racial tension in, 107; white immigration to, 123; white supremacy in, 1, 2, 4–7, 9, 11, 12, 21n22, 81, 92. *See also* African Americans; African Methodist Episcopal (AME) Church; Confederacy, the, and Confederates; Democrats: Southern; freedpeople; Ku Klux Klan; Republicans: Southern; slavery; *and individual people and states*
South Africa, 26n63, 70
South African Ethiopian Church, 70
South African Methodist Episcopal Church, 70
South Carolina, 16, 26n63, 171, 191, 200, 296–97; and 1895 South Carolina State Constitution, 219; Anderson, 227; Cape Fear river, 227; Charleston, 141, 223, 233; Columbia, 223; Edgefield county,

229; Ellenton massacre, 215, 229; federal intervention in, 229–30; Hamburg and Hamburg massacre, 142, 215, 232; Keowee, 227; Lake City, 214, 216–19, 221, 223–31, 233–34; Lancaster, 227; Lexington, 217; Newberry, 227; Phoenix, 215, 226–30, 232–34; political power in, 215, 218–20, 222, 224, 226–27, 229–34; racial violence in, 214–22, 224–34; Yorkville, 227
Soviet Union, 8
Spanish (language), 46, 62
Spanish Abolition Society, 31
Spanish-American War: *See* War of 1898
Spanish Empire, 1, 3, 17, 30–32; and army of, 44; and Black Legend, 14, 81, 83, 84; and Dominican Republic, 31, 60, 85, 86; First Spanish Republic, 79, 82, 91; and Haiti, 63; and navy of, 79, 85, 90–91; and "no transfer" resolution of 1811, 81–82, 84; and Philippines, 273; and relations with United States, 1, 14, 28, 79–104, 107, 317; and Revolution of 1895 in Cuba, 29; and Ten Years' War in Cuba, 27–53, 82; and U.S. national narrative, 83, 93. *See also* Cuba; Dominican Republic; Haiti; Hispaniola; Madrid; Treaty of Paris; *Virginius* Affair
Spencer, Herbert, 305
St. George's Methodist Episcopal Church, 56
St. John, Rachel, 4
St. Marks (FL), 83
St. Thomas, 67
Steinbock-Pratt, Sarah, 25n52, 275
Stephens, Alexander H., 124
Stevens, Thaddeus, 114
Steward, Theophilus Gould, 63–65, 76n70
Story, Moorfield, 176
Stowe, Harriet Beecher, 278
Strong, Josiah, 168, 269, 282
Stuart, Alexander H. H., 114
Summers, Mark, 107

Sumner, Charles, 87, 88, 101n65, 141, 176, 276–77, 305, 318, 319
Sumner, William Graham, 305
Swann, Thomas, 102n80

Tampa Riot, 321
Tanner, Benjamin T., 63
Taylor, A. A., 8
Taylor, John, 243, 245
Taylor, Zachary, 32
Ten Years' War (1868–1878), 13, 14, 73n12, 81, 82, 85, 86, 172, 292; beginning of, 89; and Cuban independence, 42–43; end of, 44; historiography of, 28–29; military tactics in, 40; potential U.S. intervention in, 90; and U.S. Civil War, 27–53. *See also* Cavada, Federico Fernández; Céspedes, Carlos Manuel de; Fish, Hamilton; Grant, Ulysses S.; Jordan, Thomas; Quesada, Manuel de; *Virginius* Affair
Tennessee, 141, 293–94, 298; Memphis, 35, 37; Shiloh, 204
Terrell, A. W., 171
Texas, 33, 224–25, 232, 254, 268, 297, 321; San Antonio, 123
Thirteenth Amendment, 27, 30, 33, 114, 296
Tillman, Benjamin Ryan, 16, 191–92, 200–5, 215–16, 220–29, 231–34, 258, 321, 322
Topsy, 278–79
transcontinental railroads, 15, 107, 121, 122, 123; and Central Pacific Railroad, 122; and Confederate Pacific railroad, 123; and Southern Pacific Railroad, 116, 121–22; and Southern Railroad Corporation, 122
Trautwine, John C., 30
Treaty of Paris, 200, 215, 232–34, 267, 268, 301
Trinidad de Cuba, 30, 32, 42
Tropic of Cancer, 290
Truman, Harry S, 311
Tucker, John Randolph, 14, 125–27

Turkey and Turks, 4, 165–67, 169, 171–74, 320; Constantinople, 171
Turner, Frederick Jackson, 254, 270
Turner, Henry McNeal, 70
Tuskegee Institute, 275
Twain, Mark, 136, 141, 175–76, 181, 208n28, 272, 321

Uncle Sam, 267, 278 *See also* Dalrymple, Louis: "School Begins"
Uncle Tom's Cabin, 278–79
Union, the (1861–1865), 8, 12, 13, 28, 322; army of, 141, 165, 192, 291, 301–2, 304; blockade, 111, 303; and commercialism, 119; and conservatives, 14; and economic conditions, 125; and free labor, 110, 293; and imperialism and expansion, 3–4, 9, 15, 33, 110, 268, 271, 272; and infrastructure, 122; and Irish, 152; loyalists, 112, 115, 295; navy of, 192; and patriotism, 118, 163; and peace with the Confederacy, 105, 110, 119; and slavery and abolition, 13, 45, 165, 293–97, 325; soldiers missing in action, 170; and the South, 2, 12, 293–97, 301–2, 304; victory of, 1, 2, 110, 161, 163, 164, 317, 318; and violence, 20n13. *See also* Civil War; Confederacy, the, and Confederates; Union veterans; United States, the; United States military; *and individual people and states*
Union veterans, 34, 35, 46, 109, 163, 191–95, 197–98, 201, 205, 276, 297, 304–5. *See also* Cavada, Adolfo; Cavada, Federico Fernández; Grand Army of the Republic; Woodford, Stewart; *and other individuals*
United Daughters of the Confederacy, 323
United States, the: Christian missions in, 14; empire of, 1, 2, 5, 7–11, 13, 15–16, 19n10, 27–29, 55, 71, 80, 82–84, 87–89, 94; foreign policy of, 80, 83, 84–85, 93, 107, 119, 290, 311; and free trade impe-

rialism, 104, 107, 110, 11 8–19, 120, 124, 127; geopolitical rise of, 13; and Latin America, 3, 30, 32, 33–34, 317; Midwest, 68, 116, 196; militarism, 178; national narrative of, 83; Northwest, 121; racist domestic policies of, 71; Southwest, 122–23; sovereignty in, 17; and Spain, 14, 79–104, 267, 317; and U.S.-British relations, 85, 86; West Coast, 151. *See also* Confederacy, the, and Confederates; Constitution, the; Reconstruction; Union, the; United States military; *and individual figures and states*
United States Colored Troops, 32
United States Commission of Inquiry, 73n16, 75n47
United States House of Representatives, 88, 90, 116, 118, 125
United States military: and Army, 34, 46, 126, 291–300, 304; and governance, 288, 322; and human rights, 121; and Native Americans, 319; navy of, 93, 124–25, 180; and occupation of Cuba, 93, 300–11; and occupation of Philippines, 4; and occupation of the South, 1, 17, 223, 322; and professionalization, 19n11, 287; and racism, 17; and slaveholding regimes, 33; and U.S. marshals, 227. *See also* African Americans: as Buffalo soldiers, and military service; Civil War, the; Reconstruction; South, the: federal occupation of; War of 1898
United States Senate, 87, 88, 90
U.S.S. *Maine* (ship), 174, 215, 217, 221, 267, 290
Utah, 16, 122, 239, 240, 245, 248, 249, 251. *See also* Mormons

Vance, Zebulon B., 112–13
Vallandigham, Clement, 116
Venezuela, 33–34
Virginia and Virginians, 30, 40, 105–35, 293–94, 296–97, 303; and Army of Northern Virginia, 108–9; Bedford

INDEX

County, 122; and Charlottesville Woolen Mills, 119; Chesapeake Bay, 121; and Commercial Convention Movement, 116; conservatives in, 14–15, 320–21; Cumberland County, 116; in Early Republic, 107; economic conditions in, 105, 111–16, 119, 124, 126; and federalism, 112, 118–20, 125; Hampton Roads, 124; James River in, 121; Kanawha Canal in, 121; Lexington, 112, 113; Luray Valley of, 34; Lynchburg, depression in, 111; Norfolk, 109, 111, 115; Old Dominion in, 108; and Reconstruction policies, 111; Richmond, 40, 109, 111, 112, 115, 116, 121, 195; Rockbridge County, 122; and Ruffin Agricultural Club, 116; Shenandoah Valley, 107, 114; Staunton, 116; Tredegar Ironworks in, 115, 125; and Union readmission, 115; and University of Virginia, 110, 111; and Virginia Assembly's Black Codes, 110, 296; and Virginia Military Institute, 121; and Virginia Volunteer Navy, 125. *See also individual politicians*

Virginius Affair, 79–80, 82, 85, 90–94
Vorenberg, Michael, 298

Walker, William, 325
War of 1898, 4, 14, 16, 81–82, 163–64, 174, 180–81, 191–92, 195, 199–200, 204–5, 210n66, 215, 217–21, 223–26, 233–34, 255, 288–90; beginnings of, 93; and Camp Fitzhugh Lee, 226; causes of, 79; and Confederate government, 108; and Teller Amendment, 93; and the U.S. Civil War, 3; and U.S. popular culture, 271. *See also* Mormons: military service of; United States military; *and individual colonies, countries, and empires*
Ward Beecher, Henry, 32
Warren, Robert Penn, 139
Washburn, Elihu, 114–15
Washington Bee, 217–18
Washington Post, 227

Washington, Booker T., 17, 143, 180–81, 275–76, 278–79
Washington, D.C., 3, 45, 64, 83, 84, 112, 113, 115, 117, 120, 143, 171, 173, 180, 193, 197, 227, 292, 298, 300, 310
Washington, George, 32, 83
Webster, Daniel, 84
Webster, Sidney, 86
Wells, Heber, 249
Wells-Barnett, Ida, 16, 219, 230–31
West, Elliot, 4, 325n1
West, Richard S., 266
West Africa, 67. *See also* Africa and Africans; African Diaspora; South Africa; *and individual countries*
West Point, 34, 249, 287
West Virginia, 107, 295; Allegheny mountains, 122; White Sulphur Springs, 114
Western Hemisphere, 27–30, 86, 89, 120
Western United States: 34, 88; Southwest, 88, 224–25, 268; and Westward expansion, 2, 34, 81, 83, 88, 121, 122–23, 243, 260n23, 264, 270, 287, 289–90, 319, 324, 325n1. *See also* Apache; Native Americans; Reconstruction: meaning of term; *and individual states*
Weyler, Valeriano, 172, 303
Whigs, 15, 28, 108, 114, 115, 304
White, George, 16, 219, 230–31, 233
White, Richard, 4, 11
White House, 111, 180, 194, 223, 292
White, Frank, 275
white supremacy, 15, 55, 72, 92, 136, 144, 154, 157, 179, 191, 200–3, 205, 298–300; and disenfranchisement, 215–16, 219–22, 225–27, 229–32, 234; as political supremacy, 216, 219–21, 224–26, 228–33, 288, 308–9. *See also* Democrats; Forrest, Nathan Bedford; racism; South, the, and Southerners; Tillman, Benjamin Ryan; *and other individuals*
Whitman, Walt, 136, 140
Wilberforce University, 64, 68, 78n115
Wilkinson, Morton S., 102n80

Wilkes, Barry, 122
Willard, Charles W., 102n80
Wilson, Ann Marie, 169
Wilson, James, 304–5
Wilson, Woodrow, 182, 310, 322; Wilsonian program of 1913, 119, 127
Wise, Henry A., 122–23; and Knights of Pythias, 122
Women's Mite Missionary Society, 66
Wood, Fernando, 88, 102n80
Wood, Leonard, 301–6, 308, 319
Woodford, Stewart L., 32, 33, 93
Woodruff, Wilford, 245, 247–48, 249, 250, 251
Woodward, C. Vann, 8, 137
Woody, Robert Hilliard, 8

World War I, 6, 7, 22n26, 163, 180, 182, 310
World War II, 8, 280, 310, 311
World's Fairs, 270; World's Columbian Exposition of 1893, 93, 270; World's Fair of 1851, 34
Wright, Gavin, 107

Young, Brigham, 239, 242
Young, Jr., Brigham, 246, 248, 249
Young, Richard W., 249, 252
Young, Willard, 249
Young Chief Joseph, 319

Ziker, Ann K., 280
Zimmerman, Andrew, 289
Zimmerman, Jonathan, 274

Reconstructing America
Andrew L. Slap, series editor

Hans L. Trefousse, *Impeachment of a President: Andrew Johnson, the Blacks, and Reconstruction*.

Richard Paul Fuke, *Imperfect Equality: African Americans and the Confines of White Ideology in Post-Emancipation Maryland*.

Ruth Currie-McDaniel, *Carpetbagger of Conscience: A Biography of John Emory Bryant*.

Paul A. Cimbala and Randall M. Miller, eds., *The Freedmen's Bureau and Reconstruction: Reconsiderations*.

Herman Belz, *A New Birth of Freedom: The Republican Party and Freedmen's Rights, 1861 to 1866*.

Robert Michael Goldman, *"A Free Ballot and a Fair Count": The Department of Justice and the Enforcement of Voting Rights in the South, 1877–1893*.

Ruth Douglas Currie, ed., *Emma Spaulding Bryant: Civil War Bride, Carpetbagger's Wife, Ardent Feminist—Letters, 1860–1900*.

Robert Francis Engs, *Freedom's First Generation: Black Hampton, Virginia, 1861–1890*.

Robert F. Kaczorowski, *The Politics of Judicial Interpretation: The Federal Courts, Department of Justice, and Civil Rights, 1866–1876*.

John Syrett, *The Civil War Confiscation Acts: Failing to Reconstruct the South*.

Michael Les Benedict, *Preserving the Constitution: Essays on Politics and the Constitution in the Reconstruction Era*.

Andrew L. Slap, *The Doom of Reconstruction: The Liberal Republicans in the Civil War Era*.

Edmund L. Drago, *Confederate Phoenix: Rebel Children and Their Families in South Carolina.*

Mary Farmer-Kaiser, *Freedwomen and the Freedmen's Bureau: Race, Gender, and Public Policy in the Age of Emancipation.*

Paul A. Cimbala and Randall Miller, eds., *The Great Task Remaining Before Us: Reconstruction as America's Continuing Civil War.*

John A. Casey Jr., *New Men: Reconstructing the Image of the Veteran in Late-Nineteenth-Century American Literature and Culture.*

Hilary Green, *Educational Reconstruction: African American Schools in the Urban South, 1865–1890.*

Christopher B. Bean, *Too Great a Burden to Bear: The Struggle and Failure of the Freedmen's Bureau in Texas.*

David E. Goldberg, *The Retreats of Reconstruction: Race, Leisure, and the Politics of Segregation at the New Jersey Shore, 1865–1920.*

David Prior, ed., *Reconstruction in a Globalizing World.*

Jewel L. Spangler and Frank Towers, eds., *Remaking North American Sovereignty: State Transformation in the 1860s.*

Adam H. Domby and Simon Lewis, eds., *Freedoms Gained and Lost: Reconstruction and Its Meanings 150 Years Later.*

David Prior, ed., *Reconstruction and Empire: The Legacies of Abolition and Union Victory for an Imperial Age.*

www.ingramcontent.com/pod-product-compliance
Lightning Source LLC
Chambersburg PA
CBHW032025290426
44110CB00012B/677